FAITH, HOPE,
and SUSTAINABILITY

D1596754

SUNY SERIES ON
RELIGION AND
THE ENVIRONMENT

edited by Harold Coward

FAITH,
HOPE,
and
SUSTAINABILITY

*The Greening of
US Faith Communities*

CYBELLE T. SHATTUCK

Cover photo by Ksenia Chernaya from Pexels.

Published by State University of New York Press, Albany

For information, contact State University of New York Press, Albany, NY
www.sunypress.edu

Library of Congress Cataloging-in-Publication Data
Names: Shattuck, Cybelle T., [date]- author.
Title: Faith, hope, and sustainability : the greening of US faith communities /
    Cybelle T. Shattuck.
Description: Albany : State University of New York Press, [2021] | Series: Suny
    series on religion and the environment | Includes bibliographical refer-
    ences and index.
Identifiers: LCCN 2020045642 (print) | LCCN 2020045643 (ebook) | ISBN
    9781438481999 (hardcover) | ISBN 9781438482002 (ebook) | ISBN
    9781438481982 (paperback)
Subjects: LCSH: United States—History—21st century. | Ecotheology—United
    States—Case studies. | Human ecology—Religious aspects—Christianity—
    Case studies. | Christian communities—Case studies.
Classification: LCC BR526 .S524 2021 (print) | LCC BR526 (ebook) | DDC
    261.8/80973—dc23
LC record available at https://lccn.loc.gov/2020045642
LC ebook record available at https://lccn.loc.gov/2020045643

10 9 8 7 6 5 4 3 2 1

CONTENTS

ILLUSTRATIONS

TABLES

MAPS

FIGURES

PREFACE

WHILE TEACHING IN THE RELIGION DEPARTMENT of a liberal arts college in Michigan, I developed an interest in the role that religion plays in shaping behavior toward the natural environment. Delving into the field of religious environmentalism, also called religion and ecology, I was delighted by the eloquence of writers like John Burroughs, Thomas Berry, and Sallie McFague, who advocated faith-based environmental ethics, and by the hopeful tone of scholars such as Roger Gottlieb, Mary Evelyn Tucker, and Laurel Kearns, who studied emerging eco-theologies and celebrated a greening of American religion. However, I gradually grew dissatisfied with philosophical treatises and sought information about what people were doing to put faith-based environmental ethics into practice in order to change human impacts on the environment. At that time, in 2007, there were a few intriguing accounts of religious environmentalism in action, such as: Sarah McFarland Taylor's study of "green" nuns[1] who were implementing sustainable practices on convent grounds; Roger Gottlieb's book, *A Greener Faith*,[2] which chronicled the emergence of denominational environmental statements and described a number of cases in which people of faith around the world were engaging in environmental behavior; and Jeremy Benstein's elegant exposition of the connections between Jewish teachings and environmental practices in Israel.[3] Nonetheless, it immediately became apparent that research into faith-based actions was far less comprehensive than scholarship focused on theology.

Shortly after becoming aware of the lack of empirical research on religion and environmentalism, I decided to return to graduate school for a degree in natural resources and environment. During my first semester, I read a book called *Making Collaboration Work*,[4] which compared cases of collaborative resource management from around the United States to discern factors that contributed to successful programs. The goal was to identify "best practices" that would be useful to public policy makers and to people in diverse communities seeking to develop their own collaborative management programs. It occurred to me that one could conduct a similar study of faith-based environmentalism to answer the question: When it works, why does it work? Comparing cases in which faith communities have gone beyond annual Earth Day liturgies to undertake earth-care projects could shed light on the motivations and processes that contribute to development and implementation of successful initiatives. Furthermore, this research could provide a repertoire of stories and information about best practices that would assist other faith communities seeking to develop their own initiatives.

Fortunately, when I proposed this project as a potential dissertation topic, Dr. Julia Wondolleck agreed that it would make a valuable contribution to knowledge about what motivates people to engage in environmentally beneficial behavior. With this comparative case-study model in mind, I set out to learn more about the environmental work undertaken by faith communities in the United States. While reviewing information on websites for interfaith environmental organizations like the National Religious Partnership for the Environment, Interfaith Power and Light, and GreenFaith, I discovered a trove of stories about congregations involved in environmental stewardship. All across the country, faith communities were engaging in resource conservation, land stewardship, and environmental advocacy. They were changing human behaviors and upgrading facilities to conserve energy, paper and water, buy or grow local and organic food, reduce use of toxic chemicals in buildings and grounds, produce less waste, generate carbon-free energy, restore ecosystems, and promote policies for environmental justice and climate action.

It also became apparent that while many houses of worship engaged in one or two earth-care projects, a small number of congregations scattered across the United States were implementing multiple projects and seemed to have adopted earth care as a significant element of their religious missions. Curious about how they were able to achieve so much, I visited fifteen of these remarkable faith communities to learn about the processes through which they integrated earth care into their organizations. This journey took me west to California and east to Maine, north to Minnesota and south to Virginia. I discovered wonderful examples of resource conservation, such as the first Platinum LEED-certified synagogue in the United States, built by the Jewish Reconstructionist Congregation of Evanston, Illinois. The community conserved resources during construction of their beautiful building by using materials with a lower ecological footprint like reclaimed wood siding and cabinets made from sunflower-seed shell particle board. They continue to conserve in day-to-day activities because of features like large windows that let in light and Energy Star appliances that reduce use of electricity.

I also explored land stewardship at faith communities with extensive grounds. Thus, I walked in the shade of century-old beech trees at Villa Maria Community Center in western Pennsylvania, where the Sisters of the Humility of Mary use sustainable forestry practices to manage 400 acres of woodland and grow organic produce for a market garden. Political advocacy was a less prevalent practice, often arising in response to a particular local issue, but this too was on display in several of the communities I visited. In one inspiring example of people drawing courage from their religious convictions, the Earth Care House Church at Trinity Presbyterian Church in Harrisonburg, Virginia, had decided to take on national energy policy and persuaded the Presbyterian Church (USA) denomination to advocate against coal-burning power plants that pollute the air and harm both human and environmental health.

These examples illustrate the kinds of activities undertaken by the fifteen faith communities I visited during 2012 and 2013. Each site provided an opportunity to gather information from people who have succeeded in translating environmental ethics into action. People generously shared their experiences and insights with me, explaining what motivated them to engage in earth care through the venues of their faith communities and how they had made progress toward integrating sustainability into worship, education, management, and ministry work. Visiting these communities and observing their accomplishments, seeing how they have reduced their carbon footprints and built more resilient communities both inside and outside their houses of worship, gave me a sense of hope for the future. I hope this book, with its stories of faith-based earth care and its analysis of factors that contributed to development of durable sustainability initiatives within congregation-level religious organizations, will inspire and assist others to join this great work and embark on their own pathways to sustainability.

ACKNOWLEDGMENTS

THIS RESEARCH PROJECT could not have been carried out without the support and assistance of a great many people.

First, I am deeply grateful to the people in the fifteen case-study communities who shared their stories and insights with me. They gave generously of their time, offered hospitality in guest houses and homes, took me on tours of the buildings and lands they stewarded, invited me to dine with them, and prayed for the successful completion of my project. Seeing the wonderful work that they are doing to care for the earth gives me hope that we will, indeed, create an environmentally sustainable society that supports both human and non-human life. It is a privilege for me to share their stories, to the best of my ability, through this book.

I was extraordinarily fortunate to have financial support that made it possible to do field work in communities from California to Maine, Minnesota to Virginia. Much of this support was provided by the USDA McIntire-Stennis program and the Environmental Protection Agency (EPA). This publication was partially developed under STAR Fellowship Assistance Agreement no. FP-91764701-0 awarded by the US EPA. It has not been formally reviewed by EPA and the views expressed in this publication are solely those of the author; EPA does not endorse any products or commercial services mentioned in this publication. I am grateful for financial assistance and office space from the Ecosystem Management Initiative at the University of Michigan School of Natural Resources and Environment (SNRE; now renamed the School for

Environment and Sustainability). The University of Michigan also provided financial support that made it possible to attend conferences.

This project began under the guidance of a dissertation committee that brought a range of perspectives to enrich its development. Julia M. Wondolleck made this project possible. During my first semester in the SNRE masters' program, the work she and Steven L. Yaffee did to examine factors that contributed to successful collaborative resource management projects inspired me to wonder whether one could do a similar analysis of faith-based sustainability initiatives. Julia was supportive of the idea and courageously agreed to serve as advisor for a research project that took her into the unfamiliar field of scholarship on faith-based environmentalism. Fortunately, her gift for perceiving patterns in community social behaviors was well-suited to analysis of faith communities; her insights enhanced the outcome of this project in immeasurable ways.

My thanks to Paul Mohai, who pointed out foundational questions I sometimes overlooked and helped make sure that my work was accessible to people across disciplines. I am indebted to Wayne Baker, who taught me to do field research and shared his enthusiasm for field notes—the longer and more detailed, the better. Finally, a special word of gratitude to Jim Crowfoot, whose bookshelf most closely resembles my own, for moral and intellectual support.

I owe a special debt of thanks to James Peltz, senior editor at SUNY, for stepping in to shepherd the manuscript review process after a colleague took family leave. I also appreciate the helpful comments of two anonymous reviewers. The book was greatly improved by the artistic skills of Jason Glatz, who designed the map, Carla Zorrilla, who helped with the figures, and my colleague Steve Bertman, who has a knack for analyzing the efficacy (and aesthetics) of graphic imagery.

I have been blessed with an extended network of supporters who listened patiently while this project took shape. I am grateful for the support of the world's best listener, Kathleen Karnes, and my SNRE friends, especially M'Lis Bartlett, John Graham, Shamitha Keerthi, and Samantha Shattuck. I also benefited from a group of informal mentors, which included Professor Nancy A. Falk from Western Michigan University and Professors Steven L. Yaffee, Dorceta Taylor, and Rachel Kaplan at SNRE.

One of the things that kept me going through this long process was the knowledge that there were people who wanted me to finish so they could put the research findings to use to support faith-based sustainability efforts. It has been particularly gratifying to work with the staff and board of Michigan

Interfaith Power and Light to "operationalize" my work. The opportunity to create a workshop and participate in Michigan IPL conferences helped focus portions of the book. I am especially grateful to Leah Wiste and Jane Esper Vogel, who shared in the project of creating the Sustainability Workshop for Faith Communities, and to Pastor John Schleicher and Father Jim McDougall, who brought the wisdom of their pastoral experiences to development of the Stewards of Hope program.

Finally, this work would not have been possible without the support of my husband, Brian Wilson. It was Brian who suggested that I pursue a new field when I became dissatisfied with life as an adjunct instructor of religion. He then endured seven years (instead of the two we initially expected) with a part-time spouse who split her weeks between Kalamazoo and Ann Arbor, went to conferences that conflicted with family vacations, and made long research trips during the summer. His response was to give me a Garmin for Christmas, "so you will always be able to find your way home." I am grateful for his patience and his devotion to our cats. And I am very glad that the job situation turned out quite well in the end.

INTRODUCTION

Are US Religions Going Green?

FAITH COMMUNITIES AND ENVIRONMENTAL SUSTAINABILITY

In June 2015, publication of Pope Francis' encyclical, *Laudato Si': On Care for Our Common Home,* inspired great excitement from world media, leaders of the United Nations, scientists, environmentalists, and religious organizations. The pope addressed his words to all people of the world, expressing the hope that it would "help us to acknowledge the appeal, immensity and urgency of the challenge we face" due to environmental damage, especially climate change.[1] Because encyclicals present authoritative papal teachings for the whole Catholic Church, the pope's message that being "protectors of God's handiwork is essential to a life of virtue" and that "it is not an optional or a secondary aspect of our Christian experience"[2] would now be designated as a doctrinal belief for a world religion with 1.2 billion members. Commentators speculated that *Laudato Si'* would be a "game changer" that would affect the attitudes of American Catholics[3] and motivate political leaders from around the world to reach an agreement about how to mitigate climate change during the 21st United Nations Conference of Parties in Paris in December of 2015.[4]

These hopeful discussions about Pope Francis's potential influence reflect widespread concern about the enormous global challenge of climate change. It is not just an environmental problem that will transform ecosystems; the destabilization of planetary systems is a social, economic, and political problem that will affect human and nonhuman lives in every corner of the world. Addressing it requires changes to social systems that are unlikely to occur without the involvement of leaders who can articulate cultural values that will help motivate sustained collective action. In the United States, the image of Dr. Martin Luther King Jr. hovers in the background of every leader advocating a moral obligation to change unjust social systems, reminding Americans of the role religion played in the civil rights movement and suggesting the potential for a similar transformation of political will in the present. Moreover, because some Christian politicians have cited their faith in God's sole power to determine the fate of the earth as justification for blocking efforts to support national climate action, seeing an influential religious leader take up the issue raised hopes that the same faith influences used to block action might also be able to motivate action.

RELIGIOUS ENVIRONMENTALISM

The pope's encyclical and visit to the United States does seem to have increased American support for action to address climate change,[5] however media reports that lauded the encyclical as a new frontier in environmental activism were misleading because they ignored the fact that religious leaders, including the two previous popes, had been calling on people of faith to protect the earth and its environmental systems for nearly half a century. For academics who study religion and ecology, the encyclical continues a tradition of modern American religious environmentalism that began in the late 1960s and runs parallel to the modern environmental movement.

The development of American religious environmentalism is often linked to a 1967 essay that Lynn White published in *Science*, in which he argued that Christianity had contributed to a worldview that led Western societies to exploit natural resources, degrade the environment, and create an ecological crisis.[6] Since religion played a significant role in shaping the cultural attitudes that caused problems, White thought Western society needed a new religion or a new interpretation of Christianity to help change those attitudes and solve the ecological crisis.[7] Many scholars cite the publication of White's essay as a critical moment in the emergence of American scholarly interest in the relationship between religion and environmentalism. Although there were earlier texts promoting conservation based on religion,[8] White's article garnered widespread attention because it was published in a prestigious journal at a time of "dramatic ecological change" and fit nicely with emergent countercultural critiques of Western society.[9] Consequently, it triggered strong responses within environmental, theological, and academic circles.

Some environmentalists and scholars concurred with White's assessment, although they tended to oversimplify his argument by ignoring its emphasis on historical context and focusing solely on the idea that resource exploitation in Western societies derived from an anthropocentric "mastery-over-nature" worldview rooted in the biblical creation story that gave humans "dominion" over nature.[10] In the 1970s and 1980s, this perspective coincided with academic and popular interest in a variety of spiritual traditions that seemed to offer more environmentally friendly alternatives to Christianity, such as Asian and neo-pagan religions, deep ecology, and Indigenous traditions in which Traditional Ecological Knowledge was embedded in religion.[11] Meanwhile, American and European theologians also responded to White's article. In the face of a 1970s environmentalism closely identified with wilderness preservation, some Christian leaders and theologians distanced themselves from a movement they saw as more concerned with wildlife than human welfare. Others, however, accepted White's critique of pre-modern Western worldviews but argued that biblical religion could be compatible with environmentalism. They sought to recover a biblical environmental ethic by correcting dominion-themed "misinterpretations" of scripture and highlighting passages linking the welfare of humans and nature. They also reframed Christian theology, expanding ideas of justice and human responsibilities to God to include care for nature. Since its inception in the early 1970s, this genre of eco-theology has continued to grow and has expanded to include all of the major world religions, although the majority of texts are still produced in the United States and United Kingdom.

There have also been efforts to create new ministries to implement these ethics. For example, in the 1980s, the National Council of Churches created an Eco-justice Ministry that worked to promote faith-based support for environmental justice among Protestant denominations in the United States. This ministry was a major sponsor for the People of Color Environmental Leadership Summit in 1991 and a National Black Church Environmental and Economic Justice Summit (Washington, DC) in 1993.[12]

The 1990s brought rising awareness of climate change, which transformed environmental issues into social welfare issues and inspired an upwelling of activity from religious leaders in the United States and Europe. In 1990, Carl Sagan and a group of scientists issued "An Open Letter to the Religious Community," that states, "The environmental crisis requires radical changes, not only in public policy, but also in individual behavior," and suggests that religion might be able to help create social changes that go beyond the scope of science.[13] Senior religious leaders in the US responded to the letter by forming the National Religious Partnership for the Environment in 1993, a forum in which Jewish, Catholic, Evangelical, Protestant, and Orthodox Christian organizations could share resources and support each other in promoting climate action among their members and in the wider American society.[14] In the same period, Prince Philip of Great Britain helped organize the Alliance of Religions and Conservation to assist religious organizations around the world in developing environmental programs based on their beliefs and practices.[15] In the first decade of the twenty-first century, a new organization called Interfaith Power and Light[16] emerged to promote a faith-based response to global warming through energy efficiency upgrades to US houses of worship, while the Evangelical Environmental Network organized a "What Would Jesus Drive" campaign to encourage purchase of fuel-efficient cars.[17] During this same time period, the major denominations in the United States adopted formal statements calling on their members to care for the earth and support efforts to mitigate climate change.

THE ACADEMIC STUDY OF RELIGION AND ECOLOGY

The trends in late twentieth- and early twenty-first-century religious environmentalism inspired emergence of a field of scholarship on religion and ecology, much of it predicated on the idea that "religious worldviews decisively shape environmental behaviors."[18] Research questions within the field run parallel to trends in religious environmentalism. Early work in the field focused on what role biblical religion might play in causing negative environmental attitudes and behavior, while more recent scholarship has emphasized the potential for religion to promote positive environmental actions, especially in response to climate change.

In the 1980s, social scientists became interested in exploring the "Lynn White thesis," that a biblical "mastery-over-nature" ethic contributed to a utilitarian view of nature, as a factor that might affect levels of environmental concern and activism. White's ideas may have seemed particularly apropos at a time when the newly created Moral Majority (founded in 1979) was promoting a political agenda linked to conservative Christianity. Since the Moral Majority was closely affiliated with the Reagan administration, which was removing government support for environmental programs and increasing economic development of natural resources on federally controlled lands and waters, a correlation between conservative Protestantism and anti-environmental

attitudes seemed plausible. A few social scientists tried to empirically evaluate whether belief in divinely sanctioned human dominion over nature did,
indeed, influence environmentalism. Unfortunately, efforts to use surveys to
find correlations between specific beliefs and levels of environmental concern were inconclusive. Some researchers found evidence that membership
in more conservative denominations or having greater belief in biblical literalism (also associated with conservative churches) correlated with lower levels
of environmental concern, and theorized that people in these circumstances
were more likely to subscribe to a dominion worldview, which could explain
their attitudes.[19] However, subsequent studies in the 1990s found that there
was variation within denominations and that political identity rather than
dominion beliefs might explain the differing levels of environmental concern.[20] Furthermore, as public awareness of climate change increased in the
1990s, leaders from across the spectrum of American religious denominations
became vocal advocates for environmental action. Many Christian clergy
cited the same biblical passage that Lynn White associated with Christian
anti-nature attitudes as the basis for an environmental message, arguing that
because humans were given dominion over nature, they had a divine mandate to practice sustainable stewardship of God's creation.[21]

As these eco-theologies multiplied and new religious environmental
movement organizations were established in the 1990s, more academics
began to study the intersection of religion and ecology. A contingent of
scholars became particularly interested in the potential for religion to motivate responses to environmental crises. Mary Evelyn Tucker and John Grim
organized a series of conferences on world religions and ecology that explored
religious narratives and practices that could be reframed to encourage environmental ethics. Their goal was to construct resources that could help faith
communities engage with environmental crises. To those who participated
in this constructive scholarship, the expanding body of eco-theology, prolif-
eration of environmental statements among major denominations in the US,
and emergence of religious environmental organizations seemed to indicate
that US religions were "going green."[22]

Researchers who studied the new eco-theologies and faith-based environmental campaigns speculated about whether religion would be able to
create a social movement to address climate change that would be similar to
the civil rights movement of the 1960s.[23] However, a few scholars have challenged the idea that Western religions are becoming greener.[24] They note,
for example, that people attending churches in Cornwall were unaware that

their denomination, the Church of England, was engaged in a campaign to encourage environmental action in its member congregations;[25] that many evangelicals in the United States have not heard of the Evangelical Climate Initiative and are distrustful of climate action messages from clergy they do not know personally;[26] and that surveys in the US indicate that Christians have lower levels of environmental concern than non-Christians and non-religious individuals, a pattern that did not change between 1993 and 2010.[27] These studies, which seem to indicate that denominational environmental statements have had little influence on the attitudes or actions of the people in the pews, have caused prominent scholars in the religion and ecology field to critique the idea there is an imminent greening of religion movement that will soon have significant effects on American society and advocate for much more research into how religion influences environmental behaviors.[28]

RELIGIOUS ENVIRONMENTALISM IN PRACTICE

The apparent disconnect between top-down theological pronouncements advocating earth care and denominational members' awareness is not, however, the end of the story. Some Christians, Jews, and other people of faith in the United States *are* engaging in faith-based environmental action. The number of religious environmental movement organizations in the US increased from nine in 1990 to more than eighty in 2010, by which time they were operating in most states.[29] A growing number of faith communities are working to put environmental ethics into practice. Clergy and lay members were a significant presence at the 2016 Climate March in Washington, DC, and supported the water protection movement at Standing Rock. Religious environmental action is also taking place at the local congregational level. People are making houses of worship more energy efficient, installing solar panels, and conserving water and other resources. They are restoring forests and prairies on their lands, purchasing local food, growing organic produce for food pantries, advocating for environmental justice, and participating in local climate marches. In 2018, there were 206 certified Earth Care Congregations in the Presbyterian Church USA[30] and 290 certified Green Sanctuaries in the Unitarian Universalist Association (about 30 percent of UUA churches).[31] People of faith use diverse terms such as earth care, creation care, restoring creation, being green, and practicing sustainability to describe these efforts, but what is striking is that they are taking action through the venue of religious organizations, rather than through the venue of traditional environmental organizations.

Surveys attempting to measure whether religions are becoming green by correlating religious affiliation with environmental concern do not adequately capture or explain the earth-care activities that are occurring in these individual faith communities. The fact that some Catholic parishes engage in earth care while the majority do not, despite environmental pronouncements from three consecutive popes, indicates that theology and denominational leadership are not the sole, and perhaps not even the most significant, factors in determining whether people of faith undertake environmental actions. This fact begs the question, why? Why are some faith communities going green even though most are not? And, once motivated to engage in earth care, how do people of faith turn intention into action, and what actions do they undertake?

These questions are of interest because more Americans belong to religious organizations than any other type of voluntary association[32] and, collectively, religious communities are the single most prevalent type of human organization in the world.[33] Since religions are institutions that express social values and govern behavior, they provide a platform with significant potential for advancing social change. In a world confronting the realities of climate change and the imperative for environmental sustainability, there is need for a better understanding of the role religious communities can play in facilitating institutional changes that enable resilience, adaptation, and sustainability.

A few scholars have begun to study these movements, to examine the "messiness of religious environmentalism in practice,"[34] and their research is shedding light on factors that help overcome barriers to action. Stephen Ellingson analyzed the emergence of religious environmental movement organizations in the United States between 1990 and 2010. His work revealed how these organizations adapted religious ideas to give legitimacy to religious environmentalism in ways that fit the constraints of being embedded in religious institutions.[35] Scholars are also beginning to explore religious environmentalism at the community level. Sarah McFarland Taylor described the experiences of the green sisters, a network of Catholic women religious from diverse communities in North America, whose shared knowledge and moral support facilitated efforts to incorporate earth care into convents and retreat centers.[36] These women were early adopters of an earth-care ethic and helped establish many of the precepts and practices that others later took up. Amanda Baugh delved into the empirical experiences of one specific religious environmental organization and its efforts to promote faith-based environmentalism within local congregations. She conducted fieldwork at Faith in Place in Chicago over several years and explored how race, ethnicity, and class caused variations in "the shape and meaning" of religious environmentalism in practice.[37]

A CASE-STUDY EXPLORATION OF THE GREENING OF RELIGION

This book adds to our understanding of religious environmentalism in practice. Ellingson and Baugh focused on organizations that strive to motivate action within communities of faith. To better understand faith-based environmental behavior, this study examines the empirical experiences of fifteen faith communities that heeded the call to action and integrated sustainability into their religious organizations. These communities, which include Protestant, Catholic, Jewish, and Unitarian Universalist congregations, have implemented initiatives that are designed to reduce their community's environmental impact through activities such as conserving resources, growing food, restoring ecosystems, and advocating for policies that address environmental justice and climate change. In order to understand factors that contributed to these accomplishments, the book employs case-study methods, which are particularly well suited to exploring motivations and processes that affect human behavior. As Robert Yin comments in his classic text on case-study methods, "In general, case studies are the preferred strategy when 'how' and 'why' questions are being posed," especially when trying to understand "contemporary phenomenon within some real-life context."[38] To learn why some faith communities have undertaken earth-care programs and to understand how those who are successful were able to achieve their accomplishments, it makes sense to speak with the people who were personally involved in making things happen. Therefore, this project uses field research and comparative in-depth case-study analysis to investigate factors that triggered emergence and institutionalization of faith-based sustainability initiatives as well as the reach and substantive impact of those efforts.

Key Terminology

This book uses the phrase "sustainability initiative" to describe the environmental activities undertaken by the case-study communities. The term "initiative" refers to a *set of actions* undertaken for the purpose of reducing a faith community's impact on the natural environment. Earth Day worship services or earth-care themed Bible study may serve as precursors to an initiative, but these types of activity alone do not constitute initiatives because they do not involve changes in community infrastructure or behavior that affect use of natural resources. A faith community that has undertaken a sustainability initiative is one that is engaged in activities such as conservation behavior through reduced use of water and energy, resource management through sustainable land stewardship practices, or policy advocacy work to promote regulations that protect air, water, and food.

Defining the initiatives to be studied in relation to "sustainability," the idea of "improving the quality of human life while living within the carrying capacity of supporting eco-systems,"[39] offers a broad umbrella under which to explore the diverse environmental activities being implemented by faith-based organizations. These activities range from habitat restoration to resource conservation; from support for organic, local, and fair-trade foods to social justice advocacy for policies to improve the quality of life for disadvantaged people. Faith groups use a variety of terms to describe their actions, including *restoring creation, creation care, earth stewardship, earth care,* and *being green.* Only recently have they begun speaking of *sustainability,* however, the term is gaining popularity because it avoids the social conflicts associated with references to climate change or environmentalism, which have become linked to liberal political identities in the United States. *Sustainability* is also a useful overarching term for describing a range of motives that inspire specific environmental actions. For example, one community may create a community garden to grow food as a means of reducing greenhouse gas emissions generated by transportation of non-local produce, while another community creates a garden in order to feed people who live in a food desert and have little access to fresh produce. In the first case, climate change is the motivation, whereas environmental justice is the issue in the second case, yet both can be described as actions that contribute to environmental sustainability. Therefore, this book uses *sustainability initiative* to describe programs for undertaking environmental actions within faith communities because the term is acceptable to people in diverse religious traditions and because all of the activities enacted under the various rubrics cited above can be subsumed under an overarching sustainability label.

The term *faith community* is used because this study includes both congregations and monastic communities, and because the term *congregation* has multiple meanings, which can create confusion. Congregations are "social institutions in which individuals who are not all religious specialists gather in physical proximity to one another, frequently and at regularly scheduled intervals, for activities and events with explicitly religious content and purpose, and in which there is continuity over time in the individuals who gather, the location of the gathering, and the nature of the activities and events at each gathering."[40] As faith-based social institutions, monasteries are similar to congregations except that the members are all religious specialists who have chosen to dedicate their lives to a full-time religious vocation. Because both congregations and monasteries are religious organizations with defined leadership and governance structures, memberships, locations, and fairly quantifiable material and social resources, it was possible to compare case studies from both types of faith community.

A second reason for referring to the case-study groups as *faith communities* was to avoid the potential for confusion that arises because the word *congregation* can refer to both a religious social institution (a church/synagogue/temple/mosque) and to its body of members. Thus, for example, one can say that "Trinity Presbyterian is a Christian congregation" and that "the congregation of Trinity Presbyterian meets on Sundays." To avoid confusion, this book refers to the religious social institution as a faith community and the body of members as a congregation.

The fifteen case studies in this book include ten non-monastic communities and five monastic communities. Non-monastic faith communities make up the majority of the religious organizations in the United States, and the experiences of the cases described in this study may be of particular interest for better understanding the benefits and challenges such communities face in adopting sustainability as a religious activity. Although monastic communities are less prevalent, many have been early adopters of earth-care practices and, consequently, they provide a rich source of knowledge about the long-term evolution of sustainability initiatives. Because both types of religious institutions have primary missions of supporting members' religious lives rather than being explicitly focused on environmental protection, these fifteen non-monastic and monastic communities faced similar challenges in adopting earth care as part of their community missions. The insights that emerge from comparing their experiences may be of use to people of faith in a variety of religious organizations.

Case Selection

The faith communities studied for this book were selected because they have implemented exemplary sustainability initiatives. Prior to selecting cases, I explored the range of environmental activities being conducted by faith communities in the United States by reading accounts presented on websites for interfaith environmental organizations. Brief descriptions of faith-community earth-care actions were available as Stewardship Stories on the website for the National Religious Partnership for the Environment, Cool Congregations Award winners celebrated by Interfaith Power and Light, Success Stories recounted by the Eco-Justice Program (later renamed Creation Justice Ministries) of the National Council of Churches, GreenFaith Certification Program participants listed by GreenFaith, and Engaged Projects compiled by Yale University's Forum on Religion and Ecology.[41] Analysis of 173 such stories revealed three general types of activities being undertaken by faith communities: resource conservation, land stewardship, and political advocacy. Resource conservation comprised the most widely practiced type of activity, as faith communities were: reducing use of energy, water, paper and gasoline; establishing recycling and composting programs; buying fair-trade coffee and recycled paper products; growing produce for local food pantries; and installing solar panels. Land stewardship activities were being undertaken by communities with larger grounds, where they were replacing lawns with native plant gardens, hosting community-supported agriculture (CSA) farms, and restoring prairie and forest ecosystems. Political advocacy appeared in various faith communities that engaged in actions such as writing letters to legislators to encourage support for climate action, attending municipal meetings to testify against permits for environmentally damaging projects, and submitting stockholder policy proposals to require that corporations report on the environmental effects of their supply chains.

Perusal of these stories revealed that some faith communities were engaged in environmental activities on a scale that set them apart from most congregations. The majority of the stewardship stories described faith communities that focused on one or two projects, however, a small portion had undertaken multiple activities that integrated earth care into diverse areas of their religious organizations, including worship, religious education, facilities management, and ministry work. In this subset of cases, sustainability seemed to have become embedded in the social norms that defined general behavioral expectations for the congregation. These "exemplary" cases of faith-based earth care became the focus of this research project. The goal was to compare success stories in order to identify factors that contribute to the process of integrating sustainability into a faith community's social norms. Consequently, the cases selected for this study involve faith communities with sustainability initiatives that included multiple activities and were continued for at least four years.[42] All of the cases include resource conservation actions, and most also include advocacy and/or land stewardship. The four-year criterion was added in order to examine factors that contributed to durability of initiatives.

Data Collection and Analysis

Using qualitative research methods, I collected three types of data: Fifty-two semi-structured interviews, site visit observations at all fifteen locations, and archival materials. Interviews were essential for gathering data from the people who were closely involved with the initiatives. The interview questions were developed based on information from research fields of conservation psychology, social movement theory, and collaborative resource management, which provide insights into factors that affect individual and collective action.[43] Interviewees were asked about motivations that inspired them to engage in earth care through the venue of a faith community and factors such as social networks, resources, and decision processes that enabled them to develop and sustain initiatives. Site visits were important for assessing the scale and outcome of initiatives. These visits made it possible to find out how visible earth care was in a faith community's buildings and activities, and to assess the breadth of congregational awareness of earth care through informal conversations with members who were not on the "green team" that led the initiatives or by observing how many people spent time in a community garden after worship service. The site visits also allowed me to learn about the local municipal context. Archival data provided information about the development of initiatives over time. This data included internal materials such as congregational histories, newsletters, meeting minutes, sermons, applications for green certification, brochures, and land management plans, as well as external materials such as media stories, denominational and interfaith earth-care program information, and scholarship on denominational polity. Electronic media such as webpage videos, blogs, and Facebook pages were also included in the archival materials.

The data was organized into case studies describing factors that affected development of each sustainability initiative. These case studies were then compared to identify similarities and differences across the cases. Although there was no one pathway followed by all the faith communities, comparison did reveal similar patterns of leadership and organizational factors that affected how deeply sustainability became embedded in the social norms of faith communities. In each case, initiatives began when key individuals took the lead and organized earth-care activities through the venue of their faith community. Development of the resulting sustainability initiatives was shaped by the characteristics of these individual champions and their interactions with the faith leaders, congregations, and organizations that made up their faith communities. This shared pattern provided the structure for an analytical framework to examine factors within four domains of activity—Champions, Faith Leaders, Congregations, and Organizations—that affected the emergence and implementation of the sustainability initiatives. This book recounts the stories of the remarkable sustainability initiatives undertaken by these fifteen faith communities and describes insights that emerged from comparison of their experiences in each of these four domains.

AN OVERVIEW OF THE CHAPTERS

Following on this overview of the tension between hope for an upwelling of religiously motivated environmental activity and the limited research on the practice of faith-based earth care, Part I of the book begins to describe and analyze the empirical experiences of faith communities that have developed exemplary sustainability initiatives. Chapter 1 presents an overview of the fifteen case studies, with brief descriptions of each community and its initiative. Chapter 2 describes key findings that emerged from cross-case analysis, which indicated that the initiatives were affected by factors in the four domains of activity (Champions, Faith Leaders, Congregations, and Organizations).

The rest of the book is organized into four parts that each focus on a domain of activity. Part II, Champions, comprises an introduction to the domain and Chapters 3 and 4, which examine motivations and leadership qualities that enabled individuals to effectively organize earth-care activities within their faith communities. Part III, Faith Leaders, begins with an introduction that describes the motivations that inspired clergy and leadership teams to promote earth care. Chapter 5 explores the messages through which faith leaders presented earth care as an issue requiring action from their faith communities, and Chapter 6 considers how the mechanisms through which faith leaders promoted earth-care affected initiative development. Part IV, Congregations, presents a brief summary of case-study community characteristics in the introduction, followed by two chapters that delve into factors that influenced levels of congregational support for earth-care activities. Chapter 7 focuses on community identity and historical practices, while

Chapter 8 explores variations in congregational involvement in initiatives. Finally, Part V, Organizations, examines operating procedures (Chapter 9) and organizational structures (Chapter 10) that provided opportunities, and sometimes imposed constraints, for implementation of earth-care activities. Each domain section ends with an analysis called "Summary and Domain Interactions" that summarizes specific contributions the domain made to the sustainability initiatives and examines how factors from that domain intersected with other domains to enable implementation of earth-care activities.

The Conclusion pulls together the contributions, enabling factors, and intersections from all four domains, which together form a matrix of observations, some of which suggest best practices for developing sustainability initiatives in faith communities. The chapter also includes reflections on the role of religion in these cases of faith-based earth care. It is important to remember that the primary purpose of a religious organization is to support the religious lives of its members. The case-study communities adopted earth care as an activity that was consistent with their religious purpose, but these communities are not environmental organizations; they are religious organizations working to protect the environment as an expression of their faith. Therefore, this research pays special attention to the processes through which faith communities reflected on the relationship between earth care and their religious missions, and what factors affected decisions to incorporate earth care into the religious organizations.

Part I

The
GREENING
of
US FAITH
COMMUNITIES

1 GENESIS AND EVOLUTION OF FIFTEEN SUSTAINABILITY INITIATIVES

THE FIFTEEN CASE STUDIES that provide the basis for this research share an overarching narrative: the sustainability initiatives emerged in response to specific triggering events and their development was shaped by the cultures, local geographic contexts, and resources of the faith communities. Within this common narrative, however, there is considerable variation. The triggers differed across cases: some began with one person's idea for a specific project or a small group that wanted to study connections between earth care and their faith tradition while others developed in response to a community-wide decision to adopt an earth-care ethic. The resulting initiatives progressed along divergent paths as the faith communities moved toward integration of sustainability into their congregational social norms. This chapter introduces the fifteen faith communities, giving a brief summary of how their initiatives began, how they evolved over time, and what activities were undertaken in their efforts to practice and promote more environmentally sustainable behavior. The following chapter analyzes notable similarities and differences observed across these cases and constructs an analytical framework to be used for deeper exploration of factors that enabled the emergence and implementation of these sustainability initiatives.

OVERVIEW OF THE FAITH COMMUNITIES

The sustainability initiatives examined in this project were undertaken by faith communities from across the United States. Most of the communities are in the upper Midwest/Great Lakes and northeast regions, with the exception of two congregations, one in California and another in Virginia (see Map 1.1). Study of these faith communities provided valuable opportunities to examine factors that contribute to the development of consequential and durable faith-based sustainability initiatives. As noted in the previous chapter, these case-study sites were selected because the communities have implemented initiatives that include multiple activities and they have maintained these efforts for at least four years. In addition, site selection attempted to ensure inclusion of cases representing the various types of sustainability activities that are being undertaken by faith communities in the United States. During preliminary research for this project, an examination of the range of faith-based environmental actions in the United States revealed three categories of activity. First, and most prevalent, faith communities engage in *conservation practices* in which they make changes to behavior and infrastructure in order to prevent pollution and conserve resources such as energy, water, and forests. Second, faith communities develop sustainable *land stewardship,* or resource management, systems for their lands in order to protect and restore ecosystems such as prairies, forests,

MAP 1 Map of Case-Study Sites

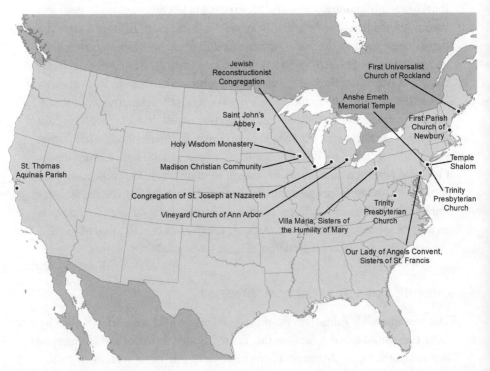

and wetlands. Third, community members engage in *advocacy* efforts to influence local, regional, or national policies related to environmental sustainability. The three categories are not mutually exclusive, and a community's focus may shift from one emphasis to another over time.

The fifteen case-study sites selected for inclusion in this research include communities that provide examples of all three types of activities. Conservation practices take center stage in the sustainability initiatives of ten urban/suburban non-monastic faith communities. Land stewardship practices are prominent in the sustainability initiatives of five monastic faith communities that have extensive land holdings. These monastic communities are religious organizations in which men (brothers) or women (sisters) have chosen to make religion the full-time focus of their lives. Four of the five communities were established in the nineteenth century and previously practiced subsistence agriculture on their lands. Advocacy efforts appear in both non-monastic and monastic faith communities but are not ubiquitous in either group.

The fifteen communities share several general characteristics: all have memberships that are predominantly white and middle-class, and all are well-established organizations, ranging in age from 39 to more than 150 years. The prevalence of white, middle-class members reflects biases in the case selection processes. Potential sites were located through use of databases created by the National Council of Churches Eco-justice Ministry, the National Religious Partnership for the Environment, Yale's Forum on Religion and Ecology, and GreenFaith. Middle-class congregations dominate the Stewardship Stories in these databases. The selection criteria of "multiple activities sustained over at least four years" may also have privileged higher-income communities over lower-income and people-of-color faith communities that engage in environmental efforts focused on a single activity or of shorter duration. Social engagement is also a shared characteristic. With the exception of one evangelical church, these communities belong to mainline Protestant, Unitarian Universalist, Jewish, and Catholic denominations that have been historically associated with social justice work in American society. Denomination was not a consideration in case selection since the research sites were chosen for the quality of their environmental activities, however, the cross-case analysis does examine denomination as a variable affecting factors that enabled the faith communities to develop their sustainability initiatives. The communities varied in size, from 40 individual members to 1,800 families, and in physical context, from an urban congregation with a building, parking lot, and no green space to a rural abbey with 2,800 acres of forest and its own zip code.

The descriptions of the fifteen cases in this chapter are divided into three clusters. Because the five monastic faith communities differ from the non-monastic cases in their emphasis on land stewardship as well as organizational structure and size of infrastructure and land holdings, it made sense to analyze patterns in the genesis and evolution of their initiatives separately from those of the non-monastic faith communities. The ten non-monastic faith communities are subdivided into two groups: a cluster of six cases in which the sustainability initiatives evolved gradually in response to ideas and programmatic structures that developed organically from within the faith communities, and a separate cluster of four cases that enrolled in green certification programs managed by external organizations that provide applicants with a standardized framework for incorporating earth care into a religious organization. Because the certification programs affected the scope and structure of the faith communities' sustainability initiatives, it was useful to describe the emergence and development of these four initiatives separately in

TABLE 1 OVERVIEW OF THE FIFTEEN CASES

CASE TYPE	FAITH COMMUNITY	LOCATION	DENOMINATION	TYPES OF ACTIVITIES
Organic structure	1. Trinity Presbyterian Church	Harrisonburg VA	Presbyterian Church (USA)	Environmental advocacy, conservation practices
Organic structure	2. Madison Christian community	Madison WI	Evangelical Lutheran Church in America and United Church of Christ (ecumenical)	Conservation practices, solar panels, community gardens, prairie restoration
Organic structure	3. Jewish Reconstructionist Congregation	Evanston IL	Reconstructionist Jewish	Conservation practices, green building
Organic structure	4. First Parish Church of Newbury	Newbury MA	United Church of Christ	Community gardens, nature-themed preschool

CASE TYPE	FAITH COMMUNITY	LOCATION	DENOMINATION	TYPES OF ACTIVITIES
Organic structure	5. Vineyard Church of Ann Arbor	Ann Arbor MI	Evangelical	Conservation practices, community garden
Organic structure	6. St. Thomas Aquinas Parish	Palo Alto CA	Catholic	Conservation practices, advocacy
Green certified	7. First Universalist Church of Rockland	Rockland ME	Unitarian Universalist	Conservation practices, CSA, Community Supported Fishery
Green certified	8. Trinity Presbyterian Church	East Brunswick NJ	Presbyterian Church (USA)	Conservation practices, community garden
Green certified	9. Anshe Emeth Memorial Temple	New Brunswick NJ	Reform Jewish	Conservation practices, environmental advocacy
Green certified	10. Temple Shalom	Aberdeen NJ	Reform Jewish	Conservation practices, solar, community garden
Monastic	11. Congregation of St. Joseph at Nazareth	Kalamazoo MI	Catholic Women	Conservation practices, land restoration
Monastic	12. Saint John's Abbey Saint John's University	Collegeville MN	Catholic Benedictine Men	Conservation practices, sustainable forestry, solar panels
Monastic	13. Villa Maria, Sisters of the Humility of Mary	Villa Maria PA	Catholic Women	Conservation practices, sustainable forestry, organic gardening, CSA
Monastic	14. Holy Wisdom Monastery, Benedictine Women	Madison WI	Ecumenical Benedictine Women	Conservation practices, prairie restoration, green building
Monastic	15. Our Lady of Angels, Sisters of St. Francis of Philadelphia	Aston PA	Catholic Franciscan Women	Conservation practices, CSA, environmental justice advocacy

order to discern patterns among the green-certified initiatives and to compare and contrast them with the cases that developed their structures organically. Table 1 provides a list of faith community names, location, size, and most prominent activities.

The brief case summaries presented in this chapter introduce the faith communities and their sustainability initiatives, with special attention to notable features of each case. The summaries describe the events that triggered the initiatives and provide an overview of each case's development, including factors such as key individuals and activities that were particularly significant for the initiatives. By comparing these case summaries, it is possible to identify themes that are shared across the cases and to discern distinctive features of initiatives that only become evident when they are juxtaposed with other cases. Identification of common themes and notable variations elucidates topics that require deeper exploration and will be taken up in greater detail in the subsequent sections of the book.

CASE CLUSTER I:
FAITH COMMUNITIES WITH ORGANIC INITIATIVES

The first six case studies describe sustainability initiatives that emerged and developed organically within their faith communities. These initiatives were inspired by a variety of triggering events. The case with the longest-running initiative began slowly when a few church members with environmental interests formed a group for shared study and worship. After several years, threats to their local environment inspired them to increased levels of action, and they developed a sustainability initiative with diverse activities focused on advocacy and conservation practices. For the other five faith communities, sustainability initiatives emerged in response to more clearly defined triggering events. In two cases, the faith communities were at crossroads in which members had to make decisions about the future of their religious organizations, and sustainability was adopted as a community focus during the decision process. For two other communities, the triggering events came from the pastors, who presented ideas for environmental stewardship to their congregations. In the final case, the triggering event came from an external source, when the regional denominational organization instituted a new program to encourage sustainability efforts among member congregations.

1 *Trinity Presbyterian Church (TPC*), Harrisonburg, Virginia*
Membership: 165

In 1996, lay members of Trinity Presbyterian Church formed a Restoring Creation House Church, which was later renamed the Earth Care House Church. House churches are small groups through which members engage in ministry work as a way to express the church's mission of "striving to be the church in the world through servant ministries."[1] Any member of the congregation may propose formation of a house church to address a perceived need such as food security or poverty alleviation. If other members share interest in the topic, the group creates a formal covenant describing the mission of the house church and the activities through which the group will fulfill its mission. The Earth Care House Church mission is "to promote Church and community awareness and involvement in restoring creation."[2] It fulfills this mission through group study of theology and environmental texts, leading the Earth Day Sunday service, and organizing outdoor activities for youth.

Along with these study and worship activities, the Earth Care House Church promotes involvement in restoring creation through community outreach and practical actions, areas of activity that have evolved over time. In the beginning, the group studied how theology connected with earth care and did outreach by sharing information on environmental issues with the congregation. After a few years, however, the group began to feel the need for increased action, especially since many of the house church participants were longtime environmentalists who were well informed about issues of pollution, biodiversity loss, and climate change.

Faith soon motivated the Earth Care House Church members to a new level of environmental action when they found that a beloved local natural area was being damaged by pollution. As outdoor enthusiasts, the house church participants often visited Shenandoah National Park. In 2001 they became aware the park suffered from air quality problems, especially acid rain. The issue could not be solved locally since the pollution came from coal-burning power plants in West Virginia; only federal legislation could regulate interstate pollution. According to Lynn Cameron, a founding member of the group, the scope of the problem intimidated them because "what could a little

---

* The name of each case study site is followed by an abbreviation that will be used in data tables. Thus, TPC designates Trinity Presbyterian Church in Harrisonburg.

house church do about such a big issue?"[3] However, their pastor, Reverend Ann Held, suggested that the Earth Care House Church might be able to gain support for addressing the issue of coal pollution if they presented a resolution to the annual General Assembly meeting of the Presbyterian Church (USA) denomination. Telling each other that "God does not call us to do little things,"[4] the members of the house church decided they had to try to protect their beloved park. They worked with the Southern Environmental Law Center to craft a resolution that called for the Presbyterian Church (USA) to educate Presbyterians about the environmental and health consequences of coal-fired power plants. It also asked all Presbyterians to exercise stewardship of the earth by urging government officials to support policies and legislation that would enforce existing clean air laws, enact new laws for power plants to reduce pollution, and end "grandfather" loopholes that exempt older coal-fired plants from current regulations. Furthermore, the resolution directed that the new policy should be communicated to power companies and that these concerns about air quality should be incorporated into the advocacy work of the Washington Office and Environmental Justice Office of the Presbyterian Church (USA). The resolution was unanimously approved by the 214th General Assembly in 2002.

Buoyed by their success, which Cameron said left them feeling that "there was no stopping us now," members of the Earth Care House Church continued to do advocacy work while also expanding their range of activities by undertaking resource conservation projects at the church. Cameron notes that environmental work often starts with being against something, but, she says, "Eventually, you have to ask, 'What are you *for*?' "[5] Study of eco-theological reports published by the Presbyterian Church (USA) such as *Restoring Creation for Ecology and Justice* (1990) and *Hope for a Global Future: Toward Just and Sustainable Human Development* (1996) set the stage for the house church members to develop a faith-based response to environmental problems that focuses on positive goals of environmental restoration, justice, and sustainability rather than simply avoiding a negative scenario.

According to Cameron, "Once the theology was within us, we could act out our faith. We could be against waste of resources"[6] and begin to organize a more diverse range of activities. They began with a strong emphasis on traditional environmental advocacy work, writing letters to legislators and speaking at public meetings. In addition, they worked to educate the wider community about subjects like air pollution and threats to local water supplies from hydraulic fracturing (or hydro-fracking, a technique for mining fossil fuels) by sponsoring town hall meetings and giving presentations at churches, universities, wineries, and other facilities. While continuing their advocacy work, they gradually added projects to conserve resources at the church by weatherizing the building, upgrading lighting, and replacing disposables with reusable dishes. They also have donated rain barrels to families with young children and grown vegetables both at home and at church to contribute to food pantries. Throughout two decades of working to restore creation, the house church has maintained a particular emphasis on working to connect youth with nature. Along with regular outings for children from the church, members of the Earth Care House Church used grant funds to organize environmental education summer programs for children from urban areas and donated trees to a local camp.

The accomplishments and durability of the Earth Care House Church have been bolstered by strong support from their faith community. Reverend Ann Held is a fervent proponent of environmental protection who enjoys outdoor activities and often incorporates reflections from her experiences of nature into her sermons. The house church structure, with its public covenant statements, ensures that the wider faith community is regularly apprised of the Earth Care group's mission and activities, and formally endorses earth care as an authorized expression of the church's mission. Due to this authorization process, the Earth Care House Church is able to publicly advocate for environmental protection as a moral issue, confident that their faith community stands behind them and will support their actions. Finally, members of the Earth Care House Church gain strength from their religious convictions. Their early years of theological study built a firm foundation from which to undertake their sustainability activities. When people have challenged them, saying that Christians should not be so focused on concerns of this world, members of the Earth Care House Church are able to explain with confidence why their faith requires them to restore God's creation.

2 *Madison Christian Community (MCC), Evangelical Lutheran Church in America and United Church of Christ, Middleton, Wisconsin*
   Membership: approximately 400

One gusty day in 2001, Reverend Jeff Wild, the new Lutheran pastor at the Madison Christian Community, found himself thinking that the church grounds would be a good location for a wind turbine. He mentioned the idea to members of the community, and they formed a task force to explore the idea. They learned that a wind turbine would not be practical but that their roof was perfect for solar panels. With grant assistance, the church installed a photovoltaic array. The solar panels were the first of many projects for a faith community that has come to see stewardship of the natural environment as part of its core mission. The ecumenical community of about 400 members, in which a Lutheran congregation and a United Church of Christ congregation share a building and six acres of land, describes its purpose as "living faithfully and lovingly with God, neighbors, and creation."[7] All the elements of this purpose statement come together in the community's environmental ministry, which includes energy conservation, extensive community gardens, and two acres of restored prairies.

The prairies are indicative of a long-term environmental ethic that was already present in the faith community when Pastor Wild arrived. The church was built in 1970 on land donated by a farmer, and the community had long felt a responsibility to care for this "gift of land," which they attributed to divine grace. When soil was excavated to create space for an addition to the building, rather than having the dirt removed, it was piled along the front edge of the parking area to form a berm. Members gathered native prairie seeds from roadsides and rural prairie patches and created a prairie on the berm. Pleased with the outcome, members worked to convert another acre of land on the side of the church into prairie. The community members have tended to these prairies since 1983, even conducting controlled burns in the spring to stimulate native plant growth and control invasive species.

In addition to this prairie restoration project, the community had a tradition of sending youth on a summer canoe trip to the Boundary Waters of Minnesota. With these traditions as background, there was already an unstated environmental ethic within the community; Pastor Wild says, "[I]t was just a matter for me to become aware of it and build on it."[8] Wild integrated environmental stewardship into religious teachings and connected those teachings to the land-heritage of the community. Members of the community who shared the pastor's environmental concerns joined the Energy Task Force to research renewable energy options and developed recommendations for reducing energy use in church facilities.

Community members take pride in their successful efforts to reduce resource use in the buildings, but the environmental stewardship activities that are closest to their hearts and most express their vision of how to live "faithfully and lovingly with God, neighbors, and creation" take place on the six acres of land around their church. Along with the two acres of prairie, the community maintains extensive produce gardens, which include a hoop house for starting seedlings in the spring, a small orchard, and a chicken coop. A community garden, where people lease plots annually, was established in the 1970s. In 2004, Pastor Wild helped plant a Children's Garden, which serves as the location for a cooperative project between the Madison Christian Community and the nearby Lussier Community Education Center. During the summer, children from the low-income Wexford Ridge Neighborhood come to the church twice a week to learn about gardening. Working closely with adults, they learn how to care for plants and chickens and how to prepare healthy meals from fresh produce. The children then take a bag of food home to their families each week. The garden also connects to prison ministry work. The heirloom plants in the garden are purchased from a prison horticultural program, and a group of prisoners comes to the church in the spring to prepare the garden beds, see where their seedlings will be planted, and partake of a lunch prepared for them by the faith community.

Pastor Wild describes the integration of environmental stewardship with faith at the Madison Christian Community as "ministry of place." Community members who tend the restored prairies, work in the gardens, walk the outdoor labyrinth, serve on environmental task forces, and participate in activities like building rainwater harvest systems are building connections to the place where they invest their effort. In the process, both faith and environmental perspectives are deepened. The relationships people build within the two congregations and with the neighborhood strengthen their sense of community. They also gain a sense of efficacy as they put their faith into action. Moreover, Wild says they have become better Trinitarians, not only focused on Jesus and salvation, but also on God as Father/Creator of the natural world and the Holy Spirit present within the environment all around them. Thus, through the ministry of place at Madison Christian Community, environmental stewardship and faith both have been enhanced.

3 *Jewish Reconstructionist Congregation (JRC), Evanston, Illinois*
   Membership: approximately 500 families; 875 adults

The Jewish Reconstructionist Congregation in Evanston is known as "The Green Synagogue." The sustainability initiative that earned it this title emerged during a period of reflection about how to deal with a building that was no longer adequate for their needs. In 2002, members of the congregation had formed an Environmental Task Force to explore connections between Judaism and environmental issues. When they learned that the Building Committee was going to recommend that the community tear down and replace its old building, the Task Force members decided to propose that the congregation follow green building practices. They presented a proposal to the board. As Rabbi Brant Rosen and the board studied the issue, Rosen became quite excited about green building as an opportunity to express religious values. He began to incorporate environmental themes into the opening prayers for board meetings. Despite some concerns about how the congregation would react to the additional costs, the board decided to present the proposal to the community. As the congregation learned more about green building, enthusiasm among the members increased.

> The more people we told about this, the more excited they became, and more people became invested in the overall project in a way they wouldn't have been ordinarily. Once this project became about more than bricks and mortar, when it became about our values—not just that we're building a building, but how we're building it—people became invested in it.[9]

Community members expressed their enthusiasm by contributing funds and skills, resulting in construction of the first platinum LEED-certified synagogue in the United States.[10]

Deciding to build a new building, and that it should be a green building, was a community-wide endeavor. Infrastructure decisions for which the community provides financial resources require full congregational participation. The proposal to follow green building practices created an opportunity for the entire community to study connections between sustainability and their religious values. All who contributed funds to the new building shared ownership in the green synagogue, and the community identification with sustainability intensified as the building drew media attention and public acclaim. Members are reminded of their community commitment to sustainability every time they visit their synagogue, where green features are beautifully apparent in natural lighting, woodwork, and windows framing restful views of foliage. Furthermore, the community uses its building as a vehicle for ministry. The congregation's website provides detailed information about the construction project, explaining the benefits of various design elements. Members of the congregation have trained to serve as docents, leading tours of the building so that others may learn about the benefits of green building.

4 *First Parish Church of Newbury (FPN), United Church of Christ,*
   Newbury, Massachusetts
   Membership: approximately 40

The Sustainability Initiative of First Parish Church of Newbury emerged from a community discernment process in 2006. The faith community had shrunk to about thirty members who struggled to keep up with repairs on a church built in 1869. The minister, Nancy Haverington, decided the community needed to consider its future, and twenty-five members met weekly for a year to reflect on their personal desires, research community demographics, listen to each other, and pray for guidance. A new community mission emerged from this process: their congregation would be Stewards of Earth and Spirit.

Uncertain of how to implement their new mission, members decided to start an organic garden behind the church. Unfortunately, the gardeners were inexperienced, the soil was stony and, after the plants went untended through the summer, the garden failed to produce. Rather than give up, however, the congregation set out to learn how to do things better. Two people in particular led the way. Erin Stack, a deacon of the church with an interest in gardening, took over management of the garden project, and the minister enrolled in training to improve her leadership skills so that she could better guide her congregation. Stack reached out to the wider community and found resources to learn about both gardening and community building. The church became a pick-up location for a local community-supported agriculture (CSA) venture, and the CSA farmers started using some of the church property for garden space. In addition, the congregation joined the newly formed Greater Newburyport Eco-Collaborative that brought together organizations and businesses to share ideas about how to foster environmental action in their area. There, church members were able to connect with the community and find people who shared their gardening interests. The garden was restarted on a larger scale, with participants from both the church and the wider community who would be present throughout the growing season. In order to facilitate gardening success, the church brought in experts to provide instruction to their fledgling gardeners. The gardens grew into a ministry called the New Eden Collaborative, which includes community gardens, eco-art projects, an environmental education program, and monthly garden parties. Knowing from their own experiences that people with an interest in gardening may need help getting started, New Eden offered organic gardening and organic cooking classes to the community.

Alongside their garden project, the faith community developed additional activities to connect the two parts of their mission to be Stewards of Earth and Spirit. They started holding some Sunday services outdoors in a tree-shaded circle of benches dubbed the "Chapel Under the Trees." Environmental awareness was incorporated into Sunday school programs for children, the youth group periodically hosted environmental speakers, and adults attended classes on topics such as simple living, local eating, and food preservation. Seeing a need in the wider community, church members decided to help create a nature-based secular preschool, utilizing the church's building and grounds. The result is Our Secret Garden, a nursery and preschool that teaches children to "care for themselves, each other, and the earth"[11] through a curriculum that emphasizes hands-on experiences of nature.

In the process of figuring out how to implement its mission to be Stewards of Earth and Spirit, First Parish Church became more active in the wider community. The church has formed partnerships with people who can teach about gardening, organizes annual community cleanups before Earth Day, and participates in the Yankee Homecoming Parade. The transformation of the church's backyard from a rocky and weedy space to a thriving community garden mirrors the transformation of the faith community from a remnant congregation just barely hanging on to a congregation actively engaged in pursuing a mission that brings them into beneficial relationship with the people around them.

5 Vineyard Church of Ann Arbor (VAA), Ann Arbor, Michigan
Membership: approximately 600

In 2007, Reverend Ken Wilson participated in a retreat that brought together scientists and evangelical ministers to discuss climate change. Although Wilson had not previously engaged in environmental activity, he had a deep interest in science-based knowledge. During the retreat, he felt great concern as he listened to the scientists describe the predicted impacts of climate change, but what most caught his attention was Dr. James (Gus) Speth's comment that the real environmental crisis had more to do with greed, pride, and apathy than pollution and climate change. Speth said what was needed was a cultural transformation, something scientists did not know how to achieve and for which they needed help from religious leaders.[12]

Inspired by Speth's words, Wilson returned to his Vineyard Church in Ann Arbor and preached a series of three sermons on creation care, explaining why Christians have a responsibility to care for God's creation and why current human behavior is environmentally unsustainable. Afterwards, a congregant named Phil Brabbs asked the pastor what he could do to respond to the homiletic message. Wilson suggested he start a green-focused "small group." Thus, Green Vineyard was formed with dual purposes of studying the scriptural basis for environmental behavior and leading efforts to make the church "greener." With support from the pastor, the church board implemented policies to incorporate environmental considerations into decision processes. The church also adopted resource conservation practices such as: reducing energy use through more efficient light bulbs, fewer hours of building and parking lot lighting, and adding roof insulation; reducing paper consumption by switching to electronic bulletins and changing office behavior; organizing participation in projects to improve local natural areas such as removal of invasive species and tree planting; and promoting use of reusable shopping bags and compact fluorescent lightbulbs (CFLs) in member homes.

Despite these early successes, Green Vineyard faced challenges. Reverend Wilson was pleased to see that Green Vineyard drew college-aged members to the church, however many of the students moved away after graduating and new members were not being added. The group was predominantly comprised of a shrinking circle of close friends and, when Brabbs had to give up leadership in order to deal with personal health problems, the original group faded away.

Despite loss of leadership and members, Green Vineyard continued because of the emergence of a new project. In 2008, a county food bank began a Faith and Food program that offered to help local congregations start community gardens if they would donate half of their harvest to feed the poor. Gretchen Marshall-TothFejel, a member of the Vineyard Church with a personal interest in organic gardening but little practical experience, attended a presentation about the program and offered to start a garden at the church. Other members who were longtime gardeners assisted with initial creation of the garden. Unlike the original Green Vineyard, which was perceived as a small group activity for a few environmental enthusiasts, the Community Garden Ministry gradually evolved into an expression of the whole congregation's Compassion and Justice ministry work.

6 *St. Thomas Aquinas Parish (STA), Palo Alto, California*
   Membership: approximately 1,800 families

In 2009, the Diocese of San Jose, on the southwest shores of San Francisco Bay, launched a Catholic Green Initiative, encouraging all parishes within the

Santa Clara Valley to adopt environmentally sustainable practices in order to mitigate the effects of climate change. Leaders of the Catholic Church, including Popes John Paul II, Benedict XVI, and Francis, as well as the US Council of Catholic Bishops, have proclaimed that the Church's social justice teachings require Catholics to respond to climate change as a moral issue because it will disproportionately affect the poor. The bishop of the Diocese of San Jose inaugurated the Catholic Green Initiative in response to a request from the local Council of Priests, who felt that they needed a way to deal with climate change issues in their parishes. Despite the proposed diocesan scope of the initiative, only a handful of parishes formed Green Committees and began to implement sustainability initiatives. Among the first to take action was St. Thomas Aquinas Parish.

St. Thomas Aquinas Parish is a complex faith community formed in 1985 by the consolidation of five smaller parishes into one administrative organization that currently has three churches (St. Thomas Aquinas Church, Our Lady of the Rosary Church, and St. Alfred the Great Church), as well as a school and a separate administrative center with two buildings. The parish is managed by a senior pastor, two associate pastors, a deacon, and a hard-working staff. In spite of three decades as one parish, the churches retain distinct identities because they are in different neighborhoods and have unique cultures rooted in their separate histories and local membership demographics. Some of the congregations predominantly consist of middle- and upper-middle-class professionals, while others have large numbers of working class and Spanish-speaking members.

The impetus for organizing a Green Committee at St. Thomas Aquinas came from Gerard McGuire. McGuire was passionate about both his Catholic faith and the need for Christians to respond to climate change. As a youth, he had studied for the priesthood and, in recent years, he trained to do public outreach on climate change issues through Al Gore's Climate Reality Project. After serving on the diocesan committee that planned the Catholic Green Initiative, McGuire pulled together a Green Committee in his home parish of St. Thomas Aquinas by reaching out to people he already knew had environmental concerns. Most of the people who joined him were members of the Human Concerns Committee, the volunteer group dedicated to alleviating social problems such as hunger and homelessness. Like McGuire, the committee members combine strong Catholic faith with deep concerns about climate change and the world their descendants will inherit. The senior pastor left management of the Green Committee in the hands of its lay members, but assigned Chuck Tully, the head of the parish's facilities staff (and, later, parish business manager), to serve on the committee. Thus, the Green Committee became a subcommittee of the Facilities Committee.

Although the Green Committee had neither administrative authority nor a budget of its own, it could research issues and bring recommendations to the Facilities Committee. This partnership with Facilities worked particularly well for implementing energy conservation projects, which were a central focus for the Green Committee due to its concerns about climate change. The parish succeeded in reducing its energy consumption through a combination of technological improvements and behavior change. One example of a technological improvement that exemplifies the cooperation between the Green Committee and the Facilities Committee is the replacement of a kitchen stove at Our Lady of the Rosary Church. Some of the women mentioned that the church had a stove with a pilot light that burned 24/7, which made the kitchen very warm even when the stove was not in use. The Green Committee raised the possibility of replacing the stove with the Facilities Committee, then did research to identify a stove with an electric ignition that would meet the church's needs and fit the budget allotted for the project. The new stove saves money and energy both by reducing gas consumption when the stove is not in use and by reducing the need for air conditioning to mitigate the heat in the kitchen area. Having the head of facilities as a liaison between the parish administration and the committee has been important for implementation of the Green Committee's energy conservation goals. Tully has not only authorized the purchase of new appliances, he has actively located grants and funds from governmental organizations to offset the costs of the upgrades, thereby making it possible to save energy without exceeding the annual Facilities budget. With these supplemental funds, he was able to upgrade the lighting to more efficient bulbs and replace the boilers with smaller, more efficient models.

Technological improvements can be a budgetary challenge for a parish with aging infrastructure and extensive charitable needs among its membership, but once the changes are in place, they mostly function automatically. Behavior change, on the other hand, is less expensive but can be slow to take hold and may require continuous renewal. Despite these challenges, St. Thomas Aquinas Parish reduced its energy use by twenty-five percent, an accomplishment that required participation from the wider congregation. The majority of this reduction came from two changes. First, the staff in the churches, schools, and administrative buildings adopted energy conservation practices such as turning off computers, printers, and copiers overnight and reducing hours of lighting inside and outside of buildings. Second, the Green Committee organized a campaign to encourage people to keep the doors of the churches closed, thereby preventing egress of heat in the winter and cool air in the summer. There is a tendency to prop church doors open, especially at the beginning and end of Sunday services, when large numbers of people are entering and exiting. In order to save energy by keeping the doors closed, community members had to be retrained to consider energy conservation and set aside old habits. The Committee wrote bulletin articles, posted signs by doors, and worked with their faith community to gradually establish new habits at all three churches.

Having multiple buildings and diverse sub-cultures presents challenges for implementing a sustainability initiative, but the Green Committee has also identified some benefits from their complex parish context. The committee members lay out a plan for the activities they will undertake each year and sometimes decide to begin a project in one church first, where they think implementation may be easier, in order to learn whether their strategies will be effective. Then they use their experiences in one church to adapt their project for the next location. Along with their successes in energy conservation, they have organized environmental education events, implemented recycling practices at the parish buildings, used recycling games and bottled-versus-tap water taste tests at the parish picnic to encourage people to change behavior at home, instituted bike-to-church days, and established a policy for replacing any trees that are removed from parish grounds.

CASE CLUSTER II:
GREEN CERTIFIED FAITH COMMUNITIES

Unlike the preceding six cases, in which the sustainability initiatives developed organically and gradually in response to individual and organizational factors, the initiatives undertaken by the next four faith communities adhered to programmatic structures prescribed by green certification processes. One is a Unitarian Universalist church in Maine that scaled up its environmental efforts by joining the Unitarian Universalist Association's Green Sanctuary Program, which provides a structured format for faith communities seeking to develop and implement sustainability initiatives. This case cluster also includes two Reform Jewish temples and a Presbyterian church in New Jersey. This trio of faith communities had ready access to the resources of GreenFaith, an organization dedicated to promoting environmental efforts through out-reach to people of faith. GreenFaith runs a green certification program that provides guidance and a general structure for integrating sustainability into religious organizations. Including these four cases in the research sample offers the opportunity to examine whether initiatives developed through certification programs differ from those that emerge organically within a faith community.

7 First Universalist Church of Rockland (UUR), Rockland, Maine
Membership: approximately 159

The sustainability initiative at the First Universalist Church of Rockland dates its origins to 2003, when Ann D. (Andy) Burt of the Maine Council of Churches asked if the congregation would join a campaign to encourage Maine legislators to support US participation in the Kyoto Protocol, an international agreement to reduce greenhouse gas emissions. Members of the church formed an Earth Care Team to coordinate their efforts, which soon expanded to include selling CFL light bulbs to community members and participation in a statewide "Be a Good Apple" program, in which people pledged to purchase ten percent of their monthly groceries from Maine food producers. After a couple years, the Earth Care Team felt the need to scale up its efforts and decided to seek Green Sanctuary Certification for their church.

Green Sanctuary is a program developed by the Unitarian Universalist Association, the denominational umbrella organization for Unitarian Universalists, to encourage sustainability activities in member congregations. To be certified as a Green Sanctuary, a congregation must complete twelve projects in four action areas: Worship and Celebration, Religious Education, Environmental Justice, and Sustainable Living. Enrolling in the certification program meant that earth care could not simply be the work of a small, committed group; the whole faith community would have to contribute. The Earth Care Team presented the idea to the congregation and received a vote of approval to begin the application process.

The activities undertaken to fulfill the certification requirements emerged from the local community context and the interests of the congregation members. Pastoral and religious education staff developed environmentally themed sermons and classes, which helped motivate participation in the larger projects organized by the Green Sanctuary Committee (formerly the Earth Care Team). Two particular project areas proved transformative for the church and its wider community: local food and energy conservation.

The Green Sanctuary Committee decided to focus on local food as an action area after organizing a meeting to ask about topics that interested congregation members. More people indicated an interest in food than any other issue. Serendipitously, shortly after that meeting, Andy Burt reached out to ask if the congregation would be interested in providing support to a young couple who wished to start a community-supported agriculture venture (CSA). The church agreed. The CSA started small, with fifteen shareholders prepaying for produce and the farmers using that money for their start-up costs. The farm was a success, and subscriptions increased from 45 in the second year to 120 in the third year and finally were capped at 200. The farm project became the basis for a motif in the church's sustainability initiatives: the team recognized that a project that started small could grow after community members saw proof of its value.

Building on the success of the CSA, members of the Green Sanctuary Committee wondered if it might be possible to add fish to their local food project. After all, Rockland had once been the heart of the midcoast Maine fishing industry and, even though the processing facilities were long gone, fishermen still worked in neighboring coastal towns. The church invited representatives of a local fishing community to speak about current industry conditions. Members were distressed to learn that the ground fishermen, who fished close to shore with small boats, were struggling to survive due to competition from large fishing enterprises, consolidation of markets and processing in distant locations, and declining fish stocks. Rather than incorporate fish into the existing CSA, the fishermen conceived the idea to experiment with a Community Supported Fishery (CSF). The church told the fishermen they thought the idea would work, but that based on their past experience, it would probably start small and then grow. The church and the fishermen decided to "take a leap of faith" and give it a try for the upcoming winter shrimp season. The church marketed the CSF to its members and rounded up subscribers to buy shrimp directly from the fishermen who promised them a fresher product than would be available in stores at a price that was lower for the consumer, yet higher than the fishermen would receive if they took the shrimp to the regular market auction. During its first year, the CSF was more symbolically than financially successful, providing just enough support for one fisherman to pay his fuel bill each week. However, it also created awareness about the opportunity for the community to support their local fishermen, and interest in the idea expanded beyond the church. The CSF grew to include fish during the summer, and by the second year there were multiple drop-off sites at community markets as well as direct sales to local restaurants.

The local food projects gave congregation members a sense of efficacy; they realized that their actions could affect conditions in their local community. For a few members, however, the food projects seemed inadequate to address the environmental concern that weighed most heavily on them: the problem of how to mitigate climate change. One of those members, Frank Mundo, finally found a meaningful project when an energy audit revealed that the church was losing heat through its basement windows. Mundo and Dick Cadwegan, another church member, built storm window inserts for the basement windows, and church energy use immediately declined. Congregation members then asked if it would be possible to build storm window inserts for their homes, which soon led to a new sustainability project. Mundo and Cadwegan formed WindowDressers, a nonprofit that works with churches to provide low-cost window inserts to people in Maine. These inserts reduce energy consumption while also reducing the cost of living in Maine, a secondary benefit that is especially important for young families and the elderly. As with the CSA and the CSF, the project started small and grew, rippling outward from the church to the wider community and beyond.

8 Trinity Presbyterian Church (TNJ), East Brunswick, New Jersey
Membership approx. 425

At Trinity Presbyterian Church in East Brunswick, a community mission discernment process inspired the community to adopt environmental stewardship as an area of church ministry. In 2007, Reverend Rob Carter, the new pastor, encouraged church members to begin a period of study to decide what their church's mission should be going forward. That year, the Presbyterian Church (USA) was recommending congregations within the denomination consider hunger, peacemaking, and environment as areas of church mission. Initially, everyone wanted to feed the hungry, which was a long-standing focus of ministry efforts at Trinity. No one was interested in environment as a mission area because they did not consider it to be a faith issue. However, a committee spent three months studying the trio of issues, exploring how many people were affected by each and what actions could be taken to mitigate them. In the process, committee members realized that all of the other issues started with the environment. People needed to learn about toxic waste, food contamination, and how to grow their own food in order to address issues of hunger and conflict. At the end of their study process, the committee voted unanimously to adopt stewardship of creation as a mission focus for their church.

Debbie O'Halloran, who had led the study process, became co-chair of a new Trinity Earth Shepherds group working to integrate stewardship of creation into the faith community. The Earth Shepherds organized some activities such as educational events to teach community members how to recycle and collecting sneakers for recycling through a Nike program, however, they soon decided that their committee was not knowledgeable enough about environmental issues to effectively educate the congregation. They sought help from GreenFaith, a New Jersey nonprofit organization dedicated to helping people of faith take a leadership role in developing a more environmentally sustainable world. Trinity enrolled in the GreenFaith Certification Program, which provides a framework and support to help congregations "integrate environmental themes into their worship, religious education, facility maintenance, and social outreach."[13] After three years of work, they became the first congregation in the United States to be certified as a GreenFaith Sanctuary and, in 2010, they were also certified as an Earth Care Congregation through a new program developed by the Presbyterian Church (USA).

Because Trinity's earth-care initiative emerged from a community mission discernment process, from its inception the congregation regarded it as an aspect of the church's mission, not a separate project for a small group of environmentalists. Once they enrolled in the GreenFaith program, they were able to implement their new mission by using that program's structure and ideas to integrate earth care into their religious organization. The first step was to create an environmental mission statement to explain how earth care fit into the community mission. Their statement expressed the faith foundation that motivated their work and the types of activities that a faith community could contribute to environmental efforts: "We, as a family of faith, believe that it is the responsibility of all to Care for God's Creation through environmental education, conservation and community outreach."[14]

Environmental education became a core area of activity for the church. They started with member education about ways to care for the earth through programs on topics such as pollution, environmental justice, and hydro-fracking. Because GreenFaith required congregations to conduct an environmental justice project, they organized a tour of the Ironbound District, a low-income area of New Jersey with extensive pollution from its long manufacturing history. Trinity members were shocked to discover that there were areas of such poverty and pollution just a few miles from their church. They also learned that the Ironbound residents were looking for partners who would help them lobby for regulation enforcement and contamination cleanup, not "saviors" who would rescue them.[15] In addition to adult education, the church arranged to sponsor a faith-based preschool program that would incorporate earth care into its curriculum. The Little Earth Shepherds preschool made use of the church's classroom space as well as its new community gardens.

The gardens and a variety of conservation practices emerged in response to the interests and concerns of several church members. The GreenFaith Program requires that communities undertake activities to "green" their operations and provides a list of action ideas to help communities find options that best suit them. Ideas on these lists helped Trinity office staff and committee members adopt practices to reduce paper use, increase recycling, and conserve water and electricity. They also applied the ideas to community events by switching to reusable dishes, which volunteers washed by hand, and hosting vegetarian church suppers. Some of the biggest projects, however, took place on the grounds. One church member was concerned about the increasing endangerment of butterflies in North America so, in 2010, he and his family created a 12,500 square-foot butterfly garden in the wide grassy area beyond the church parking lot. Then a young church member got the idea to create a community garden as his Eagle Scout project. In 2011, he built thirty-eight 10'x10' beds and a surrounding fence in the open area between the church and the new butterfly garden. Church members signed up for plots in which to grow food, and families with surplus produce shared it with other community members. Some people also grew flowers, which were used to decorate the church. These gardens were especially popular with young families who would bring their children down to the garden after Sunday services.

The new outdoor projects changed the look of the church grounds and served as a visible witness to the congregation's mission to be stewards of the earth. According to Reverend Rob Carter, the community takes sustainability and creation care to heart.[16] They did not adopt earth care on a whim; they went through an extensive study process, decided that earth care was important to them as people of faith, and "covenanted to Care for Creation."[17] Adopting earth care through a covenant, a formal obligation to God, made it a core part of the community's religious mission. As a result, when describing the church's organizational practices, the pastor noted that environmental stewardship affected the management of the church and its ministries: "Our church family feels a personal responsibility to Care for God's Creation. Everything that is done in the church, is done through an environmental lens—meaning, what is best for God's Creation, is always a consideration in our decision-making."[18]

9 Anshe Emeth Memorial Temple (AET), New Brunswick, New Jersey
Membership: approximately 550 families

Anshe Emeth Memorial Temple is one of the oldest Reform Jewish faith communities in New Jersey. In the 1960s, as most of its members moved to the suburbs, the community made a conscious decision to remain in its historic Moorish-style building. By the twenty-first century, fewer than 20 of the approximately 550 member families resided in New Brunswick, yet this commuter temple remains a vibrant, multigenerational faith community.

In 2010, the Union for Reform Judaism in New Jersey, a regional organization for Reform Jewish congregations, formed a partnership with GreenFaith, the interfaith organization dedicated to promoting environmental sustainability in faith communities. The Union for Reform Judaism offered to provide grants to offset application costs for Reform temples that enrolled in the GreenFaith certification program. The senior rabbi at Anshe Emeth Memorial Temple brought up the opportunity with his temple board, which included an environmental educator named Michael (Mike) Chodroff. The board supported the idea, and Chodroff agreed to chair a Green Team and guide the temple through the green certification process.

GreenFaith certification requires congregations to undertake actions in areas of Spirit (worship and education), Justice (education and advocacy), and Stewardship (conservation behavior related to energy, transportation, food, water, waste, toxics, and grounds maintenance). Enthusiastic support from clergy and members of all the committees that manage the temple's programs and operations facilitated implementation of greening efforts at Anshe Emeth. The associate rabbi took the lead on worship elements, beginning with a sermon about the GreenFaith program on Rosh Hashanah, one of the high holy days in the Jewish calendar during which the majority of the community is present at the temple. Green Team members from custodial and administrative staff helped integrate sustainability into temple operations by instituting use of nontoxic cleaning supplies, exploring the potential for installation of solar panels, changing purchasing policies to emphasize paper products with recycled content, replacing mailed annual reports with electronic texts, and increasing efforts to recycle.

Anshe Emeth has strong educational programs for both children and adults, both of which became venues for greening the temple. Chodroff created a high school elective on Jews and Ecology that taught temple students about the intersection of Judaism and ecology through time in order to "explore our responsibilities as Jews in the twenty-first century."[19] As part of the course, which took place during fall of 2010, the students were encouraged to apply what they were learning by developing projects to green the community. One project they initiated was a carpool program for students attending religious school classes. In addition to the high school course, the director of religious education, who was also on the Green Team, added environmental themes to the educational programming for younger children. Finally, Chodroff gave four presentations for adults under the auspices of the temple's tradition of Monday night Kollel, or Jewish learning.

The Green Team at Anshe Emeth was able to incorporate environmental elements into a number of regular temple activities. Each December, the temple organizes a Mitzvah Day, an annual day of volunteer service for congregation members of all ages. The Green Team organized a Green Mitzvah Day that combined community service with environmental education through: an environmental justice tour to a nearby Superfund site followed by a panel discussion and advocacy project for adults; green crafts, recycling games, and storytelling with environmental lessons for kids; and an informational display on organic foods and energy conservation created by the teens in the Jews and Ecology course. They also used the annual food donation campaign as an opportunity to distribute reusable shopping bags with the Anthe Emeth Green Team slogan, *Anshe Emeth Shomrei Adamah* (People of Truth, Protectors of Earth). The Green Mitzvah Day illustrates the community-wide nature of the sustainability initiative at Anshe Emeth; the organizers included leaders from administrative, worship, education, and social action areas who created a program that connected to the spiritual, educational, and social service traditions of their temple.

10 *Temple Shalom (TS), Aberdeen, New Jersey*
Membership: approximately 300 families

Temple Shalom is a Reform Jewish congregation that was established more than fifty years ago by Jewish residents of a new suburb near the Atlantic coast of New Jersey. The temple was built in 1967 on land donated for that purpose by the developers who built area homes. The faith community includes some founding members and their descendants as well as many "newcomers" who have moved to the area over the last half-century. It is an affluent congregation with strong religious education and social action programs.

Like Anshe Emeth Memorial Temple, the sustainability initiative at Temple Shalom emerged in response to the Union for Reform Judaism's campaign to encourage congregations to "go green" by offering grants to offset the cost of enrolling in the GreenFaith certification program. The vice president of the temple board introduced the idea of applying for the program and received support from the rabbi and board members. The vice president asked Margo Wolfson, a community college biology professor, lifelong environmentalist, and active volunteer in Temple Shalom's religious education program, to lead a Green Team. Wolfson jumped at the opportunity. She had occasionally included environmental ethics in her third- through sixth-grade classes and had previously helped organize two Earth Day programs at Temple Shalom. The GreenFaith certification program would make it possible to expand these efforts to the entire temple.[20]

As noted above, GreenFaith certification requires activities in areas of worship and education (Spirit), advocacy and social outreach (Justice), and resource conservation through modifications to facilities and administrative practices (Stewardship). The Temple Shalom Green Team set two major goals for its certification plan: 1) To inspire and educate the faith community about environmental issues and to show that environmentalism is a Jewish cause; and 2) To green the synagogue and lead by example, showing that living "greener" is attainable.

The sustainability activities implemented to fulfill these goals at Temple Shalom reflected the human and physical resources of the faith community. The Green Team had strong support from the rabbi and robust representation from the religious education and social action committees. Rabbi Malinger led the Spirit component with several sermons linking sustainability to Jewish obligations to help repair God's creation. He also developed a Jewish Food Justice Program for Teens, while Wolfson worked with other members of the religious education program to include environmental themes in classes and activities for all age levels.

The physical context also shaped green efforts at Temple Shalom. The building sits on almost three acres of land in a suburb of Aberdeen, just a few miles from the Atlantic coast. There are green spaces on the north and east sides of the building, and the parking lot on the building's south side slopes down to a wetland. The temple roof provided a good site for solar energy, and congregation members contributed installation knowledge and funds to set up a solar array. In the green space on the north side of the building, Lenore Robinson, chair of the Social Action Committee, organized an interfaith community garden to raise fresh produce for donation to a local food pantry. Although Robinson had little prior gardening experience, the Gan Tikvah, or Garden of Hope, brought together people from three faith communities and, among them, they had the knowledge, gardening tools, and volunteer numbers to make the project successful.

CASE CLUSTER III:
MONASTIC CASE SITES

The monastic case studies, which focus on communities in which women and men have chosen to dedicate their lives to God as sisters/nuns[21] and brothers/monks, have greater emphasis on land stewardship through sustainable resource management activities than the non-monastic cases. These five cases, which are the longest-lived initiatives among the fifteen cases studied, emerged among faith communities with land holdings, where concerns about the natural environment motivated the members to undertake ecosystem restoration projects and adopt sustainable management practices for forests and farmlands. In some of these cases, land stewardship practices were inspired by community members with formal education in the natural sciences who encouraged the larger community to adopt new practices. In others, however, a general ideal of caring for the earth emerged from the community as a whole and led to development of new management systems. As environmental concerns in the United States shifted toward increased awareness of climate change, these sustainability initiatives were expanded to include additional conservation practices such as recycling, energy conservation, and renewable energy generation.

11 *Congregation of St. Joseph at Nazareth (CJN),*
Sisters of St. Joseph, Kalamazoo, Michigan
Membership: 191 sisters

Concern for the environment has been a theme for the Sisters of St. Joseph at Nazareth for more than four decades. This community of Catholic women religious dates back to 1889, when the first sisters arrived in Kalamazoo, Michigan, to establish a hospital. They founded the congregation of Sisters of St. Joseph at Nazareth on 400 acres of farmland. The Nazareth campus, which once included an orphanage, school, and college (1914–1992), is the mother-house from which the sisters have conducted ministries in healthcare, social work, education, pastoral care, and spiritual development. Many of the former orphanage and school buildings have been converted to new uses through agreements with secular organizations. At the time of this study, the campus still included a retreat center, administrative facilities, and housing for the sisters. In 2007, seven separate communities of the Sisters of St. Joseph joined together to form the Congregation of St. Joseph, which is distributed across several states but retains separate motherhouses for each historical group.

Sister Virginia (Ginny) Jones fostered recognition of the importance of environmental sustainability as a religious value among the Sisters of St. Joseph at Nazareth. Jones arrived in 1968 to serve as an environmental science teacher for Nazareth College. At that time, the Sisters of St. Joseph were responding to Vatican II (1962–65)[22] by expanding their ministry to address new social concerns, which included the environment. The sisters hosted Kalamazoo's first Earth Day celebration at the Nazareth campus in 1970, and, over the years, they have applied sustainable management principles to two parcels of land. The first is a sixty-acre wetland preserve on the edge of the main Nazareth convent campus. In her role as science teacher, Jones turned the prairie fen wetland into an outdoor classroom for Nazareth College. Her students built trails and planted trees in the wetland, which was dedicated as the Bow in the Clouds Natural Area in 1973. Jones selected the name to express the idea that humans and nature are all one in their relationship to God: "The name Bow in the Clouds comes from the Bible (Genesis 9:13) where God set a 'bow in the clouds' as a sign of the new covenant between Him and the earth."[23]

The second property under sustainable management practices is a former dairy farm the sisters purchased in 1948. Nazareth Farm, which is about three miles from the convent, once provided dairy and beef products for Nazareth College, Borgess Hospital, and other institutions operated by the sisters. In 1993, when the farm products were no longer needed, most of the land was enrolled in the Federal Conservation Reserve Program. The sisters began efforts to restore some of the lands by planting trees and vegetative cover and, with assistance from a wildlife biologist, they developed a wildlife management plan designed to attract pheasants and maximize wildlife diversity.[24]

Religious values motivated the sisters to restore these former farmlands, even though it meant losing income that had previously been generated by leasing their land to farmers. The mission of the order is based on the idea that "all are one," from the scriptural passage: *"That all may be one as You,*

Father, are in Me, and I in You; I pray that they may be one in Us (John 17:21)".[25] Among the Sisters of St. Joseph at Nazareth, this oneness is understood to include non-human species as well as human beings. Therefore, the sisters feel an obligation to care for the wildlife on their lands as well as the people in their local community. They also see connections between healing the natural environment and healing people, thereby linking their environmental work with their order's long heritage of medical ministry.

Earth care was formally incorporated into the Nazareth community goals in 1989, when the sisters added concern for environmental issues to the directional statement guiding their work. The statement described environmental problems as part of a larger pattern of imbalance:

> There is a sense that many of our relationships with each other, with the earth, and with our God have become distorted by our consumer society and by the philosophy that the "earth" is ours to do with as we will. We see environmental issues as spiritual issues calling us to deep conversion of spirit, a change of perspective, and we recognize a call to share these insights with other people of good will.[26]

In order to address this imbalance, the leadership team asked Sister Ginny Jones to develop some environmental programs. The result was formation of a Center for Ecology and Spirituality that provided spiritual retreats and educational resources for the local community, as well as continued expansion of land stewardship practices. Thus, the community's focus on healing included both humans and nature: the earth healing processes enacted through practice of land stewardship could contribute to human spiritual healing, and both types of healing were necessary to "restore a sense of balance and relationship with the whole earth community."[27]

In 2007, when the aging community decided it no longer had the people power to maintain the sixty-acre wetland preserve, the sisters donated Bow in the Clouds to the Southwest Michigan Land Conservancy so the land would be cared for while remaining open to the public. According to Jones, the sisters hope people will use it for "re-creation" of spiritual wellbeing: "We know many people today are separated from religious tradition, and we respect that. We also know that before formal religion existed, people encountered something of the holy in the natural world. And that something—that peace, solitude, and wisdom—is what we believe people can still find here."[28]

Although Jones was the strongest advocate for environmental stewardship at Nazareth, the community of sisters has supported her work because they share her beliefs about the importance of protecting nature. The community expressed its environmental values by providing an endowment for maintenance of the lands it donated to the Southwest Michigan Land Conservancy. Furthermore, in addition to their land stewardship, the sisters pursue conservation practices in their community lives. They conserve water and energy, recycle and require use of recycled products in their facilities, buy fair trade goods, use soy-based inks, mandate chemical-free landscape management, ensure that construction projects on their properties follow eco-friendly processes, and replace their gas-powered cars with hybrids as opportunity arises. They also work with community organizations to promote local environmental awareness and engage in advocacy work, petitioning elected officials to protect the Earth from climate change.

12 *Saint John's Abbey (SJA), Order of St. Benedict, Collegeville, Minnesota*
Membership: 153 monks

Saint John's Abbey, a Catholic Benedictine monastery in the Avon Hills of central Minnesota, has an arboretum that comprises 2,700 acres of forests, wetlands, and prairie that are managed sustainably for the benefit of the land and for the purpose of educating people about land stewardship. The arboretum is a joint project between the abbey monks, who own the land, and Saint John's University, which administers its educational programs. The university, which was begun by the monks who previously served as teachers and administrators, is now a separate institution, but the two contiguous organizations are economically intertwined through agreements to share facilities and services.

Establishment of the arboretum in 1997 marked the fulfillment of a vision that originated with Father Paul Schwietz. Schwietz had been actively concerned about natural environments since his undergraduate days at Saint John's University in the 1970s, during which he studied the natural sciences. He entered the monastery after graduation, was ordained in 1982, and earned a master's degree in forestry from the University of Minnesota in 1985 so he could become the abbey land manager. He immediately began to implement habitat restoration projects, putting in two dams to recreate a wetland on sixty acres that had previously been drained for agricultural use and restoring an adjacent area of prairie. These projects were part of Schwietz's larger vision: the monastic community could "strengthen the witness of our commitment to sustainability"[29] by creating a natural arboretum through which to teach about land stewardship. After a decade of work, demonstrating processes of land restoration and articulating connections between the abbey's Benedictine heritage and stewardship ideals, Schwietz's vision took shape as the Saint John's Arboretum.

The arboretum's joint purposes of preservation and education were a good fit for Saint John's. The abbey was founded in 1856 by German monks who used the land for food and timber as they built a monastery and school. The Benedictine tradition emphasizes stability, the idea of staying in one place to pursue religious life, and has a long heritage of farm-based monasteries. Since the founding of Saint John's Abbey, the monks have used lumber from the forest in their woodshop and furniture business and engaged in activities such as bee keeping, orcharding, maple sugar production, and bird watching. Agricultural activities tapered off in the 1950s, as the monastery, university, and Saint John's Preparatory School grew too big to be self-sustaining, and much of the cleared farmland reverted to forests. This abbey history, combined with the Benedictine heritage of place-based religious practice, provided a basis for affirming connections between sustainable land stewardship and the spiritual purposes of the abbey.

Father Schwietz articulated these connections between religious values and land stewardship in his proposal for creation of a natural arboretum. He also emphasized the importance of using the arboretum to educate people about land management, an idea that evoked the abbey's long history of educational work and fit with emerging academic trends. The period in which Schwietz began his tenure as land manager coincided with development of an environmental studies program at Saint John's University. This program quickly became one of the university's identifying characteristics due to its exceptional resources; abbey lands provided opportunities for field study, and abbey records provided rare longitudinal data on local plant species.

By emphasizing the confluence of spiritual heritage with perceived benefits from preserving the land and using it for educational purposes, Schwietz and other members of the community (in the monastery, university, and neighboring area) succeeded in building support for creation of the Saint John's Arboretum. The stewardship and education programs proved successful and fostered a sustainability ethic that gradually expanded throughout the Saint John's community. In 2009, the university established an Office of Sustainability to implement changes to infrastructure and behavior at the university and abbey. New sustainability activities include switching the campus power plant fuel from coal to natural gas; creation of a revolving loan fund for sustainability projects; and development of a campaign to inculcate conservation behavior among students as an expression of Catholic values. As of 2017, the abbey hosts a twenty-seven-acre solar farm that produces 3.4 megawatts of energy through a partnership with Xcel Energy.[30]

13 Villa Maria (VM), Sisters of the Humility of Mary, Villa Maria, Pennsylvania
Membership: 158 sisters

Sister Barbara O'Donnell began exploring connections between sustainable land care and spiritual life at Villa Maria Community Center in western Pennsylvania in 1990. At the time, however, it was not clear how her mission could be incorporated into any of the order's extant ministries. Over the next decade, through self-education and a fruitful partnership with the Villa Maria land manager, O'Donnell created new environmental ministry and education programs, established an organic food program, and helped the convent formalize sustainable land stewardship systems for its 736-acre holdings. Today, the Villa includes 400 acres of sustainably managed forests, 300 acres of farmland that is mostly managed in accord with organic practices,[31] and an organic produce garden.

O'Donnell was ready to begin a new ministry after she retired in 1990 from a career in education and administration. She felt called to "educate for the earth" but was not sure how to turn that calling into a viable practice.[32] She found support from Frank Romeo, the community's land manager, and from the librarian, both of whom helped her uncover the history of the community and its land. In 1864, when the Sisters of the Humility of Mary first arrived from France and bought a 250-acre farm, they practiced subsistence farming while developing ministries in education and medicine. During the twentieth century, most sisters worked in schools and hospitals, but the Villa continued to produce food. At its height in 1970, the order's farm had expanded to more than 700 acres, including 300 acres of grain and hay, cattle, hogs, 10,000 laying hens, ten acres of orchards, and four acres of vegetable gardens. It was the largest diversified farm in the county until changes in both agricultural systems and the local community led to severe cutbacks in 1983. At that time, all the farm workers except Romeo were laid off, and the lands were shifted to a limited production of crops for charitable donation.

Arguing that organic food production fit with their heritage, O'Donnell convinced her order to let her experiment with an organic gardening initiative.

Romeo, who had managed the farm during its heyday and longed for an opportunity to "bring it back to life,"[33] provided instruction and assistance in the garden project. The garden was so successful that it gave rise to a produce market and expansion of production. O'Donnell continually tried to integrate spirituality into her garden project because, for her, "the spirituality of the land is so real."[34] Motivated by her sense of being called to educate for the earth, which now included a desire to share her experiences of awe at the workings of nature and her discovery of the history of the Villa lands, she envisioned a new ministry that would combine spirituality and education with organic gardening. This vision brought together care for the earth, the strong educational tradition of the Sisters of the Humility of Mary, and the farm heritage of Villa Maria. The ministry, originally named Ecology and Faith and later renamed EverGreen, became part of the Villa Maria Retreat Center programming. Together with a companion program in Farm-Based Environmental Education, EverGreen helped make sustainability a core part of the mission of the Sisters of the Humility of Mary.

14 Holy Wisdom Monastery (HWM), Benedictine Women of Madison, Madison, Wisconsin
Membership: 3 sisters; 350 lay members (Sunday Assembly attendees)

The Benedictine Women of Madison live in an ecumenical women's monastery with a mission of "weaving prayer, hospitality, justice, and care for the earth into a shared way of life."[35] Their mission is carried out in a platinum LEED-certified monastery building surrounded by 138 acres of land comprised of 100 acres of restored prairie, a small glacial lake, woodlands, an orchard, and an organic vegetable garden. The three sisters who comprised the membership in 2013 were at the center of a community that included a small staff, volunteer board members, nearly 200 affiliated lay oblate men and women who apply the Rule of Benedict to their lives outside the monastery, and a Sunday Assembly congregation of about 350 people (approximately 200 attended worship services each week). The community of volunteers, oblates, and Sunday Assembly members grows each year, a testament to the value that people find in the spiritual practices and ministries of Holy Wisdom Monastery.

The earth care practices of the monastery emerged from a combination of influences. First, the sisters had a deep attachment to the place where they lived. A small group of Benedictine sisters had settled on ninety acres of land near Madison, Wisconsin, to establish a Catholic high school in the 1950s. These daughters of Midwestern farmers had planted trees and gardens, building personal connections to the land. Second, as developers moved into the area in the 1970s and 80s, the sisters watched surrounding farmland transformed into suburbs and mourned the loss of the old landscape. Finally, in 1985, a developer proposed building a golf course on top of the hill behind the monastery. The offer prompted a period of contemplation, in which the sisters pondered the question: "What would God want us to do?" Their high school had been transformed into a retreat center in 1966, but the building was large and expensive to operate. If they sold the land, they could use the money to start a new ministry elsewhere. After prayer and reflection, the sisters decided they wanted to remain on the land. Moreover, they decided that the land should be for all people, not for a wealthy few. In 1990, they began a formal discernment process to develop a vision for the future in which their community could live in place, make a living, and serve people. According to Sister Mary David Walgenbach, "Having said no to selling off land in the 1960s, '70s, and '80s, we now said yes to doing more with it."[36] They would open their community to Christian women from non-Catholic traditions and care for the land by converting their 100 acres of cornfield into prairie.

They found, however, that it is easier to articulate a vision for land restoration than to act on it. The monastery director (leader of a volunteer board of directors) set up a plan, calling for ten acres of farmland to be restored to prairie each year for a decade, but no one at Holy Wisdom actually had any idea of how to go about restoring a prairie. To implement their plan, the monastery consulted with local experts from organizations such as the Wisconsin Department of Natural Resources and The Prairie Enthusiasts, a nonprofit organization dedicated to protection and management of native prairie in the Upper Midwest. The monastery groundskeeper spent time with the ranger at a park near Holy Wisdom to learn about prairie restoration processes and then organized volunteer work groups to collect and plant seed. Year by year, from 1996 to 2006, with design assistance and grants from the county, advice and financial support from the state Department of Natural Resources, funds from bird protection organizations and the community, and lots of volunteer labor, 100 acres of fields were converted into prairie that protects Lake Mendota from polluting runoff, houses wildlife, and provides visitors with natural areas for reflection.

As the prairie restoration neared completion, the sisters decided it was time to do something about the monastery buildings. Since the old school building was too large for their needs and their location was not suitable for renting out space, the best course of action seemed to be tearing it down and constructing something more suitable. They worked with an architectural firm to plan a green building that would support core activities of worship and community interaction while connecting people with nature. Ninety-nine percent of the old building's materials were recycled. The new building houses a chapel, kitchen, dining area/meeting space, offices, and library. It is platinum LEED-certified, with geothermal heating and cooling and solar panels providing a portion of the electricity. Skylights, windows, and natural materials in floors, walls, and ceilings conserve resources while integrating indoor and outdoor environments.

The efforts to care for the earth have enhanced the community at Holy Wisdom Monastery. Volunteers who work on the land build relationships with people and place. People who visit for religious services and retreats enjoy the simple beauty of the building and the peacefulness of the prairie, woods, and lake. They comment that they feel they are on holy ground. To Walgenbach, caring for the land advances the spiritual work of the monastery: "People come out and just walk the land. They have a place to stay in our retreat center. For people whose modern lives leave them tired and stressed, this space in creation helps them open up their interior space. Being out in nature restores them."[37]

15 *Our Lady of Angels Convent (OLA), Sisters of St. Francis of Philadelphia, Aston, Pennsylvania*
   Membership: 450 sisters

The Sisters of St. Francis of Philadelphia established Our Lady of Angels convent in the 1870s in the rolling hills near Aston, Pennsylvania. In the 1990s, development pressures in the area and increasing concern about climate change inspired the sisters to think about how the environment fit into their religious mission. The community decided that care for the environment was important to them because, as followers of St. Francis, who called animals and birds his brothers and sisters, they had a duty to care for all of God's creation. They developed an environmental mission statement explaining their call to care for the environment:

> Based on our Franciscan worldview, we believe that Jesus Christ came as brother to all created reality, and as Sisters of St. Francis of Philadelphia we

acknowledge our oneness with the universe. We call ourselves to proclaim in a viable and tangible manner our belief in the Cosmic Christ. Therefore, we commit ourselves: to reverence all that exists; to preserve the integrity of the land entrusted to our care; to dialogue and explore with others the implications of eco-spirituality; to promote positive environmental behaviors; and to celebrate our oneness with the universe.[38]

In order to put their mission into practice, an environmental task force created a set of guiding principles for action based on four ideas: Interconnectedness, Sustainability, Education, and Witness. The community would fulfill their environmental mission with awareness that their actions affected the whole creation (Interconnectedness), that actions must not compromise the resources and choices of future generations (Sustainability), that their actions could serve to educate others about personal and corporate responsibility toward the environment (Education), and that actions related to their own land use and lifestyle should reflect their values (Witness).[39]

The Sisters formed subcommittees to research potential activities in areas of education, land use, and sustainable living. They hired Sister Corinne Wright to serve as manager of their Environmental Initiative. In education, the sisters collaborated with faculty from Neumann University to develop the Franciscan Center for Earth Education to provide a venue for ecological education within a Catholic Franciscan context. That center evolved into a Care of Creation program managed by faculty, staff, and students at the university. Land use was one area where Wright decided the initiative could be particularly effective because it was an area that was under the sisters' control. The sisters owned 295 acres of land, 180 acres of which were still undeveloped, so they decided to preserve those lands as wildlife habitat and to adopt new practices for the developed lands to make them more hospitable to wildlife.

To achieve these goals, the sisters developed new policies for managing the lands. New development would only be approved if it did not damage ecosystems. Thus, when some hermitage buildings were added to the convent's retreat center, the small residential units were built on platforms extending out over the edge of a hill so that the soil would not be disturbed. Similarly, new walking trails were carefully designed to take visitors through the woods in the ravine area below the hermitages without causing erosion to the steep slopes. In this way, the retreat center was designed to incorporate nature into material and spiritual practices. New policies also increased environmental health on lands that were already developed. Native meadow plants and trees that would provide food and shelter for wildlife replaced areas of lawn, and native plants that would benefit local animals and insects supplanted non-native ornamentals in garden areas. Wright used information from Pennsylvania State University's agricultural extension services to develop an integrated pest management plan so the lands could be maintained without toxic chemicals to control weeds or insects.

In the area of sustainable living, the sisters adopted a range of activities. In 2000, they hired a farmer to start a community supported agriculture venture on six acres of land. Red Hill Farm received material support from the convent, which purchased a tractor and paid for the farm manager's salary, thereby making it easier to start a new business that would eventually be funded by shareholders. Several of the sisters purchased individual shares in the CSA, and the convent kitchens also purchased fresh produce to use in the sisters' retirement home. By 2003, the farm had a stable membership of approximately 120 local families, and the annual harvest festival had become a major social event that brought community members and sisters together. For a while, the convent's kitchen waste was sent to a composting facility to be transformed into compost that would be sent back to enrich the soils at Red Hill Farm. This program eventually dissolved when the composting company went out of business.

Our Lady of Angels convent also incorporated conservation into other aspects of its daily operations. The administrative offices purchased supplies with high recycled content and developed programs to recycle aluminum, paper, plastic, batteries, furniture, motor oil and light bulbs. Custodians switched to nontoxic cleaning supplies, and the sisters installed solar panels on the roof of the barn to reduce their carbon footprint. On a more global scale, the Sisters of St. Francis integrated care of creation into their social justice ministry work by adding it to their Corporate Social Responsibility (CSR) ministry. In this ministry, the sisters purchase shares in corporations, then attend stockholder meetings to submit proposals asking the companies to adopt policies that require them to track the social impacts of their supply chains. Once the community made care for the environment part of its mission, the members who worked in CSR began adding environmental impacts to the information they requested from corporations. They also began to lobby for regulation of hydraulic fracturing, a fossil fuel extraction technique that has polluted water supplies in some of the poorest regions of Pennsylvania.

Many of these activities did not have an immediate financial return on investment, yet the Sisters of St. Francis undertook them because of their "commitment to the environment based on their Franciscan charism, which sees all of creation as sister and brother."[40] This sense of connection between faith and earth care was reinforced through religious activities. Sisters visited Red Hill Farm to offer prayers in the spring, when the farm was prepared for the new growing season, and joined in the harvest festival in the fall. On the grounds where they restored native flora to create habitat for wildlife, a trail winds past the Stations of the Cross. This allows visitors to participate in a traditional devotion as they walk among native ferns that grow in the shade of magnificent oaks. Nearby, the Canticle of the Sun garden offers opportunities to contemplate God's presence in creation with quotations from St. Francis' prayer in which God is "praised though all your creatures" including Brother Sun, Sister Moon, and the elements of wind, water, fire, and earth.

CONCLUSION:
FAITH COMMUNITIES AS STEWARDS OF SPIRIT AND EARTH

The purpose of a faith community is, first and foremost, to assist its members in cultivating their spiritual lives by providing opportunities to participate in collective and individual activities of worship, spiritual study, and ministry work. The communities of faith in this study integrated sustainability into their organizational missions and incorporated environmental activities into their organizational behavior, thereby becoming communities in which people see themselves as stewards of both spirit and earth. Although the summaries presented here are brief, they provide an overview of the genesis and evolution of each sustainability initiative by describing triggering events, leadership, activities undertaken, and notable characteristics of each faith community's environmental efforts. The following chapter compares the fifteen cases to identify similarities and differences in the processes through which these initiatives emerged and became integrated into the communities of faith.

2 MANY PATHS TO SUSTAINABILITY

Cross-Case Analysis

ALTHOUGH THE DETAILS OF the fifteen sustainability initiatives vary, the overarching narratives of their emergence and development are remarkably aligned. Each case is a story in which an event *triggered* a response from *individuals* who implemented activities within the *organizational context* of their faith communities. Together, these three elements—triggering event, individual responses, and organizational context—shed light on factors and processes that enabled the initiatives to take root in these communities of faith.

TRIGGERS OF INITIATIVE EMERGENCE

The fifteen initiatives emerged in response to five triggers that created opportunities to take action through the venue of a faith community: prompts from faith leaders, reaction to a local environmental threat, projects associated with an individual's career goals, community discernment processes, and opportunities provided by external organizations. The first four triggers were *internal* to the faith communities, arising either from individual and affinity group responses to environmental issues or from congregational responses to periods of community transition. The fifth trigger came from sources *external* to the faith communities, such as interfaith organizations and regional denominational organizations that invited the faith communities to participate in an activity or program. The following comparison of the cases is organized according to these five triggers in order to identify key

TABLE 2 TRIGGERS FOR SUSTAINABILITY INITIATIVES

TRIGGER LOCUS	TYPE OF TRIGGER	ORGANIC CASES	GREEN-CERTIFIED CASES	MONASTIC CASES	TOTAL
Internal	1. *Faith leader prompt*	2			2
Internal	2. *Local environmental threat*	1			1
Internal	3. *Career-related projects*			3	3
Internal	4. *Community discernment*	2	1	2	5
External	5. *Opportunity from external organization*	1	3		4

factors and patterns that shaped the development of the sustainability initiatives (see Table 2).

This analysis makes a distinction between triggers that motivated individual actions and triggers that led to sustainability initiatives. An individual may have experiences that cause environmental concerns and lead to personal actions, which may in turn inspire members of the wider faith community to undertake environmental activities. In this chain of events, the trigger for the sustainability initiative is the action that inspired the community, not the preceding experience that affected the individual. For example, in several of the cases, a few community members formed study groups to explore shared interests in the environment, however these groups were focused on reading and discussion rather than action and, therefore, the founding of a group does not qualify as emergence of a sustainability *initiative*. These study groups could, however, serve as precursors to initiatives if the members eventually undertook actions that triggered emergence of initiatives within the communities. Because this chapter focuses on triggers that led to emergence of initiatives, experiences that affected individuals personally are noted only for their role in motivating individuals to act in ways that triggered initiatives within their faith communities. These personal experiences are, however, important for understanding initiative development and will be examined in more depth in the next chapter.

1 FAITH LEADER PROMPT AS TRIGGER

At the Madison Christian Community (MCC) and Vineyard Church of Ann Arbor (VAA), actions by clergy who became concerned about climate change triggered environmental efforts. At Vineyard, the prompt took the form of a series of sermons about the Christian obligation to care for creation and address climate change. At Madison Christian Community, the prompt came from the minister's interest in exploring the possibility of installing a wind turbine on the church grounds. In both cases, the pastors presented ideas about people of faith as environmental stewards, which triggered formation of small groups to explore implementation of sustainability efforts in church facilities.

The sustainability initiatives in these two faith communities evolved along similar trajectories: affinity groups developed a project or activity in response to the originating trigger, which then led to further activities and adoption of sustainability as an area of ministry for the religious organization as a whole. At Madison Christian Community, the pastor's interest in alternative energy to mitigate climate change led to installation of solar panels and adoption of energy conservation practices. The following year, the pastor helped expand the community garden to include areas for the Children's Garden and food pantry ministries. At Vineyard Church of Ann Arbor, the minister's climate change sermons motivated the formation of Green Vineyard, a lay group that worked to make the church more sustainable through building upgrades to improve energy efficiency and institution of practices such as recycling and energy conservation. Just as declining membership was causing Green Vineyard to lose steam, a new leader emerged to organize a Community Garden Ministry that became the focus for a renewal of the church's commitment to sustainability.

2 LOCAL ENVIRONMENTAL THREAT AS TRIGGER

A small group also led the way at Trinity Presbyterian Church in Harrisonburg (TPC), where concern about environmental damage in Shenandoah National Park motivated members of the Earth Care House Church, a group that had formerly focused on outdoor worship and study of connections between theology and environmental ethics, to engage in policy advocacy. In this case, the prompt came from lay members who noted the threat to their local environment and brought the issue to the attention of their community. Their pastor helped them develop a means for responding to their concerns by suggesting they present a resolution at the annual General Assembly of the Presbyterian Church (USA). After successful passage of their resolution, which required distribution of information on the health effects of coal-burning to member churches and encouraging all Presbyterians to advocate for clean air regulations, the Earth Care House Church members went on to engage in further environmental advocacy regarding local concerns about hydraulic fracking, and implemented conservation practices at the church to reduce the ecological footprint of their religious organization.

In this case, as in the two cases that emerged in response to clergy prompts, there is a pattern of interaction between clergy, who provide inspiration and guidance, and affinity groups that form to develop and implement actions. The three cases also follow similar trajectories from originating project to community initiative: as new activity ideas were implemented, the sustainability initiatives expanded and became more embedded in the communities, each of which came to include environmental stewardship in its community mission. Clergy contributed to the processes of integrating sustainability into their communities by advising environmentally focused lay groups (TPC, VAA), proposing and participating in projects (MCC), and presenting sustainability as a faith issue (all three). Hence, the processes by which these three initiatives evolved, growing from their origins with a few activities related to the concerns of individual members (clergy and laity) into community-wide sustainability social norms, were shaped by four elements: individuals who championed and led the initiatives; clergy who played roles in fostering initiative development; congregations that became involved with an issue that originated from a small group; and organizational structures, such as house churches and task forces, through which individuals took action.

3 CAREER-RELATED TRIGGER

Career-related personal interests triggered the shift toward land stewardship in three monastic communities, which followed similar paths from single project to community-wide sustainability ethos. At Nazareth (CJN), Saint John's Abbey (SJA), and Villa Maria (VM), individual community members began projects related to their careers within the faith organizations, and those projects gradually grew into community-based initiatives. Sister Ginny Jones established the Bow in the Clouds Natural Area as an outdoor classroom for her biology classes at Nazareth College and later developed retreat programs focused on eco-spirituality, which laid the foundations for her community of sisters to consider care for the earth as a facet of their religious lives. The community then applied those values to restoration of their former dairy farmland and later invested financial resources to ensure that the lands they had cared for would be preserved into the future. They also instituted conservation practices in organizational facilities to reduce use of natural resources. At Saint John's Abbey, Father Paul Schwietz took up the position of land manager and began restoring ecosystems in areas that had once been used for agriculture. His activities helped establish land stewardship as a community value and, ultimately, led to formation of an arboretum dedicated to educating people about sustainable land management. This land stewardship paved the way for conservation practices such as replacing coal-based electricity with power from natural gas and solar panels. At Villa Maria, Sister Barbara O'Donnell's post-retirement experiment with organic gardening led to a rebirth of agricultural activity at the convent, in which organic farming and sustainable forestry were combined with new environmental education and spirituality programs. Building on these programs, the community established a formal land ethic and integrated sustainability into administrative and facilities management.

As in the non-monastic cases, early projects undertaken to address the interests of individuals paved the way for development of community-wide sustainability ethics. The path from first project to community initiative was not, however, either smooth or straightforward since the monastic organizations had to be reorganized to accommodate new career paths and activities. Employee positions were adapted (for example, land manager at Saint John's Abbey and Villa Maria), new employee positions were created (for example, coordinator of newly formed eco-spirituality retreat ministries at Villa Maria and Nazareth), new organizational committees were formed to develop land ethics and oversee land management, and employees were hired to implement new ventures such as the Saint John's Arboretum and the Villa Maria Farm. Thus, the organizational structures within which the initiatives were implemented had significant influence on their development.

In order to make these innovations possible, the individuals who championed sustainable land stewardship had to cultivate support for their ideas within their faith communities. That process of building support was facilitated by "faith leaders," a term used here to describe the people who serve as the organizational and spiritual leaders in communities. These faith leaders fulfilled two key roles played by clergy in non-monastic cases. First, people in organizational leadership promoted sustainability by giving permission for individuals to take up new career paths and providing resources for implementation of proposed projects. Second, people in spiritual leadership roles led study groups to explore connections between faith and environmental issues and coordinated task forces to develop formal sustainability plans. These spiritual leaders included women religious (who are not ordained as clergy in the Catholic Church) as well as clergy and scholars from both inside and outside the community membership who were invited to contribute to monastic planning processes. The actions of these faith leaders, the processes though which the congregational membership became involved with the initiatives, and the organizational structures all shaped development of initiatives that began in response to the career goals of these monks and nuns.

4 COMMUNITY DISCERNMENT PROCESS AS TRIGGER

In contrast to the previous six cases, with their slow transition from first project to adoption of sustainability as a community-wide initiative, the five initiatives triggered by community discernment processes were perceived as community-wide activities from their inception. These discernment processes occurred during periods of transition in which the faith communities evaluated how to address particular community needs that would affect the future of their religious organizations. Consequently, there was extensive congregational involvement in the discernment processes as the communities defined long- and short-term goals, with particular emphasis on where to focus ministry efforts or how to address disjunctions between organizational needs and infrastructure. Once sustainability was introduced into the discussion, these discernment processes provided opportunities for extended community study of sustainability as a faith issue, which led to widespread endorsement of a sustainability ethic before the communities undertook their initiatives.

Broad congregational support for sustainability initiatives did not, however, guarantee a smooth transition from ethic to initiative implementation. Among the three non-monastic faith communities that adopted sustainability ethics through discernment processes, the ease with which a community realized its sustainability goals depended on the issue that had prompted the discernment process. Development of the initiative at the Jewish Reconstructionist Congregation was fairly straightforward because implementation focused on green building practices to address the infrastructure needs that had triggered the discernment process. Once the rabbi and governance board presented the idea for a green building to the congregation and received a positive response, implementation followed a standard process for new construction. A building committee worked with a construction firm to design a synagogue that would meet community needs and conform to LEED construction guidelines.

For communities in which sustainability was adopted as a component of the community mission, but for which there was no specific environmental project or concern underlying that decision, transforming ethic into action proved more challenging. At Trinity Presbyterian Church of East Brunswick, members of the Trinity Earth Shepherds group, which was created to carry out the community's new mission to practice stewardship of creation, realized they lacked the knowledge necessary to fulfill their task. They enrolled in the GreenFaith Certification program, which provided leadership training, a programmatic structure, and informational resources that enabled them to transform practices at their church. At First Parish Church of Newbury, the community did not have a specific project in mind when it adopted a mission to be "Stewards of Earth and Spirit."[1] The tiny congregation of thirty-five members decided to create a community garden behind the church, but their first attempt withered due to lack of experience, poor soil, and neglect. Only when a member of the church took the lead and enlisted aid from experienced gardeners in the region did the garden become a venue for successfully enacting the community's stewardship mission.

Initiatives undertaken as a result of discernment processes in two monastic communities followed similar patterns: once the community adopted sustainability as an ethic, members had to figure out how to integrate the new value into their practices. The Sisters of St. Francis at Our Lady of Angels (OLA) in Aston resolved that care for the earth was important to them and then had to determine how to implement that resolution on their property and through their ministries. Even a community-wide discernment process that led to adoption of a sustainability ethic with a specific focus could be challenging to implement. At Holy Wisdom Monastery (HWM) in Madison, a desire to remain in place and care for the land gave rise to the idea for restoring monastery farmland to prairie. Only after the idea had been adopted did the sisters and their staff set out to learn what they would actually have to do to fulfill their new mission.

The role of staff in these two initiatives highlights a distinction between monastic and non-monastic cases: monastic communities could assign responsibility for initiatives to full-time workers, whereas the non-monastic communities generally relied on volunteers to organize and implement their environmental efforts. At Holy Wisdom Monastery, lay staff learned new skills in order to restore prairieland. At Our Lady of Angels Convent, the community hired people for new positions in native plant landscaping and farm management, which were created to implement their plan for sustainable land stewardship. Additionally, sisters in administrative positions added stewardship of creation to organizational practices and facilities management. The role of staff in these cases illustrates the significance of organizational structure as a factor affecting implementation of initiatives.

Whether staff members or volunteers, champions who took leadership roles were just as significant for the development of the five discernment-triggered initiatives as for the six cases that grew out of projects related to clergy prompts, local environmental threats, and individual career interests. Individual champions (FPN, HWM) and affinity groups (JRC) introduced the idea of sustainability into discernment processes, did preliminary research before asking their communities to adopt sustainability as a value (TNJ, JRC, OLA), and took responsibility for incorporating sustainability into their religious organizations. These champions often had to acquire new knowledge and locate resources for activities such as prairie restoration (HWM), recycling (OLA), gardening (FPN), and greening their religious organization (TNJ, OLA). Faith leaders and clergy also played pivotal roles by setting the stage for discernment of new mission areas (FPN, TNJ, HWM, OLA) and promoting sustainability as a faith issue once the idea was introduced (JRC, HWM).

The progression of these five discernment-based initiatives was similar to the progression of the six that emerged from individual interests: despite the broad scope of their visions for a community-wide sustainability ethic, the initiatives started with a few projects and gradually expanded to include an array of activities. Members of Holy Wisdom spent a few years practicing stewardship of earth by restoring a prairie on former agricultural lands, then decided to follow green construction guidelines when they replaced their outdated monastery building. Our Lady of Angels began by hiring people to transform a section of land into the Red Hill Farm CSA; a few years later, they used green building techniques for construction of retreat facilities and incorporated environmental justice into their social justice advocacy work. First Parish Church of Newbury planted a few garden beds, which grew into a community garden and a nature-themed preschool. The Earth Shepherds at Trinity Presbyterian Church started with some educational programs and distribution of compact fluorescent lightbulbs and eventually led their church to become the first GreenFaith certified congregation. Only the Jewish Reconstructionist Congregation moved directly from adoption of sustainability as a goal to construction of the green synagogue that expressed their environmental ethic.

Despite the similarities in the evolution of the eleven cases, there are notable distinctions between initiatives that grew out of individual/affinity group projects and those that emerged from discernment processes. Discernment processes increased levels of congregational involvement and expanded the scope of the sustainability mission, particularly during early stages of the sustainability initiative. Thus, comparing initiatives that emerged from discernment processes with those that grew out of individual members' interests highlights some factors that shaped the eleven initiatives. The initiatives followed similar progressions, evolving from a few projects to an extensive set of activities, and individual champions played significant roles in their creation and implementation. However, development also varied due to differences in levels of involvement from faith leaders and the wider congregation, as well as variations in organizational structures.

5 EXTERNAL OPPORTUNITY AS TRIGGER

The final trigger differs from the other four in that it came from outside the faith communities. Four cases have sustainability initiatives that originated when external organizations presented the communities with opportunities to participate in local environmental programs. Among these initiatives, the decision to join the proffered activities came from grassroots membership in two cases and from organizational leadership in the other two.

Grassroots Responses

At both First Universalist Church of Rockland and St. Thomas Aquinas Parish in Palo Alto, lay members of the faith communities responded to outreach from an external organization and formed affinity groups to participate in the opportunities presented by the external organization. At First Universalist Church, a representative from the Maine Council of Churches asked if the community would join its advocacy campaign focused on climate change legislation, and some church members formed an Earth Team to facilitate participation in that advocacy effort and subsequent Maine Council projects. At St. Thomas Aquinas Parish, members formed a Green Committee in response to the Catholic Green Initiative for the Santa Clara Valley, which encouraged all parishes in the Diocese of San Jose to adopt environmentally sustainable practices.

Despite similar origins, development of these two initiatives was quite different due to their respective community contexts. The Earth Team at First Universalist Church became dissatisfied with the scale of environmental activities available through the Maine Council of Churches and enrolled in their denomination's Green Sanctuary Program in order to expand their efforts into a community-wide initiative. The certification program provided a structure for integrating sustainability throughout the faith community by requiring activities in worship, education, social justice ministry, and facilities management. The certification program expanded the scale of the sustainability initiative from a small group activity to a community ethic, realization of which involved support from clergy, staff, members of relevant committees, and the congregational membership.

The Green Committee at St. Thomas Aquinas Parish also envisioned its sustainability initiative as a parish-wide mission. The Catholic Greening Initiative of the Diocese of San Jose, which triggered their initiative, provided legitimacy for designating sustainability as a religious value and offered resources for prayer, study, and actions to address a suite of environmental issues such as resource conservation, climate change, and pollution prevention. In spite of the committee's broad mission, committee resources and organizational structures (for example, designating the Green Committee as a subgroup of the Facilities Committee) channeled the parish greening initiative toward energy conservation through technology upgrades, and resource conservation through behavior changes among staff. There was little opportunity to incorporate sustainability into worship, education, or social ministries. Therefore, although the sustainability groups at St. Thomas Aquinas and First Universalist Church both envisioned their initiatives as mechanisms for implementing community-wide sustainability ethics, development of their respective environmental activities was affected by their community contexts, especially the organizational structures and differing modes of involvement from clergy and congregations.

Organizational Leadership Responses

In contrast to the grassroots origins of the preceding two cases, the sustainability efforts in the final two cases began when organizational leaders responded to external opportunities. In New Jersey, Anshe Emeth Memorial Temple and Temple Shalom undertook sustainability initiatives because board members proposed that their temples participate in the GreenFaith certification program. In both cases, the board members were reacting to outreach from the regional branch of the Union for Reform Judaism, their denomination's umbrella organization, which had decided to provide support for enrollment in the GreenFaith program as a means of promoting environmental action among its member congregations. Once the leadership boards of the temples approved enrollment in the certification programs, they enlisted community members known to be strong environmentalists to lead their green initiatives.

Juxtaposing the two temple cases reveals similarities and differences in the unfolding of their sustainability initiatives that illustrate how factors within faith communities can affect development of sustainability initiatives. These communities have notable similarities: they belong to the same religious denomination, are located only thirty miles apart, and have memberships dominated by middle-class professionals. Both initiatives were coordinated by environmental educators and had support from rabbis who led environmentally themed worship services and incorporated environmental issues into youth programs. Despite this shared emphasis on educational programming, the processes by which resource conservation activities were implemented differed from one community to the other. Temple Shalom's accomplishments took the form of a series of distinct projects under the auspices of different committees, including installation of solar panels (Facilities Committee) and creating a community garden (Social Action Committee). In contrast, although some activities at Anshe Emeth were particular to one segment of the organization (for example, youth education), other projects like the Green Mitzvah Day were cooperatively developed by organizers from administration, education, worship, and social justice areas of the faith community.

The differences in the processes for creating and implementing activities at the two Reform temples highlight the influence of individuals, congregational involvement, and opportunities and constraints related to organizational context. Despite using a common programmatic structure, differences among their communities caused variations in the development of the initiatives. Each had a Green Team comprised of community members with ties to various areas of the organization, and the activities they undertook intersected with structures that existed to implement the mission and ministries of their respective faith organization. So, for example, incorporating sustainability into a pre-existing annual community service program (AET) or having strong support from the chair of the Facilities Committee (TS) shaped the types of activities undertaken within each community. Even the physical context determined constraints and opportunities that affected environmental activities. The roof at Anshe Emeth Memorial Temple was not strong enough to support solar panels, whereas Temple Shalom had a structurally sound roof with ample southern exposure. Temple Shalom had extensive grounds, which facilitated efforts to establish a community garden, while Anshe Emeth, which has a parking lot but no green space, hopes to become a pick-up location for a Community Supported Agriculture project.

AN INTERPLAY OF FOUR CRITICAL DOMAINS

These fifteen sustainability initiatives emerged in response to a variety of triggers ranging from personal career aspirations to community discernment processes, from concern about an environmental threat affecting a beloved place to concerns about climate change as a threat to entire global systems. Some were proposed from the top, by senior clergy or board members, while others emerged from the grassroots, through community member interests. A few began as community-wide missions while others started with narrower foci and gradually expanded. The variability of these perceived opportunities for action and the processes by which initiatives developed in response to the opportunities, demonstrates that triggers alone do not explain why these sustainability initiatives began or why they evolved into durable initiatives encompassing multiple activities. Certainly, it seems clear that the emergence of sustainability initiatives in response to these triggering events was not inevitable. There are more than 300,000 congregations in the United States,[2] yet only a handful engage in comparable initiatives, with multiple activities sustained over periods of at least four years.[3] Therefore, it is particularly interesting to ask why consequential and durable initiatives developed in these fifteen cases.

One essential element in the emergence and development of these initiatives is the role played by individuals. Individuals were the champions who organized and implemented the initiatives through the venue of their faith communities, regardless of whether they were triggered by outreach from external organizations or by internal community discernment processes and personal environmental concerns. Individuals took the lead in responding to clergy prompts, protecting local environments, and developing career resources. In some cases, individuals introduced sustainability into discernment processes and, when community discernment processes resulted in adoption of sustainability as a community mission, individuals and affinity groups were responsible for translating ethic into action. Finally, when external organizations presented opportunities for participating in environmental activities, individuals coordinated community engagement with those opportunities. These individual champions did not, however, act in a vacuum. The case studies show that these sustainability initiatives were created by champions in interaction with the clergy/faith leaders, congregations, and organizational structures that made up their faith communities.

These domains of activity—champions, faith leaders, congregations, and organizations—provide an analytical framework that can be used to better understand the factors that contributed to the emergence and development of these exemplary sustainability initiatives (see Figure 1).

FIGURE 1 The Four Domains of Activity

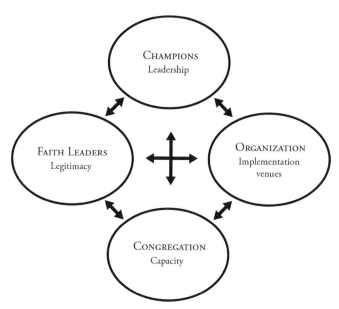

Champions

In the Champions domain, each initiative had champions who turned idea into action. Without them, the initiatives would not have come into existence. It is notable, however, that there are significant variations among the people who championed sustainability from community to community. Depending on the case, the individuals who played this pivotal role were clergy, staff, or laity; some were the originators who proposed adopting sustainability as a faith issue and others were community members responding to a request to lead a program proposed by someone else; some were longtime environmentalists while, for others, the environment was a new issue. Because champions are so prominent in these fifteen cases, their role begs deeper examination. Cross-case analysis can help answer questions about motivations and characteristics that enabled individuals to successfully organize and implement these initiatives, thereby providing a better understanding of factors that affected the role of champions in these cases.

Faith Leaders

Faith leaders played a particularly significant role in establishing the legitimacy of sustainability as a faith issue; hence the contributions of faith leaders influenced the adoption of sustainability as a social norm within the faith communities. There was, however, great variation among modes of involvement by faith leaders in the fifteen cases. In some cases, clergy led development of the initiatives. In others they provided support or advice while leaving the initiative in the hands of a lay group. Similarly, in some monastic communities, theologically astute spiritual leaders among the brothers and sisters led development of the initiatives with varying levels of involvement from administrative leaders. Thus, levels of personal interest and modes of involvement by faith leaders varied across cases. Even sermons, the most obvious type of clergy contribution, ranged from consistent, long-term preaching on environmental themes to short-term or occasional reflections from the pulpit, and even no preaching at all. These variations raise questions about the ways motivations and personal characteristics influenced faith leader participation, and how their divergent modes of involvement affected development of the initiatives.

Congregations

Similarly, the involvement of the congregation, the body of members in a faith community, was significant in all cases, but the modes and levels of engagement varied from one community to another. Involvement of the congregation affected a faith community's capacity for action, the scope and scale of its sustainability initiatives, because levels of support from the congregation members determined the availability of volunteers and material resources. Congregational participation in the processes through which sustainability initiatives were developed was not uniform. Some cases had community-wide discernment processes or used other mechanisms to include the wider congregation in initiative planning, while others relied on small groups or coalitions of committee chairs to organize their initiatives. The scale of congregational involvement in initiative implementation also differed in level (from extensive to minimal) and duration (from long-term to short-term). In light of these variations in the modes and levels of involvement by the congregations, there is need for additional analysis in order to better understand how factors in this domain influenced development of the initiatives.

Organizations

The initiatives developed within the context of a fourth domain, the faith organization, which affected the behavior of the champions, faith leaders, and congregations. Organizational structures shaped the processes through which initiatives emerged, the venues through which activities were implemented, and the interactions among community members. In some cases, environmental activities were carried out by temporary task forces researching specific projects and, in other cases, by permanent committees created to fulfill organization-wide missions. Depending on the community, the greening efforts might be implemented under the auspices of a religious mission committee, a facilities committee, or through a small group ministry. These variations in the scale of the effort to integrate sustainability into the organization and in the location of the green team within the organization, illustrate some ways the structures of the faith organizations shaped development of the sustainability initiatives. Hence, the role of organizational structure in providing the venues through which an initiative was developed and implemented begs deeper examination.

CONCLUSION

Comparison of the fifteen case studies indicates that the initiatives followed a general pattern in which passionate individuals responded to triggering events by organizing environmental activities through the venues of their faith communities. There was, however, no single, simple process through which sustainability became integrated into the faith organizations. Instead, the initiatives emerged and evolved through complex processes that were shaped by a dynamic interplay among the individuals who championed sustainability, the organizational structures within which the initiatives resided, and the faith leaders and congregations that comprised the communities of faith. Factors within these four domains of activity, and the interactions among them, affected the emergence, evolution, and outcomes of the initiatives described in the case studies. Hence, to fully comprehend the processes through which consequential and durable sustainability initiatives developed in these faith communities requires a deeper understanding of elements within each domain and of the dynamic interplay among them. The next four parts of this book examine each of these four domains in depth.

Part II

CHAMPIONS

Leaders of Sustainability Initiatives

INTRODUCTION

"Educate for the earth." The sound of these words, spoken in her own voice, jolted Sister Barbara O'Donnell awake and set her on a path to create and nurture a sustainability initiative at the Villa Maria convent in western Pennsylvania. That path was not, however, either clearly marked or smooth. Despite a deep conviction that the words she had heard were a calling from God and that they came in answer to her prayers about what new ministry work she should undertake after retiring from her career in academic administration, O'Donnell was uncertain of how to proceed because, she says, "There was no model for 'educating for the earth.'"[1] Over time, O'Donnell and the faith community at Villa Maria developed their own model, encompassing land stewardship, organic gardening, farm-based environmental education, and eco-spirituality programs. However, when the journey began in 1990, the sisters had to educate themselves about sustainability before they could "educate for the earth."

This combination of conviction about the need to pursue faith-based environmental action and uncertainty about how to proceed is a common theme in accounts about the origins of the sustainability initiatives in the fifteen case studies. The initiatives arose and grew into programs of consequence for their communities because of individuals who did not turn away from a challenge.

They sought out information, asked advice, found allies and resources, experimented, and persevered, thereby providing the leadership necessary to get these initiatives started and carry them forward. Without these champions, sustainability might have remained an ideal with little practical expression in these faith communities. Therefore, the stories of these faith-based sustainability initiatives begin with the individuals who set them in motion and shaped their development. In order to understand the role champions played in development of these initiatives and the factors that enabled them to be successful leaders, chapter 3 asks: Who were these sustainability champions and why did they take action through faith communities? Chapter 4 then delves into characteristics that contributed to their success, including resources that helped them overcome challenges along the way and the personal benefits people experienced from participating in earth care efforts.

3 PEOPLE OF FAITH, STEWARDS OF EARTH

I see the Earth as a gift from God to us, and it is our obligation to be good stewards and take only what we need with no waste, so that it is sustainable for future generations.

—KATIA REEVES, St. Thomas Aquinas Parish

THE INDIVIDUALS WHO CHAMPIONED EARTH CARE in these fifteen cases took on the challenges of developing initiatives for their faith communities because they perceived these sustainability initiatives as a means through which to address personal interests. Although particular interests differed from person to person, they can be organized under general themes of environmental and religious interests, which interviewees had come to see as intertwined. The individuals who led these initiatives did not, however, all follow the same path to arrive at the conviction that environmental issues are faith issues and that faith communities should be venues for environmental activities. In some cases, people with long-standing environmental interests did not perceive connections between their environmental concerns and their faith communities until they encountered an opportunity to explore the topic. In others, people of faith who had not paid much attention to environmental issues in the past became passionate about earth care because of new circumstances linking environment to their religious lives. The divergent paths individuals traveled toward perception of a connection between faith and earth care shaped the development of the sustainability initiatives, affecting implementation processes and the types of activities undertaken. Therefore, it is important to look deeper into the factors that motivated the individuals who took on the task of developing and implementing these initiatives for their faith communities.

MOTIVATIONS: INTERTWINED PERSONAL INTERESTS

The personal interests that individuals described in discussing what motivated them to participate in a faith community's sustainability initiative fall into three categories: environmental interests, religious interests, and personal windows of opportunity (see Table 3). These categories are not mutually exclusive, since, as stated above, religious and environmental interests became intertwined for the initiative leaders in the fifteen cases, and most interviewees described multiple interests that came together in their faith-based sustainability work. However, individuals usually mentioned specific topics or concerns that were particularly important to them and, when these core interests became connected to additional interests, they felt the need to take action. Thus, the interconnection of these personal interests is a significant factor in explaining what motivated these individuals to champion earth care in their faith communities.

TABLE 3 CHAMPIONS' MOTIVATIONAL INTERESTS

TOPICS MENTIONED BY INDIVIDUALS (ONE PERSON MAY CITE MORE THAN ONE TOPIC)	NUMBER OF INDIVIDUALS
1. *Environmental Interests*	
General concern for the environment	9
Protection of local environment	5
Interest in forestry	2
Concerns about climate change	12
Preserve world for descendants	6
Interest in gardening	9
2. *Religious Interests*	
Social justice ministry must include sustainability	11
Religious duty to care for creation	5
Stewardship as a religious calling	5
Pursuing religious vocation (career)	4
3. *Personal Windows of Opportunity*	6

1 ENVIRONMENTAL INTERESTS

Most of the individuals who led sustainability activities in these fifteen religious organizations had environmental interests that preceded their involvement in the faith-based initiatives. Some described themselves as longtime environmentalists who focused on protection of the natural environment and belonged to organizations such as the Sierra Club. Others had more recently become concerned about the environment due to awareness of climate change and its predicted effects on the world their children would inherit. A subgroup had an interest in gardening, especially growing organic food. These environmental interests merged with religious life as the individuals found opportunities to connect the two topics.

Traditional Environmentalism: Protecting Nature

Some of the earliest sustainability initiatives to emerge among these fifteen cases were founded by individuals who had long-standing ties to the environmental movement. Sister Ginny Jones of the Congregation of St. Joseph and Father Paul Schwietz of Saint John's Abbey both became environmentalists as undergraduates majoring in biology. Jones combined her environmental concerns with her religious life among the Sisters of St. Joseph of Nazareth, where her calling to do environmental stewardship found expression through her work as a biology teacher at Nazareth College. She helped organize citywide activities for the first Earth Day in 1970 and created a nature preserve on convent lands in 1973, which served as an educational resource for her students. After the college closed in 1992, she made a detour into hospital administrative work before returning to her environmental calling by developing eco-spirituality programs that became part of a new retreat center ministry at the convent. Schwietz also forged a connection between his concern for the environment and his religious vocation. After becoming land manager for Saint John's Abbey in 1985, he introduced sustainable land management practices for the Abbey forests and began doing restoration work in some areas that had once been used for farming. Both Jones and Schwietz created careers that allowed them to incorporate their environmental interests into their religious vocations.

A similar theme of linked environmental and faith vocations runs through the story of Lynn Cameron, one of the founders of the Earth Care House Church, the group that carries out environmental ministry at Trinity Presbyterian Church in Harrisonburg, Virginia. Cameron uses religiously evocative language to describe her environmentalism, saying she "always felt a calling to care for the earth."[1] It was the opportunity to combine this environmental vocation with her faith tradition that motivated her to join Trinity. Cameron and her husband first met the Trinity pastor, Reverend Ann Held, at an environmental festival where the Camerons were tending the Sierra Club display table. Discovering that Pastor Held shared their environmental concerns, the Camerons visited Trinity and decided to join the congregation, leaving their previous church where the environment was never discussed. With support from Reverend Held, in 1996 Lynn Cameron and two other environmentalist congregation members founded the Restoring Creation House Church (later renamed Earth Care House Church) to explore connections between Christianity and the environment.

For the sustainability champions in these early initiatives, combining environmental interests with their faith traditions was not clear-cut, especially since there was little precedent for the combination in the societies around them. Consequently, Jones and Cameron both noted that theological study was an important step in the development of their faith-based sustainability work. Jones drew on the writings of Catholic theologians like Teilhard de Chardin and Thomas Berry to explain why stewardship of the environment was an appropriate activity for Catholics. Cameron and the members of the Restoring Creation House Church studied Presbyterian Church (USA) reports and other theological texts that described why care for the environment and sustainable development were moral obligations for Christians.[2] Through this study, Cameron found that her religious and environmental interests were drawn together: "We started with the biblical foundations, and I think it was important to get clear that those foundations were there. I kind of lost faith in college, and finding these biblical foundations was important to getting my faith back; it gave me a way to connect faith with my concerns."[3] Linking environmental concerns with theological teachings not only strengthened her faith, it motivated her and the house church members to take environmental action through their faith community because, according to Cameron, "Once the theology was within us, we could act out our faith." As she explained, "Some of the theology we read was really dense and hard to understand. Then, after a couple years of study, people wanted to do something. It is not enough to be *against* things, we needed to be *for* things. A lot of environmental work starts with being against something. But what are you for? I guess for us, it's the idea of sustainability."[4] Having established a faith foundation for environmental action, the members of the house church were motivated to pursue sustainability as an expression of their religious mission.

New Environmentalism: Greening Organizations

Long-term environmentalists also took the lead in two of the most recently formed initiatives, at Temple Shalom and Anshe Emeth Memorial Temple. In these cases, however, their efforts began with a new area of environmental practice, the greening of organizations. Both of these Reform Jewish communities enrolled in a certification program offered by GreenFaith, an organization that promotes sustainability in faith communities, and both tapped environmental educators in their communities to lead the certification processes.

At Temple Shalom in Aberdeen, New Jersey, when the board decided that the congregation should pursue certification as a green congregation, the vice president asked Margo Wolfson to lead the effort. She "jumped at the chance" because she was passionate about the environment. "I am an environmentalist from way back, starting in high school, when I had a wonderful biology teacher. I went on to teach biology myself. I joined the World Wildlife Fund and the Sierra Club when I was just a teenager. I think, being a city girl living in Brooklyn, I had an especially strong longing for the outdoors."[5] For Wolfson, leading the GreenFaith certification process provided an opportunity to engage with a topic of personal interest under the auspices of her faith community. Previously, she had organized efforts to incorporate the environment into Temple Shalom through Earth Day celebrations, observation of Tu BiShvat, the "Jewish Arbor Day" that has come to be linked with environmental concerns, and activities on seed-planting and water conservation in the religious education classes that Wolfson taught for third through sixth graders. However, prior to enrollment in the certification program, Wolfson felt that the environment was "kind of a piece off to the side but was not welcome in the main door" of the temple. Leading the GreenFaith certification process gave her "permission to bring it in the main door."[6]

Whereas champions like Cameron and Jones went through gradual processes of theological study to lay the groundwork for their actions in an era when the idea of faith-based earth care was little known in their communities, Wolfson was able to begin her temple initiative confident that Judaism endorsed sustainability. Due to her long-standing interest in environmentalism, she was already well versed in teachings about connections between Judaism and ecology that had developed in the 1990s. She was familiar with the work of the Coalition on the Environment and Jewish Life (COEJL), an "organization that deepens and broadens the Jewish community's commitment to stewardship and protection of the Earth through outreach, activism, and Jewish learning,"[7] having used some COEJL resources for the Earth Day and Tu BiShvat services she had previously organized. Moreover, Temple Shalom belongs to the Reform Jewish tradition, which affirms that protecting the environment is an important aspect of the Jewish practice of *tikkun olam*, "repairing the world." Even before the temple joined GreenFaith, Wolfson had identified environmental texts in the new Siddur, the book of daily prayers used by Reform temples, so that she could point them out to the children in religious education classes. For champions like Wolfson, the connections between religious values and environmentalism were well established before they encountered opportunities to take action in their faith communities.

Climate Change Transforms Environment into a Faith Issue

Interviewees in eight of the ten suburban communities mentioned climate change as an issue that motivated their efforts. For individuals at St. Thomas Aquinas Parish and Vineyard Church of Ann Arbor, climate change was the subject that transformed environmental issues into faith issues. Gerard McGuire, who helped organize the Green Committee at St. Thomas Aquinas Parish, said his environmental and religious interests developed separately but came together in response to climate change. "My awareness of environmental issues was separate [from religion]; it was shaped by Al Gore and the environmental movement. The two were on parallel courses."[8] McGuire became involved in Gore's Climate Reality Project, through which he trained to give public presentations about climate change. He began telling his brother, who is a priest, that he ought to address the issue of climate change when he preached. In contrast to environmental issues, which were a fairly new interest for McGuire, religion had been important to him throughout his life. He had studied for the Catholic priesthood in his youth, then pursued other paths, which included exploration of Eastern religions, before returning to his Catholic religious roots. Although eco-theology was not part of his Catholic theological training, McGuire had come to see care for the environment as integral to his religion because he saw the whole world as a manifestation of God and, "if you're part of the greater whole that is God then you have to respect it all." Because climate change damages God's world and is most harmful to the poor and oppressed, the very people Jesus worked to help, McGuire argued that living more sustainably is an expression of Christian values. He even went so far as to state that "you can't call yourself a Christian without being an environmentalist."

While McGuire's statement may be extreme, it demonstrates the strength of his conviction that the moral teachings of his faith require him to take action in response to the predicted impacts of climate change. The two individuals who inaugurated the sustainability initiative at Vineyard Church came to a similar conclusion, as will be described below.

Individuals with a strong personal interest in growing organic food played significant roles organizing garden projects in seven cases. The majority of these gardeners had previous experience with home gardens, but a few were completely new to the activity. In the beginning, Erin Stack of First Parish Church of Newbury was such an amateur that she had to enlist help from experienced gardeners in the local community to teach her and other members how to plan and care for the community garden they established at the church. Stack found the work so rewarding that she eventually founded a Community Supported Agriculture venture and became a farmer. Sister Barbara O'Donnell came to organic gardening without previous experience but benefited from the guidance of Frank Romeo, the land manager at the Villa Maria convent. The more she learned and the more time she spent in the gardens, the more enthusiastic she became. "I was going up to the farm every day to watch things. I went regularly to watch the birthing of an eggplant. It really is like a birth, the way the fruit emerges from the flower; that was fascinating to me. And the miracle of composting as 'waste' becomes fresh, black, and fragrant. It was like the new me, becoming rooted in the soil."[9]

As O'Donnell's language indicates, gardening was a spiritual activity for her. She felt connected to the divine through her awe at the workings of God's creation. She also saw her labor as an expression of her faith community's ministry work; part of the mission of the Sisters of the Humility of Mary is to care for the poor, and the new organic gardens became a resource for food donations. Other individuals also mentioned that gardening was both a personal passion and a venue through which to practice ministry. Lisa Bauer, who coordinated care of the chickens in the gardens at the Madison Christian Community, reflected on the role of interactions with nature as part of the spiritual development of her children: "My girls, six and nine, are enamored with the chickens. They beg to go see them daily and jump right into chore mode. My youngest daughter has taught some to roost on her shoulder, so she walks around as the chicken whisperer. She loves the idea that she can be a farmer someday. In my mind, that is a great ministry—connecting people with nature and our agricultural heritage."[10]

An interest in organic food and teaching their children where food comes from motivated some young families like the Bauers to participate in garden projects, however, the majority of the leaders and volunteers were older. In the Children's Garden at the Madison Christian Community, most of the volunteers were women, often recently retired, for whom the garden had become "their passion."[11] Many of them lived in apartments or condos and had little yard space at home. Female, and some male, retirees were also prevalent among the workers in the food pantry garden and the group tending the restored prairie. Some volunteers had grown up with gardens and were delighted to have an opportunity to reengage with an activity from their pasts. Their enjoyment was furthered by the conviction that the work in the garden was an expression of their religious values to care for others. As one member commented, "People enjoy gardening because they feel connected to the earth and they find satisfaction in feeding people."[12]

2 RELIGIOUS INTERESTS

Across the fifteen cases, the individuals who took on the challenge of leading sustainability initiatives in their faith communities had strong faith components to their lives. The sustainability champions included men and women with full-time religious vocations in monastic communities, pastors and rabbis for whom religion defined their worldviews, and lay people who were deeply invested in their religious traditions and sought to live their values in their daily lives. In the words of Gerard McGuire, "Because I am a 'recycled' Catholic [who returned to his natal religion as an adult], I see my faith in a different way; I want to be active."[13] For these people of faith, seeing connections between religion and sustainability created a significant motivation to take action in order to address environmental issues.

Katia Reeves, leader of the Green Committee at St. Thomas Aquinas Parish at the time of this study, noted that she was educated by nuns from kindergarten through tenth grade and, consequently, her faith "probably motivates everything I do and shaped who I am." Reeves described her sustainability activities as an expression of her religion. "I see the Earth as a gift from God to us, and it is our obligation to be good stewards and take only what we need with no waste, so that it is sustainable for future generations. Drastically reducing our CO_2 emissions is a huge part of this effort. I have three small grandsons and I wonder what will the natural resources be when they are my age?"[14] Although her primary motivation may be the welfare of her grandchildren, she links her personal desire to protect them with a transpersonal value of working for the common good of future generations, which is framed as a moral obligation under her religion. Thus, for Reeves, the parish sustainability initiative brings together personal interests related to family, environment, and religion.

Religious interests dominate the stories of the individuals who led sustainability initiatives in the monastic cases, but even in these cases, religion is intertwined with a variety of other personal interests. Sister Barbara O'Donnell described the experience that inspired her to take up environmental work as a calling from God. On retreat in 1990, after having retired from a career in teaching and academic administration, she was praying for guidance about what kind of work to take up as her next vocation. It was in this context that she awakened one morning to hear her own voice saying out loud, "Educate for the earth."

As with Reeves and those with pre-existing environmental interests, O'Donnell's sustainability work brought together interests related to personal relationships, environment, and religion. She had a long-standing sense of connection to nature and to the land at the Villa Maria convent. As a child, her mother had taught her to see God's hand in nature: "She used to hold blooming flowers between her cupped hands and say, 'Oh, God has made this.' "[15] O'Donnell's sense of a connection between nature and spirituality was further nurtured by her extensive collection of nature-themed mandalas, images used to focus the mind for meditation. She also felt a special connection to the lands at Villa Maria, where she had spent several years as a novice. At the time of her novitiate, the order still had a large working farm, and all novices were required to contribute their labor by gathering eggs from the commercial chicken houses. Throughout her career, O'Donnell had looked forward to retreats and opportunities to return to Villa Maria, so developing a ministry focused on organic gardening, farm-based education, and eco-spirituality using the Villa lands was a delight for her. Furthermore, because her previous work had been as an educator in schools run by the sisters, the combination of environmental education and eco-spiritual ministry brought together multiple personal interests connected to faith and sustainability.

Although individuals with pre-existing environmental interests led thirteen of the fifteen initiatives in these case studies, there were two cases in which people of faith with no prior environmental background became sustainability champions once they became convinced that environmental issues were also faith issues. For Pastor Ken Wilson of the Vineyard Church of Ann Arbor, that transition in perspective came in 2007, when he attended a retreat convened by the Center for Health and the Global Environment (Harvard

Medical School) and the National Association of Evangelicals. After various scientists described evidence for climate change and its predicted impacts on human beings, James Gustav (Gus) Speth, dean of the School of Forestry at Yale, spoke about why the scientists needed assistance from faith leaders. According to Wilson:

> Gus Speth said words to this effect: Thirty years ago, I thought that with enough good science we would be able to solve the environmental crisis. I was wrong. I used to think the greatest problems threatening the planet were pollution, biodiversity loss, and climate change. I was wrong there too. I now believe the greatest environmental problems are pride, apathy, and greed. For that, I now see that we need a cultural and spiritual transformation. And we in the scientific community don't know how to do that. But you evangelicals do. We need your help.[16]

Wilson described his personal response to Speth's words as a moment of spiritual awakening. "That's when it happened: the conviction of Holy Spirit. The tightening of the throat. The raising of the hair on my arms. The watering of the eyes. How could I have been so blind?"[17] In that moment, Wilson realized that he had previously considered caring for the environment in passive terms and had not been actively engaged because he saw "environmentalists" as more concerned about spotted owls and wildlife than the social issues that were important to him. However, he now perceived the falsity of that presumed dichotomy. "What was I thinking? That if I cared less about polar bears or other endangered species, I'd somehow care more about the vulnerable unborn?"[18] In response to his new conviction that care for the environment was not separate from his faith values, Wilson did further research on climate change and decided he needed to take action. He prepared a series of three sermons on creation care for his congregation, describing why Christians are obligated to be stewards of God's creation, the evidence for climate change, and the need for changes in human behavior.

In response to Wilson's sermons, one of his congregation members felt called to take action as well. Phil Brabbs approached the minister to ask what he could do to care for creation. Wilson suggested he organize a small group ministry at the church. Brabbs and some like-minded congregants founded Green Vineyard, a group that engaged in Bible study to explore the scriptural basis for creation care and undertook sustainability activities to put their beliefs into practice. Members of Green Vineyard worked to conserve resources at the church through energy efficiency, waste reduction, recycling, and changes in supply purchases, and to promote conservation behavior in people's homes through distribution of CFLs and reusable shopping bags.

Both Brabbs and Reverend Wilson felt concerned about climate change because they were fathers who worried about the world their children would inherit, and yet neither took significant interest in the topic until it was presented as an issue that required a faith-based response. Only after climate change was framed as a religious issue did both men experience a sense of being called to take action. A similar pattern is evident for Debbie O'Halloran, although she does not use the language of calling to describe the transformation of perspective that led her to promote a faith-based sustainability initiative.

O'Halloran is a lifelong member of Trinity Presbyterian Church in East Brunswick, New Jersey. In 2006, she led a discernment group to consider possible missions for the church to focus on in the future. The environment, hunger, and peace-making were the three topics under consideration. Environment was on the list because the Presbyterian Church (USA) denomination had recommended its member congregations consider adopting the environment as a mission area, not because any member had proposed it. O'Halloran had never been an active environmentalist and did not see why the subject was relevant, however, as she and her group researched the topic, her perspective changed. "When we started the discernment process, none of us were certain of why environment connected to our faith. No one voted for it as our mission focus at first."[19] But they studied all three issues, breaking them down, considering statistics, looking at how people were affected by the issues, and determining what a church could do in response. Much to her surprise, they found their perspectives changing: "By the end, we voted unanimously to choose environment as a mission. No one wanted to do anything unless we addressed environment first because it was connected with all the other issues, like feeding the hungry."[20]

Like Wilson and Brabbs, O'Halloran was motivated to develop a sustainability initiative because she came to see responding to environmental issues as intertwined with fulfillment of her faith work, particularly in relation to Bible passages advocating love of neighbors and care for the poor. Although environment was not previously "on her radar," through the mission study she came to the conclusion that care for the environment is something Christians are called to do. O'Halloran's association of environment with the social justice issues of poverty and hunger highlights the role community context played in shaping connections between faith and sustainability. Interviewees described the religious bases for sustainability in terms of theological ideas associated with their community's pre-existing ministries. Hence, O'Halloran emphasized social justice, a long-standing focus for her Presbyterian church, whereas Wilson described a "religious duty to care for creation" that fit with the evangelical emphasis on personal behavior. The ways theology and ministry practices affected initiatives will be examined in more detail in chapters 5, 7, and 10.

3 PERSONAL WINDOWS OF OPPORTUNITY

Personal windows of opportunity added to some individuals' interest in taking action and enabled them to devote time and energy to environmental activities. A number of sustainability champions in these cases mentioned that they became leaders of their community initiatives at a time in their lives when they were looking for new projects. Debbie O'Halloran got involved in organizing her church's environmental mission because she was at a point in her life where "I needed something, and something presented itself."[21] She went on to describe the circumstances in more detail saying, "My children had gone off to college and I was floundering. I went to the minister and told him I was looking for a project. Then I went to a Bread for the World[22] presentation and felt that we needed to do something. That something ended up growing into this whole greening of the church. I never knew it would be this big."[23] Similarly, Gerard McGuire noted that his children were grown and out of the house and he was partially retired, which meant that he had time for greater involvement in activities at his church. Although much younger than O'Halloran or McGuire, Gretchen Marshall-TothFejel cited the need for a new project as part of her motivation for founding the Community Garden that became a core activity for Green Vineyard. Because she had just been laid off from her job, she "had extra time and needed something positive to do."[24]

Unlike Marshall-TothFejel, the majority of the sustainability champions in the non-monastic faith communities were in their fifties or older. For many of them, retirement created the window of opportunity to become more involved in activities at their churches and synagogues. In several cases, retired couples volunteered in their faith communities, either working together on projects related to a shared interest, such as gardening, or serving separately on committees that made use of skills from their previous careers.

Windows of opportunity were also a theme in the stories of Father Paul Schwietz, Sister Ginny Jones, and Sister Barbara O'Donnell. In these cases, however, the timing had to do with opportunities to develop careers rather than availability of free time outside of work and family. Shortly after joining the monastic community, Schwietz established a career path at Saint John's Abbey by applying his training in biology and forestry to the new position of land manager. Jones first took up care of the prairie fen that would become Bow in the Clouds Nature Preserve by using it as an educational resource when she began teaching at Nazareth College. Later, after a career in both teaching and hospital administration, she founded a new ministry for her convent with programs on eco-spirituality; this new ministry coincided with a new career in retreat leadership. O'Donnell was motivated to learn how to "educate for the earth" when she sought a new ministry after retiring from her previous career in administrative work. Like Jones, she developed an outdoor activity, organic gardening in this case, which led to a new ministry career coordinating eco-spirituality retreats and environmental education programs. Thus, in these monastic communities, the individuals who championed sustainability did so during windows of opportunity related to their careers, in which they were able to incorporate environmental activities into jobs within their faith organizations.

EFFECTS:
COMMITMENT TO SUSTAINABILITY INITIATIVES

Interviewees' answers to questions about what motivated their efforts to organize and implement sustainability initiatives describe diverse personal and religious interests. Some emphasized personal concerns for family, local environments, and careers, which were linked to wider environmental and religious interests. For individuals with strong connections to their faith traditions, developing a conviction that environmental issues are faith issues was a key factor in motivating them to take action through the venue of a faith community. Lynn Cameron, a longtime environmentalist, illustrates this experience in her description of the Earth Care House Church as a place where her calling to religious life and calling to care for the earth intertwined and "the two threads of my life came together."[25]

For these individuals, promoting sustainability through their faith communities was an opportunity to address intertwined personal interests related to both environment and faith. Consequently, they brought a deep personal commitment to their sustainability work, which was evident in their investment of considerable time, effort, and creativity. For some champions, that commitment was augmented by a window of opportunity in their personal lives that meant they were ready to take on new projects. An indication of the level of commitment is apparent in the willingness of these champions to seek external resources in order to fulfill their goals when personal knowledge proved insufficient. They enrolled their faith communities in green certification programs to acquire structure and informational resources, enlisted aid from local experts to set up gardens or install solar panels, consulted professionals to learn about prairie restoration and sustainable forest management, attended workshops on organic farming and storm window construction, researched recycling and office supply options, and learned to write grant applications in order to fund projects.[26] Even the two leaders who were professional environmental educators had to acquire information about best practices and available resources that would fit their religious organizations. Thus, a key factor affecting the success of these initiatives was the presence of champions with a deep sense of commitment to earth care who were willing to do research and develop new skills in order to implement activities that would address their intertwined environmental and faith interests.

4 LEADERS WHO MAKE THINGS HAPPEN

See, that's the thing, things happened because someone has an idea and is passionate and is able to bring others along. They are able to show how it fits with the mission of the community. A lot of it comes from individuals.
—TOM MATTHEWS, Madison Christian Community

PERSONAL INTERESTS INSPIRED INDIVIDUALS with a sense of commitment to faith-based earth care, but commitment alone does not guarantee that a person can effectively develop a project, especially if the project requires managing a group of people and navigating the processes that govern an organization. The champions who led these sustainability initiatives shared characteristics that enabled them to be effective initiative leaders. They also found ways to face and respond to challenges along the way. Ultimately, they felt their work as leaders and participants engaged in faith-based earth care was important to their communities and meaningful to their religious lives.

LEADERSHIP CAPACITY

Interviewees across the cases cited the presence of dedicated individuals who were able to provide leadership as a significant factor contributing to the accomplishments of their sustainability initiatives. Tom Matthews, the maintenance person for the Madison Christian Community, attributed the success of the sustainability activities in his faith community to people he called "spark plugs," who get things started and keep them going. These spark plugs inspired others because they had ideas and passion and, perhaps most important, the leadership skills to bring others along as they turned those ideas into actions. Chuck Tully, facilities manager for St. Thomas Aquinas Parish, also commented on the importance of leadership for getting enough people involved to make it possible for an initiative to be successful. He had noticed that levels of volunteer participation were higher in the presence of strong leaders and theorized that "people recognize their leadership and are interested in working with them."[1] Similarly, at Anshe Emeth Memorial Temple, one of the Green Team members asserted that the whole temple was supportive of the idea to seek GreenFaith certification, however what made it possible for that idea to become reality was having an effective leader in Mike Chodroff: "It was his baby, but he delegated well, and we are proud of him."[2]

The comment about Chodroff's ability to delegate reinforces Matthews' and Tully's observations that leadership is not simply a matter of doing all the work oneself; it involves the ability to work with others in a range of situations. Comparing the cases suggests that the individuals who led these faith-community sustainability initiatives shared three characteristics that contributed to their leadership capacity (see Table 4). First, many of the initiative leaders were knowledgeable about environmental issues and sustainability. Second, most of the individuals exhibited leadership skills derived from prior experience working for the religious organization. Third, nearly all were long-time members who were embedded in their communities, which positioned them to assume leadership roles.

TABLE 4 CHARACTERISTICS THAT CONTRIBUTED TO LEADERSHIP CAPACITY

ENABLING CHARACTERISTICS	NUMBER OF CASES
1. *Sustainability Knowledge*	8
2. *Leadership Skills* Institutional knowledge Project management	14
3. *Embedded in the Community* Trust Relationships/networks	15

1 *Sustainability Knowledge*

Eight of the individuals who led initiatives in their faith communities were knowledgeable about sustainability due to backgrounds in environmental work. Five initiatives emerged because of community members who started activities related to their environmental interests. Training in biology and forestry provided knowledge that enabled Sister Ginny Jones and Father Paul Schwietz to implement land restoration projects in monastic communities, and experience with environmental organizations like the Sierra Club and Al Gore's Climate Reality Project assisted Lynn Cameron and Gerard McGuire in organizing groups to take up faith-based sustainability activities in their churches. Individuals with environmental knowledge were also recruited and asked to implement sustainability initiatives in cases for which a leadership board or a community discernment process had adopted a sustainability ethic. Anshe Emeth Memorial Temple and Temple Shalom both enlisted environmental educators to lead their green certification processes, and the Sisters of St. Francis of Philadelphia turned to Sister Corrine Wright, an educator with a degree in biology, to manage implementation of their Environmental Initiative. Thus, environmental knowledge enabled some individuals to lead specific activities or participate in development of plans for making their communities more sustainable. Moreover, because these individuals had academic training, careers in environmental education, and experience with environmental organizations, faith community members perceived them as knowledgeable about sustainability and trusted them to lead initiatives.

2 *Leadership Skills*

Although sustainability knowledge conferred authority for leading initiatives, when interviewees described factors that contributed to the successful development of their earth care efforts, they mostly focused on leadership skills that were well suited to the context of their religious organizations. Comparing the cases suggests that leadership, in the context of a faith community, was enhanced by two sets of leadership skills: 1) institutional knowledge, which facilitated the process of taking action through the venue of a religious organization, and 2) project management skills, which enabled champions to organize projects and people.

INSTITUTIONAL KNOWLEDGE. In fourteen cases, the sustainability initiative leaders had prior experience serving on committees, which gave them "institutional knowledge," practical knowledge about how their religious organizations were structured and how to manage groups in accord with organizational social norms. When Trinity Presbyterian Church in New Brunswick engaged in a discernment process to update the church's mission foci, Debbie O'Halloran led a three-month study exploring hunger, peacemaking, and environment as potential mission topics. Drawing on her past experience with Bible study groups, she ran the discernment process like a Bible study class, a format that was familiar to members and provided an effective process through which a core group could explore ideas and present information to the wider community. The group read denominational reports and information from the internet, discussed what they had learned and how it connected with their faith, and then "sat with it" to reflect. At the end of this process, the study group took a vote and unanimously elected environment as a mission area because they had become convinced that neither hunger alleviation nor peace could be achieved without also addressing environmental issues. O'Halloran then made a presentation to the Session, the elected board of elders that governs the church, to explain what the discernment committee had learned and why it was recommending adoption of environment as a church mission.

As the Trinity example demonstrates, institutional knowledge was not simply a matter of knowing how to lead a meeting, it also included knowledge of how to appropriately introduce sustainability as a topic for the community's consideration and how to work through organizational structures to foster community engagement with earth care as a faith issue. Most of the individuals leading the initiatives in these cases were able to draw on prior experiences as volunteers or employees within their faith communities for institutional knowledge that enabled them to be effective sustainability champions. O'Halloran was familiar with Bible study class social norms and congregational governance systems because she was a lifelong member of Trinity Presbyterian Church. Like her mother before her, she was an active participant in the community who volunteered to serve on committees. These characteristics of long-term membership and prior committee service were also evident among initiative leaders in other faith communities. Mike Chodroff, a life-long member of Anshe Emeth Memorial Temple, was serving on the board of trustees when he took up the task of coordinating the temple's GreenFaith certification process. Erin Stack, who organized the community garden for First Parish Church of Newbury, was a longtime member and served as a deacon (lay minister) for the congregation. Several of the sustainability champions had experience as volunteers in religious education programs. In the monastic cases, sustainability champions drew on experiences in community planning committee work as well as management experience from previous administrative work at schools, hospitals, and parishes run by their faith communities.

With the exception of Vineyard Church of Ann Arbor, all of the initiatives were led by individuals who were long-time members with a history of community service that provided them with practical institutional knowledge. They were familiar with normative processes for organizing small groups to accomplish projects and governance systems for making decisions. This institutional knowledge not only equipped sustainability champions with knowledge about how to lead meetings and planning processes, it also enabled them to engage with the wider congregation and integrate sustainability activities into organizational structures. Thus, individuals' institutional knowledge was an enabling factor that intersected with factors in the Congregation and Organization domains, as will be discussed in subsequent chapters.

PROJECT MANAGEMENT. When interviewees described the importance of having people with leadership skills as key to the successful implementation of their projects, they mentioned two skill sets that assisted with project management. First, project planning required meeting management skills such as setting agendas, taking notes, and keeping track of progress toward completion of proposed activities; these meeting management skills were enacted in accord with organizational norms, as described in the discussion of institutional knowledge. The second skill set that contributed to project management had to do with coordination and effective use of volunteers. Among the fifteen cases, individuals' project management skills were important factors in holding the initiatives together and moving them forward.

Individuals gained meeting management skills from previous experiences within the faith organization as well as experiences in other contexts. As noted above, most of the champions leading these sustainability initiatives were familiar with their faith community's normative group processes because of previous volunteer committee service. These group norms included meeting management practices such as use of agendas and note-taking as well as processes for setting committee goals, planning actions, and allocating responsibility for project implementation to specific people. Sustainability champions in the monastic communities also drew on management experience from previous administrative work at schools, hospitals, and parishes run by their faith communities. Others drew on project management skills from secular venues such as prior participation in Sierra Club campaigns or Al Gore's Climate Reality Project. One initiative leader had a long history of advocacy work for LGBT rights, which provided insights into group management and advocacy strategies that could be used to build community support for sustainability.

In addition to the meeting management skills through which individuals organized their green teams to plan initiatives, sustainability champions developed creative approaches to coordinating volunteers, which assisted with implementation of initiatives. Garden projects offer a good example of the combination of personal commitment and volunteer coordination that enabled these champions to be effective project managers. Garden maintenance requires steady work over a long period of time, and much of that time commitment is during the summer, when attendance at religious services is low and variable. The need for workers to assist with watering and harvesting is highest in late summer, when members are most likely to be out of town for vacation. The productive community gardens in these case studies all had a few dedicated project leaders who took responsibility for planning and regular maintenance throughout the growing season. In addition to their own labor, these leaders were able to nurture large-scale gardens because of skillful management strategies that allowed a large number of people to contribute according to their capacity. Margo Wolfson ascribed the success of the community garden at Temple Shalom to Lenore Robinson's management skills. "Lenore is passionate about [the garden]. When she speaks to people, she is able to get them involved. She uses an email list of volunteers and gets them all organized. There are people who don't want to be on a committee but will come and dig in the dirt. There are some who come just for planting in the spring or just to help with harvest in the fall."[3] By creating a system in which volunteers were able to contribute brief periods of labor, Robinson made it possible for people to share in the gardening project in ways that fit their schedules and personal capacities.

At the Madison Christian Community, leaders of various garden projects also developed management techniques to make it easier for volunteers to participate even if they had limited time. Pastor Wild described the importance of leaders like Jean Einerson, who coordinated the upper garden at the church: "She is a clear communicator and she thanks people—it makes working in the garden enjoyable, which attracts more people, so there is a core group now."[4] One of the methods Einerson used to make it possible for diverse community members to share in the garden work was to post lists of tasks on a white board on the edge of the garden where they are available to anyone dropping by with some spare time and a desire to pitch in. Kim Eighmy, who coordinated the MCC Kids in the Garden project, said she recognized that community members were busy, and she felt a need to honor the time commitment they made when they chose to volunteer by ensuring that they had a positive experience. To that end, she took responsibility for managing some of the challenges inherent in a project that intermingles people from different age and cultural groups. During the summer, Kids in the Garden brings children from a neighborhood community center to the church for a program in which they learn about caring for plants and preparing healthy snacks. The children work closely with adult volunteers from the church. Eighmy developed creative methods for calming rambunctious children so volunteers would not feel overwhelmed. One method that proved especially effective was photography: the children loved to have their pictures taken and would settle down to pose for the camera. Eighmy also intervened when she found that her volunteers were distressed because a few of the neighborhood center's staff members spoke disparagingly about the children in their care. Eighmy worked with the center's leadership to improve staff training so there was a better understanding of behavioral expectations for members of the two organizations.[5]

3 Embedded in the Community

The previous committee experiences that contributed to leadership capabilities indicate another characteristic shared by the champions who developed these initiatives: they were embedded in their faith communities. As long-time members who participated in worship, education, and community service, they had extensive personal relationships with other members of their religious organizations. Consequently, organizational leaders and members were familiar with the individuals' interests and abilities and trusted them to organize initiatives. Furthermore, these personal relationships enhanced individuals' ability to recruit participants and build support for the initiatives across diverse areas of the religious organizations. Thus, embeddedness helped champions create initiatives and integrate them into the community.

TRUST. As longtime members and active volunteers, the champions who organized these initiatives were known and trusted members of their communities. Scholarship focused on collaborative processes has identified trust as a significant factor that contributes to peoples' willingness to try new practices and facilitates development of interpersonal relationships that are essential for viable collaborations.[6] In these faith communities, community leaders and congregations were willing to support proposals for sustainability initiatives that came from trusted members. Furthermore, the champions' longtime membership meant that they had extensive interpersonal relationships that enhanced levels of participation by the wider community. For example, at Anshe Emeth, the board and rabbis made the decision to enroll in GreenFaith before consulting the congregation; once informed, the congregation was supportive because they knew and trusted Mike Chodroff, the leader of the project. According to Asher Siebert, a member of the Green Team, "This is a large but close-knit congregation. They knew this [sustainability] was Mike's thing and had faith in us to create this program."[7]

NETWORKS OF COMMUNITY RELATIONSHIPS. In addition to trust, being embedded in their faith communities meant that sustainability champions could draw on networks of community relationships to facilitate development and implementation of initiatives. Those relationships played a role in forming green teams and building support networks to implement sustainability initiatives. For initiatives that began in response to individuals' concerns, the discovery of shared concern for environmental issues often led people to form environmental affinity groups. At Trinity Presbyterian Church in Harrisonburg, the founding members of the Earth Care House Church discovered a shared interest in exploring connections between their faith and environmental concerns while participating in a retreat together. Similarly, at the Jewish Reconstructionist Congregation, the Environmental Task Force formed after a few congregation members discovered their common desire to explore environmental issues from a Jewish perspective. For cases that began with a vision for a community-wide initiative rather than a small study group, green team formation often commenced with recruitment of people known to be concerned about the environment. For example, at St. Thomas Aquinas, McGuire had been active as a volunteer in the parish in the past and was able to organize the parish Green Committee by contacting people on the Human Concerns Committee[8] who he already knew had an interest in environmental issues.

Previous service to the faith community also enabled members of green teams to implement sustainability initiatives. At Anshe Emeth, Chodroff was on the board of trustees when he began organizing the temple's green certification process, which facilitated his ability to coordinate with temple leadership. He was able to interact with the rabbis regularly and worked with them to integrate the green certification process into the religious and educational programming at the temple. Because previous service in the temple meant that Chodroff knew people on various committees, he was able to enlist support from committee leaders, who organized their own activities as part of the community greening initiative. The Anshe Emeth Green Team also benefited from inclusion of a member of the office staff, which made it easier to communicate with the wider congregation by getting articles into the newsletter and placing information on the temple website. In addition to relationships based on community service, personal ties facilitated initiative implementation across areas of the faith communities. At Temple Shalom, Wolfson's husband was chair of the Facilities Committee during the period in which they worked toward GreenFaith certification, and his committee undertook a number of projects that contributed to the greening process. At Trinity Presbyterian Church in Harrisonburg, friendships between Pastor Held's family and the Cameron family increased opportunities for communication between the community's faith leader and the Earth Care House Church.

Thus, networks of relationships among individuals aided formation of green teams and created opportunities for cooperation between green teams and other units within a faith community. The role of these relationships conforms to scholarship on social capital, which finds that networks facilitate cooperation within or among groups.[9] Through these networks, the champions enlisted support from other members of the community, thereby aiding the process of integrating sustainability into multiple areas of the religious organization. The influence of these networks of community relationships draws attention to the significance of the congregation and the organizational structures as factors shaping development of initiatives, topics that will be examined in more detail in Chapters 7–10.

The relationship networks and trust that arose from a champion being embedded in the community were closely intertwined with leadership capabilities of institutional knowledge and project management skills. The importance of both embeddedness and leadership capabilities as complementary factors that enabled individuals to be effective sustainability champions may be illustrated with the example of one individual who developed these personal resources *after* founding an environmental activity. When Gretchen Marshall-TothFejel proposed creation of a community garden on the grounds of Vineyard Church, Ann Arbor, she was a young, devout woman with a personal interest in organic gardening and a recent job loss that opened a window of opportunity for taking on a new challenge. Thus, she brought commitment, time, and energy to the project. However, she had little prior experience with gardening and, because she was not a longtime volunteer in her church, she lacked institutional knowledge or networks of relationships within the religious organization. Given her youth and unproven abilities, she expressed surprise that the pastors supported her proposal to start a food pantry garden. "[Pastors] Ken and Nancy just trusted this twenty-two-year-old with the backyard of the church! We discussed practical issues, like leaving enough distance between the garden and the children's education areas, and they said, 'Okay, go ahead.'"[10]

The subsequent evolution of the garden project illustrates the importance of relationship networks, institutional knowledge, and project managements skills as factors that affected an individual's ability to lead an initiative. Marshall-TothFejel, like so many other sustainability champions in these cases, was committed to the project because of her personal interests. She sought out people with expertise who could help set up the garden, however those supporters soon moved out of town, and it was difficult to recruit a stable volunteer workforce during that first summer. Her ability to engage people in the garden project improved in subsequent years, as she began building networks of relationships and connecting the garden to other areas of the religious organization. To broaden awareness of the garden, she worked with the music minister to include biannual spring and harvest prayers in Sunday services and became involved with the membership classes for new members of the church: "Recently, I started helping in the kitchen during the membership class. It turned out to be a good way to get conversation started, to let new people know about the garden. The produce goes to the kitchen and when it is served, people are told, 'This was grown in our garden.'"[11] Integrating the garden into services and membership classes embedded the project in the organization and made it more visible. Visibility also increased as Marshall-TothFejel built personal connections with other members of the church. She described benefits from interactions with a woman on the prayer ministry team who helps in the garden:

"I wanted her opinion on the prayer garden I am trying to get started. It will be a quiet area with native plants. She walked around the area and said, 'I'm getting Jesus bumps; whatever you have been doing here is awesome.' She started telling others about that space, and other people have begun to come spend time there because of the word of mouth."[12]

In addition to advantages from a growing network of relationships and integration with different areas of the organization, the Garden Ministry benefited from Marshall-TothFejel's development of creative project management skills. Although the primary purpose of the garden is to provide produce for the local food bank, she tried to find ways to make the gardening experience rewarding for volunteers so they would enjoy themselves and wish to continue.

> Last year I created some designated beds with greens, radishes, spinach—things that grow quickly. These were not for donation; they are not things the food bank wants. They were for the volunteers. I thought it would help if they got some tangible reward for their work, something that can be harvested early. Before last year, we focused more on the goal of donating to the food bank, but I was hoping to create more of a connection to the idea of food for the volunteers. The garden is also used for our summer camp. We have cooking and gardening projects for the kids. They harvest carrots and make muffins.[13]

These examples indicate that although Gretchen Marshall-TothFejel did not begin her leadership of the Garden Ministry with all the advantages that made older champions trusted, effective initiative leaders, she soon developed a similar suite of leadership capabilities and formed relationships that embedded her in the community. Increased embeddedness and leadership skills, combined with deep personal commitment, facilitated her ability to manage the garden successfully.

SUSTAINING INITIATIVES:
CHALLENGES & RESPONSES

All of the interviewees were asked about the kinds of challenges that they had encountered in developing their sustainability initiatives. Their responses described a variety of issues related to communication and levels of support within their communities as well as access to resources (funds, volunteers, and knowledge) that affected their capacity to implement and sustain activities. Several of these challenges intersected with factors in the Faith Leader, Congregation, and Organization domains, and will be discussed in subsequent chapters. This section examines challenges that affected champions personally, thereby making it more difficult for them to develop, implement, and sustain initiatives in their faith communities.

The personal challenges that champions described can be divided into three categories: knowledge deficits, emotional challenges, and changes of personnel (see Table 5). Knowledge deficits posed a challenge for implementing initiative goals in several cases. Interviewees indicated that they began with a desire to make their congregations more sustainable but often had no real idea of what to do. Burnout, often accompanied by despair over the magnitude of environmental crises, was the most frequently cited emotional challenge. A few individuals also mentioned frustrations with perceived lack of interest and support from clergy or committee leaders in their faith communities. Changes in personnel due to job changes, health problems, or the need to care for family members, affected some cases. Loss of green team members could increase the workload and hasten burnout for those who remained on a downsized team. In a few communities, changes in staff or faith leadership created challenges by reducing administrative support for sustainability or shifting the dynamics of interpersonal relationships as new employees replaced initiative founders.

TABLE 5 CHALLENGES THAT AFFECTED CHAMPIONS

CHALLENGES	CASES CITING ISSUE
1. *Knowledge Deficits*	
How to enact a specific activity (e.g. garden)	7
How to connect sustainability with spiritual practices	2
How to make the organization more sustainable	3
2. *Emotional Challenges*	
Burnout	6
Lack of interest from faith community	3
Despair at magnitude of environmental crises	4
3. *Personnel Changes*	
Loss of Green Team leaders	4
Changes in clergy and staff	3

Translating a general desire to live more sustainably into a sustainability initiative that will affect individual and collective behavior not only requires motivation to act, it also requires knowledge about *how* to make the organization more sustainable. Environmental psychology researchers describe "procedural knowledge," knowledge about how to take action, as a significant factor that determines whether an individual will actually engage in behaviors that fulfill a personal intention to care for the environment.[14] Interviewees mentioned that they faced challenges early in the process of developing their faith-based initiatives because they were uncertain about how to integrate sustainability into their faith communities. In particular, they described problems due to lack of knowledge about how to undertake specific environmental activities, how to connect sustainability with spiritual practices, and how to make their religious organizations more sustainable.

As recounted earlier, Sister Barbara O'Donnell felt called to "educate for the earth," but no such ministry existed in her religious order and she was not certain what kind of work she could do to fulfill her calling while also contributing to her community. At the Jewish Reconstructionist Congregation, the newly formed Environmental Task Force wanted to explore connections between faith and sustainability, but the lay group was not sure how they could connect concern for the environment with their community's spiritual practices. At Trinity Presbyterian Church in East Brunswick, the congregational discernment process had identified stewardship of creation as a core mission area, but the leaders of the Earth Shepherd team that formed to implement this mission were not certain what actions to take. At First Universalist Church of Rockland, the Earth Care Team, which had been founded in response to a Maine Council of Churches' campaign to promote legislative support for the Kyoto Protocol, was no longer content to write occasional letters to senators and encourage congregation members to use CFLs but was not sure how to step up its level of activity.

In these four cases, individuals and affinity groups were uncertain how to shift from personal study and small group activities to community-level action. They were able to overcome these challenges when they found resources that provided ideas and guidance for potential paths forward. Sister Barbara O'Donnell returned to Villa Maria, the motherhouse of her order (the Sisters of the Humility of Mary), where she discussed her calling to educate for the earth with members of the community's leadership team. They were sympathetic but also thought it would be best if she took a job through one of the existing organizations run by the order, which would guarantee her a salary. Because O'Donnell's sense of being called was so strong, she persisted in seeking a way to fulfill her mission to educate for the earth. With assistance from the convent librarian, she began to study the history of the order, which had once farmed its lands, and spoke to the land manager, Frank Romeo, to learn more about the land. Romeo became her teacher and partner, sharing his firsthand knowledge of the convent's past and present land management and guiding O'Donnell in her efforts to start an organic garden. Both the garden and O'Donnell's passion for learning about how to grow food flourished; she went on to take courses in permaculture and environmental education. With her new knowledge, she and Romeo gradually created programs in environmental education and eco-spirituality that developed into Evergreen, an environmental ministry for the Villa Maria Retreat Center. Alongside the new spiritual programs, the garden project became an opportunity for Romeo to bring the convent's 300 acres of farmland back into production, raising food for charity and providing a context for farm-based environmental education for children.

Like O'Donnell, the members of the Environmental Task Force at the Jewish Reconstructionist Congregation were uncertain how to integrate their exploration of connections between religion and sustainability into the structure of their faith community. They asked their rabbi for help. Rabbi Rosen suggested that they could start organizing an annual Tu BiShvat service for the congregation, thereby connecting environmental concerns to one of the regular observances in the Jewish liturgical cycle, the calendar of religious celebrations. He also helped his congregants contact Rabbi Fred Dobbs, a leader in the American Jewish environmental movement, who could assist them in developing their first Tu BiShvat program. Through this program, the Task Force was able to integrate sustainability into the spiritual practices of their faith community and share their conviction that Judaism includes an environmental ethic.

For Trinity Presbyterian Church in East Brunswick and First Universalist Church of Rockland, the knowledge deficit had less to do with making connections to spiritual practices than with figuring out how to develop a community-wide sustainability initiative. Debbie O'Halloran, who led the creation of Trinity's Earth Shepherds program, had a background in nursing and secretarial work but no prior experience with environmental activity.

However, she had become convinced that Christians have a responsibility to care for God's creation and, "Once you believe in something, you find a way to make it happen."[15] After trying some basic projects like teaching the congregation members about recycling, the Trinity Earth Shepherds realized their committee was not educated enough about sustainability to educate the congregation. They reached out to GreenFaith, an interfaith organization that promotes resource conservation in congregations. O'Halloran went through the GreenFaith Fellowship training program to gain knowledge about faith-based sustainability, and the church enrolled in the GreenFaith Certification program. Similarly, after working on small projects like selling CFLs to congregation members and writing letters to encourage Maine politicians to support US endorsement of the Kyoto Protocol, the leaders of the Earth Care Team at First Universalist Church of Rockland decided to "step up" their sustainability efforts by enrolling in the Unitarian Universalist Association's Green Sanctuary Certification program. These green certification programs provided procedural knowledge in the form of frameworks with which to define goals, requirements for actions in all areas of congregational activity, examples of potential actions, and metrics for assessing progress.

Lack of knowledge about how to develop and implement a sustainability initiative often required that individuals seek information from experts outside of the faith context. Even following through on one specific project might require assistance if the community decided to focus on an activity for which no members had sufficient prior experience. At Holy Wisdom Monastery, the sisters decided that they would restore their farmland to prairie as part of their newly articulated mission to care for the earth, only to realize that neither they nor their staff members knew how to go about restoring a prairie. Fortunately, the monastery land manager rose to the challenge. He shadowed a ranger at a nearby state park to learn about prairie restoration techniques, then shared his new knowledge with the sisters and groups of volunteers who assisted with annual prairie project workdays. At First Parish Church of Newbury, the community decided to plant a garden to implement its mission to be Stewards of Earth and Spirit, but they had little knowledge of the work required and, since most people left for the summer, the neglected garden failed to produce. The following year, deacon Erin Stack took the lead in organizing a renewed garden. She sought out garden experts from the wider community to learn about organic gardening and organized speakers to give presentations at the church so that those who participated in the church's community garden would be equipped to care for their plots of land. In both of these examples, an individual from the faith community took the lead and acquired procedural knowledge in order to implement activities undertaken as part of a community-wide sustainability initiative.

In all of the cases described above, the champions who were committed to making their faith communities more sustainable sought out resources to help them address knowledge deficits. Thus, willingness to seek new knowledge, as needed, was another personal characteristic that enabled these individuals to be effective initiative leaders. The accompanying enabling factor was availability of resources that made it possible for these individuals to develop initiatives and implement specific activities despite their prior lack of knowledge. Interfaith and denominational programs like GreenFaith and the Green Sanctuary Program as well as secular programs on relevant topics like farming, forestry, and green building were all vital to the champions' ability to turn intention into action.

2 Emotional Challenges

Several interviewees mentioned emotional challenges that made it difficult to persevere with sustainability activities over time. Burnout, a perceived lack of interest from the faith community, and despair over environmental crises were closely intertwined issues that affected individuals in several of the cases.

BURNOUT. Six interviewees mentioned burnout as a personal challenge. Several individuals who led faith communities through certification processes found themselves worn out by the end of the process. Asked whether Temple Shalom would continue to engage in environmental activities now that they had completed their GreenFaith certification, Margo Wolfson said there would be a hiatus because she did not have time to organize new activities, explaining, "I dropped the ball this year. I have two jobs, so I don't have much time, and I just felt that it takes lots of energy—more than I have right now. Like for the Water Certification, I wanted to do that and I gave a presentation, but there was such a lack of enthusiasm that I figured we just needed a break."[16]

Wolfson's comments indicate that several intertwined factors contributed to her burnout: her daily work did not leave much time for additional tasks at the temple, and low levels of participation by the congregation undermined her intention to continue. The heavy workload was the result of problems with Green Team recruitment. The team that took on the task of planning the activities for the GreenFaith Certification process at Temple Shalom included people who represented committees that were required to contribute in order to meet program mandates. Several team members who lacked personal environmental interests soon dropped out, leaving Wolfson, as coordinator of the process, to shoulder much of the burden for organizing projects and writing up reports for the certification application. Since Wolfson also worked full time and assisted with the temple's religious education program, it is not surprising that the certification process left her feeling worn out.

LACK OF INTEREST FROM THE COMMUNITY. Wolfson's burnout was further exacerbated by the perceived lack of interest from many members of her congregation, an emotional challenge mentioned by interviewees in several communities. She did not blame people for their disinterest, since she considered it natural that some people had other concerns and felt that "parents are pushed so many ways these days, they just don't have time" to participate in extra events at the temple.[17] Nevertheless, knowing that there was little community desire to participate in environmental activities, she could not muster enthusiasm for taking on any new tasks after completing the certification process.

The challenges posed by burnout and lack of interest were closely tied to participant numbers as a factor that affected the durability of sustainability initiatives. In communities where sustainability affinity groups were larger and better established, members could share the workload and take breaks to avoid burnout. Malcolm Cameron mentioned that he had periodically taken a year off from participating in the Earth Care House Church at Trinity Presbyterian Church. He felt comfortable taking breaks because, in a group that had between twelve and sixteen members each year and regularly rotated leadership among those members, he could be confident the work would continue even if he was not there. Achieving a "critical mass" of green team members seems to have been a factor that sustained initiatives over time for several reasons. First, it reduced the workload for individuals and distributed responsibility for maintaining the sustainability initiative across a larger group, which prevented burnout. Second, the larger group made it possible for individuals to take restorative breaks when they felt burnout might be imminent. Third, a high level of participation by community members gave the green team members a sense that their concerns were shared by a significant portion of their community, which bolstered their enthusiasm for persevering with the initiative. Levels of participation by congregation members, which determined whether a green team reached critical mass, were affected by factors in the Faith Leader and Congregation domains and will be discussed further in the next two sections.

DESPAIR AT THE MAGNITUDE OF ENVIRONMENTAL PROBLEMS. A third emotional challenge, also closely linked to the problem of burnout, arose from the despair individuals felt in the face of overwhelming environmental crises. Malcolm Cameron cited "despair; not becoming discouraged" as his core challenge and one reason he periodically took a year off from participating in the house church. Frank Mundo at First Universalist Church of Rockland also spoke of his struggle with despair over the magnitude of environmental crises: "We were anguishing over the environment, over how it's going down the toilet . . . The situation is so terrible, and I felt so hopeless. But we're trying to do something."[18]

Individuals described a range of ways to alleviate despair and find the strength to take action despite feeling overwhelmed by environmental issues. Religion provided one significant resource for counteracting despair. Lynn Cameron cited a key pastoral message that helped members of the Earth Care House Church:

> [Reverend] Ann has a saying, "God calls us to be faithful, not successful." We just have to try. Even if it does not work out, at least we've tried. The resolution against coal power was like that. We thought, "We're just a little house church, we can't do much." But we don't want to just do little things like picking up litter from the side of the highway. There are big problems like acid rain and air quality, so we thought we should try. And it worked. That taught us that it's okay to try for big things.[19]

Members of Trinity Presbyterian Church drew on Reverend Held's message for courage to attempt actions that seemed beyond their reach, taking comfort in the idea that their efforts would have value even if the results were uncertain.

Sister Ginny Jones at the Congregation of St. Joseph also shared a spiritual message that she drew on for inspiration when environmental crises seemed too big to be addressed by individual actions. She recounted a story told by Joan Chittister, a Benedictine nun and author. In the story, travelers encounter a small bird lying on its back with its feet in the air, so they stop to find out what the bird is doing. The bird tells them it has heard that the sky is falling. They laugh, asking if the tiny creature really thinks it can hold up the entire sky with its feet. The bird responds, "One does what one can."[20] Jones often tells this charming tale to students to convey a message that is very similar to Held's: even if individual contributions seem too small to affect a crisis like climate change, it is still important to do what one can. In her own life, she too does "what she can."[21]

Worship was another aspect of faith that enabled some individuals to avoid despair. In the words of Lynn Cameron:

> Here is another thing about being faith-based: there is this reminder that this is God's creation. So, we take time to celebrate it, to enjoy it. You can't be frantically fighting all the time. We want to be hopeful. The worship and the hymns, the scriptures, they help us to be hopeful. The Sierra Club likes to take people on outings, to connect them to nature and show them what they are preserving, but that is not the same as thanking God and realizing that you are related to all of creation.[22]

Approaching sustainability through the context of religion created a celebratory, reverent attitude toward nature that helped individuals persevere.

A second antidote to despair was the fellowship that emerged out of participating in a faith community. The Earth Care House Church took time at the beginning of its meetings to ask each member about how their lives were going. People might talk about particular environmental issues that worried them and, even if the problem was something the group could not solve, there was benefit in knowing that others understood and sympathized. Frank Mundo described a similar fellowship resource at First Universalist Church, where he helped organize an environmentally-themed chalice circle, a small group for spiritual development. He recalled that, "The Green Chalice Circle started after a group of us got together at a church retreat. . . . We wanted to form a group, not to do any specific activity but to be mutually supportive of our concerns. . . . We read books like Bill McKibben's and we discussed them. After a while I stopped doing the reading because it was too depressing, but I still went to the meetings."[23] Even though Mundo found the readings distressing, he continued to attend meetings because the group fellowship salved his anguish.

A third method for reducing despair, and the solution that finally made the greatest difference for Mundo, was to take meaningful action. He was depressed because he was deeply concerned about climate change and did not perceive local food projects or writing letters to politicians as actions that would have adequate or immediate effects on greenhouse gas emissions.

However, he became involved in a project to build storm window inserts for his church, to reduce heat loss through the basement windows. That project became the basis for establishing the WindowDressers, a nonprofit organization working with congregations to provide window inserts for churches and homes in several towns. As the project expanded, Mundo became more hopeful because he was doing something that would directly reduce energy use in Maine, thereby having an immediate impact on greenhouse gas emissions. Moreover, the results were readily apparent in the completed window inserts and reduced energy bills. "This is something that is physical, direct, and personal," he said. "You have control over it; you're not asking someone else [i.e. politicians] to do something for you at some point in the future."[24]

Faith, fellowship, and meaningful work, the solutions to despair cited by these individuals, may also be described as enabling factors that enhanced champions' abilities to undertake and sustain environmental activities. Religious messages that affirmed the moral value of taking action, even if the actions were imperfect or too small to solve large-scale environmental crises, provided impetus for individuals to overcome their feelings of being overwhelmed and begin to "do something" by organizing environmental activities. Fellowship with like-minded members of their faith communities helped them persevere with their efforts and kept them involved even when they were frustrated by the inadequacy of the actions available. Finally, meaningful work, in the form of projects that addressed personal environmental and faith interests, gave champions a sense of efficacy that motivated them to continue their efforts.

3 Personnel Changes

Changes in personnel created challenges for individuals in several of the sustainability initiatives either by jeopardizing the viability of a green team or affecting initiative support from other areas of the religious organization. Green team viability was affected by loss of leaders and member attrition, both of which usually resulted from transitions in individuals' lives and demonstrate the importance of personal "windows of opportunity" as a factor that influenced initiatives. Changes in clergy or staff affected networks of personal relationships within faith communities, which led to shifts in social dynamics within the groups carrying out environmental activities as well as differences in levels of engagement from new organizational leaders.

CHANGES IN GREEN TEAM LEADERSHIP AND MEMBERSHIP. Six green teams lost their original leaders and had to regroup. In some cases, new leaders stepped up to take over. The Green Committee at St. Thomas Aquinas Parish went through a lull when its first leader left, but continued to meet and plan, and emerged with renewed energy as Katia Reeves stepped up from member to leader. In contrast, at Vineyard Church of Ann Arbor, the Green Vineyard initiative stalled when Phil Brabbs became ill and was unable to continue leading the group. Subsequent efforts to restart the initiative have not proven durable. The difference between the two communities may be due to window-of-opportunity factors that affected the size and continuity of the green teams. The original Green Vineyard participants, and the subsequent short-term members, have mostly been college students who soon graduate and leave town. This regular attrition has prevented Green Vineyard from achieving a critical mass to provide for leadership succession or group continuity. The Green Committee at St. Thomas Aquinas, on the other hand, is composed of long-term parish members who are nearing the end of their careers or are newly retired. Despite some attrition due to family illnesses, each year there has been a core group of about six people, which seems to provide the critical mass necessary for continuity over time.

In three cases, completion of green certification processes coincided with reduced activity by former sustainability champions. After Temple Shalom completed its certification, the Green Team that had formed for that purpose disbanded, and Wolfson had no energy for organizing a new team to take on new activities. The one group project that continued was the community garden, which was organized by a passionate gardener. Shortly after Anshe Emeth Memorial Temple became green certified, Chodroff moved to a new teaching job, which drew his attention and energy. He arranged for another member of the temple to become his co-chair on the Green Team in order to ease the transition to new leadership, however the number of activities declined. At First Universalist Church of Rockland, the original leaders of the Green Sanctuary Committee stepped back from their leadership roles after the church was certified. As a result, the church ceased to develop new projects. Lucie Bauer, a former committee leader, suggested that it was natural for a community to go through phases of activity followed by lulls, and that new leaders would emerge if they were needed. In the meantime, two of the major projects the Green Sanctuary Committee had helped develop were continuing quite successfully under the leadership of people who were deeply invested in those particular activities.

These changes in leadership generally occurred because windows of opportunity had closed. Leaders left or reduced their levels of activity because of jobs, health, or family needs that meant they no longer had the time and energy to participate. The same types of issues affected continuity of membership on green teams. The teams often suffered from member attrition as individuals graduated from college and moved out of town for new jobs, or as individuals reduced their volunteer hours in order to care for family members. Reductions in team membership increased the workload for remaining members, putting them at greater risk of burnout, especially in cases where lack of critical mass on green teams meant there were few people available to take over leadership roles. The challenges posed by loss of personnel indicate that continuity of leadership and group membership, which was lacking in some cases, was a sustaining factor that contributed to the durability of other sustainability initiatives.

CHANGES IN CLERGY AND STAFF. Lack of continuity among faith leaders and staff created stresses for the champions leading four sustainability initiatives. In cases where organizational leaders were strongly supportive of initiatives, staff losses were replaced by people chosen for their ability to continue the work. At Saint John's Abbey, people were concerned that the untimely death of Father Paul Schwietz would undermine the newly formed arboretum. Fortunately, the abbey hired a professional arboretum/land manager with extensive experience in science-based sustainable forestry to replace Schwietz, and the arboretum has flourished under his care.[25] Staff replacements could, however, lead to tensions. In one case, a staff person's retirement meant dissolution of a partnership with a sustainability initiative champion that had been important for the development and implementation of the community's initiative. The challenge of building a new relationship with the replacement staff person made continuation of the environmental programs more difficult.

Whereas changes in staff affected implementation of specific projects, changes in organizational leadership affected integration of sustainability into the wider community. In two cases, changes in clergy meant the green teams had little active support from their organizational leaders. Neither of the new pastors objected to the initiatives, but they were not personally interested in environmental issues. Green team members felt that the lack of a voice from the pulpit promoting sustainability as a faith issue undermined their ability to attract new committee members or increase levels of community engagement.

This insight into the role of clergy in building congregational support for initiatives will be examined further in chapters 5 and 6.

SUSTAINING FACTORS REVEALED BY RESPONSES TO CHALLENGES

Interviewee descriptions of the resources that helped them respond to the personal challenges they encountered reveal a number of factors located in other domains of the faith community that intersected with the Champions domain and contributed to individuals' abilities to persevere in their initiative leadership. Sustainability champions sought out experts in the congregation and in the wider community to help them address knowledge deficits related to specific activities as well as complex issues like how to green a religious organization. Faith leaders provided advice to champions who were uncertain about how to connect sustainability with a community's spiritual practices. Moral support to mitigate emotional challenges came from faith leaders' religious messages and from fellowship with congregation members. The level of support from the congregation affected the size of the green team, which determined whether the group attained a critical mass sufficient to allow individuals on the verge of burnout to take breaks. Continuity of personnel proved to be a factor that sustained initiatives, an issue made evident by the decreased levels of activity in communities that lost their green team leaders. Critical mass helped mitigate the effects of personnel changes by increasing the availability of members who could step up to replace a departing leader, and sometimes pastors (faith leaders) recruited members of the congregation to take over when green teams lost leaders. Continuity of clergy and staff personnel also helped sustain initiatives by ensuring stable relationship networks and consistent levels of support across the organization.

EFFECTS ON CHAMPIONS: PERSONAL REWARDS

Personal rewards arising from participation in sustainability initiatives played a significant role in motivating champions to persevere, which helped sustain initiatives over time. In response to a question about how participating in initiatives affected them, interviewees described a sense of satisfaction that came from using their skills, often in activities they enjoyed, to address issues of personal concern. The result was a sense of personal efficacy. Their satisfaction was further increased by tangible results indicating that their efforts were benefiting people and communities, and the conviction that, through these activities, they were living out their religious values (see Table 6). Research in environmental psychology indicates that experiences of satisfaction due to a sense of efficacy (or "competence") and acting in accord with values can motivate sustained behavior change, which suggests that these personal rewards were additional factors that enabled champions to persevere in leading initiatives.[26]

TABLE 6 EFFECTS ON INDIVIDUALS WHO PARTICIPATED IN INITIATIVES

EFFECTS	SATISFACTION
Sense of Efficacy	Addressing personal concerns Engaging in enjoyable activities Using skills Tangible results
Living Values	Building relationships Helping individuals Helping community

As noted in the discussion of gardening earlier in this chapter, champions often became involved in environmental activities they enjoyed. Some of these activities allowed them to repurpose skills developed in careers and hobbies. Frank Mundo and Dick Cadwegan, who organized the WindowDressers project for First Universalist Church of Rockland, were able to apply their wood-working hobbies and home basement workshops to construct storm window inserts using measurements calculated through a computer program written by Mundo, a retired programmer.[27] Tom Matthews, a farmer's son trained in computer technology during a stint in the military, had a knack for tinkering. After retiring from a career in sales, he had taken the position of maintenance person at the Madison Christian Community, where the church's sustainability initiative provided opportunities to exercise his mechanical gifts. One of the pastors had lots of ideas about how to practice sustainability but turning those ideas into reality often required mechanical creativity. According to Matthews, "[Reverend] Jeff has been an idea fountain. He'll say, 'What would happen if we. . . .' My contribution is to figure out how to do it without spending too much; how to make it feasible." This symbiotic relationship made his work at the church "a super job for an old guy."[28]

Thus, individuals applied their accumulated skills as computer programmers, gardeners, teachers, preachers, administrators, policy advocates, artists, geologists, musicians, and community activists in pursuit of creating more sustainable religious organizations. Tangible evidence of successful outcomes inspired a sense of efficacy and increased individuals' enthusiasm for continuing their efforts. When the Earth Care House Church from Trinity Presbyterian Church in Harrisonburg succeeded in persuading the Presbyterian Church (USA) to adopt their resolution against coal-based air pollution, it showed them that it was possible for a small group to accomplish big things. For Lynn Cameron, the high point of the coal resolution came from its effects: Southern Company, a major utility, felt the need to defend its environmental record, and Presbyterian lobbyists worked to change a legislative policy:

> Southern Company, a major polluter, heard about it [the anti-coal resolution] and contacted the Presbyterian Church. They wanted to meet with representatives to talk about it, and we were invited to participate. Southern Company showed this PowerPoint to explain how wonderful they were, how they give money to Boy Scouts to plant trees, and we weren't buying it because they are still polluters [who are] damaging ecosystems.
>
> I think it's important for perpetrators to meet the people they affect . . . . The resolution did have an impact. Southern Company heard about it, and that led them to have a dialogue with us. They met us face-to-face.
>
> And information about the resolution was communicated to senators on an energy committee that was about to make a vote on some legislation. I don't remember exactly what it was. But there were some Presbyterians on the committee, and the legislation passed by one vote. Maybe the resolution helped it get through that subcommittee.[29]

The results of advocacy work are often difficult to quantify, so knowing that a utility company felt its reputation was under threat and that lobbyists were following through on the resolution were particularly gratifying outcomes. Other initiatives also produced results that gave sustainability champions a sense of efficacy. At Holy Wisdom Monastery, where the sisters, staff, and volunteers restored ten acres of farmland to prairie each year until they had completed 100 acres, success could be measured in the decreased volume of runoff. Where precipitation had once carried pollutants into Lake Mendota, all rain now filtrated into the soil to nourish native plants, a transformation further made apparent by annually increasing numbers of flowers and birds.[30] Restoring a prairie inspired a sense of efficacy through hands-on activities and tangible results. Champions experienced similar feelings of efficacy by purchasing solar panels, washing reusable dishes, paying lower utility bills after installing storm window inserts, or seeing the banner indicating a community was green certified. All of these tangible outcomes gave interviewees a sense of efficacy; they were taking meaningful action to address environmental concerns.

Individuals also found satisfaction in their work because, in addition to benefiting the environment, they were benefiting people. At the First Universalist Church of Rockland, church sponsorship of a young couple starting a community-supported agriculture farm was motivated by an interest in local food and a desire to have a relationship with the food producers. The success of the farm was, therefore, not just measured in produce, it was also measured in the friendships that grew up between church members and the farmers, who eventually joined the church. At the Madison Christian Community, gardeners are fond of recounting a story about ten-year-old Ruth, a participant in the Kids in the Garden program, who told one of the adults, "You can't lie to the earth. The earth knows when you are lying. I might tell you I watered, but the plants know I didn't. And they will tell you I didn't."[31] Narratives like Ruth's are perceived as evidence that the garden program fulfills its objective of "nourishing soil and soul" by teaching gardening skills and values.

As Ruth's story indicates, individuals involved in faith-based initiatives placed great emphasis on the importance of earth care as a means to live out their religious values and practice compassion for others. Consequently, it makes sense that Reverend Jeff Wild considered building relationships among church members and between church and community to be among the significant effects that explained why individuals found satisfaction in their gardening labors:

> Working in the garden—it's a really rewarding experience for people. They find it meaningful; it's meaningful work. And through it their relationships with one another are strengthened and they get to work with children they would not meet otherwise. It generates a sense of what is meant by the Greek word "hilarity." This doesn't mean laughter in the popular sense, it means "deep gladness." What we do here facilitated a sense of deep gladness.[32]

This description of gladness nicely sums up the sense of joyful satisfaction that many individuals expressed as they spoke about their participation in faith-based sustainability initiatives.

SUMMARY AND DOMAIN INTERACTIONS

How Champions Affected Initiatives

CHAMPIONS PLAYED A CRUCIAL ROLE in the emergence and development of these fifteen sustainability initiatives by providing the leadership that turned idea into action. Chapters 3 and 4 examined what motivated individuals to develop and participate in sustainability initiatives, why they chose to act through the venue of their faith communities, what enabled them to effectively lead initiatives, and how participation in faith-based sustainability initiatives affected them. This section summarizes the findings from these two chapters and delineates how the factors that enabled individuals to be effective sustainability champions were influenced by contributions from other domains.

CHARACTERISTICS THAT ENABLED CHAMPIONS TO LEAD INITIATIVES

Cross-case analysis indicates that personal factors in three key areas contributed to individuals' role as leaders of sustainability initiatives. First, personal interests created a deep sense of *commitment* to sustainability that motivated these individuals to take action. These champions were passionate about their sustainability efforts because they provided a means to address multiple personal interests, including caring for family and community; protecting local and global environments; and acting on religious values of responsibility for people and God's creation. The conviction that environmental issues are faith issues made it natural to undertake sustainability initiatives through the venues of faith communities, especially for individuals who had prior experience as volunteers serving on administrative committees and working in faith-community ministries. Personal windows of opportunity also meant that many of these champions had time and energy to invest in a new project.

Second, these sustainability champions had knowledge and relationships that contributed to their leadership capacity, which enabled them to effectively organize and implement initiatives through the venue of their faith communities. Many individuals had personal experience in environmental education or advocacy work that provided foundational knowledge for developing sustainability efforts. They also drew on leadership skills comprised of institutional knowledge and project management expertise acquired through previous service on committees in their faith communities. As longtime, active members who were embedded in their communities, these champions were known and trusted by their faith leaders and congregations. Trust and networks of personal relationships facilitated their ability to enlist support for initiatives from people in diverse areas of a faith community, while institutional knowledge and project management skills assisted champions in implementing and sustaining activities.[1]

Finally, using their leadership skills to address personal interests resulted in a sense of satisfaction that sustained individuals and helped them persevere in their efforts to implement sustainability initiatives.

DOMAIN INTERACTIONS

The personal factors that affected champions' commitment, leadership capacity, and sense of satisfaction were also influenced by contributions from Faith Leader, Congregation, and Organization domains (see Table 7).

Faith leaders strengthened individuals' sense of commitment by sharing messages that affirmed a religious obligation to care for the earth and by assuring champions that their efforts were valued as expressions of faith, regardless of their efficacy. Faith leaders also enhanced individuals' leadership capacity by authorizing initiatives and providing advice on how to take action through the venue of the religious organization. The organization, with its procedural norms for managing committees and venues for enacting values, provided the context within which individual champions applied their institutional knowledge and interacted with their relationship networks. The congregation, with its body of members, provided volunteers

TABLE 7 LEADERSHIP FACTORS AND THEIR INTERACTIONS
WITH OTHER DOMAINS

FACTORS THAT ENABLED LEADERSHIP	INTERACTIONS WITH OTHER DOMAINS THAT CONTRIBUTED TO CHAMPIONS' LEADERSHIP	EFFECTS ON THE CHAMPION
Commitment: Personal interests Environment, Religion Windows of Opportunity	*Faith Leaders:* religious messages *Congregation:* fellowship, moral support	*Motivation to take action*
Leadership Capacity: Sustainability knowledge Leadership skills Institutional knowledge Project management Embeddedness Trust Relationship networks	*Faith Leaders:* authorization, advice on actions *Congregation:* support due to relationships and trust; critical mass *Organization:* venue for institutional knowledge; networks help integrate earth care into multiple areas	*Effective leadership:* Ability to organize and implement initiatives in a faith community
Sense of Satisfaction	*Faith Leaders:* religious messages *Congregation:* affirmation	*Sustained participation*

to serve on those committees and support earth care activities, which, in turn, influenced the network of relationships through which sustainability was integrated into the faith community. Furthermore, fellowship with like-minded members of the congregation strengthened individuals' sense of commitment and provided moral support that enabled them to persevere in spite of emotional challenges.

The interplay between champions and other domains, which affected relationship networks and levels of community involvement, also influenced their ability to sustain initiative leadership over time. The impact of these contextual factors became particularly evident when personnel changes in the organization or on the green team created challenges for initiatives. Although changes in organizational leadership or staff did not directly affect the personal leadership capabilities of champions, they did affect the milieu within which they worked, especially the relationship networks through which they implemented environmental activities. Loss of supportive staff relationships could complicate implementation and maintenance of projects. Durability of initiatives was also affected by the Congregation domain, which influenced participation on green teams. Low levels of congregational involvement could lead to inadequate critical mass for a durable green team, thereby increasing likelihood of individual burnout and lack of continuity for team leadership and membership. Hence, the interaction of elements from various domains affected champions' ability to organize and sustain initiatives within their faith communities. Figure 2 illustrates the interactions between champions and the other three domains.

Despite the challenges, interviewees persevered because of the personal rewards they experienced while participating in the initiatives. Through these sustainability activities, individuals were able to use their knowledge and skills to address intertwined personal interests: they were protecting people and places they loved while acting on their religious values. Those actions often involved enjoyable activities, strengthened their relationships with other members of the congregation, and generated tangible results that benefited people and communities. These outcomes produced a sense of efficacy and gave people hope that they could make a difference in spite of the magnitude of the world's environmental problems. The satisfaction engendered by these personal rewards motivated them to persevere in their efforts to promote sustainability, thereby helping to sustain the initiatives.

FIGURE 2 Interactions between Champions and the Other Domains

Chapters 3 and 4 identified characteristics within the Champions domain that contributed to the commitment, leadership capabilities, and satisfaction that enabled individuals to be effective sustainability champions within their faith communities. They also revealed an interplay of factors across domains that affected individuals' ability to organize and sustain initiatives. These interactions illustrate the importance of understanding the faith-community context, comprised of faith leaders, congregation, and organization, within which these initiatives arose. Factors within the Champions domain interacted with contributions from the Faith Leader and Congregation domains to create the sense of commitment that motivated individuals to campaign for sustainability. Contributions from Faith Leader, Congregation, and Organization domains also interacted with the personal characteristics that enabled individuals to be effective initiative leaders. Therefore, understanding the processes through which these sustainability initiatives developed requires deeper analysis of the contributions from these other three domains. What kind of religious messages did faith leaders contribute? What factors influenced congregational support and whether religious organizations were appropriate venues through which to implement sustainability initiatives? The next section will examine the Faith Leaders domain to better understand how it contributed to the process of embedding sustainability in these faith communities.

Part III

FAITH LEADERS

Legitimators of Sustainability Initiatives

INTRODUCTION

While it was lay members of the Jewish Reconstructionist Congregation (JRC) in Evanston who started an environmental initiative that eventually led to construction of the first Platinum-LEED certified[1] synagogue in the United States, they could not have achieved this outcome without assistance from Rabbi Brant Rosen. A few members had formed an environmental task force to explore connections between their religious tradition and care for the environment. Although they were able to study on their own, they turned to their rabbi for advice about how to incorporate environmental stewardship into Jewish spiritual practices. Rosen suggested they develop a community celebration of Tu BiShvat, a festival in the Jewish liturgical cycle of holy days that has become associated with environmental themes, and helped the group find the information they needed to carry through with the idea. Later, when the Environmental Task Force proposed that the community consider following green building practices in the construction of their new synagogue, Rabbi Rosen played a key role in advocating for the idea with the board of trustees and the congregation. He continued to promote the idea during the building planning process by beginning board meetings with environmentally themed scriptural readings and by writing blog posts explaining how sustainability dovetailed with the social justice ministries of his congregation. Thus, the rabbi provided vital support for the development of the Jewish Reconstructionist Congregation's sustainability initiative in two ways. First, as a religious authority, he was able to legitimate sustainability as a Jewish value and help integrate it into the community's religious practices. Second, as manager of the religious organization, he exerted influence on the community's decision processes.

As the JRC story illustrates, faith leaders made key contributions to the process of integrating sustainability into these fifteen faith communities. Religion is central to the purpose of these organizations; their mission is to encourage people to develop personal religious beliefs and apply religious values to their daily lives. Therefore, any new area of activity had to be connected to the religious tradition that is foundational to a faith community's purpose and sense of identity.[2] "Faith leaders," in this study, are the people with authority to define the beliefs and values of a religious community and make decisions about community practices based on those values. Their faith leadership includes the two roles, religious authority and organizational manager, that Rabbi Rosen used to facilitate the adoption of earth care as an area of activity at the Jewish Reconstructionist Congregation. It should be noted, however, that whereas both roles were fulfilled by the same individual pastors in eleven of the cases, the roles were distributed among several people in the four women's monastic communities.

Defining who qualifies as a faith leader is somewhat complicated in a study that includes several religious traditions. In most US congregations, faith leaders are clergy who have been officially ordained after completing a formal training program that includes study of a religion's scriptures[3] and philosophical teachings.[4] Protestant Christian clergy are usually called ministers, Catholic and Episcopal clergy are called priests, Jewish clergy are called rabbis, and all of these traditions use the job title of pastor for clergy who serve congregations. Faith communities may also rely on groups rather than individuals for faith leadership. Many Quaker meetings and congregations of Catholic and Episcopal women religious, which emphasize egalitarianism among their members, designate committees or voluntary groups of lay members to periodically review and revise statements that define a congregation's beliefs. Because the Catholic Church does not ordain women as clergy, faith leaders in women's religious orders are, technically, lay leaders. In many women's monastic communities, decisions about how to apply values to community management practices are mediated by leadership teams that are elected to serve for a designated period of time, a practice that has replaced the older system in which a single mother superior (or prioress or abbess) held supreme authority. These leadership teams draw on the religious values and mission statements of their communities as guidelines for administrative decisions.

Both types of faith leaders, clergy and lay leaders, were represented among the cases in this study. Clergy served as the primary faith leaders at Saint John's Abbey and in the ten non-monastic congregations, where their dual roles as religious authorities and organizational managers provided them with a range of opportunities to establish the legitimacy of sustainability as a focal area for their communities. The two roles were fulfilled separately in the women's monastic communities: sustainability champions among the membership led efforts to define the religious bases for faith-based sustainability, and leadership teams served as the organizational managers who authorized earth care initiatives. Together, both champions and leadership teams contributed to the process of exploring the relationship between earth care and an order's religious mission and promoting integration of sustainability into their faith communities.

MOTIVATIONS FOR PROMOTING SUSTAINABILITY

In all fifteen cases, interviewees mentioned the importance of faith leader support for the development of their initiatives, but the types and continuity of that support varied. Nine of the non-monastic congregations had active clergy support for their sustainability initiatives, and the tenth had passive support. Among the five monastic communities, four had active support from community leadership and the fifth had support from a task force exploring faith and environmental stewardship. Although faith leaders across the cases affirmed the importance of sustainability, the strength of their commitment to promoting the issue and the amount of energy they invested in community sustainability initiatives varied in accord with their motivations for promoting their community initiatives. Motives fell into three categories (see Table 8). The first category included personal interests, such as traditional environmental concerns about protecting natural areas or responding to environmental crises, and enthusiasm for outdoor activities. The second category centered on faith community interests, including support for individuals and affinity groups with environmental agendas, or responding to a community vision. The third category emphasized fulfillment of regional denominational goals by joining green certification programs run by external organizations or by the denomination.

TABLE 8 FAITH LEADER MOTIVATIONS FOR
PROMOTING SUSTAINABILITY

		NUMBER OF CASES		
MOTIVATIONS		NON-MONASTIC	MONASTIC	TOTAL
1. *Personal environmental interests*	Environmental concerns	9	5	14
	Outdoor activities	2	3	5
2. *Faith community interests*	Support individuals/ groups	5	3	8
	Response to community vision	2	4	6
3. *Fulfill denominational goals*	Participate in external program	2		2
	Participate in denominational program	1		1

1 *Personal Environmental Interests*

Concerns about specific environmental issues and enjoyment of outdoor
hobbies were the most prevalent motivations for faith leader involvement in
sustainability initiatives. In fourteen out of fifteen cases, faith leaders took
up sustainability as a faith issue because of concerns about climate change,
pollution, or development that threatened local natural areas. As described
in the chapter on sustainability champions, two pastors served as champions
and prompted creation of sustainability initiatives as a way to respond to
their personal concerns. In most cases, however, the initiatives were led by
lay people with support from faith leaders who shared their environmental
concerns. Some faith leaders also had personal interests in outdoor activities that motivated them to participate in sustainability projects and support
the development of initiatives. Reverend Jeff Wild (MCC) and Sister Mary
David Walgenbach (HWM) were avid gardeners; Reverend Ann Held (TPC)
was fond of hiking and camping; and Abbot John Klassen (SJA), who had a
doctorate in bio-organic chemistry, spent considerable time in the gardens
and forests of the abbey. These personal interests, both in addressing environmental crises and in outdoor activities, motivated faith leaders to encourage
the sustainability champions in their communities and inspired them to com-
pose sermons and writings on environmental topics.

Some faith leaders were motivated by a desire to support environmentally minded individuals, affinity groups, or the faith community as a whole after it had identified sustainability as an issue to be addressed by the religious organization. In these cases, leaders were working to fulfill their pastoral roles by fostering members' religious lives and promoting the welfare of the religious organization. Thus, the relationship between the faith leaders and the community members ran in two directions: the faith leaders were responsive to community interests, and the community was responsive to the guidance of its leaders.

In five non-monastic cases, clergy provided advice and support for affinity groups and individuals who sought to organize environmental activities under the auspices of the faith community. For example, at Trinity Presbyterian Church in Harrisonburg, the pastor advised members of the Earth Care House Church about how to bring the problem of air pollution from coal-based energy production to the attention of their denomination.[5] She also applauded their environmental work in the congregation and shared information about their accomplishments with people outside the faith community. Clergy also provided support to individuals who told them of their desires to integrate personal environmental interests into their faith traditions. Several years before Anshe Emeth Memorial Temple enrolled in the GreenFaith certification program, Mike Chodroff had a conversation with his rabbi in which they discussed Chodroff's desire to connect his work as an environmental educator with his religious life. Consequently, when the opportunity to pursue green certification arose, the rabbi knew that Chodroff would be interested in leading the program.[6]

In three monastic communities, organizational leaders tried to balance support for individual members' desires to pursue environmental interests with community needs. The abbot of Saint John's Abbey sent Father Schwietz to school to earn a master's degree in forestry as preparation for employing him as abbey land manager, a position that fit within the structure of the monastic organization. Schwietz's subsequent proposal to create an educational arboretum was more difficult since it required making changes to the organization. Schwietz lobbied for his idea for a decade and, eventually, the abbot authorized a study to discern whether such a project would enhance the work of the abbey and university. When Sister Ginny Jones worked for Nazareth College in the early 1970s, leaders of her religious community were supportive of her project to create the Bow in the Clouds Nature Preserve, but it was largely a one-woman initiative, and the preserve became overgrown with invasive plant species when Jones moved from teaching to hospital administrative work. By 1990, however, there was growing interest in environmental issues among the members of the organization, and the leadership team asked Jones to "begin some type of 'environmental' program."[7] She created a ministry in eco-spirituality that became part of the organization's new retreat center and, during the same period, she was able to begin restoring Bow in the Clouds.

As these monastic cases demonstrate, organizational leaders were more supportive of environmental efforts when the subject was of interest to a larger number of community members.[8] The breadth of that interest often became apparent when communities revised their missions. For example, all four women's monastic communities engaged in formal mission discernment processes that led to adoption of care for the earth or environmental stewardship as a community-wide ethic. As a result, leadership teams provided resources such as staff time and funds to implement initiatives that fulfilled their community environmental ethics. Clergy in two of the non-monastic communities also took up the task of implementing an earth care mission after their congregations adopted a sustainability ethic through a community discernment process. As in the cases in which faith leaders supported individuals and affinity groups, a community ethic could motivate faith leaders who did not have a prior personal interest in the environment to endorse sustainability initiatives because of their responsibility to support the spiritual lives of their community members.

3 Fulfill Denominational Goals

In three cases, clergy encouraged congregational involvement in sustainability initiatives in response to regional denominational organizations that encouraged local congregations to take up earth care practices. Two Jewish congregations participated in an external green certification program that was promoted by their denominational leaders, and a Catholic parish participated in a program established by the regional diocese, or district, to which it belonged. When the regional branch of the Union for Reform Judaism encouraged member congregations in New Jersey to enroll in the GreenFaith program, Rabbi Bennett Miller, senior pastor at Anshe Emeth Memorial

Temple, embraced the idea. According to members of his green team, the rabbi considered adoption of the idea a "no brainer" because it fit with the community's religious ethics, and he had an environmental educator and a junior rabbi in his congregation who would be able to lead the effort.[9] Rabbi Laurence Malinger at Temple Shalom had a similarly positive response; he too knew he had some members who would embrace the idea. The senior pastor of St. Thomas Aquinas Parish in Palo Alto, California, also authorized a community sustainability initiative because of a regional denominational movement. In 2009, the bishop of the Diocese of San Jose, to which the parish belongs, organized a Catholic Green Initiative to encourage all parishes in the Santa Clara Valley to adopt more sustainable practices. Consequently, when lay members of St. Thomas Aquinas asked for permission to form the parish's Green Committee, the senior pastor acquiesced even though he did not have much personal interest in environmental activities.

Once faith leaders responded to these motivations and decided to support a sustainability initiative, they took action in ways that fit with their roles as leaders within faith communities. First, through their status as religious authorities, they articulated the reasons that sustainability should be considered a religious issue to be addressed by their communities. Second, as organizational managers, they helped integrate earth care into the practices of their faith communities. The following two chapters explore the contributions that faith leaders made to the development of sustainability initiatives within the fifteen case-study communities. Chapter 5 focuses on the messages that were used to legitimate sustainability as a religious issue and motivate community members to engage in earth care activities. Chapter 6 examines the mechanisms through which faith leaders were able to promote implementation of earth care activities within the context of their faith communities. Together, the chapters elucidate how faith leaders contributed to development of a sustainability social norm for their communities.

5 LEGITIMATING SUSTAINABILITY AS A FAITH ISSUE

It's important to make sure that everything we do is theologically under-girded. We know we need to care for the environment, but we have to ask why should we, as people of faith, have concern for the environment?
—REVEREND JEFF WILD, Madison Christian Community

ONE SIGNIFICANT CONTRIBUTION that faith leaders made to the sustainability initiatives was to legitimate sustainability as a faith issue that required a response from members of their faith communities. Faith leaders conferred legitimacy on sustainability through their roles as religious authorities who interpret religious teachings and apply them to modern life. The primary purpose of a religious organization is to support the development of its members' religious lives. One of the inherent challenges for integrating environmentalism into Christian and Jewish traditions is that these religions base their teachings about moral behavior on scriptures and interpretive commentaries that were written long before modern environmental crises emerged. Consequently, they do not directly address issues such as climate change. However, the same challenges pertain to many other aspects of modern life that are not directly addressed in texts written for pre-modern social systems, so clergy and lay faith leaders continually update teachings about religious ethics, the moral behavior incumbent on members of a tradition, by using the core values of their faith traditions as an interpretative framework for addressing current issues. In the case studies, faith leaders adhered to this tradition of interpretation to present sustainability as an issue that needed to be addressed because of their community's pre-existing religious ethics. The ways faith leaders framed their earth care messages were influenced by two key factors: the denominational teachings of their religious traditions and the traditional ministries of their faith communities.

FRAMING SUSTAINABILITY AS A FAITH COMMUNITY ISSUE

In all fifteen cases, faith leaders explained that sustainability was closely linked with their religious tradition's foundational values, however the specific message frames used to describe why people of faith ought to engage in environmental activities varied due to differences in denomination, community mission, and faith leaders' personal interests. Despite these variations, the messages expressed four thematic motifs (see Table 9): First, a stewardship ethic motif was used to explain that people have a religious duty to care for the natural world. Second, a nature spirituality motif described the necessity of protecting nature because it is a place where people have spiritual experiences. Third, a social justice motif stated that people have a responsibility to aid the poor and disadvantaged, who are harmed by environmental degradation.[1] Fourth, some leaders also called for action on the grounds that people of faith had a special role to play in creating a more environmentally sustainable society. The lines between themes could be porous, and faith leaders often shifted from one to another depending on context. For example, pastors might emphasize stewardship when speaking about ethics and emphasize spirituality when describing personal experiences in nature.[2]

TABLE 9 FRAMING SUSTAINABILITY AS
A FAITH COMMUNITY ISSUE

MOTIF	RELIGIOUS FRAME	NUMBER OF CASES
1. *Stewardship ethic*	Fulfill Commandments	
	Dominion/stewardship	5
	Bal tashchit ("Do not waste")	3
	Recognize interdependence of people and nature	1
2. *Nature spirituality*	Become aware of Creator	9
	Nature is sacred/Spirit is present in nature	3
	Learn religious precepts	4
	Care for sacred places	5
3. *Social justice*	Protect the poor and disadvantaged	15
4. *Special role of religion*	Confront the powerful	2
	Provide a positive vision	3

1 Stewardship Ethic

One of the most prevalent frames used to explain why sustainability is a faith issue was the idea that stewardship of the earth is included in the moral obligations incumbent on members of a religious tradition. For Christian and Jewish faith communities, this moral duty was linked with biblical commandments, or *mitzvot* (singular *mitzvah*), that delineate proper religious and social behavior. For Unitarian Universalists, who draw on multiple sources of spiritual knowledge and moral precepts, stewardship was described as a way to live in accord with the Seven Principles that define their religion's values.

In American Jewish and Christian environmental organizations, the idea of environmental stewardship has become closely linked with the biblical creation story,[3] and this theme appeared in most of the cases. In the three Jewish communities, rabbis articulated a Jewish duty to care for the earth during Rosh Hashanah, the New Year festival that celebrates creation. In their sermons, they described the beauty of God's creation but then pointed out that human behavior was damaging the world and therefore was out of sync with God's plan. As Rabbi Rebecca Epstein explained:

> The activities that we have undertaken as we have filled up the earth and have become fruitful and multiplied—our use of natural resources, our use of toxic chemicals and dangerous energy sources—have resulted in dramatic changes to our air, water, our forest, and to the many other species with whom we share Creation. We have gone too far. We have become dangerous not only to the atmosphere and the ocean and the animals, but to ourselves, and to our own children. We are not fulfilling God's blessing. And it is NOT good.[4]

All of the rabbis in this study stated that Jews had an obligation to respond to the earth's environmental crises and referenced two texts as bases for a Jewish responsibility to care for the earth. The first text was the biblical creation story. In Genesis 1:28, God gives human beings "dominion" over other living beings, a passage that has often been cited to suggest that biblical religions may encourage people to exploit natural resources.[5] The rabbis argued that the passage should be interpreted to mean that people are given the responsibility to be stewards of God's creation, an interpretation that is reinforced by Genesis 2, in which God instructs the first human beings to "tend the garden." Rabbi Epstein expressed these ideas in a sermon for Rosh Hashanah:

God took the *adam* [the man[6]], and placed him in the Garden of Eden: to till it, and to protect it. The *adam* was commanded by God to be *shomeir Adamah*, a protector of the earth. So, too, we are commanded to be *Shomrei Adamah*, protectors of the earth. Living according to that commandedness, along with sustaining awareness of our intimate connection and ultimate dependence on Creation, are vital, I believe, to our existence.[7]

The second text used to prove humans have a divine mandate to care for the earth comes from a rabbinic *midrash*, or commentary, that expands on the Genesis creation story. In the words of Rabbi Laurence Malinger of Temple Shalom:

> There is a Midrash, a rabbinic story, that says: When God created the first people, He showed them all the trees of the Garden of Eden, saying, "See My handiwork, how beautiful and choice they are . . . be careful not to ruin and destroy my world, for if you do, there is no one to repair it after you." (*Midrash Rabbah Ecclesiastes* 7:13)
>
> We are, according to tradition, the descendants of Adam and Eve, and that voice speaking to them in the garden is speaking to us, right now. There is no one to repair it after us. Our very existence demands that we are stewards of this great planet.[8]

The rabbis in the case-study communities provided further legitimation of sustainability as a Jewish issue by citing a passage from the book of Deuteronomy that has become the basis for the modern Jewish environmental ethic of *bal tashchit*, "Do not waste." Deuteronomy 20:19–20, which occurs in a list of rules governing warfare, says that those who lay siege to a city must not destroy (*bal tashchit*) the fruit-bearing trees belonging to the city. Rabbi Brant Rosen explained that the rabbinic tradition had transformed this command into an environmental commandment:

> Indeed, the sages of the Talmud would eventually apply the term *bal tashchit* ("do not destroy") to issues far transcending concern over fruit-bearing trees during wartime. The concept "*bal tashchit*" eventually became a Jewish legal term referring to the destruction of natural resources on a wide scale, ranging from the wanton killing of animals (Talmud Hullin 7b) to the wasting of fuel (Talmud Shabbat 67b).[9]

Rabbi Malinger also used this rabbinic teaching to legitimate the idea that sustainability was "a Jewish issue." He noted that the medieval scholar

Maimonides "emphasizes the gravity" of violating this biblical prohibition against needless destruction by teaching that a person who commits acts of wanton destruction should be "administered a disciplinary beating imposed by the Rabbis (Mishneh Torah 6:10)."[10] According to Malinger, the strength of the punishment illustrates the importance of the ethic: "Our sources make it very clear that it is not just an ethical issue, or a personal choice, but a *Jewish* imperative, a legally binding prohibition not to waste the precious resources of our planet."[11]

Pastor Ken Wilson, Vineyard Church of Ann Arbor, also used the idea of fulfilling God's commandments to explain why evangelical Christians have a duty to be environmental stewards. He noted that for Christians, the "first and greatest commandment" given by Jesus is: "Love the Lord your God with all your heart and all your soul and with all your mind" (Matthew 22:36). According to Wilson, caring for creation is included in this command:

> For many evangelicals, loving God means spending time in worship and prayer. This is foundational. But there is another way to express our love for God. Jesus tells us: "If you love me, keep my commands" (John 14:15). Loving God means caring about what happens to God's creation because God cares about it and because God gave us the job of caring for it. We worship God by caring for creation.[12]

Furthermore, Wilson indicated that people would be held accountable for how well they looked after the world that the Creator had left in their care.

Unitarian Universalism places much less emphasis on commandments and formally defined beliefs than Judaism and Christianity, however it does affirm Seven Principles that express the values of its members. The pastor of the First Universalist Church of Rockland cited the Seventh Principle, "recognition of the interdependent web of life of which we are all a part," to explain how their religion affirmed the importance of environmentally sustainable behavior:

> We hold up respect for the interdependent web of all existence of which we are a part. In response to this principle we are called to live as people who respect the earth. We're called to live as people who recognize the damage our technological shortsightedness has done—and will continue to do—to the earth until we radically transform our ways. We recognize that we do nothing in isolation, that everything we do has an impact on our surroundings because we are interconnected.[13]

In addition to citing biblical commandments as evidence that people have a religious duty to be environmental stewards, Christian and Jewish faith leaders emphasized the need to care for the natural world because it is a place where people have spiritual experiences. Four themes appeared in teachings related to nature spirituality. First, the world is God's beloved creation and provides a means to interact with God. Second, God is present in nature because the earth is a divine manifestation. Although these two ideas are theologically distinct (the first emphasizes divine transcendence while the second emphasizes immanence) both themes were used to explain why caring for the earth was a type of religious practice. Third, nature is important because it provides a context for learning about religious precepts. Fourth, some faith leaders noted that places where people engaged in spiritual practices came to be perceived as sacred places, which added to the impetus to protect them. Across these four themes, there was an overarching sense that people have a reciprocal relationship with nature: nature nurtures people mentally and spiritually, and, in return, humans are called to care for nature.

As an example of the first theme, Pastor Wild explained that, "The garden offers opportunities to be a biblical witness. It's really symbiotic: it's something we do because we're guided by our Christian faith and we want to care for God's creation, but then the experiences in the garden reveal God's grace."[14] Similarly, according to Reverend Wilson, "We worship God by caring for creation. We don't worship creation. God created the world for his glory, and because of this, it reveals his glory to us: 'LORD, our Lord, how majestic is your name in all the earth! You have set your glory in the heavens' (Psalm 8:1)."[15]

By carefully explaining that care for creation is a means of honoring the Creator, Wilson forestalls a traditional Christian criticism of environmentalists as idolaters who worship nature. He bolsters his case by citing numerous biblical passages from the Psalms and Genesis describing the wonders and beauty of the world, noting that these passages indicate God's love for the flora and fauna He created. Consequently, observation of nature may serve as a way for humans to become aware of the Creator and lead them to recognize that they have an obligation to protect the diverse creations with which they share the planet.

Faith leaders in a subset of cases went farther than Wilson and described the natural environment as sacred because God is present within His creation.

This theme was most common in three of the women's monastic communities, where it emerged from study of theologians such as Saint Bonaventure, Father Thomas Berry, and Zachary Hayes, OFM. The Sisters of St. Francis cited the idea of the "Cosmic Christ" as foundational to their mission to care for the earth. According to Sister Margaret Pirkl, "The Cosmic Christ can be defined as that aspect of God which pervades all of creation, the Christ who 'fills the universe in all its parts' (Ephesians 1:23)."[16] She derives this idea from Bonaventure's interpretation of the Trinity, the idea of God as three persons, in which "the First Person of the Trinity, the Father-Mother Person, is Love, the Source of all that is good," and the Second Person, Christ, is "God's self-expression as the Word." Because "the Word expressed outwardly is God's creation of the world," the material universe is understood to be an external embodiment of the Word of God.[17] This teaching reflects a passage in the Gospel of John in which "all things were made through him [the Word]" (John 1:3). The Third Person, the Spirit, is God "living and active in this world." Pirkl explains that this Trinitarian theology indicates that the earth and everything in it is sacred: "Bonaventure's teaching leads us to an almost incredible conclusion. Every leaf, cloud, fruit, animal, and person is to be seen as an outward expression of the Word of God in Love! Thus, each creation has its own identity, integrity, and dignity. Each is sacred because it holds something of the Word of God, Christ, in a unique way."[18]

Those who recognize that everything that exists is sacred, are obligated to change the way they behave toward the physical world. As Pirkl points out:

> If every being somehow carries the divine (the Cosmic Christ in the Franciscan tradition), every being is basically sacred. If we truly believed this, we would change our ways, be more thought-full, walk with a lighter step, and show our love and gratitude and concern for sister thrush, brother cloud, sister water, sister star, and the rest of the family. Such is the sometimes difficult but always life-giving challenge placed before Earth's people and, especially, those of us who are Franciscan at heart.[19]

Although Pirkl equates the Cosmic Christ with Franciscan teachings, Sister Ginny Jones also described Thomas Berry's teachings about the cosmic creation story as important for framing sustainability as an issue of concern to the Sisters of St. Joseph. Her community takes its mission from the biblical message, "That all may be one, as You, Father, are in Me, and I in You; I pray that they may be one in Us" (John 17:21). After studying the teachings of Berry, the Sisters of St. Joseph determined that the idea "all are one" extended to all life on earth, not just humans, and therefore, their congregational mission to live and work "that all may be one" included care for the earth.

Several interviewees described the sacredness of nature in relation to its role in generating spiritual knowledge and wellbeing. Sister Mary David Walgenbach noted that Christianity has a long tradition of viewing nature as a vehicle for spiritual knowledge. For example, "in the writing of Clement, he says there are two books: the first is the book of life, which is Creation, and the second is the book of the scriptures."[20] To her, time in nature was one of the best ways to wake people up when modern, urban life left them numb:

> If you're dead inside, then the hope is for relationships to wake you up. That includes relationships with people and with nature. Then you can get out in your dinghy boat and get out to where you can find life. That includes getting out into nature. You know, I feel so bad for the kids in cities who don't get a chance to experience nature. People come out here [to Holy Wisdom Monastery] and they just walk the land and they have a place to stay. Having a space in Creation helps them open up their interior space.[21]

Sister Ginny Jones also thought time in nature was beneficial to people's spiritual lives. In describing the importance of making the Bow in the Clouds Preserve accessible to people outside the convent, she explained, "before formal religion existed, people encountered something of the holy in the natural world. And that something—that peace, solitude, and wisdom—is what we believe people can still find here."[22]

Along with the idea that exposure to nature can nurture people's spiritual lives, a number of faith leaders drew on experiences with nature to illustrate religious precepts. Although these illustrations were part of a larger body of teachings on faith-based morality and often were not specifically focused on promoting sustainability, they reinforced the idea that nature played a significant role in spiritual life. For example, Reverend Held described how she had used a story about precautions to avoid polluting a lake to illustrate her message in a sermon on the interconnectedness of humans and nature:

> I just did a sermon series on Psalm 8. I came back from spending time at a lake in Wisconsin, and it inspired me to preach on God's grace and majesty and what it means to be human. What makes us unique is that we are co-creators. In South Africa, there is this idea of *ubuntu*, "I am human because I belong." Humanity is expressed through relationships with others.

They also recognize their interconnectedness with nature, their relationships with the natural world. I pointed out that this means that if I pollute the lake with shampoo, I am harming it and not acting as a person who belongs to the lake.[23]

Moral lessons could also be derived from experiences with nature on church grounds, as in the Madison Christian Community story of ten-year-old Ruth who, as described in the previous chapter, shared her realization that, "You can't lie to the earth,"[24] while taking part in the MCC Kids in the Garden program.

It is notable that faith leaders who regularly spent time engaged in outdoor activities were the most likely to incorporate their experiences with nature into religious teachings. Reverend Wild commented that his congregation appreciated stories from the church garden: "People resonate with . . . stories about the land and chickens. I talked about 'hen love' instead of the 'fox love' of Herod. That's good theology. It's an opportunity to preach about powerless love that can overcome loveless power."[25] Like Wild, many clergy and lay spiritual teachers found opportunities for reflecting on lessons from nature while gardening, camping, canoeing, walking dogs, visiting the seashore, doing ecological restoration work, or gazing out a church office window to watch native plants gradually greening a prairie after a controlled burn to remove invasive species. By sharing their experiences with their faith communities, they raised members' awareness of connections between faith and nature and encouraged community members to see the environment as a venue for spiritual practice.

Spiritual experiences with nature were particularly prominent incentives for land stewardship among the communities that engaged in sustainable land management. Faith leaders described their properties as sacred places where the community grounds had become part of their religious work. For example, the Sisters of the Humility of Mary consider the grounds at the Villa Maria Education and Spirituality Center to be "a sacred setting where God's grace is nurtured and abundant life unfolds."[26] For Sister Barbara O'Donnell, "the spirituality of the land is so real" at Villa Maria that she feels a deep obligation to be a good environmental steward of that land. When she and other sisters with an interest in environmental ministry walked the boundaries of their property with the land manager, she recalled feeling that, "It was so awesome—to stand in the woods and realize what a responsibility we have to care for them."[27] That sense of responsibility could also include the idea that a piece of land had come to the community as a gift from God, which meant that they had a special religious duty to care for it. This was the case for the

Madison Christian Community, which received six acres of land that was set aside for building a church in a new suburb.

Being associated with a religious organization added to the sense of sanctity ascribed to the lands in these cases. As Paul Boutwell, land manager at Holy Wisdom Monastery commented, "All land is sacred. But it does make a difference—what the land is being used for. It affects the way people see it and what they feel when they are there."[28] In his opinion, visiting the monastery was different from visiting the neighboring park: "People see the land differently. They come in past the sign that says 'Holy Wisdom Monastery' and that affects their perceptions of how to behave and what the land means. It's a different experience than going into 'Governor Nelson Park.' Naming matters. Calling something a park tells you something about what you expect there."[29] But even more than the name, Boutwell believed that the way land is cared for and used affects the way people feel when they visit it. In his experience, "It's something that you know when you walk on a piece of land that someone has cared for—there is a sense of the soul of the land and person that you connect to." Thus, a place like Holy Wisdom, where people gather for spiritual activities, and where the land is being restored to native prairie and savanna as an expression of the sisters' Benedictine mission, becomes a special place that feels sacred to those who spend time there.

3 Social Justice

Faith leaders across all cases cited religious obligations to pursue social justice as a reason for people of faith to address environmental crises. Christian leaders invoked the foundational teaching that requires Christians to "Love your neighbor as yourself" (Matt 22:39). As Reverend Wilson explained:

> Loving my neighbor, according to the parable [of the Good Samaritan], includes responding to the needs of someone who has been hurt. We are to feed him, clothe him, care for his wounds, and provide for him. . . . Nothing could be clearer than Jesus' words in Matthew 25:36–44. Jesus tells his disciples that on Judgment Day, we will stand before God and answer for the way we treated those who were hungry, naked, and sick, and for those who were strangers and prisoners: "Truly I tell you, whatever you did for one of the least of these brothers and sisters of mine, you did for me" (v. 40). And, on the other hand, Jesus says, "Truly I tell you, whatever you did not do for one of the least of these, you did not do for me" (v. 45).

There are millions of suffering people in the world, and thousands of Christians who offer them assistance. Unfortunately, the realities of climate change mean that those suffering millions may become billions. All of us who follow Jesus will need to respond.[30]

Environmental activities were also perceived as extensions of community social justice missions among the women monastics. At Villa Maria, Sister Barbara O'Donnell framed environmental issues as social justice issues in her role as a spiritual teacher leading community programs focused on faith and sustainability. She described connections between her identity as a Sister of the Humility of Mary and her calling to environmental education, noting that her work developing the gardens and environmental ministries fit with the Sisters' mission to bring "more abundant life to God's people, especially those who are poor."[31] Therefore, the sustainability programs were designed so that large portions of the produce from the gardens and the farm were donated to local food pantries, and the environmental education programs offered opportunities for low-income children to spend time in nature. Similarly, because the Sisters of St. Francis of Philadelphia perceived connections between their social justice mission and earth care, the sisters who were charged with fulfilling the organization's Corporate Social Responsibility work began incorporating the environment into their justice work. As they explained: "We engage in Corporate Social Responsibility in order to fulfill the congregation's mission to 'direct our corporate resources to the promotion of justice, peace, and reconciliation' and thereby to effect change toward social and environmental justice."[32] In order to promote socially just corporate behavior, representatives of the order would attend shareholder meetings for corporations in which they held stock and present resolutions requesting that the corporations do more analysis of financial risks related to investments in hydraulic fracturing or provide better regulation of work conditions and environmental impacts throughout their supply chains.

Jewish faith leaders also spoke of the connections between environmental issues and social inequities, noting that the effects of pollution and climate change fall disproportionately on the poor and on future generations. Rabbi Epstein described her awakening to awareness of how the environmental damage caused by past generations affects the young when her infant daughter was tested for lead exposure. Such testing is mandatory for all children in New Jersey, which has widespread pollution issues due to its long manufacturing history. Epstein incorporated this personal experience into a broader message, calling on her congregation to become Protectors of the Earth because of unjust harm to the planet, the poor, and future generations: "God can be heard from the atmosphere, calling out to us to be *shomrei adamah* [protectors of earth]. God can be heard in the voices of the poor on our Earth—the poor who are most affected by all of this—calling out to us to be *shomrei adamah*. God's voice can be heard in our own children, calling out to us to be *shomrei adamah*."[33]

The rabbis defined sustainability as a social justice issue by linking it to the Jewish tradition's foundational social justice teaching of *tikkun olam*, "repairing the world," and the various practices through which their communities were already working to make the world whole. At the Jewish Reconstructionist Congregation in Evanston, Rabbi Rosen summed up the connections by saying:

> JRC has always considered itself committed to *tikkun olam*, to making the world better, and environmentalism is just part of a larger vision that we don't accept the world at face value. Reconstructionism teaches that the world is as yet not fully created. We are G-d's partners in creation and that is what it means to be a Jew, and it is a very sacred enterprise. Making and remaking the world, creating and recreating the world, and repairing the world in the places it needs to be repaired, whether working in a soup kitchen, marching in a rally for immigrant rights, or building a new building in a green way, it's all a part of the same ultimate sacred tradition.[34]

Rosen not only connected the green building project with the overarching Jewish value of *tikkun olam*, he linked it to specific ministry efforts that his community had undertaken in the past. This connection integrated sustainability into the faith community's extant practice of social justice.

Reverend Mark Glovin, First Universalist Church of Rockland, followed a similar approach by placing his church's environmental work in the context of their local social justice ministries:

> Our work in founding and supporting AIO [Area Interfaith Outreach food pantry] in feeding the hungry in our community; the Unitarian Universalist movement to teach healthy human sexuality; our movement to welcome gay, lesbian, bisexual and transgender people, to ordain them to ministry, to bless their marriages; our movement to confront racism and the legacies of colonialism—each of these efforts seeks to heal massive social and spiritual wounds whose deepest roots lie in the soil of humanity's great turning away from right relationship with the earth.[35]

In their descriptions of sustainability as a faith issue, some faith leaders emphasized that faith communities had a special role to play in helping the wider American society respond to environmental issues. In doing so, they emphasized two themes. First, there is a history of religious voices challenging unjust social systems, and second, people of faith are known for taking on difficult tasks and working to make the world a better place.

Rabbi Rosen, a strong proponent of faith-based social justice work, provides an example of the idea that religion can promote sustainability by challenging the status quo:

> In this, I believe our religious communities have a critical role to play. As the popular saying goes, religious communities don't only exist to comfort the afflicted, they also exist to afflict the comfortable. Hasn't this been the job of religion at its best from time immemorial? To warn against the deification of human power? To affirm that no matter how powerful we may become, there will always be a Power greater than even our own? To remind leaders and nations that in the end, it is not by might and not by power that God's world will be sustained?
>
> For the Jewish community, [Rosh Hashanah] is a season of new beginnings, of new opportunity, new hope. If this will be a truly new year, it will not just be up to our leaders to make it so—it will be up to us as Americans, as people of faith, as communities of conscience—to do what we must to promote a vision of sustainability in our country.[36]

Pastor Wilson sounded a similar theme, noting that Christianity can counter entrenched social systems. He stated, "God's creation is being plundered, and the gospel is the answer because it has power to transform hearts, confront [the] powers that be, and change the course of history."[37]

In addition to "confronting power," other faith leaders echoed Wilson's conviction that religion could transform hearts and minds, which would help people live more environmentally sustainable lives. Abbot John Klassen of Saint John's Abbey commented that, "To really understand and live environmental sustainability requires a fundamental conversion: of thought, of the ordering of our values and desires, of our understanding, and of practice."[38] In an article for *Catholic Rural Life Magazine*, the reporter described the abbot's conviction that teachings from the rule of St. Benedict could provide the basis for a shift in values that would prepare Catholics to live more sustainably: "Humility puts us in right relationship with God and the planet, underscoring our radical dependence. Stability creates the conditions needed to have a greater awareness of the environment in which we live. And frugality helps to undermine what Abbot John called 'the dominant culture of consumerism' that insists that we use too many of the earth's resources for our lives."[39]

Faith leaders also stressed that being people of faith equipped their communities for the difficult task of making the world more sustainable. Rabbi Malinger expressed this idea for his Jewish community in a Rosh Hashanah sermon, preaching, "We Jews never give up hope and belief in our capacity to change ourselves and change the world. Even if something seems utterly inevitable, we pray, we act, we behave as if we can alter the outcome. This is what it means to be God's partners in creation. On this Rosh Hashanah, this New Year, we have potential in a very real way to save the world."[40] Similarly, Reverend Glovin at First Universalist Church of Rockland suggested that Unitarian Universalism provided its members with valuable preparation for building a more sustainable society. Rather than relying on technology, he suggested that the key to mitigating climate change was to recognize that "we are our brother's and sister's keepers, and that it's time to take better care of each other," a task for which their years of social justice work had trained them.[41] In a sermon, he said, "This is why Unitarian Universalist congregations like ours and a thousand others are so necessary in this moment. Because we know how to work together amidst amazing diversity, know how to focus on what connects us instead of what separates us, know how to build bridges across vast difference. This is the work to which we are called."[42]

A recurrent theme threading through these pastoral messages emphasized that sustainability was part of a larger religious vision in which people of faith were called to build a better world. In this context, environmental stewardship became a component of a tradition's mission to heal the world, establish the Kingdom of God, or build the beloved community.[43] Thus, for example, Rabbi Malinger described sustainability as a facet of the traditional Jewish mission to heal the world: "As the midrash states, we are partners in God's glorious universe, here to repair, protect, and perfect the world."[44] Reverend Glovin also described environmental activities as part of an overarching vision of the new earth that the First Universalist Church community was called to create:

We are called to engage in bringing forth an environmentally sustainable, spiritually fulfilling, and socially just human presence on this planet. We're not here to find a magic bullet. There is no magic bullet . . . but there is hope that together we can forge a new way. Socrates said: "The secret of change is to focus your energy not on fighting the old, but on building the new." . . . When we see our members and friends picking up their CSA veggies on a sunny summer morning, we are witnessing the building of the new earth. When we institute composting and recycling and energy-saving devices at our church, we are witnessing the building of a new earth.[45]

Reverend Wild, whose faith community had one of the longest-running sustainability initiatives in this study, suggested that equating earth care with the positive vision of a long-range religious objective was necessary in order to sustain members' commitment to stewardship efforts. Although early environmental activities at the Madison Christian Community focused on energy conservation and installation of solar panels in an effort to address concerns about climate change, Wild's framing of environmental stewardship as a faith issue soon broadened beyond climate. He shifted his message of environmental ministry to emphasize positive goals of land stewardship and building community instead of the "negative" goal of mitigating the worst effects of climate change. He did not make this change to devalue the issue of climate change, but rather because the multi-year projects of his community required a different type of message. He said, "Acting on the basis of positive affirmation is an alternative to fear-driven motives to 'save the world.' Fear-driven motives—though justifiable given the grave condition of creation—are difficult to sustain, for avoiding disaster is the best we can hope for."[46]

This tendency to frame environmental efforts as part of a positive religious vision may have helped sustain people's participation in the case-study initiatives. Research suggests that fear-based appeals for action in response to climate change are unlikely to have long-lasting impacts because the initial sense of urgency soon declines,[47] an effect that may be exacerbated because climate change is a complex problem that many Americans perceive as distant in time and space.[48] Some scholars have suggested that "nonthreatening imagery and icons that link to individuals' everyday emotions and concerns" may be more effective than fear for motivating genuine personal engagement with climate change.[49] Incorporating environmental activities into the ministry work of a religious community conforms to this recommendation. Religions have well-established traditions of engaging in activities that contribute to long-term pursuit of a distant ideal goal. Although centuries of effort have not yet succeeded in creating a perfectly just and peaceful society, people of faith continue to strive to make the world better. Thus, in contrast to actions taken out of fear, Reverend Wilson theorized that people of faith could draw on their sense of hope for the world in order to motivate climate action among themselves and in the wider society:

> The gospel prepares us to face the future with hope. And hope is in even shorter supply than energy these days. Those who are in touch with the global environmental crisis—the rampant pollution, the millions of people without any access to clean water, the global poor who will be hit hard by the widespread effects of climate change—are hard pressed to be hopeful. We can join this effort and bring our hope with us, the hope of a gospel that is truly good news on a global scale.[50]

FOSTERING AN INTENTION TO ENGAGE IN EARTH CARE

Comparison of the messages through which faith leaders called on their communities to work toward creating a more environmentally sustainable society indicates that three elements contributed to the efficacy of their messages. First, they legitimated sustainability as a faith issue by grounding it in their religious tradition's core theologies. Second, faith leaders in the case studies went beyond general religious values such as justice and charity to connect sustainability to the identity of each specific faith community. Third, they emphasized the special role that faith communities could play in creating social change.

1 Grounding Sustainability in Core Theologies

As the quotes from sermons and blogs cited earlier make clear, faith leaders legitimated sustainability as a faith issue by grounding it in core theological teachings of their religious traditions. This process fits the strategy of "frame bridging," creating links between two unconnected frames, which Stephen Ellingson uses to describe how religious environmental movement organizations "weave environmentalism into existing religious ethics."[51] The teachings cited in each case reflected denominational affiliations. Rabbis emphasized the relationship between earth care and the Jewish ethic of *tikkun olam*, healing the world.[52] Mainline Protestant and Catholic faith leaders connected environmental issues with social justice. Reverend Wilson at Vineyard Church of Ann Arbor framed his call for a Christian response to climate change as a means to love and obey God by fulfilling divine commandments, thereby connecting it to the evangelical emphasis on personal relationships with God. Pastor

Glovin at First Universalist Church of Rockland stressed the need for actions that were consistent with the Seventh Principle of Unitarian Universalism, affirming "the interconnected web of life." By invoking these core teachings, which the communities already understood to be central to their religious traditions, the faith leaders provided a solid foundation for establishing the legitimacy of sustainability as a faith issue.

2 Connecting Sustainability with Community Identity

In addition to providing general theological foundations for earth care, clergy and lay faith teachers framed sustainability as an issue that connected with the identity of their specific faith communities by directly connecting it to extant ministry work. Hence, sustainability was not simply something the congregation ought to consider because they were Jews, Unitarian Universalists, or Christians; sustainability was incumbent on them as members of a particular faith community because it was tied to their community mission and the ministries through which they enacted that mission. The rabbis stressed the alignment of sustainability with social justice work that already formed the core of their specific communities' service activities, such as providing food to the poor or advocating for improvements in immigration policy. Reverend Glovin noted that sustainability fit into the First Universalist Church of Rockland's long-standing vision of creating a just society, which they worked toward by advocating for marriage equality and supporting programs to alleviate poverty. The mission of the Green Committee at St. Thomas Aquinas Parish described its sustainability initiative as a continuation of preexisting ministries to care for disadvantaged people, a connection made explicit by having the chair of the Human Concerns Committee that focused on local poverty issues also serve as chair for the Green Committee.

For the monastic communities, sustainability was legitimated when faith leaders linked it to the *charism*, or mission, that was foundational to each community's identity. At Saint John's Abbey and Holy Wisdom Monastery, in addition to general Benedictine values such as stability, faith leaders in both communities invoked community-specific values. For Saint John's Abbey, that meant connecting to their heritage as caretakers of the forest where their predecessors had planted evergreens grown lovingly from seed. For Holy Wisdom, it meant deciding that there was a reason they had repeatedly refused to sell their land to developers, and reframing that decision so that "no sale" became the basis for care of their land as part of their mission. As

Franciscans, faith leaders at Our Lady of Angels legitimated sustainability by invoking St. Francis, the patron saint of ecology who addressed earth, sun, and animals as brethren. Thus, all parts of creation were seen as brother and sister, and care for the earth was connected to previous social justice work focused on care for the poorest members of the human family. For the Sisters of St. Joseph at Nazareth, sustainability came to be understood as part of their mission to live and work in order that "all may be one," once faith leaders articulated the idea that "all" included all of creation, not just human beings. At Villa Maria, lay faith leaders developed the idea that there were connections between humus and their core value of humility. Care for the garden *humus* from which food grew had special meaning for the Sisters of the *Humility* of Mary, who could use their land to produce food, host spiritual retreats, and provide educational benefits through which to fulfill their mission to "bring more abundant life to God's people, especially the poor."[53]

Defining sustainability as a religious issue laid the foundation for calling people of faith to engage in environmental activities, however, it did not necessarily require that those activities be undertaken through a faith community. Individuals could have taken action by joining secular environmental organizations or making changes to behavior in their homes and workplaces. Therefore, connecting sustainability to faith community identity and linking it with extant missions was important for defining earth care as an area of action to be undertaken within the religious organization. In effect, the faith leaders expanded the missions of their faith communities to include earth care.[54] This aspect of the faith leader messages conveyed an expectation that members of a congregation would adopt sustainable behaviors, and that those behaviors would be integrated into the practices of the religious organization, with participation and support from the congregation. Messages integrating sustainability into community identity may, therefore, be a characteristic of faith-community-level sustainability initiatives that distinguishes them from other types of religious environmental movement organizations.[55]

3 Special Contributions of Faith Communities

The call to community-based action was further strengthened by the message that faith communities could make special contributions to the campaign to create a more sustainable society through their role as voices of morality and justice. This message made earth care accessible; it suggested that individuals did not need expertise in science or engineering to take action, they could do important work by changing hearts and minds. By citing historical examples of instances in which people of faith provided moral leadership during times of social change, faith leaders furthered the perception that sustainability was a faith issue that their communities could and should address. In the process, they motivated members to take action and increased congregational support for initiatives.

Thus, by grounding sustainability in core theologies, connecting it to community identity, and arguing that people of faith have special contributions to make in the movement to build a more sustainable society, faith leaders legitimated earth care as a faith issue that required action from their community members. In the process, they created an implicit definition of a sustainability ethic: to protect people and ecosystems from pollution and the effects of climate change, and to interact with the environment in ways that would restore balance to the natural order. In other words, they defined sustainability as an expression of moral behavior, to be achieved by living in accord with ethical precepts that define what it means to be in right relationship with God (for theistic traditions), other human beings, and the environment.

Once earth care was defined as a faith issue, many community members felt a desire to take action. Lynn Cameron, a lay faith leader at Trinity Presbyterian Church, described the importance of religious messages for motivating action among members of the Earth Care House Church. Her words, already mentioned earlier, bear repetition:

> We started with the biblical foundations, and I think it was important to get clear that those foundations were there. . . . But then people wanted to do something. It is not enough to be against things, we needed to be for things. A lot of environmental work starts with being against something. But what are you for? I guess, for us, it's the idea of sustainability. . . . Once the theology was inside us, we could act on our faith.

By presenting sustainability as an area for community activity, faith leaders played an important role in establishing sustainability as a new social norm, an area of activity that members were expected to support and participate in. How deeply sustainability became embedded in the social norms of each community was affected by the actions faith leaders took to present these religious messages and express support for initiatives. The next chapter examines the mechanisms through which faith leaders took action and contributed to the development of the initiatives.

6 MECHANISMS FOR LEGITIMATING SUSTAINABILITY

[Reverend] Ann has been great about weaving earth care into the services. She does that too often to count.
—JUDY LEPERA, Trinity Presbyterian Church

BY PRESENTING THE MESSAGE that earth care was a faith issue that required a response from their community, faith leaders sought to influence members' attitudes toward sustainability in order to motivate them to take action. Thus, faith leaders were advocating for adoption of sustainability as a social norm, an expected behavior, for members of their communities. How well they succeeded in embedding sustainability in the social norms of their congregations was affected by the mechanisms through which they promoted earth care. Those mechanisms also shaped the actions available to the faith leaders. An additional factor affecting faith-leader contributions to initiative development concerned the intensity with which they promoted earth care, a topic that will be examined toward the end of the chapter.

MECHANISMS FOR PROMOTING SUSTAINABILITY

To promote sustainability initiatives, faith leaders employed an array of mechanisms related to their dual roles as religious authorities and organizational managers (see Table 10). As religious authorities, clergy used sermons to convey messages to the whole community. Lay faith leaders often participated in study groups where they led explorations of religious teachings and developed resources for sharing the idea of faith-based sustainability with congregation members. Some leaders also used newsletter articles or blogs to share religious reflections or to keep the wider community updated on various projects. Alongside these intellectual presentations, which articulated connections between sustainability and religious values, faith leaders encouraged engagement with earth care by making it a visible part of community religious practice. They did this through affirmations, in the form of announcements and celebrations of environmental actions, and by developing rituals related to earth care.

In their role as organizational managers, faith leaders helped implement initiatives. They authorized the creation of initiatives and advised champions about ways to incorporate sustainability into religious practices and organizational systems. They also advocated for support of initiatives from administrative boards and other committees within the religious organization.

TABLE 10 MECHANISMS FOR PROMOTING SUSTAINABILITY

FAITH LEADER ROLE	MECHANISM	NUMBER OF CASES
1. *Religious Authority*	Sermons	11
	Study groups	10
	Blogs, newsletters	7
	Public affirmations	10
	Rituals	10
2. *Organizational Management*	Authorize initiatives	12
	Advise champions	3
	Advocate for community support	4

1   *Mechanisms Related to Religious Authority*

Because the purpose of a faith community is to foster members' religious lives and promote moral behavior, proposed activities must be understood to contribute to the organization's religious mission. In their role as religious authorities responsible for interpreting religious beliefs and practices, faith leaders had the power to legitimate sustainability as a faith issue that required a response from the community. They conveyed this message through a variety of mechanisms that were available to them as clergy and, to a lesser extent, as lay leaders.

SERMONS. As the numerous homiletic quotes in Chapter 5 indicate, sermons were a prominent mechanism through which faith leaders promoted sustainability as a faith issue. Sermons are a natural venue for encouraging development of new social norms; pastors use sermons to explain how traditional religious teachings can be applied to current circumstances and issue injunctions regarding individual and congregational behavior. Thus, sermons were an especially effective means of promoting sustainability as a faith issue because members expected that the pastor, an authority on religion, would provide information about connections between their faith tradition and emergent social concerns. Sermons also had the advantage of reaching the majority of the community since they are a central aspect of the worship rituals that members attended each week.

Clergy in nine of the ten non-monastic cases and two monasteries presented homilies with environmental themes. The previous chapter provided examples of passages from sermons in the non-monastic communities. Similarly, care for the earth was a regular topic at Holy Wisdom Monastery, where various speakers took turns delivering sermons during the Sunday Assembly, and at Saint John's Abbey, where the abbot occasionally preached about connections between sustainability and Benedictine traditions. In contrast, women interviewed at the three Catholic convents that relied on priests to perform mass did not mention homilies as a source of information about faith-based sustainability.

Annual liturgical cycles affected the size of the audience exposed to homiletic messages. Ann Cohen commented that Rabbi Rebecca Epstein "was a big factor in bringing the issue [of sustainability] to the congregation through the pulpit" at Anshe Emeth Memorial Temple. "She spoke from the Bimah [podium] several times and she even did a sermon during High Holy Days when the house was packed. She did periodic sermons throughout the GreenFaith certification process."[1] By speaking about sustainability during one of the major holidays, Rabbi Epstein reached a greater number of community members than she could have during a regular Sabbath service.

STUDY GROUPS. Study groups served as mechanisms for lay faith leaders to share messages about earth care as a faith issue. In the three Catholic women's convents, where the sisters rely on local priests to lead Sunday mass, study groups were more important than sermons for presenting connections between sustainability and faith traditions. In these cases, sisters who were sustainability champions participated in study groups during mission discernment processes, where they introduced other sisters to texts that explained theological bases for earth care.

Study groups also provided an opportunity for laity in non-monastic cases to develop earth-care messages that they used in their roles as sustainability champions when they proposed initiatives to their communities. Lay leaders organized Bible studies to explore the scriptural context for sustainability as part of Green Vineyard and the Trinity Earth Shepherds (Trinity Presbyterian Church, East Brunswick). Study was also central to the Earth Care House Church at Trinity Presbyterian Church in Harrisonburg, Virginia, where lay faith leaders organized study of theological and inspirational texts every year as part of their house church mission. Similarly, the idea for building a green synagogue at the Jewish Reconstructionist Congregation came from an Environmental Task Force study group that had been founded by laity interested in exploring connections between Judaism and environmental issues. In each of these cases, the study group served as a community of interest in which people explored religious teachings that legitimated sustainability as a faith issue, thereby enhancing their ability to present earth-care proposals in ways that would motivate congregational support. Lynn Cameron described the effects of theological study in the Earth Care House Church:

> In the early environmental movement, there used to be an anti-environment sentiment in churches—people said the resources were there for us to use. There was that idea that humans were given dominion over the creation. It was really helpful for me to have knowledge of theology so I could articulate a response to that. I needed to know what I could say that's based in the Bible. That helped get people to think differently, so all that reading was really helpful.[2]

NEWSLETTER ARTICLES AND BLOGS. Some faith leaders included sustainability messages in newsletter articles and blogs, often in response to a particular event such as a holy day, an environmental activity at the house of worship, or a campaign to enlist member support for a project. For example, leaders seeking to encourage integration of environmental behavior into the daily lives of community members might use the religious calendar to talk about specific practices. Ann Cohen described the efficacy with which one of the rabbis at Anshe Emeth Memorial Temple used newsletter articles to connect environmentally sustainable practices with Jewish holiday traditions: "During the GreenFaith certification process, Rabbi Epstein would do a piece on how each holiday connects to the environment. Like Passover—lots of people do cleaning at that holiday, so she talked about the savings that come with homemade [nontoxic] cleaning products."[3]

Environmental activities at houses of worship also provided occasions for messages about faith and sustainability. The dramatic changes in the prairie at the Madison Christian Community, as it re-grew after a controlled burn to remove invasive species and stimulate fire-adapted native plants, inspired Pastor Ticia Brown to write several prairie-themed entries for her weekly blog.[4] During construction of the new building for the Jewish Reconstructionist Congregation, Rabbi Brant Rosen maintained a Construction Diary blog with entries that included photos and explanations of green features as they were added to the building. For example, in Construction Diary #26, Rosen wrote:

> The next two pix down show our building's white reflective roof. Most homes and buildings in America, in fact, are built with dark roofs that absorb heat, forcing air conditioners to work up to 20% longer and use a fifth more power. JRC's reflective roof will help our air conditioning system to work more efficiently, especially during peak usage hours. The small domed items on the second pic down are Solartube skylights that will let natural light into our kitchen.[5]

In some of these blog posts, Rabbi Rosen articulated connections between Judaism and sustainability, explaining that, "our new synagogue building is a green shul [synagogue], having been built according to sacred Jewish values of environmental sustainability."[6] He also described how the building served as an expression of the JRC community's values. One blog entry that illustrates this connection recounts how the children contributed to the construction project:

> We discovered last year that the soil on our property was soft and sandy—definitely not suitable for supporting a large three-story building. This necessitated drilling of [eighteen] caissons: concrete pillars driven deep into the ground that will serve to stabilize the structure. . . . Just before the caisson drilling commenced, our congregation's president, Alan Saposnik, came up with an inspired idea. Since we are constructing pillars to support our congregation, why not create eighteen symbolic "pillars" of our community—spiritual values that we could somehow connect to the physical caissons?
>
> I took Alan's idea to our fourth and seventh grade religious school students . . . What, I asked our students, would you consider to be the eighteen "pillars" upon which our congregational community stands?
>
> Then together we brainstormed eighteen spiritual values of our JRC community: God, Judaism, Joy, Prayer, Hope, Respect, Partnership, Song, Tikkun

Olam, Community, Study, Freedom, Friendship, Spirit, Learning, Peace, Growth, and Love. Afterwards, I wrote out the values on separate pieces of paper and each one was placed by the construction crew into a separate caisson shaft to be mixed together with the concrete, becoming a permanent part of JRC's support structure.[7]

PUBLIC AFFIRMATIONS. In addition to defining environmental issues as faith issues through religious teaching, faith leaders legitimated sustainability initiatives by publicly affirming the importance of the activities undertaken by sustainability champions. These "affirmations" were faith-leader actions that called attention to sustainability efforts such as making announcements that promoted upcoming events, celebrating accomplishments during worship services, and mentioning the community's environmental efforts in venues such as denominational and interfaith meetings.

Clergy often demonstrated their support for community greening efforts by reminding people of upcoming activities and encouraging them to get involved. One member of the Green Team at Anshe Emeth Memorial Temple noted that although the senior rabbi left responsibility for green sermons to the junior rabbi, he actively supported the congregation's GreenFaith certification program by publicizing the project. In the words of Asher Siebert, "He's good about advertising events. The whole issue of our becoming GreenFaith certified was brought to people's attention on Fridays" during the regular Friday evening worship services.[8]

Faith leaders further affirmed the value of sustainability efforts by celebrating their community's accomplishments. In all four green-certified communities, the pastors organized worship services to mark the attainment of certification as a green congregation. During these celebrations, they commended the green teams for their work, reiterated messages connecting earth care with the community's religious values, and emphasized that completion of the certification process was a beginning, not an end, to the community's sustainability initiative. Sustainability-themed celebrations also marked completion of green construction or renovation projects, installation of solar panels, spring planting and fall harvests in community gardens, and relief work in areas damaged by major storms.

Celebration of accomplishments often included affirmations in which faith leaders expressed their appreciation for the work individuals did. These personal affirmations were especially important when champions felt that their efforts were not having a significant impact on the wider faith community. For example, at Anshe Emeth, Rabbi Bennett Miller reassured the Green Team that the Interfaith Earth Day program they organized was important even if few members of the congregation had attended. Ann Cohen described how the rabbi affirmed the value of their accomplishment: "But our rabbi says it's not about numbers. He says that if you put together a good program and only a few people come, those people will talk about it and others will wish they had been there."[9]

In addition to activity reminders and celebrations within the community, some faith leaders further supported their community sustainability efforts through affirmations that took place outside the congregation. The Earth Care House Church members attributed much of their success to the support they received from their minister and noted that one way she helped them was through publicly affirming the importance of their work. According to Lynn Cameron, "She shows us off at mission meetings and tells people about the work we are doing."[10] By mentioning the Earth Care group as an example of the good work going on at Trinity Presbyterian Church, Reverend Ann Held reinforced the importance of earth care as an expression of her church's religious mission.

RITUALS. Rituals served as another mechanism through which faith leaders conveyed the idea that environmental actions belonged in a community's religious practice. Some faith leaders led rituals to highlight specific environmental activities either during special ceremonies or by incorporating nature-themed rituals into regular worship services. Special ceremonies drew congregation members outdoors to witness green accomplishments such as installation of solar panels or restoration of ecosystems, and these ceremonies provided an opportunity to reinforce the value of those activities. When Abbot Jerome Thiessen participated in a dedication ceremony for the restored wetlands at Saint John's Abbey, he gave a brief sermon in which he described stewardship as the guiding principle for abbey land management,[11] thereby establishing a theme that would be continued by the abbots who succeeded him.

Earth-care rituals could also be incorporated into the regular rhythm of faith-community worship. In congregations with community gardens, clergy and nuns often blessed the gardens when they were planted in the spring and offered thanksgiving prayers during fall harvest season. Vineyard Church of Ann Arbor developed a harvest ritual in which two young members would carry garden produce up the center aisle and place it at the front of the church where the minister would offer a prayer of gratitude. At First Parish Church of Newbury, summer services were held in an "outdoor chapel" comprised of a circle of benches in a shady arbor between the church building and the community garden. Through these actions, faith leaders raised the visibility of their community's environmental activities and reinforced the idea that earth care should be considered a form of religious practice.

2 Mechanisms Related to Organizational Management

In their roles as chief executives for religious organizations, faith leaders had opportunities to encourage adoption of sustainability as an organizational priority. In non-monastic communities, senior clergy stand at the top of the organizational structure. Although they have boards and leadership committees to assist them, in most faith communities, pastors have considerable influence on board decisions. As one congregation member noted, "We have a volunteer board so it's not very authoritative; the people only serve for three years, but the ministers are permanent members."[12] In other words, pastors have managerial authority over term-limited volunteers. Monastic communities have a variety of leadership structures, but all of them assign authority to specific leaders who manage their organizations. The abbot at Saint John's Abbey stands at the top of the abbey administrative hierarchy, with a council to provide advice on organizational decisions. Holy Wisdom Monastery has a prioress who makes decisions in consultation with the other sisters and a lay advisory board. The three Catholic women's communities have elected leadership teams that serve for specific terms of four to six years and are charged with the duty of implementing mission priorities that have been developed by their faith communities.

In the case studies, faith leaders drew on their authority as organizational managers to promote sustainability in several ways. First, they authorized activities by individuals and affinity groups interested in exploring connections between faith and environment. Second, they provided advice to assist affinity groups seeking to integrate sustainability into spiritual practices or take action in response to environmental concerns. Third, they advocated for support of initiatives from boards of directors and other groups within the community.

AUTHORIZATION OF SUSTAINABILITY INITIATIVES. As chief executives, faith leaders authorized development of sustainability initiatives either by supporting enrollment in external green programs or by empowering their own communities to examine sustainability as a possible area of action. In the four green-certified cases, clergy expressed support for the idea of enrolling in certification programs during board meetings, thereby prompting congregational participation. The pastors at Trinity Presbyterian Church in East Brunswick and First Parish Church of Newbury encouraged their communities to engage in the mission discernment processes that led to adoption of earth care as a core focus. At St. Thomas Aquinas Parish, the senior pastor gave permission for the establishment of a Green Committee to lead participation in the bishop's greening initiative, and the ministers of Trinity Presbyterian Church in Harrisonburg and the Madison Christian Community endorsed formation of groups dedicated to earth care.

In the monastic cases, administrative leaders authorized formation of task forces to examine how earth care intersected with community missions. At Saint John's Abbey, the abbot approved a task force to examine whether an arboretum would be of value to the religious and educational missions of the community. At Villa Maria, the leadership team allowed Sister Barbara O'Donnell to experiment with organic gardening and eco-spirituality programming while also granting permission for a task force to study how the order's mission intersected with environmental issues. For the Sisters of St. Joseph at Nazareth, it was the leadership team itself that asked Sister Ginny Jones to develop eco-spirituality programs. Leadership teams for Holy Wisdom Monastery and Our Lady of Angels also authorized examination of the relationship between earth care and their community missions during formal discernment processes focused on evaluating options for their future ministry work.

ADVISING SUSTAINABILITY CHAMPIONS. When individuals in non-monastic cases developed a desire to address environmental concerns through the venue of their faith communities, they often consulted their pastors for ideas about how to take action. At the Vineyard Church, Phil Brabbs asked Reverend Ken Wilson what he could do to act on the pastor's message that Christians have a responsibility to care for God's creation. It was Wilson who suggested that Brabbs form a small group that would combine scriptural study and environmental activities. At the Jewish Reconstructionist Congregation, the Environmental Task Force began as a study group in which people gathered to examine connections between faith and sustainability. When they felt a desire to take action and incorporate Jewish environmentalism into their spiritual lives, they turned to Rabbi Rosen for advice. He suggested that they could organize annual Tu BiShvat services for the congregation, and he put them in touch with Rabbi Fred Dobbs, a Jewish environmental leader, who could serve as a resource for them. When members of Trinity's Earth Care House Church were agonizing over the enormous challenge of protecting Shenandoah National Park from acid rain, it was Reverend Ann Held who suggested they leverage the power of their denomination's national membership by presenting a resolution at the General Assembly of the Presbyterian Church (USA).

In these examples, Faith Leader and Organization domains intersected. Clergy drew on their knowledge of the structures and practices in their religious organizations to advise environmental affinity groups about potential paths of action. Reverend Wilson helped Phil Brabbs start Green Vineyard using a small-group format that was already well-established at his church. Rabbi Rosen provided information about how to incorporate environmental themes into Jewish spiritual practices by fitting it into the worship cycle of the Jewish liturgical calendar. And Reverend Held shared information about resources available to the house church through their congregation's membership in a national denomination, thereby prompting the Earth Care group to pursue a new course of action.

ADVOCATING FOR COMMUNITY SUPPORT. In several cases, clergy facilitated development of initiatives by encouraging community groups such as committees or boards of trustees to support earth-care efforts. In two cases, pastors requested that their congregational board of trustees/directors act on sustainability initiatives. Clergy who made these requests combined their authority as interpreters of religion with their stature as chief administrators to argue that the organization's administrative board had a moral obligation to adopt policies that were consistent with the community's faith values. Rabbi Rosen demonstrated the persuasive power of combined religious and administrative authority at the Jewish Reconstructionist Congregation, where he offered environmentally themed prayers at the beginning of each board meeting to endorse the idea of incorporating Jewish environmental values into his congregation's decisions about how to address their need for a new building.

A similar combination of religious and managerial authority was evident in the processes through which the board at the Vineyard Church of Ann Arbor adopted sustainability as a guiding principle for the religious organization. The spiritual mission of the Vineyard Church was shaped by the leadership of Ken Wilson, the founding pastor. When he became concerned about climate change and the damage that human beings were doing to God's creation, he not only preached a series of sermons introducing creation care as a Christian obligation, he also asked his church board to integrate sustainability into governance policies. The request to the board, like the sermon series, included the pastor's testimony about the process of Bible study and prayer that had brought him to the conviction that Christians must take action in order to care for creation. Some members of the board, who were politically conservative and employed in extractive resource industries, were hesitant. They took time to pray and reflect for several days before eventually deciding that they agreed with their pastor and would, indeed, integrate environmental concerns into organizational management policies. This process of biblical justification followed by prayer and reflection is consistent with normative decision processes in an evangelical church. By following this paradigm, both the pastor's request and the board's acquiescence gained legitimacy. The positive outcome illustrates how clergy could combine religious and managerial authority to promote community adoption of sustainability as a new social norm.

This combination of religious and organizational authority marks another place where the domains of Faith Leaders and Organization intersect. A faith community has specific organizational structures designed to aid in fulfillment of its mission. Once governing boards adopted sustainability as a community emphasis, the senior managers (clergy and monastic leadership teams) could encourage people in other areas of the organization to support the environmental activities. At St. Thomas Aquinas Parish, the pastor assigned the parish facilities manager to serve on the Green Committee, thereby providing staff support for the lay-led effort to green the organization. At Temple Shalom, the rabbi interceded with the community's volunteer service organizations to encourage their participation in the temple's sustainability initiative. Rabbi Malinger and the board of trustees had decided that their congregation should seek GreenFaith certification, a process that requires support from clergy, staff, and lay committee members in order to implement activities in worship, education, social justice, and facilities management. The men's and women's service organizations did not initially perceive environmental stewardship as their responsibility; they had their own traditional slates of activities and considered the new sustainability initiative to be the purview of the Green Team. As chief administrator of the temple, Rabbi Malinger was able to request their support by explaining that the certification project was a congregational goal, and that the service organizations had the obligation to contribute for the benefit of the entire community.

SUSTAINABILITY INTEGRATED INTO VALUES AND PRACTICES

Using these mechanisms, which were available through their roles as religious authorities and organizational managers, enabled faith leaders to weave sustainability into the religious life of their communities in three significant ways. First, through sermons, study groups, and newsletter articles that presented theological bases for earth care and connected it to extant ministries, they defined earth care as part of their community's values. Second, through affirmations that highlighted activities taking place in a faith community and enactment of rituals that brought earth care into worship services, they made sustainability a visible element of community religious practice. Third, the message that earth care was an expression of faith in action was reinforced when faith leaders exercised their role as organizational managers and helped implement initiatives by authorizing their creation, advising individuals about how to take action within the context of a religious organization, and advocating for community support.

The emphases on values and practices worked together to foster a sustainability social norm. Environmental psychology research indicates that messages about the importance of specific actions, especially when presented by people like pastors, whose opinions carry weight with congregational members, affect individuals' attitudes and increase their intention to take action.[13] That intention to act becomes much stronger if there is also a perception that the prescribed actions are in accord with normal behavior for people in the community.[14] These insights suggest that affirmations and rituals were just as important for motivating community action as theology. By drawing people's attention to the practices of earth care taking place in their communities, faith leaders made those practices more visible and fostered a perception that environmental activities were normative behavior for community members.

Highlighting the community's environmental activities had an additional benefit: it made it easier for people to take action. One barrier that hinders adoption of new behaviors is a lack of knowledge about how to take action.[15] Faith community members who felt motivated to act but uncertain of *how* to engage in earth care could participate in accessible projects managed by their green teams. Faith leaders contributed to members' sense of competence to act both through the affirmations that reminded people of opportunities for action and through the advice that helped sustainability champions select courses of action that were well suited to the religious and organizational venues of their faith communities. Thus, faith leaders integrated earth care into community social norms both through injunctions calling on people of faith to fulfill religious obligations and through descriptions of practical actions with which to enact those obligations.

EARTH CARE'S EFFECTS ON FAITH LEADERS

Although most faith-leader interviewees emphasized ways sustainability initiatives affected their faith communities, adopting an earth-care social norm also had an impact on some of the faith leaders themselves. In accord with the previous discussion of motivations that inspired faith leaders to address earth care, some commented that they were able to fulfill their roles as spiritual guides by helping individual congregants find ways to connect their dual interests in faith and environment, thereby keeping religion relevant to members' lives. As organizational managers with responsibility for the welfare of their communities, they appreciated opportunities to save money through resource conservation and to build a public image of their faith communities as places where religion was addressing current issues. Several pastors noted that adopting an emphasis on earth care had drawn new members to join the congregation or had coincided with revitalization of the community.

A few ministers also spoke of personal benefits that emerged as involvement with environmental activities enriched their ministry work. For Nancy Haverington, pastor of First Parish Church of Newbury when it adopted its earth stewardship mission, earth care became the means to revitalize a shrinking congregation by creating innovative worship services and cultivating a distinctive community identity. Similarly, Reverend Jeff Wild of the Madison Christian Community found that focusing on care for creation enriched his personal theology and led him to develop a new ministerial calling. He explained that, "For myself, I think it helped me develop a more Trinitarian theology. Lutherans are especially Christocentric, and our relationship with this place and this sense of place has led me to think about God as the Creator and have more of a sense of the Spirit. It broadens our sense of Christian perspective and identity."[16] Christian theology describes God as a Trinity, one divine being with three aspects of Creator (Father), Redeemer (Christ, Son), and Holy Spirit. God is understood to be the Creator of the universe who entered the world temporarily as Jesus Christ in order to bring salvation to human beings and remains eternally present in the physical world in the form of the Holy Spirit. As Wild's personal understanding of God expanded to include a greater awareness of the world as a divine creation and of the Holy Spirit immanent in the natural world around him, he incorporated these new insights into his sermons.

In addition to theological insights, Wild found a special ministerial calling through his congregation's environmental activities. He realized that as the church members cared for their two acres of restored prairie and cultivated gardens to feed the hungry, they were building relationships with a physical space and its church community.[17] These activities created a sense of place for members, a sense of belonging and attachment that strengthened the faith community. Recognizing this sense of place as a valuable component of religious life, Wild came to see his pastoral work as a "ministry of place." He described the effects of this ministry: "To feel at home somewhere, to have roots in a place that nourish one's sense of selfhood; to be sustained by the beauty and fruitfulness of one's local landscape and the work and companionship of one's neighbors, can be experienced as holy gifts and occasions for gratitude and praise of God."[18] Wild attributed much of the organizational stability of the Madison Christian Community to the environmental activities that fostered a sense of place among its members. At the time of this study, most North American churches were shrinking, but the Madison Christian Community had a stable, multigenerational membership. Consequently, Reverend Wild felt a calling "to talk about a sense of place" and share insights about the benefits of place-based ministry with other pastors. To that end, he worked with theologian Peter Bakken to develop an adult education curriculum for congregations,[19] and together they wrote a book called *Church on Earth: Grounding Your Ministry in a Sense of Place*. Thus, the experiences of a pastor who promoted an earth-care social norm in his community were offered as a resource for other ministers seeking to build religious ministries that would be meaningful for modern Americans.

SUMMARY AND DOMAIN INTERACTIONS

How Faith Leaders Affected Initiatives

FAITH LEADERS MADE AN ESSENTIAL CONTRIBUTION to the initiatives by legitimating sustainability as a faith issue, thereby making earth care an appropriate area of activity within the context of a faith community. Chapter 5 described the message frames that faith leaders used to define sustainability as a faith issue and, in particular, to explain why it fit into a community's sense of identity. Chapter 6 examined the mechanisms through which they presented those messages to the members of their faith communities. This section summarizes the findings of the two chapters and describes the domain interactions through which faith leader contributions affected development of sustainability initiatives.

FOSTERING A SUSTAINABILITY SOCIAL NORM

Faith Leaders legitimated sustainability as a faith issue and defined it as an appropriate area of activity for their communities through their dual roles as religious authorities and organization managers. Domain interactions contributed to the efficacy of faith leader actions: their advocacy for faith-based earth care influenced champions and congregations, and they exercised their dual roles within the context of the religious organization. (see Table 11).

In the role of religious authority, faith leaders drew on theological teachings from their respective traditions to explain that earth care is incumbent on people of faith who want to live in accord with their religion's values. They also personalized earth care by linking it with specific ministries already practiced by their faith communities. In addition, they made the idea of earth care more accessible by evoking historical traditions of religious leadership in advocating for social change, which suggested that people of faith could make a special contribution to the great work of building a more environmentally sustainable society.

TABLE 11 FAITH LEADER CONTRIBUTIONS AND
THEIR INTERACTIONS WITH OTHER DOMAINS

MECHANISMS FOR LEGITIMATING SUSTAINABILITY AS A FAITH ISSUE	EFFECTS ON THE INITIATIVE	INTERACTIONS WITH OTHER DOMAINS
Religious Authority: Religious messages (sermons, blogs, newsletters) connect earth care to: Theology Community identity Special role of faith communities	Legitimated sustainability as a faith issue requiring community action by connecting it with community values	*Champions:* strengthened commitment *Congregation:* increased support *Organization:* opportunities to share religious messages
Religious Authority: Public affirmations (announcements, celebrations) Rituals	Integrated earth care into religious practices	*Congregation:* increased support *Organization:* opportunities for adding earth care to practices
Organizational management: Authorization, advice, advocacy within the community	Facilitated action in a faith community	*Champions:* increased efficacy *Congregation:* increased support *Organization:* venue for organizational management

In their role as organization managers, faith leaders were able to help integrate sustainability into the practices of their religious organizations. They had the authority to approve formation of environmental task forces focused on specific projects and to authorize discernment processes to explore adoption of earth care as a community mission. They could also advocate for support of sustainability initiatives with boards of directors and ministry committees. Finally, due to their comprehensive knowledge of religious organizations, they were able to advise individuals about how to take action within the context of a faith community.

These messages legitimating sustainability and promoting earth-care action were shared through multiple mechanisms that combined to foster a sustainability social norm. Religious messages presented through sermons, blogs, newsletters, and study groups connected earth care to a faith community's values. Earth care was also integrated into religious practices through public affirmations such as announcements and celebrations, as well as rituals that drew attention to the actions taking place within the faith community. By raising the visibility of community earth-care activities, faith leaders fostered the perception that sustainability was part of the community's social norms, its behavioral practices, and not just an abstract theological principle. Furthermore, by reminding members of upcoming events, they provided information about how people could engage in earth-care action. Thus, religious messages explained why earth care fit into a faith community's values, and public affirmations helped integrate earth care into religious practices, thereby encouraging members to participate in initiatives.

DOMAIN INTERACTIONS

The mechanisms through which faith leaders promoted earth care as an area of activity for their faith communities interacted with other domains to contribute to development of initiatives. Champions who participated in initiatives described the support of faith leaders as a key element in their success because it raised awareness and increased congregational involvement. Implicit in their comments is a second vital effect: faith leader support affected the champions themselves. Religious messages and public affirmations strengthened individuals' commitment to environmental efforts by validating their actions as expressions of religious life. This positive feedback created a sense of satisfaction both through external validation and the internal satisfaction of living their values. When Lynn Cameron described the importance of her pastor's support and mentioned that Reverend Ann Held "shows us off at mission meetings, tells people about the work we are doing," one can hear the gratification that comes from this validation of Trinity's Earth Care House Church.[1] As noted in Chapter 4, religious messages from faith leaders also helped sustain champions so they could persevere in the face of challenges. For example, Reverend Held's maxim that "God calls us to be faithful, not successful" not only motivated members of the House Church to tackle the complex problem of air pollution, it provided comfort when some projects did not go well. Malcolm Cameron noted that this message was "particularly important for issues where we've tried and failed."[2] Interviewees at Anshe Emeth Memorial Temple made a similar comment about the importance of their rabbi's encouragement after they organized an interfaith Earth Day event that few members of their congregation attended.

His reassurance that their efforts were valuable in spite of the low congregational involvement helped them continue their work.

The religious organization, as the context in which initiatives developed, offered opportunities for faith leaders to promote earth care by exercising their roles as religious authorities and organizational managers. As will be discussed in more detail in the Organization section, organizational structures provided the worship service and newsletter venues through which faith leaders shared messages about earth care as a faith issue. Similarly, the governance structures of the religious organizations were the venues in which faith leaders authorized initiatives and advocated for support from boards and other committees. Finally, it was knowledge of the religious traditions and governance practices of their religious organizations that enabled faith leaders to advise sustainability champions about appropriate options for integrating earth care into their faith communities.

Contributions by faith leaders were particularly crucial for the development of initiatives because their actions affected the levels of congregational support. They framed earth care as a faith issue that required action in ways that resonated with their communities, grounding it in theology and relating it to extant ministries that expressed community identity. They also made earth care accessible by suggesting people of faith could make a special contribution to the effort to build a more sustainable society through their role as voices of morality. Faith leaders used sermons and newsletters as mechanisms through which to convey messages about how earth care fit into the community's normative values, then encouraged members to act on those values by using affirmations and advice as mechanisms through which to integrate earth care into normative practices. By legitimating sustainability as a faith issue and connecting it with community values and practices, faith leaders encouraged their congregations to adopt earth care as a social norm. Congregational acceptance of an earth-care social norm increased member investment of time, talent, and funds in environmental activities, which were key factors in development and maintenance of initiatives. Figure 3 illustrates the interactions between Faith Leaders and the other three domains.

THE IMPORTANCE OF MESSAGE CADENCE

The efficacy of faith leader efforts to promote earth care in their congregations was affected by the frequency and consistency with which they employed the action mechanisms that were available to them. Message cadence differed

FIGURE 3 Interactions between Faith Leaders and the Other Domains

across cases due to variations in the motivations that inspired faith leaders to promote sustainability, as well as the influence of current events and the liturgical cycles of specific religious traditions. These differing patterns influenced the development and durability of initiatives.

Faith leaders who were passionate about outdoor activities such as camping, gardening, and forestry found spiritual meanings in their engagement with the natural environment, which they then integrated into their pastoral work. Consequently, they returned to environmental themes regularly, year after year, in response to their recurrent personal experiences. Clergy used stories of their experiences with nature in sermons and blogs, while lay faith leaders incorporated nature into retreats and presentations in monastic communities. For example, Reverend Ann Held of Trinity Presbyterian Church, who enjoyed hiking and camping, frequently drew on these experiences to illustrate ethics toward people and the natural world. Judy LePera, a member of Trinity's Earth Care House Church, commented on the consistency of Reverend Held's environmental messages: "Ann has been great about weaving earth care into the services. She does that too often to count."[3]

Faith leaders who did not engage in regular outdoor activities tended to focus on environmental issues such as climate change or health threats from pollution that dovetailed with personal interests in social justice and community wellbeing. In these cases, clergy were most likely to speak about sustainability when circumstances brought environmental issues to their attention. Major news events such as environmental catastrophes and international climate change negotiations inspired periodic homilies with environmental justice themes. Environmental issues could also be temporarily elevated to a higher position on a pastor's ladder of personal concerns due to the need for a new building or the opportunity to achieve certification as a green congregation. Once the desired result had been achieved, sustainability seemed to drop to a lower level in the hierarchy of pastoral themes. This decreased emphasis was not necessarily conscious. When asked whether he would continue to focus on environmental themes now that his congregation had completed its certification, one pastor indicated that he planned to address the topic every few months. Analysis of the sermons he delivered that year, however, showed sustainability was not mentioned.

Liturgical cycles could also trigger presentations with sustainability themes because particular scriptural passages are closely associated with environmental ethics. Rosh Hashanah, the New Year festival that is one of Judaism's major holy days, brings an annual assessment of ethical behavior and a retelling of the creation story, both of which may inspire reflection on the responsibility to care for the earth. Although it is a less important holiday, Tu BiShvat, the spring festival associated with tree planting in Israel, often became an opportunity for a message about earth stewardship. Additionally, the annual cycle of Torah readings could trigger environmental sermons and blogs. For example, a verse on meat eating in the book of Deuteronomy (12.20) inspired Rabbi Rosen to comment on dietary choices that affect the environment,[4] while the *bal tashchit* passage prohibiting destruction of fruit trees (20.19–20) prompted him to deliver a treatise on environmental ethics.[5] Christians were less consistent in connecting sustainability with specific passages in the liturgy, perhaps because the topic does not fit as easily with New Testament readings as with Old Testament texts describing agricultural life in ancient Israel. Nevertheless, both Christians and Unitarian Universalists regularly focused on sustainability during worship services near Earth Day in April.

Variations in the cadence with which faith leaders iterated the importance of sustainability as a faith issue seemed to affect the scope and durability of initiatives: there is evidence that participation in environmental activities fluctuated in communities that did not regularly hear environmentally themed sermons. For example, in three of the four green-certified communities, clergy messages dropped off and green committees disbanded soon after achieving certification. Without regular prompts from the pulpit, committees found it difficult to replace members who moved on to other projects. The fourth green-certified community, in which the Green Committee remained active despite decreased homiletic support, benefited from continuity of lay leadership and a large committee that provided the critical mass necessary to sustain their efforts.

As the differences in durability of the initiatives among the four green-certified cases illustrate, levels of congregational involvement also had significant effects on a faith community's earth-care activities. The introduction to the Faith Leader Domain described motivations that led faith leaders to promote earth care and noted that there was a two-way relationship between faith leaders and congregations. On the one hand, faith leaders who promoted earth care did so by explaining why it should be a topic of interest to their congregations while, on the other hand, faith leaders' incentives to promote earth care were influenced by the level of interest within the congregation. The next section focuses on the Congregation Domain and delves into factors that affected levels of support from the body of members in the case-study communities.

Part IV

CONGREGATIONS

Arbiters of Initiative Capacity

INTRODUCTION

In 2011, the Madison Christian Community (MCC) realized that the future of a core program in their sustainability initiative was in jeopardy. During a community meeting, Pastor Jeff Wild, who had provided the impetus for numerous environmental activities and served as full-time coordinator of the community's extensive garden projects, announced that he could no longer maintain the same level of involvement in the garden and still fulfill his duties as a pastor. He was overextended and "needed to decide if I was a gardener or a minister."[1] The community had a choice: Wild could continue to be the primary organizer of the Children's Garden and do less ministerial work, or the garden programs would have to be scaled back. After some discussion of whether it would be best to replace the Children's Garden with individual plots since there were few volunteers helping with the kids, the community decided that the children's program was important to their religious mission. Consequently, they hired a plant biologist to take over the garden coordination for the first year after Wild stepped down. The biologist systematized plant selection and established organizational systems that made it easier for volunteers to chip in small amounts of time, such as setting up a white board with a list of tasks on the edge of the garden so anyone with some spare time could stop in and lend a hand. Other volunteers took over management of specific garden areas: there were separate coordinators for the lower garden, the upper garden, and the children's program.

According to Sonja Keesey-Berg, the community secretary, the momentary crisis marked an important turning point for the Madison Christian Community's sustainability initiative.[2] When the community had to make a decision about the Children's Garden, it forced them to break out of the lull they had fallen into. Deciding to maintain all of the garden projects meant that the members made a commitment, which led to an increase in the number of volunteers and an expansion of the program; the Children's Garden and the upper garden now produce even more fruits and vegetables for donation to a neighborhood food pantry. In essence, the community took ownership of programs that the pastor had begun and managed for nearly a decade.

This moment of truth at the Madison Christian Community reveals the importance of congregational support for developing and maintaining a sustainability initiative. Individual champions often began the environmental projects in the case-study communities, but the scale and durability of initiatives were affected by levels of support from the congregation, the body of people who make up a faith community. Prior to Pastor Wild's announcement, MCC members were proud of their community's environmental initiative, but many people took the activities for granted and relied on a small group of sustainability champions to make them happen. The 2011 meeting forced the congregation to make a conscious choice about whether they would support the initiative by investing resources of time, energy, and funds. The congregation at MCC decided that creation care was an important part of their community mission, and volunteers stepped up to share the workload.

Across the case-study communities, the level of support initiatives received from congregations affected their capacity by determining what human and material resources were available for implementation and maintenance of environmental activities. As the Madison Christian Community story demonstrates, two key factors affected levels of congregational support: First, whether sustainability was perceived as an expression of a faith community's mission, and second, to what extent the congregation participated in the decision to adopt earth care as an area of community activity. Both factors will be examined in the following chapters.

CHARACTERISTICS OF THE CASE-STUDY CONGREGATIONS

Before delving into these developmental processes, it is important to note some characteristics of the case-study congregations that affected their engagement with earth care (see Table 12). The ten non-monastic congregations (1–10) were predominantly white and middle-class. Recent research has demonstrated that race and class do not necessarily correlate with variations in levels of environmental concern[3] or support for policies to reduce greenhouse gas emissions,[4] however socio-economic status likely contributed to the communities' financial capacity for implementing sustainability initiatives.[5]

With the exceptions of Anshe Emeth Memorial Temple and St. Thomas Aquinas Catholic Parish, the non-monastic faith communities were located in middle-class suburban or urban areas. The Anshe Emeth Memorial Temple building was constructed in 1930 in New Brunswick, an urban area that gradually shifted from middle to lower income. Although the members migrated to more affluent residential suburbs, in the 1970s the congregation voted to preserve their historic temple in its current location rather than build a new structure in a suburb. That decision was reaffirmed when the faith community elected to renovate and expand the Temple's building in 2006.[6] St. Thomas Aquinas Parish has considerable economic and ethnic diversity in its membership because five parishes were consolidated into one in the 1980s, resulting in a single religious organization serving several neighborhoods with different economic demographics. However, even at St. Thomas Aquinas, middle-class parishioners were prominent among committee leaders and volunteers carrying out the ministry work of the community. All ten cases had a mix of ages, but, like most faith communities in the United States, older members and families with young children made up the majority; young adults were the least represented.

For the five monastic case studies, the term *congregation* is used here to designate the body of members who make decisions about the activities of the community. This includes all members in residence at the monastery or convent but may also include members who live off campus in nearby housing or in small communities located in distant cities where they run ministries such as schools and health clinics. These non-resident members usually travel to the main campus to participate in formal processes for deciding future directions and leadership of their faith communities.

Among these monastic communities, changes in demographic characteristics affected congregational attitudes toward sustainability initiatives. Between

TABLE 12 CONGREGATION CHARACTERISTICS

	FAITH COMMUNITY	DENOMINATION	SIZE	LOCALE
1	Trinity Presbyterian Church (TPC)	Presbyterian Church (USA)	165 members	suburb
2	Madison Christian Community (MCC)	Evangelical Lutheran Church in America and United Church of Christ	400 members	suburb
3	Jewish Reconstructionist Congregation (JRC)	Reconstructionist Jewish	500 families	city
4	First Parish Church of Newbury (FPN)	United Church of Christ	40 members	suburb
5	Vineyard Church of Ann Arbor (VAA)	Evangelical	600 members	suburb
6	St. Thomas Aquinas Parish (STA)	Catholic	1800 families	suburb
7	First Universalist Church of Rockland (UUR)	Unitarian Universalist	159 members	suburb
8	Trinity Presbyterian Church (TNJ)	Presbyterian Church (USA)	350 members	suburb
9	Anshe Emeth Memorial Temple (AET)	Reform Jewish	550 families	city
10	Temple Shalom (TS)	Reform Jewish	300 families	suburb
11	Saint John's Abbey (SJA) Benedictine Men	Catholic	153 monks	rural
12	Congregation of St. Joseph at Nazareth (CJN) Sisters of St. Joseph	Catholic	191 sisters	suburb
13	Villa Maria (VM) Sisters of the Humility of Mary	Catholic	158 sisters	rural
14	Our Lady of Angels (OLA) Sisters of St. Francis of Philadelphia	Catholic	450 sisters	suburb
15	Holy Wisdom Monastery (HWM) Benedictine Women of Madison	Ecumenical Benedictine	3 sisters 350 lay members	suburb

1970 and 2014, the number of Catholic women religious in the United States declined dramatically from approximately 180,000 to about 50,000, a 72 percent change.[7] The number of priests and monks (male religious) has also declined, although at a slower rate of 35 percent. These national trends were mirrored in the membership of the five case sites, where novices entering the communities have become rare. As the median age shifts higher, greater portions of community resources are allocated to senior residential facilities and healthcare. In response to these demographic changes, the communities are finding it necessary to think creatively about how to sustain the hospitals, schools, and social work ministries that they have founded because soon there may not be enough sisters or brothers to run them. Thus, for example, recognition that "there will be no new vowed women" caused the Sisters of the Humility of Mary to decide that they wanted to find ways to live in community with the wider society.[8] Similarly, at Holy Wisdom Monastery, the sisters created a hybrid congregation that includes a non-monastic Sunday Assembly of people who come for worship services as well as the nuns who reside at the monastery (three at the time of this study, six in 2018). Consequently, decisions at Holy Wisdom are made by the sisters in consultation with a board that includes representatives of the non-monastic congregation.

Congregations determine what resources are available for activities undertaken in communities by deciding whether to provide funds, time, and talent to support specific committees and projects. Therefore, congregational support was a significant factor affecting the scope and durability of the sustainability initiatives studied here because of its impact on material and human resources for implementing earth-care activities. The next two chapters examine factors that affected levels of congregational support. Chapter 7 explores circumstances that influenced congregational perceptions as to whether sustainability fit with a community's identity and mission. Chapter 8 looks at ways that involvement in initiatives affected congregations, and what kinds of challenges undermined congregational support for earth-care efforts. The section ends with an analysis of the contributions that supportive congregations made to initiatives.

7 COMMUNITY IDENTITY AND CONGREGATIONAL SUPPORT

So much of the sustainability ethic was already in place that it was just a matter for me to become aware of it and build on it.
—REVEREND JEFF WILD, Madison Christian Community

SUPPORT FROM THE CONGREGATIONS significantly affected the development and maintenance of sustainability initiatives in the case-study communities. Initiatives in communities with high levels of support had more participants, included a greater variety of activities, and were more durable. Moreover, high levels of congregational support facilitated establishment of earth care as a new social norm, a behavioral expectation for members. One of the factors that affected the level of congregational support was the extent to which congregation members perceived earth care as a community issue rather than the purview of a core group of environmentalists. Cross-case analysis indicates that this perception emerged as faith leaders and sustainability champions presented earth care as an activity that aligned with a community's identity and, therefore, fit into its mission. Aspects of community history that came to be defined as precursors to earth care often provided foundations for perceiving sustainability as an issue that fit into community identity.

CONNECTING EARTH CARE WITH COMMUNITY IDENTITY

Integrating sustainability into a community's sense of identity was a key step in the process of reaching the perception that earth care was an issue for the entire community. Webpages on which faith communities describe "Who we are" indicate their identities are comprised of two essential elements: 1) the religious tradition, with its particular beliefs and rituals; and 2) the history of the faith community. The previous section described the role of faith leaders in addressing the first element by making connections between sustainability and a community's religious tradition. In particular, it noted that faith leaders not only framed earth care as a faith issue due to its alignment with scriptural teachings, they also linked it with community identity by emphasizing that caring for the earth was related to the religious ministries through which the community put its faith into action. Thus, they connected earth care to a community's religious values and practices.

Comparison of the cases indicates that the second element, community history, influenced whether congregation members were likely to embrace the idea of a connection between earth care and community identity. Each congregation had stories of its founding and historical traditions that set it apart from other houses of worship. In several of the case studies, practices from these histories came to be seen as precursors to earth care. Thus, in addition to the widespread focus on extant social justice and service ministries as foundations for an environmental ethic (described in Chapter 5), champions fostered congregational support by invoking prior environmental activities and historical land uses as means to demonstrate that earth care fit into a community's identity (see Table 13).

TABLE 13 FOUNDATIONS FOR EARTH CARE IN COMMUNITY IDENTITY

FOUNDATIONS FOR EARTH CARE	NON-MONASTIC CASES	MONASTIC CASES	TOTAL
Previous environmental activities	1	1	2
Historical land use	1	5	6
Social justice and service ministries	10	5	15

BUILDING ON PREVIOUS ENVIRONMENTAL ACTIVITIES. In two cases, congregational support was fairly easy to cultivate because previous environmental activities had laid the foundations for an environmental ethic. The Madison Christian Community had long engaged in land stewardship and outdoor activities, although these had not been formally defined as environmental/sustainability projects. The Sisters of St. Joseph at Nazareth also had a history of environmental activities undertaken by one member that gradually came to be seen as evidence of a congregational environmental ethic. These pre-existing traditions facilitated adoption of earth care as a new social norm for the Madison Christian Community and Sisters of St. Joseph.

Pastor Wild said that the sustainability initiative at the Madison Christian Community took root and grew quickly because "so much of the sustainability ethic was already in place that it was just a matter for me to become aware of it and build on it."[1] In David Keesey-Berg's history of MCC, he describes how gratitude for the original gift of land, donated just as the two congregations were struggling to find resources to begin their ecumenical community,[2] made attention to the land part of the community's spirituality. This foundational experience, in which their land seemed a miraculous gift, formed the basis for a "creation spirituality" embraced by members and pastors.[3]

The community developed a number of practices through which they expressed their sense of connection between religion and nature, the most visible of which is the cultivation of restored prairie on part of their six-acre grounds. When the building was expanded, the earth displaced in the construction process was mounded along the front edge of the property in the shape of a bird with outstretched wings. The congregants saw the bird shape as a way to honor the native peoples who had once lived in the area and practiced lifestyles that were in harmony with the earth. MCC members planted the mounded earth with native prairie plants, a project that required them to gather seeds from remnant prairie patches along railroads and on "goat prairies," hillsides too steep for cultivation. A few years later, a second prairie restoration project covered a gently sloping acre of land on the east side of the property. The two prairie areas are labeled with signs so those who visit or live nearby will understand that the non-lawn landscape is intentional and meaningful. The Madison Christian Community website describes the symbolism of this land stewardship:

> [P]art of our mission to care for our earth, this prairie preserves a part of the natural diversity that thrived before European settlers came to this part of southern Wisconsin. It provides cover for small mammals, insects, and birds that are losing their habitat as the west side of Madison develops. Walking in this small prairie, we can experience the land as our ancestors did when they first saw this "sea of grass."[4]

Community members labor to maintain these restored prairies. During the growing season, volunteers come for a few hours each Saturday and, every few years, controlled burns help replicate the natural conditions vital to regeneration of prairie plants.

The community's environmental ethic was further developed by ministers who perceived nature as a place for religious experiences. Dan Schmiechen, the first Community of Hope (UCC) pastor at MCC, established a tradition of taking high school youth on an annual trip to the Boundary Waters of Minnesota. Another pastor was fascinated by wildlife tracking and brought ideas from that skill into his homilies. With this background, Keesey-Berg said, environmental awareness was "very much a part of the spirituality of the community, and out of it morphed concern for climate change" and other environmental issues.[5]

These pre-existing environmental activities, which were unusual among the cases studied, help explain why the two congregations that make up the Madison Christian Community were so supportive of Pastor Wild's sustainability initiative. When the minister suggested putting in a wind turbine to reduce reliance on fossil fuels, his proposal struck a chord. Within months, a task force was exploring renewable energy options. Member participation on the task force and financial contributions to purchase solar panels are two indicators of congregational support, but the aspect of the project that is especially noteworthy concerns behavior change. The task force examined energy use in the church buildings and created a list of recommendations for conserving energy, such as ensuring that the sanctuary lights were turned off before starting the dishwasher in the kitchen. These recommendations were immediately adopted and have become standard procedures for members of the church, an indication of strong member support for enacting earth care values.

Community history also facilitated development of the Children's Garden project. When Pastor Wild first proposed creation of the garden, he imagined it as a means for building a connection between the church and people beyond the congregation. His idea to create a garden did not, however, emerge from thin air; there was already a thriving neighborhood garden on the church property. This community garden had been established in 1973, when twenty-one families responded to a proposal to make plots available for church members. In the 1990s, as the area near the church developed into a residential neighborhood, open plots in this "lower garden" were periodically made available to non-members through the Community Action Coalition, a community action agency dedicated to reducing poverty.[6] Thus, since the lower garden had gradually evolved into a neighborhood garden where church members and the wider community interacted, there was precedent for using a garden to foster relationships among church members and between the church and external community. This previous history meant that gardening was already part of the community identity at the Madison Christian Community, which made it more likely that the congregation would perceive support for the Children's Garden as a part of its community religious practice.

For the Sisters of St. Joseph at Nazareth, congregational support for adoption of formal sustainability initiatives also seems to have been enhanced by previous environmental activities that linked earth care with community identity. When she was a biology teacher at Nazareth College, Sister Ginny Jones helped organize the first Earth Day celebrations in the town of Kalamazoo in 1970 and established the Bow in the Clouds Nature Preserve on the convent campus in 1973. These projects became part of the historical record of the congregation's contributions to the wider community. Participation in environmental education expanded to include more of the sisters in 1990, when the congregation's leadership team asked Jones to develop an environmental ministry. The resulting eco-spirituality programs introduced the sisters to theological teachings about the interconnectedness of all life on earth, which they incorporated into their mission to work "that all may be one" in God. Eco-spirituality retreats often included outdoor work in the Bow in the Clouds Preserve or on the grounds, which created hands-on experiences with earth care similar to those taking place in the prairie and gardens at the Madison Christian Community. These teachings and experiences influenced the congregation's decisions to require that the farmers who leased their land follow organic farming practices and to take some land out of production for restoration of wildlife habitat. The land stewardship practices established earth care as a community value that paved the way for integrating sustainability into the religious organization through practices such as resource conservation and green energy purchases.

REFRAMING HISTORICAL LAND USES. For the Madison Christian Community, previous environmental activities, especially land stewardship, served as an effective foundation for integrating sustainability into community identity. Similar patterns were evident in all five monastic cases, where congregational support for initiatives was strengthened by reframing historical land uses as evidence for a community heritage of sustainable land stewardship. The monastic communities developed narratives that rooted their new environmental ethics in stories of their founding and past practices of forestry and agriculture.

When Father Paul Schwietz presented the idea for turning 2,400 acres of land at Saint John's Abbey into an educational arboretum, he described the project as a way the monastic community could "strengthen the witness of our commitment to sustainability."[7] For the monk who would come to be known as the "Padre of the Pines," land stewardship was an expression of a sustainability ethic that was part of his community's identity. He stated that "Our stewardship is rooted in Gospel values and the vow of stability. Thus, designating our property as an arboretum springs from who we are as a monastic community. In a transitory and disposable culture, we witness/proclaim stability, longevity, and sustainability."[8]

Even though Schwietz saw the arboretum as a natural extension of abbey practices, he met resistance from his community because some monks were concerned about changes that would come with it. Schwietz and his supporters embarked on an eleven-year campaign to build community support for the Abbey Arboretum, which was formally established in 1997. A key element of that campaign came from the combination of Benedictine heritage and abbey history. Schwietz and the abbot cited the 1,500-year-old Benedictine tradition of stability, in which monks remained in one place and often farmed their lands in order to be economically self-sufficient, as the basis for a heritage of land stewardship that had shaped Saint John's Abbey. The Bavarian monks who established the abbey in the Avon Hills of Minnesota in 1864 selected the location because it provided resources for a self-sufficient community: lumber for building the abbey and college and to supply a furniture woodshop; fuelwood for heat and making bricks; fields for crops; water power for milling grain; pasturage for livestock; and trees to produce maple syrup.

Over time, shifting community needs had led to changes in land use as unused farmland reverted to forest. By the mid-twentieth century, concrete replaced wood in construction of buildings while fuelwood gave way to coal and, later, natural gas. In spite of the changes, Father Schwietz and those who supported his vision of creating an educational arboretum were able to cite the abbey's history of forestry and farming to argue that sustainable land management was part of their community heritage. The abbey website emphasizes this heritage theme in its description of the arboretum history: "The pioneer monks carefully managed the surrounding forests, fields, and lakes to provide shelter and food for the community while at the same time preserving these resources for our enjoyment today."[9] Arboretum advocates also stressed that the abbey had a long tradition of scientific woodland management. Some of the founding monks had relatives who worked as foresters in Germany and provided management advice to their brethren. In 1894 a tornado knocked down trees on abbey grounds, and comrades in Germany sent seeds of Norway spruce, Scotch pine, and white pine, which became the earliest documented conifer plantation in Minnesota. The brothers later raised seedlings and planted conifers on former pastureland in the 1930s.[10] By 1949, the abbey had developed a forest management plan that followed Minnesota Department of National Resources recommendations for best practices in management of oak trees. That plan formalized a tradition of seeking out expert advice in order to manage the forest in accord with the latest knowledge, which provided a natural foundation for developing an educational arboretum that would demonstrate sustainable land management practices.

The tree-planting history rooted the monks to long-term care for the land. In spring of 2003, Brother Christian Breczinski, OSB, helped plant northern white cedars as a barrier between the Arboretum and Interstate 94. In an interview with a reporter, he noted that during tree planting events, older monks would tell him about the history of other trees at the abbey:

> When he strolls through the woods with his older confreres, they often point to a towering white pine and tell him, "I planted that tree during my novitiate." Last spring, Br. Christian performed the same ritual. "I can imagine how these cedars will look in 20 or 30 years, but I know I won't live long enough to see them fully mature and that's okay," he reflects. "Someone else will see them and enjoy it. That gives me a sense of peace."[11]

In addition to forestry, many abbey monks engaged in outdoor work and hobbies that contributed to their sense that land stewardship was part of community identity. Activities that connected monks to the natural resources of the abbey included orcharding, woodcutting, beekeeping, maple syrup production, and birdwatching. Brother George Primus, who worked as a bookbinder for the Liturgical Press and as abbey tailor, also served as the unofficial supervisor of the apple orchard and provided fruit for both monks and students. In addition, Primus enjoyed hiking, snowshoeing, and collecting diamond willow, which he used to make walking sticks and other crafts. Asked about his connections with the outdoors, he said, "I enjoy the peaceful surroundings; it's relaxing. But most of all, I love watching things grow. It's miraculous."[12] Because he saw himself as "a woodsman at heart," he was pleased with the efforts to restore areas of oak savanna as a means to fulfill a religious obligation "to take care of what God gives us."[13]

Numerous current activities link monks to their community's historical use of natural resources. Brother Lewis Grobe started a beehive in response to stories about colony collapse disorder, the condition that began decimating crop-pollinating bee populations at the beginning of the twenty-first century. Beekeeping had been a major activity at the abbey in the 1940s and 1950s, with over 100 hives producing honey and beeswax for candles. The resurgent interest in honey production derived from a combination of popular environmental concern about loss of bees and interest in recreating a piece of abbey history. Grape growing and produce gardening followed similar patterns. In the early 1900s, an abbey monk crossed a Minnesota wild grape with a Concord grape to create the "Alpha Grape," a hybrid that could survive Minnesota winters. The abbey preserved this heritage by maintaining a stand of the Alphas on a pergola in the monastery gardens, but grape cultivation ended long ago. Then, in 2005, the landscape manager revived the tradition with ten new varieties of grapes, which are used for making wine, jelly, and juice.[14] There is also a revival of food production because the mainstream farm-to-table movement inspired several monks to take up gardening. The abbey's ten-acre truck garden had been discontinued decades ago, when rising labor costs and commercial competition made it uneconomical, but the new gardeners are motivated by concerns about food quality and reducing reliance on an unsustainable commercial agricultural system rather than profit.

These diverse personal experiences of gardening and tree planting created a pool of monks who were sympathetic to the idea that resource stewardship was part of the abbey lifestyle. Their connections to the land, along with Schwietz' invocation of stories about the abbey's founding and history of resource management, contributed to the community's growing perception of sustainability as a value that fit with their community heritage. Thus, community history and personal environmental activities helped build congregational support for adopting sustainability as a community ethic, and that is now part of the official abbey mission. The website for Saint John's Abbey describes the community as a group of men who, "Seek God through a common life of prayer, study, and work, giving witness to Christ and the Gospel, in service to the church and the world. Called together by Christ, we support each other under the Rule of Saint Benedict and our abbot. Our life together encourages learning, creativity in the arts and trades, and *care for God's creation* (emphasis added)."[15]

The history of a religious organization's founding and members' experiences of working on the land were also important contributors to congregational support for the sustainability initiative at Villa Maria. When Sister Barbara O'Donnell was trying to figure out how to act on her calling to educate for the earth, she began to research Villa Maria history. In the archives, she came across some loose pages that had been written by Father Begel, the priest who founded the Sisters of the Humility of Mary (HM) and accompanied the first members when they migrated from France and settled on land near Youngstown, Pennsylvania, in 1864. During its early years, the community practiced subsistence farming while gradually building a school and medical clinic. Much to O'Donnell's delight, Begel described the original state of the lands and also recorded his plans for creating agricultural fields, planting an orchard, and establishing vineyards. Along the way, he described how to manage the forests, stating which trees had value for food, construction, or fuel, and how to use decayed organic matter (compost) and manure for fertilizer.[16]

These notes became the basis for an organic gardening initiative. They provided evidence of a heritage that made it possible for O'Donnell to say to other women in her order, "See, it's not a whim. This project is true to our charism[17] and history. As women of humility, we should have an interest in humus."[18] The history of the convent also included development of a farming operation that provided income to the community from 1955 to 1983. At its height, it was the largest diversified farm in the area, with 11,000 laying hens, 500 hogs, 75 head of beef cattle, 300 acres of grain, and 12 acres of orchards. During that period, one advantage the Villa had over other farms was a ready supply of labor from novices who were required to work there during their first year in the order. The young women were assigned to gather eggs and pick beans. The farm was drastically scaled back in 1983, when industrialization of agriculture and declining numbers of novices made it difficult to compete for market shares. Moreover, malodorous farm operations were incompatible with the residential high school and retreat center that had been constructed to fulfill the sisters' new ministry interests.

Even though the farm operations ceased, most of the sisters in the order shared the experience of having worked on the farm during their novitiate, which gave them a personal connection to the agricultural heritage of the community. According to John Moreira, land manager at the time of this study, the mother superior once told him that she hated digging potatoes as a novice but she also considered that experience to be "part of who she is."[19] These personal experiences on the farm gave the women a sense of connection to the land of Villa Maria, the place where they trained for their vocations, spent time in periodic spiritual retreat during their careers in education and health care, and the place to which they would eventually retire to live out their final years in community.

O'Donnell built on this foundation of attachment to the Villa by educating her community about the founders' efforts to cultivate the land and the history of their land's management. In partnership with Frank Romeo, the long-time land manager who had been affiliated with the Villa since childhood, she organized community education activities. She and Romeo gave presentations about Villa history and described how care for the land connected with the order's spiritual traditions. Romeo led "boundary tours," in which a group would visit sections of the property by car and foot to learn about the diverse ecosystems of meadow, wetland, and forest that belonged to their community. Prior to O'Donnell's initiative, land management was a background activity carried out by staff, and few of the sisters ventured beyond the residential campus and gardens. As they learned more about the history of their community and its lands, the women developed an active interest in protecting the property under their care. This new awareness of their heritage, combined with novitiate experiences of farm work that connected them to the land, contributed to implicit congregational support for land stewardship, including both organic farming and sustainable forestry, as activities that fit their community identity. Eventually, that connection between heritage and land care became explicit as it was incorporated into a formal Land Ethic that defined sustainability as a community mission: "We, Sisters of the Humility of Mary, claim our history of being connected to the land of Villa Maria, Pennsylvania. Our Land Ethic is rooted in and flows from Scripture, HM heritage and charism, church documents, Catholic Social Teaching, and contemporary theology and spirituality. It affirms the prophetic call to ecological sustainability and nonviolence in all our relationships."[20] This Land Ethic is designed to serve as "a guide for decisions made by the entire congregation and by those in congregational leadership regarding the land for which we are responsible."[21]

Historical land management also provided foundations for adoption of sustainability ethics by the women of Holy Wisdom Monastery, Nazareth, and Our Lady of Angels, all three of which owned farmland that was eventually taken out of production as needs changed. In the early 1950s, a small group of Benedictine sisters established the monastery that would come to be known as Holy Wisdom on 138 acres of land in the hilly countryside north of Madison. The land had previously been farmed, and the sisters, who were running a high school/retreat center, continued to lease much of the land for agricultural use. Their land management followed contemporary soil conservation practices, a history that was later interpreted as a precursor to their current creation care mission. Neal Smith, the monastery's former financial adviser and long-time community participant, described the evolution of monastery management practices in a newsletter article explaining that the sisters had a long tradition of caring for the land:

> Until the sisters owned the property, the land was farmed, and only a few trees existed on the initial parcel. The process of returning the land to a more pre-settlement existence soon began. It started with the gradual elimination of farming, developing a plan to attract native wildlife and planting trees and bushes. In the early 1970s, conservation practices began, including the contouring and planting of grass waterways in the areas still farmed. With the 1980s came the conversion of highly erodible hillsides to woodland and savanna areas, using the government Conservation Reserve Program (CRP).[22]

Smith's account of historical land care emphasizes replacement of farming with ecosystem restoration; however the timeline indicates that the sisters were not opposed to farming during the first four decades of the monastery. Farming did not actually cease until after 1995, when the Benedictine Women decided to make earth care a central focus of their mission and developed a master plan for the grounds that included the decision to "eliminate the balance of the farming lands and restore all possible acres to native prairie and wetlands."[23] As the sisters incorporated creation care into their mission, the past history of land management, with its emphasis on soil conservation and application of sustainable agricultural practices, was reframed to emphasize a community heritage of land stewardship.

Like Villa Maria, the Sisters of St. Francis, who founded Our Lady of Angels in the hills near Philadelphia in 1973, farmed part of their 298 acres to feed their community. In the 1950s, when an arsonist burned their barn, they decided not to rebuild because they had greater need for educational facilities to train nuns for their core work in academic, medical, and administrative fields. They constructed a college on former farmland, and, over the years, the college expanded while the fields shrank. Although very few of the remaining sisters worked on the farm, that agricultural history contributed to community support for creation of Red Hill Farm, a community-supported agriculture venture on six acres of their land. Similarly, among the Sisters of

St. Joseph, many of the women who retired to the motherhouse at Nazareth in southwestern Michigan had fond memories of working in the orchards during their novitiate days. Sister Ginny Jones also recalled that retreat participants had contributed a great many "woman hours" of labor to build the earthen berm on the edge of the Bow in the Clouds Nature Preserve. Through these labors, the women became personally invested in care for their lands.

Thus, even in communities where participation in farming and forestry did not approach the scale of congregational activity at Saint John's Abbey and Villa Maria, members did have personal experiences of gardening and landscaping on community grounds that contributed to a desire to protect their lands. According to Prioress Mary David Walgenbach of Holy Wisdom, "Our sisters came here in the 1950s and bought the first forty acres. Then they bought ninety acres more in the 1960s. They planted trees and did gardening and took good care of the land, so periodically someone would want to buy part of it and they always said 'no.' "[24]

Walgenbach's comment reveals an additional motive for congregational support of earth care: the desire to protect beloved lands from development.[25] Her community took up the project of restoring prairie on former farmland partly in response to new developments on lands bordering the monastery that were causing runoff pollution into Lake Mendota. Similarly, Sister Corinne Wright, manager for the sustainability initiatives at Our Lady of Angels, commented that development was a cause of widespread concern in her community:

> People that pay attention see the demands on the land. For example, the township wanted to use some of our land to build a ball field, and Neumann University [the college built on the convent's former agricultural lands] wanted another field for soccer. We were trying to do earth ministry and ended up in conflict with all these people who wanted to put our property to use. We didn't want to develop the last few acres of forest; we wanted to protect the land and preserve it as habitat.[26]

Some members of the Sisters of St. Francis of Philadelphia had already begun doing environmental education work, but the development pressures during the 1990s helped increase community interest in doing more to protect the environment. Consequently, in 1996, the leadership team assigned the environment as a topic to be considered during the community discernment process, and the congregation developed a formal environmental initiative as part of their mission. Wright stressed that the Franciscan community was willing to participate in civic projects that would not change the land, such as creation of walking trails, but felt it important to preserve habitat for the animals and birds that St. Francis had called brother and sister.

LINKING SUSTAINABILITY TO SOCIAL JUSTICE AND SERVICE MINISTRIES. Previous environmental activities and historical land-use practices enhanced efforts to demonstrate that earth care fit into community identity, however, only six of the cases could draw on such precursors to sustainability. The other cases had to look elsewhere within their community practices to find a framework for fitting earth care into community identity, and the most prevalent motif in these nine cases was to posit connections between earth care and the ministry work through which a community fulfilled its religious mission. As Chapter 5 demonstrated, faith leaders made these connections by describing earth care as a form of social justice or community service. This message resonated in the case-study communities, all of which had long-standing traditions of service ministry. Among the non-monastic cases, the communities had justice or community service ministries that were usually managed by committees of volunteers from the congregation, while the monastic communities employed congregation members as staff to administer service ministries. Through these ministries, community members worked to provide food, housing, job training, education, and healthcare to low-income people in the US and developing countries. Linking earth care with the ministries through which these communities enacted their religious values was an effective means to demonstrate to congregation members that sustainability fit into their community identity.

PLACE AND COMMUNITY IDENTITY

The emphasis on community identity as expressed through founding stories, histories, and previous traditions of ministry work reveals an additional factor that contributed to congregational support for sustainability initiatives: these stories are reminders that these communities of faith are also communities of place. The members' sense of community identity was tied to histories of actions in particular places. Framing sustainability as a means to care for those places resonated with the congregations.

Attachment to place might seem most obvious for monks and nuns who live and work in their communities and engage in land stewardship activities; because they are caring for the places where they will spend their lives, they are motivated to protect their lands from development that would dramatically transform the character of the landscape. Sarah McFarland Taylor has described the sustainability activities of green sisters as a process of "reinhabiting" the landscape. The term was coined by bioregional environmental philosophers to describe a process of relearning how to "live in place" by developing communities that are integrated into their local ecosystems and work to conserve and restore natural resources for the welfare of present and future generations.[27] Taylor expands this idea of reinhabiting to include place, religion, and culture. The sisters not only reinhabit the physical landscape, they also reinhabit the vows and missions of their religious orders by integrating earth care into them and reinhabit their community culture by greening their daily practices.[28] Hence, being part of a residential community with historical ties to a landscape would naturally create a sense of place attachment that could lead to a desire to practice land stewardship and other green actions.

Recognizing the significance of this sense of place in the monastic cases draws attention to place attachment as a factor in the non-monastic cases. It elucidates the Jewish Reconstructionist Congregation's decision to tear down and replace their building rather than move, even though selling and using the proceeds to purchase another building would have been less expensive. It helps explain why the congregation of the First Parish Church of Newbury chose to stay and embark on a new mission of earth care even though they had shrunk to a tiny membership and faced enormous maintenance costs for their nineteenth-century church building. And it was a prominent theme in the First Universalist Church of Rockland's efforts to support local farmers and fishermen.

Place attachment seems to have been a factor in decisions to take action and implement earth-care efforts through the venues of these faith communities: the members wanted their places of worship to express their community values. These communities of faith were also communities of place for which the house of worship and its setting were elements of community identity. Thus, communities with land holdings instituted sustainable land management activities that fit with their heritage as stewards of land resources, while those with smaller properties started community gardens that fit with traditional ministries in poverty alleviation and food ministry. Some communities undertook large green building projects, while others retrofitted old buildings or installed solar panels to reduce their carbon emissions and protect the poor from the effects of climate change. Those without resources for large infrastructure projects adopted conservation practices to reduce use of energy and water in their buildings and grounds and used space in their buildings to sponsor educational programs to teach about earth care. They also created displays about earth care for public spaces in their houses of worship. Through these activities, the places associated with faith community identity became venues for enacting the earth care ethic of the congregation.

Earth care both expressed place attachment and fostered place attachment. As a component of community identity, earth care motivated some members to engage in sustainability initiatives through their place of worship while, at the same time, participation in environmental activities increased place attachment for many people. Volunteers who tended gardens, restored prairies, planted trees, weatherized buildings, and served as docents for green building tours felt a deep connection to the lands and buildings they cared for. Hands-on land stewardship cultivated a community identity so strongly rooted in the prairies and gardens of the Madison Christian Community that interviewees spoke extensively about their outdoor earth care activities while rarely mentioning the energy conservation features of their lovely building unless asked about them. Similarly, members of the Jewish Reconstructionist Congregation became deeply invested in their place during their green building project, with the result that the congregation now identifies itself as the People of the Green Synagogue. These communities of faith are also communities of place where attachment to place has been enhanced by the activities through which the congregations engage in earth care.

EFFECTS:
INTEGRATING EARTH CARE INTO COMMUNITY IDENTITY

Chapter 5 examined the messages through which faith leaders defined earth care as an issue that fit into a community's religious identity and, therefore, required action from community members. Faith leaders legitimated sustainability as a religious issue by connecting it to their community's values and practices; they drew on theological precepts to explain that people of faith had a moral responsibility to take action and pointed out that earth care was consistent with pre-existing ministries in social justice and community service. This chapter provided examples of cases in which previous activities that served as precursors to earth care contributed to congregation members' perception of whether earth care fit community identity (see Table 14) The influence of previous environmental activities and historical land uses were particularly evident among the cases where land stewardship became a significant area of environmental activity. Stories of founders who practiced pre-modern, sustainable farming and forestry provided a basis for claiming a heritage of land stewardship and adopting modern sustainable resource management practices. These community histories increased congregational support for earth care by encouraging members to see sustainability as a community practice rather than an activity for a small group of environmentalists. They also explain the popularity of activities such as organic gardening, community supported agriculture, beekeeping, and sustainable forestry, which replicated historical practices.

TABLE 14 FACTORS THAT CONTRIBUTED TO CONGREGATIONAL SUPPORT

FACTORS	BENEFITS	EFFECTS
Previous environmental activities	Able to build on a pre-existing environmental ethic	Extensive member participation Development of related activities
Historical land uses	Connected earth care with community heritage	Foundation for land stewardship and resource management
Social justice and service ministries	Perception earth care fit into community mission	Extensive member participation Connect with other committees
Place attachment	Faith community as venue for earth care	Two-way relationship: place attachment inspired earth care and participation in earth care strengthened place attachment

In cases without overtly environmental past activities, champions and faith leaders associated earth care with extant ministries in social justice and community service. Since justice and service activities were more common than environmental activities among the cases studied, it is not surprising that messages linking earth care with social ministries were the most widely used means of connecting sustainability with community identity, especially among non-monastic communities. These messages resonated with members who actively supported or participated in justice and service work and helped increase congregational perception that earth care was a community activity, not just an environmental project for a core group. The case of Trinity Presbyterian Church in East Brunswick illustrates this process.

The congregation had no previous environmental activities or land use heritage to provide a foundation for integrating earth care into their community identity, however study and reflection convinced them that none of their ministries in poverty alleviation or peace could be achieved without also addressing environmental issues. Consequently, there was widespread support from the congregation when they enrolled in the GreenFaith certification program. Once the community was certified, the Trinity Earth Shepherds started to scale back their initiative, but congregation members protested and made it clear that they wanted the initiative to continue. According to Debbie O'Halloran, "We went to the Session and said, 'Okay, we're certified. Should we keep going?' They were appalled at the suggestion we might stop. It is just part of who we are now."[29]

8 CONGREGATIONAL INVOLVEMENT IN INITIATIVES

You need to bring people along and you need to do it in a way that people are comfortable. Not like it's being imposed on top of them but like they are being involved in the process, and we are learning about it together.
—RABBI BRANT ROSEN, Jewish Reconstructionist Congregation

CONGREGATIONS DETERMINED the capacity of sustainability initiatives through their contributions of human and material resources for enacting earth-care actions, and, therefore, factors that affected a congregation's level of support for earth-care shaped development of initiatives. Faith leaders and sustainability champions drew on extant ministry work and community history to define earth care as an activity that fit into community identity. Whether congregations accepted these ideas and put resources into earth care was influenced by levels of congregational involvement in advancing sustainability as an area of activity. In most of the case-study communities, congregations actively participated in the decision to adopt earth care as a community ethic and had a say in selecting the types of activities to be undertaken. There was, however, a subset of cases in which the congregations did not play an active role in initiative development. These differences in congregational involvement correlate with different levels of congregational support.

CONGREGATIONAL INVOLVEMENT IN ADOPTING EARTH CARE

Congregations were actively involved in the adoption and formation of eleven out of fifteen sustainability initiatives. In five communities that took up earth care when individuals or affinity groups proposed projects to address environmental concerns, congregations formally endorsed these activities as expressions of their community's religious mission. Among six other cases, congregations were actively engaged in the process for adopting earth care as a community-wide ethic, a decision that set the stage for development of sustainability initiatives. Where congregations were involved in adopting earth care, they were also likely to participate in selection of activities through which to implement sustainability initiatives. These eleven cases stand in contrast to two cases in which pastors were solely responsible for authorizing creation of environmental groups and two cases in which boards of directors made the decision to engage in green certification projects with minimal congregational input. Table 15 summarizes the roles various parties played in decisions about adoption of earth care and selecting activities across the cases.

TABLE 15 EARTH-CARE DECISION MAKERS

DECISION	DECIDER	NUMBER OF CASES
1. *Authorize earth care project*	Congregation	5
	Pastor	2
	Board	2
2. *Adopt earth care community ethic*	Congregation	6
3. *Activity selection*	Congregation and green team	7
	Congregation approved green team ideas	4
	Green team only	4

1   *Congregation Authorized Earth-Care Projects*

In five cases, congregations participated in decisions to authorize earth-care projects and, in the process, formally endorsed sustainability as an area of ministry for their faith communities. In two of these cases, individuals with environmental concerns involved their faith communities in development of sustainability initiatives by asking the congregations to approve formation of a green team to implement earth-care actions. In the other three cases, congregations authorized and supported specific projects that grew into full-scale initiatives.

AUTHORIZING EARTH CARE MINISTRY GROUPS. At the First Universalist Church of Rockland, the Earth Team originally came together to participate in projects sponsored by the Maine Council of Churches. Eventually, the team decided they wanted to scale up their efforts and proposed enrolling their church in the Green Sanctuary Program run by the Unitarian Universalist Association, their denominational organization. One of the first steps in this program is to seek congregational support, which the Earth Team did by presenting the idea during the annual community meeting. The congregation had an opportunity to discuss whether earth care fit their mission before voting to pursue certification as a Green Sanctuary and formally adopting sustainability as a community value.

Similarly, the congregation at Trinity Presbyterian Church in Harrisonburg evaluated whether authorizing formation of an Earth Care House Church ministry fit their community mission. Houses churches are small groups formed by lay members who see a ministry need. A new house church is "called" when a group presents a proposal to the congregation for its approval. The proposal is in the form of a covenant, a document that includes a formal mission statement describing the purpose of the house church and information about study and actions that will be undertaken to fulfill that mission (this covenant and process is described in more detail in Chapter 9). If the congregation accepts the proposal, all members of the house church sign the covenant, which is witnessed by the Session (congregation) as well as the communicator and clerk. At the end of the year, members of a house church do an assessment to review how well they met their goals and decide if they will apply to recall their ministry group for the next year. They present their annual review to the congregation, which shares in the decision about whether that particular house church should continue its mission.

Through this covenanting process, the Trinity congregation formally affirmed that earth care was a ministry need in keeping with the mission of Trinity Presbyterian Church. By endorsing the Earth Care House Church, the congregation committed itself to support its mission to "promote Church and community awareness and involvement in restoring the creation."[1] Because the covenant approval and review process recurred each year, the congregation regularly reiterated its endorsement of earth care as an area of ministry and reflected on the accomplishments to which its support had contributed. The strength of the Trinity congregation's support was evident in the longevity of this environmental ministry: at the time of this study, the Earth Care House

Church was the largest house church at Trinity, averaging sixteen members[2] annually (one tenth of the congregation), and had been re-covenanted every year since its formation in 1996.

AUTHORIZING SUSTAINABILITY PROJECTS. The sustainability initiatives at the Madison Christian Community, Jewish Reconstructionist Congregation, and Saint John's Abbey followed slightly different paths than First Universalist and Trinity Presbyterian because they grew up around specific projects to install renewable energy, construct a green building, and establish an educational arboretum instead of formation of an Earth Care ministry group. Nevertheless, these communities had similar levels of congregational involvement in decisions to enact earth care.

The Madison Christian Community's sustainability initiative began with the pastor's suggestion that the church would be a great location for a wind turbine to produce clean energy and reduce greenhouse gas emissions. When an individual at this ecumenical faith community comes up with an idea for a new project, that person checks to see if others share interest in it, and, if so, they form a task force to research costs, benefits, and drawbacks. For any expense over $10,000, the bylaws require that there be a meeting with a quorum of the congregation membership so the congregation can formally approve it. Tom Matthews, church maintenance person, said that the community has spirited discussions about whether to take on proposed projects, but there is trust and respect among them and "nobody gets mad if the decision does not go their way."[3]

Through this process, the community debated the merits of the solar panel project that the energy task force determined was more appropriate than a wind turbine. Consequently, by the time the project was approved, it had full support from the congregation. The solar project set a precedent for congregational backing of additional environmental activities such as the Children's Garden, food pantry garden, and rooftop rainwater collection system. Then, in 2014 when the church needed re-roofing, the congregation was asked to consider whether to reinstall the previous solar panels or increase the size of the array. They collectively decided to increase the array, which now covers the entire south-facing roof area.

Major infrastructure changes can provide an opportunity for environmental action that involves an entire congregation. Because buildings account for approximately 40 percent of annual energy use in the United States,[4] they offer a venue through which to significantly reduce environmental impacts, and because infrastructure changes are expensive, they require widespread congregational support. For the Jewish Reconstructionist Congregation, the resolution to "build green" was only the first step in a community-based process that involved the members in decisions about how to apply green construction practices to their synagogue.

The building process at the Jewish Reconstructionist Congregation began in the traditional way. The board created a building task force to assess options for addressing the inadequacies of their old building, which was no longer large enough. The task force engaged the congregation in extensive discussions about the community's needs and hired a consultant to assess the community's fundraising capacity so they could explore options that balanced needs with financial constraints. After looking at the three options of renovation, moving to a new location, or tearing down the old building and replacing it, the community decided they wanted to create a new building on the old site. About that time, members of the environmental task force attended a presentation on green building and conceived the idea of asking the board to consider building a "green" synagogue. Green building practices include recycling materials from buildings that are deconstructed, minimizing waste and using renewable materials in construction, and creating a structure that conserves energy and water in daily operations. The environmental task force took its idea to the president of the synagogue, and she told them to write a resolution and present it to the board. The task force took the draft resolution to the rabbi, who became excited about the idea of following construction practices that "really reflected the values that are important to us"[5] and provided support by articulating connections between sustainability and Jewish teachings. This encouraged the board to take the idea to the congregation.

The community began a multi-year campaign to raise funds for a new building and provide the congregation with information so it could decide what kind of building to construct. The fundraising materials included information about green construction, describing what green building entailed and how it connected with Jewish values. According to Rabbi Rosen, "That's how it all started. The more we learned about it, the more committed we became— as Americans, as global citizens, as Jews—to this notion of sustainability."[6] Along with the religious message, the task force presented practical information so the community could make an informed decision. Julie Dorfman, who served on the environmental task force, said, "It helped to explain to congregants that the building would cost just five percent more than a conventional structure and would save 40 percent in energy costs in five to ten years over a conventional building."[7] After extensive community discussion to allay members' concerns, the congregation agreed to solicit bids for a green building.

Members were just as thoroughly involved in the adoption of sustainability as an area of activity at Saint John's Abbey, where the scope of the proposed project, to designate 2,400 acres of the abbey as an educational arboretum, would affect the entire community. Decision processes at the abbey emphasize consensus among the monks, which is especially important for issues involving abbey property and resources that are owned communally by the entire monastic body. Moreover, all proposals that affect the abbey must be evaluated for their potential effects on the long-term wellbeing of the monastic community. When Father Paul Schwietz first proposed creation of an arboretum, his vision was not widely supported. According to land manager Tom Kroll, "he had to sell the idea pretty hard" because the monks were concerned that designating the land as an educational arboretum, with programs to be run by Saint John's University, would give the university control over their land.[8]

It took more than a decade of campaigning to gather support among the monks, faculty at Saint John's University, and laypeople from the external community who enjoyed visiting the abbey lands. Finally, in 1995, Abbot Timothy Kelly appointed a committee to explore the idea of an educational arboretum. The Arboretum Task Force, which included representatives of the various interest groups that would be affected by creation of an arboretum, examined how such a project would fit with the abbey mission and the curriculum at Saint John's University and Preparatory School. The report they produced stated that an arboretum would align with the mission of the abbey by fostering spiritual values such as celebrating the beauty of creation, which reflects its divine maker, and providing an environment for repose and contemplation. This assessment reassured monks that opening abbey grounds to outside visitors would not detract from the brothers' use of the land for spiritual practice. The report further emphasized that sustainable land management was itself a means of practicing Benedictine spirituality since Benedictines settle in a particular place and "dedicate themselves to a program of stewardship which encompasses preservation, sustainability and biodiversity."[9] The university would also benefit since an arboretum would be a natural laboratory for field research that would distinguish the school from other colleges. Furthermore, as a project of leadership in the local community, an arboretum could serve as a means to cultivate greater interaction with people outside Saint John's and be a positive instrument of public relations through which the abbey would become better known in association with an endeavor dedicated to the common good.[10]

Due to these potential benefits, the Chapter (the full body of monastic community members) agreed that designating the lands as a natural arboretum would be beneficial and called for a committee to develop an acceptable administrative structure. Schwietz worked with several monks and lay supporters to devise plans for an organizational structure to manage an arboretum and presented a draft proposal to the abbey's Senior Council in March 1997. Council members expressed concerns about the need to more clearly define issues of ownership and authority between the abbey and the university. The plans were revised to address these concerns and presented to the entire Chapter for discussion in April 1997. Only after the Chapter approved the organizational structure did the Saint John's Arboretum became a reality.

Through this lengthy, deliberative process, the entire monastic community participated in the decision to put their community resources into the arboretum initiative. The Chapter (whole community) authorized a representative committee to develop a proposal, which was revised in response to feedback from members of the Senior Council before the committee presented the revised proposal to the Chapter for approval. Along the way, the brothers carefully weighed the benefits and costs of the project and assiduously addressed members' concerns in order to reach consensus. Consequently, by the time the Saint John's Arboretum was dedicated, it had extensive support from the community. Brother John Kulas described the community's affirmation of the arboretum in the ceremony celebrating its establishment on May 9, 1997:

> The entire Saint John's community assembled at the oak savanna to designate and consecrate Abbey lands and waters as the Saint John's Arboretum. Words lauding the preciousness of the natural area were proclaimed. This property was claimed for the extended community of monks, faculty, SJU/CSB students, neighbors, friends, supporters, benefactors—one community in one sacred place.[11]

2 Congregation Adopted an Earth-Care Ethic

Six case-study communities set out on the path toward sustainability by developing formal statements defining earth care as a community mission prior to engaging in extensive environmental activities. These initiatives emerged from mission discernment processes in which congregation members were actively involved in discussing the future mission work of their faith communities. Two of these discussions were triggered by declining membership and concerns about long-term community viability while the remaining four occurred during periods of regular communal reflection.

ADOPTING EARTH CARE AS A COMMUNITY MISSION. The sustainability initiatives at First Parish Church of Newbury and Holy Wisdom Monastery emerged from discernment processes undertaken at a time when the members needed to decide if their communities would continue to exist in their historical locations. In both cases, there was widespread congregational participation in the discussions and decisions about the future of their communities.

When First Parish Church of Newbury embarked on a year-long discernment process, the community was "dying physically, spiritually, and financially."[12] Membership had dropped to about thirty people, and the community was as worn down as its church building, which dated back to 1868. The minister, Reverend Nancy Haverington, initiated a community discernment process in which twenty-five people, almost the whole congregation, met weekly for a year to consider their future. According to the minister, for the first three months they focused on self-analysis: "We conducted a strategic and prayerful look at who we were and what we were about. We took a good hard look at ourselves. We conducted a self-critique. We looked at what we did well, and what we did lousy. We kept putting things on the board."[13]

After this evaluation of their faith community's strengths and weaknesses, the congregation began analyzing local community demographics and researching what other churches in the area were doing so they could assess what they might offer that would distinguish them from other houses of worship. As they brainstormed, they also prayed and reflected together, and listened for the "still small voice"[14] of divine inspiration. In the Congregationalist tradition, each member of a congregation has an equal vote in decisions, but the goal is to reach a consensus rather than practice majority rule because divisions are perceived as evidence that a community has not yet discerned the will of God. The denomination teaches that a community of believers should work together to discern God's will through "habitual study of scripture, habits of worship, and practices of prayer that involve opening the heart as well as listening for clarity."[15] Reverend Haverington described the way the First Parish congregation used this process to discern a shared vision of a new mission: "We started each meeting with a scripture reading, and then we went into silent prayer, asking God what God's purpose was for us. Then someone stood up and stated that they had heard the answer. We were here to be an environmental church. We discussed it right then, and there was unanimous agreement."[16] The idea was put to a vote and approved by the entire congregation; their community adopted a mission to be "Stewards of Earth and Spirit."

In the 1990s, the Benedictine Women of Madison went through a similar experience as they set out to determine whether to continue their monastery in Madison, Wisconsin. Even though the official "congregation" at Holy Wisdom Monastery only comprised two sisters at that time, the discussions involved a wider community of supporters who joined them in a visioning process because, according to Prioress Mary David Walgenbach, "We've always believed in consultation and letting others help us discern how to proceed."[17] Participants included local people, like their long-term financial advisor, as well as academic and monastic religious thinkers from both Catholic and Protestant traditions. These friends and colleagues were invited to the monastery for a meeting in which they were asked to help the sisters envision options for their future. Seven options emerged from the brainstorming session and, after prayer and discussion, the sisters "chose the path that seemed best, with the affirmation of that group."[18]

UPDATING A MISSION TO INCLUDE EARTH CARE. Three women's monastic communities and one Presbyterian church adopted earth care as a mission after exploring the topic during discernment processes focused on updating their areas of ministry. These discernment processes engage congregation members in assessment of a faith community's activities in relation to its mission, thereby making the community responsible for determining what kinds of work it will undertake to express its religious values. In each of the three communities of Catholic women religious, the entire congregation participated in these decisions. Trinity Presbyterian Church in East Brunswick had less direct congregational involvement because the community relied on committee members and elected representatives to make decisions about its future mission emphases. Nevertheless, the Trinity congregation perceived the outcome as an expression of the whole congregation's religious values.

For Villa Maria, Nazareth, and Our Lady of Angels convents, community members participated in evaluation of earth care as a potential area of activity through the periodic Chapter meetings in which the sisters update their ministries in response to changing circumstances.[19] At Villa Maria every four years, the Sisters of the Humility of Mary (HM) hold a Chapter to "reflect on our heritage in light of the times, to set direction and to elect a leadership team to facilitate the implementation of that direction."[20] In 1989, care for environment was identified as a direction for community action, and during the 1990s, groups of sisters participated in Chapter discussions exploring how to reframe the order's vows in relation to cosmology. In study group and community meetings, individuals with environmental concerns shared theological texts that described the cosmos as a divine creation in which all beings are interdependent, thereby creating opportunities for the members to reflect on how the spiritual calling of the Sisters of the Humility of Mary related to sustainability issues.[21] This internal process of reflection on eco-theology and mission was further shaped by Sister Barbara O'Donnell's research into the community's early land care, Frank Romeo's presentations on the HM community's farming heritage, and external news reports on global warming. In 1997, these reflections culminated in the congregation's adoption of a new Direction Statement: "We will claim the depth and significance of our *charism* of humility which connects us with the whole earth community and unites us in our ministries on behalf of the poor."[22]

The Sisters of St. Joseph at Nazareth also adopted a community-wide earth-care ethic during their Chapter meeting in 1989. During the meeting, the community evaluated how to update its directional statement in relation to its founding charism of "unity and reconciliation" as it pertained to the world's current spiritual and environmental conditions. As a result, the members revised their directional statement to include concern for ecological systems as well as human beings, with the understanding that at that time in history, their charism was a "mandate for helping us and others restore a sense of balance and relationship with the whole earth community."[23]

At Trinity Presbyterian Church in East Brunswick, the congregation was less directly involved in adopting earth care as part of its mission. There, a committee of lay church members explored three potential missions and, after study and prayer, recommended to the board that the church adopt earth care as a community-wide mission. The board, comprised of elected elders and the pastor, decided to follow the committee's recommendation. Later, however, the newly formed Trinity Earth Shepherds directly involved the congregation in its environmental initiative. When the Earth Shepherds decided that enrolling in the GreenFaith certification program would better enable the group to fulfill its mission to help Trinity and its members grow in their ability to care for God's creation, they asked all the commission chairs, who were responsible for leading other mission areas of the community, to support the program. Debbie O'Halloran described the importance of engaging the church committee network in their earth-care efforts, saying, "When we joined GreenFaith, we wanted to be sure we had across-the-board support from the congregation so we got all the commission chairs to sign off on it. That was done consciously to make sure they would participate in the process. By getting them to sign off on enrolling in GreenFaith, we got their buy-in."[24]

3 Congregational Involvement in Activity Selection

The eleven cases in which congregations were involved in decisions to approve earth-care projects or adopt an earth-care ethic also had congregational participation in selection of sustainability activities. In some communities, this participation mostly comprised approval of specific projects proposed by green teams, such as solar panels at Madison Christian Community or the organic market garden at Villa Maria. However, in seven cases, congregations were actively involved in proposing topics or selecting actions from a range of options.

After the congregation at First Universalist Church of Rockland voted to enroll in the Green Sanctuary Program, the Green Sanctuary Committee (formerly the Earth Team) invited congregation members to a brainstorming meeting in which they asked about people's environmental concerns. As Lucie Bauer explained, "We did an open meeting and about thirty people came. We asked them what their concerns were. We had people with different perspectives on what aspects were of most environmental concern, but lots were worried about food. So, we set out and did all manner of programs on local food."[25] The Green Sanctuary Committee organized the community brainstorming session because they felt that including the congregation in the process of selecting areas of action was important to their community values, which emphasized democratic processes and congregational ownership of church ministries. Moreover, they thought people would be more likely to get involved in activities that addressed their interests. In addition to programs on food preservation, this meeting led to a major project in which the church helped a young couple establish the first community-supported agricultural (CSA) farm in Maine, a project that flourished because of congregational support in the form of CSA subscriptions.

At the Jewish Reconstructionist Congregation, the congregation actively participated in decisions about the details of the green building they had decided to build. Because the structure would be unconventional, community leaders moved slowly and included the congregation in discussions about what options to include in the building. Rabbi Rosen's description of this process, part of which was quoted at the beginning of the chapter, explains the importance of engaging with the community:

> When we started the process (of planning the building) it was before environmentalism and green building were really on the radar. It felt a little fringy. There were conversations we needed to have, and we needed to do it step by step. One of the things we learned from the policy discussions is to say, OK, this is too much too soon. You need to bring people along and you need to do it in a way that people are comfortable. Not like it's being imposed on top of them but like they are being involved in the process, and we are learning about it together.[26]

Making this green building project acceptable meant that the board could not just hire a construction firm and sit back; the congregation had to be involved in the construction process. Community members served on a planning committee that participated in the construction planning by learning about green building and discussing tradeoffs among various options in order to make the best use of their funds. Because this committee shared the rationale behind their decisions with the wider congregation, many individual members became knowledgeable about green building techniques. According to the rabbi, by the end of the building construction, "People here could tell you about T5 florescent light bulbs and VOC carpet and fly ash cement (all sustainable components of buildings) and all kinds of things that we just had a crash course in learning about that we really didn't know much about previously. In the process, it raised people's consciousness."[27]

As the contractor developed plans and outlined costs for specific features, the newly educated community was able to make decisions about what features to prioritize and which to cut in order to stay within budget. For example, they realized that solar hot water would have little conservation value in a situation where hot water was not used much during the week but was needed in large amounts on weekends. Instead, they conserved electricity by installing a highly efficient water heater and dishwasher, as well as windows, motion sensors for lights, and efficient fluorescent lighting. They also decided that a white reflective roof was preferable to a green roof because the light color would reduce urban heating without adding weight to the roof, whereas a green roof with soil and plants would require additional structural supports, which would mean adding columns that blocked sight lines in the sanctuary. These types of decisions were made after researching construction options and considering what features would provide the greatest value in the context of the synagogue's use patterns. The decisions were then shared with the congregation so members understood the reasons behind the decisions.

At Our Lady of Angels, the entire membership of the Sisters of St. Francis of Philadelphia helped design the structure of their community sustainability initiative. During the 1996 Chapter, their periodic mission discernment process, the leadership team assigned the environment as a topic to be addressed. The community had already been involved in environmental education but that year they began a process of brainstorming about what else could be done to care for the earth. First, the congregation participated in the development of a community Environmental Vision Statement and Guiding Principles that proclaimed: "We believe that Jesus Christ came as brother to all created reality, and as Sisters of St. Francis of Philadelphia we acknowledge our oneness with the universe. We call ourselves to proclaim in a viable and tangible manner our belief in the Cosmic Christ."[28] Belief in the Cosmic Christ, present in every aspect of the created universe, meant that the sisters felt called to care for creation.

Second, the sisters set up committees to research potential activities to answer that call. According to Sister Corinne Wright, "We looked at all kinds of things that we might be able to do. For example, groups went to visit places to see what they were doing, like with hermitages constructed using green building techniques. That was how we started to develop the sixteen areas of the Environmental Initiative."[29] With the information gathered by these groups, the congregation worked together to select tangible action areas that would be viable given the resources of their community and, by the end of the Chapter process, the congregation had approved its Environmental Initiative with specific strategy areas. The sisters would: promote communication and support regarding their environmental vision with internal and external groups; expand on their past efforts to develop Franciscan-themed environmental education; address members' desires to protect convent land from development and restore wildlife habitat; promote sustainable lifestyles through activities such as organic food production, increased attention to sustainability of food consumed by the community, renewable energy, recycling, and waste management; and develop a formal land use policy and explore options for ensuring that future care of the land would continue to adhere to a Franciscan world view.[30]

CHALLENGES THAT AFFECTED CONGREGATIONAL SUPPORT

Levels of congregational support were not consistent across the fifteen cases and could fluctuate within a specific faith community. Support was lowest and initiatives were less durable in the four cases where the congregations were not involved in the decisions to develop sustainability initiatives. However, even in communities with extensive congregational participation in the decision to adopt earth-care ethics, initiatives encountered challenges related to congregational support. The most common challenge interviewees mentioned was a lack of consistency in the congregation's interest in sustainability, an issue that was sometimes exacerbated by the aging of community members. A second challenge had to do with tensions that emerged when members realized that a community ethic might affect individual behavior.

LACK OF CONGREGATIONAL INVOLVEMENT IN ADOPTING EARTH CARE. Four cases stand in contrast to the eleven described above because the congregations were not involved in decisions to develop sustainability initiatives. At the Vineyard Church of Ann Arbor, a lay member founded Green Vineyard in response to a series of sermons on creation care. Reverend Wilson authorized creation of the group and encouraged its efforts to implement conservation practices such as reducing paper waste and improving the building's energy efficiency. The pastor also asked the board to adopt creation care as an organizational policy that would be taken into consideration when making decisions about building maintenance and administrative practices. The congregation was not involved in the decisions to start Green Vineyard or to adopt an earth-care policy, which likely contributed to the perception that Green Vineyard was an activity for a core group of people with environmental concerns rather than an area of activity for the whole community.

A similar lack of congregational participation marked development of the initiative at St. Thomas Aquinas Parish. There, the senior pastor acquiesced to a request from a few laypeople who wanted their church to join the bishop's Catholic Greening Initiative. With pastoral permission, the laypeople formed the Green Committee by advertising in the parish bulletin and inviting known sympathizers to join. The committee shared its mission with the congregation through regular articles in the bulletin, hosting educational presentations, and sponsoring activities at the annual parish picnic. However, the congregation had no role in deciding whether the parish would join the bishops' initiative or choosing what kind of activities should be undertaken in the parish.

At Anshe Emeth Memorial Temple and Temple Shalom, community leaders responded to denominational encouragement to enroll in a green certification program. In each case, a board member brought up the opportunity for participating in the program, and the board, comprised of rabbis and elected lay leaders, decided to pursue certification. They then tapped known environmentalists within their communities to serve as program coordinators. Mike Chodroff, the environmental educator who led the program at Anshe Emeth, described how his congregation learned about their enrollment in the GreenFaith program:

> Twice a year, we have a congregation meeting. It's really a board meeting that is open to the whole congregation. In June 2010, we got grant approval for joining the GreenFaith program and I did a presentation on environment at the next congregation meeting. I started by reading a *Time* magazine article describing environmental damage and then asked people to guess what year it was written. They all thought it was recent, but it was from 1989, the issue with the earth on the cover. I described the condition of some of the places mentioned in the article, like a lake that had gone dry. Then I described GreenFaith, the process and the goals. It was a way of introducing it to the congregation.[31]

This presentation was designed to inform members of the congregation about the certification program and to ask for their support and participation. However, it was not a participatory process in which the congregation voted on the program after pondering whether it fit with their community mission. Nor were the members asked to help select the activities that would be undertaken by the Green Team.

The lack of congregational participation in the decision to pursue certification may be one reason that there was limited congregational involvement in environmental activities in these two cases. Both communities developed wonderful environmental education programs, especially for children, and integrated conservation practices into their organizations to achieve significant reductions in energy consumption, water use, and waste generation. However, other than the parents of children involved in greening projects, few congregation members attended events. Apparently, the congregations perceived sustainability as the purview of a small group of environmentalists rather than an area of activity for all members of their community and, once they became certified, there was not enough interest among congregation members to sustain engagement at the same level as during the two-year certification program.

Anshe Emeth Memorial Temple has continued to organize annual environmentally themed youth seders for Tu BiShvat, the Jewish festival of trees, however the Green Team did not list any new activities on its webpage during 2013–14 and does not seem to be developing new projects at the time of this study. During this same period, environmental themes disappeared from Sabbath services because the junior rabbi, who had preached on the subject, left for another position. Similarly, at Temple Shalom, a few of the activities that were established during the GreenFaith certification program have continued: the solar panels on the roof deliver electricity, the rabbi leads a service at the beach during the summer, and the garden coordinator raises food for donation to a food pantry as part of the community's social justice work. However, it is notable that when the temple developed a new website in 2014, sustainability became much less visible as an element of the community's public identity. Unlike the previous website, which had the GreenFaith certification logo on the homepage, the new website does not include any indications that the community is green certified. Furthermore, there are no pictures of the solar panels or the garden, and no links to sermons or theological statements about Jewish environmental ethics. If sustainability had been perceived as an important element of Temple Shalom's community identity, members of the congregation would have ensured that their environmental accomplishments were more visible on the website[32] through which they present their community values and practices to the public.

FLUCTUATING LEVELS OF CONGREGATIONAL SUPPORT. In communities where congregations did participate in the decision to adopt earth-care ministries, congregational support for earth-care action was not necessarily constant. Within most of the case-study communities, there were times when rising awareness of environmental crises, prompts from faith leaders, or discernment processes shifted the balance so that a larger proportion of members were interested in sustainability. However, after adopting an environmental ethic, levels of interest would rise and fall as attention shifted to other topics such as dealing with an economic recession or fighting human trafficking. These fluctuations, which reflect human nature, were common enough at Our Lady of Angels that the community developed a policy to help address them. According to Sister Corinne Wright, "The level of community interest in a specific topic can change over time, but once we adopt an issue, those of us who are interested in it can continue to work on it. A facilitator clarified this point for us: 'Anything you have adopted but not voted out is still on the agenda.' "[33] This policy affirming the continued validity of a formally adopted mission area ensured that sustainability champions could continue to work on environmental activities under the auspices of the faith community.

A more intractable challenge was caused by demographic shifts that affected how many members were available to participate in earth-care activities; a decline could result in decreased congregational involvement. In four of the monastic communities, age reduced the number of members who participated in outdoor activities, and green teams in some of the non-monastic communities mentioned that age was changing the types of activities they could do. In some cases, aging memberships motivated communities to find outsiders who would continue their work. Thus, the Sisters of St. Joseph donated their Bow in the Clouds Preserve to the Southwest Michigan Land Conservancy when they realized they no longer had the womanpower to maintain the prairie fen themselves. This decision meant that the land they had cared for would continue to be preserved and used for the benefit of the public, in conformity with the values of the sisters. However it also meant that the congregation no longer spent time working in the fen or making decisions about its care during their community meetings.

Wright identified a similar pattern at Our Lady of Angels, where she noted that physical limitations were changing the relationship between her community and its property: "It's also getting harder to maintain the connection to the land. Only a few people can walk it anymore; most seem to prefer to sit on their porches."[34] She noted that even in the gardens near the residential buildings, "People make use of the grounds and go outside but not like they used to. There used to be circles of people sitting outside. But some have died, and others maybe are just too busy."[35] With fewer community members outside, no one noticed that a new gardener had replaced the native vines on a pergola with wisteria or that mowing practices were encroaching on areas that had been restored to wildlife habitat. Thus, in several cases, the aging of community members affected congregational engagement in two ways. First it reduced the number of members who were physically participating in earth-care activities and, second, it reduced the extent to which members were aware of what was happening with the implementation of activities in their community. These cases suggest that there is a correlation between participation and levels of interest: as fewer members participate in or observe earth-care activities, sustainability may become less salient to the congregation and levels of interest may decrease.

TENSIONS BETWEEN COMMUNITY ETHICS AND PERSONAL BEHAVIOR.
As an abstract idea, adopting an environmental ethic seems simple, however, deciding how to implement that ethic within a community may create
tensions when policies begin to affect individual behavior. The Jewish
Reconstructionist Congregation adopted a sustainability ethic as a way to
define the values that guided their decision to construct a green synagogue.
After the building was completed, some community leaders began discussing
policy changes that would integrate sustainability into other community activities, and their proposals sparked a vigorous community discussion about
how to implement the ethic. In an interview with Pauline Yearwood for the
Chicago Jewish News, Rabbi Rosen described the resistance that arose when
JRC tried to develop policies that would affect people's behavior: "When we
developed our first green policy statement, I'll tell you frankly, some people
freaked out. But our thinking was, if we're going to be the greenest congregation in the world, we should have a green policy that's commensurate with
the commitment we made."[36]

Undertaking a sustainability initiative in a faith community raises questions about expectations for behavior in members' daily lives. Religions have
a long history of behavioral codes that affect marriage, occupation, food,
clothing, and even hairstyles. In the United States, however, faith communities
are voluntary associations, and levels of adherence to doctrinal injunctions
vary across denominations and even from one congregation to another within
a denomination. Many Americans dislike the idea of having their individual
actions "policed" to determine whether they are living up to religious ideals.
Moreover, there is disagreement about which religious precepts are most
important and how modern believers should interpret behavioral codes created in pre-modern societies. The voluminous rabbinic literary corpus, which
records two millennia of analyses and debates over how to interpret biblical
behavioral precepts, attests to the complexity of these issues.

At JRC, the community discussion about how the congregation's sustainability ethic should affect community behavior began with questions about
policies that would mandate environmentally beneficial practices within the
synagogue. Rabbi Rosen described some of the proposed ideas and members' responses:

> Do we want our *bar* and *bat mitzvah* families to use caterers that will only
> use recyclables? Are we going to tell them they can't use Mylar balloons in
> celebrations? Are we going to extend this to fair trade—economic sustain-

ability as well as environmental sustainability? People went, "Whoa, we're going to ask members to make that kind of commitment?" And the answer was, "Why shouldn't we?"[37]

Having decided that sustainability was a Jewish value, it made sense to apply it to practices in daily life, however, Rosen discovered that defining best practices within a house of worship was easier than getting agreement about living more sustainably at home. Nevertheless, he felt it important to bring up the issue since values do not stop at the door of the synagogue.

> "It's one thing to live green in synagogue, then you get in your SUV and drive home. Are we going to extend our green philosophy to touch on other aspects of people's lives?" [Rabbi Rosen] compares these issues to others faced by more traditional Jewish congregations—how far should they go in monitoring an individual's level of *kashrut*,[38] for example? Not all of these questions need to be answered, Rosen says, but he believes it's important to ask them. "These are good questions and they are difficult because they go to the heart of our own personal freedoms, independence and liberties and also to being part of a community that's based on values. This is the sacred value of environmentalism, and if we are going to commit to it in how we build our building, I believe we need to have serious discussions about how each and every one of us is going to carry it into our own lives as well," he says.[39]

Rabbi Rosen's description of the conversations that arose at the Jewish Reconstructionist Congregation illustrates a challenge that remained in the background for the other sustainability initiatives. It was easier to develop policies and practices for the religious organization than for the members. Few other congregations engaged in such explicit discussions of the issue, however, the topic was present across the cases, as evidenced in interviews during which people described activities to encourage more sustainable behavior in homes by selling CFLs and reusable shopping bags, organizing workshops on home weatherization, and developing campaigns to educate members about environmental issues related to consumption of products like beef or bottled water.

FACTORS THAT HELPED MITIGATE CHALLENGES

There were no simple solutions for the challenge of an aging membership, however congregational involvement appeared to help some communities address fluctuating levels of interest and concerns that faith community policies might impinge on personal behavior. Brother Lewis Grobe noted that monks at Saint John's Abbey were not uniformly enthusiastic about sustainability, especially when it affected them personally, explaining that, "There are 150 monks, and they run the gamut in their interests and perceptions. Some are progressive and others think it's a bunch of rubbish."[40] Changes at Saint John's Abbey had to be deliberative and intentional so the community could reach consensus. According to Grobe, they succeeded in making changes by involving members in discussion of new ideas and continuing these discussions until all came to agreement about how to proceed:

> Even in the abbey community, sustainability is not always easy. When we switched from paper to cloth napkins, that required three years of deliberation before we could make the move. People get into habits and it is difficult to change things. Sometimes you have to ask, where do you want to draw the line? What is appropriate to the monastic way of life? One good thing about the abbey is that here we are open to discussing these things so that, gradually, change can happen.[41]

Although the process could be slow, participating in a well-established tradition of study and discussion assisted the abbey monks in evaluating whether behaviors needed to be adapted to better conform with their community's religious values. The monks' system for cultivating consensus was similar to the process of study and discussion through which the Jewish Reconstructionist Congregation fostered support for their green building project; in both examples, the congregation took an active role in evaluating potential actions before deciding what would be done. By sharing in decisions about actions, the members were invested in the decisions and were more likely to help implement the earth-care activities.

EFFECTS: CONGREGATIONAL OWNERSHIP OF INITIATIVES

Cases in which congregations were involved in adopting and enacting earth-care ethics had higher levels of congregational support during implementation of their initiatives. The congregational support associated with participatory decision processes seems to derive from two factors. First, a greater number of community members developed personal convictions about connections between faith and earth care and how the initiatives fit with their faith community's identity and mission. Second, individuals' uncertainties about courses of action and potential effects on the community, especially its finances, were addressed. Consequently, the congregation members had a sense of ownership for the initiatives, which were perceived as community projects that would benefit the entire faith community, rather than activities for a small group of environmentalists.

In relation to the first point, participatory processes gave community members a chance to ponder whether sustainability was important to them as people of faith. In addition to hearing sermons on the topic, they became active learners who engaged in study, discussion, and prayer to understand how environmental issues intersected with their religious traditions. Like the committee at Trinity Presbyterian Church in East Brunswick, study led people to determine that unsustainable resource use affected their ministry work to obey God, care for the poor, promote social justice, and lead lives that reflected their spiritual values. Because a large portion of the membership actively came to the conclusion that sustainability was a faith issue, the congregation was committed to supporting its sustainability initiative.

The second factor was also important for initiatives: people needed to learn about options for action, and address concerns about whether environmental activities would negatively affect their communities, before making a commitment. Often this exploratory process meant going slowly and giving people time to become familiar with environmental issues and potential responses. Thus, Father Schwietz spent eleven years promoting his vision of an educational arboretum and, in the meantime, he restored a wetland and a prairie area, which served as examples of sustainable land stewardship and made the arboretum idea less abstract. Similarly, members of the Jewish Reconstructionist Congregation took their time in developing construction plans that were supported by their community. The building committee studied materials and took field trips to see samples of green building techniques so they could explain options to their community and make the best choices for the new synagogue. Across the cases, green teams organized numerous educational events with guest speakers to inform their congregations about climate change, energy efficiency, energy policy, food production, environmental justice, and green building. Examples of shared learning were prevalent in interviewees' descriptions of congregational involvement in the development of initiatives, especially during processes in which the whole congregation decided to adopt an earth-care ethic or helped decide what kinds of actions should be taken to incorporate sustainability into the practices of their faith communities.

As a result of these two factors—widespread personal conviction and mitigation of concerns—members of congregations that had extensive involvement in decisions to adopt earth care had a more unified perspective about the importance of sustainability as a faith issue and a sense of ownership for their community's earth-care efforts. That ownership increased congregational support for initiatives and made it easier to implement environmental activities because more members contributed resources and engaged in various actions to make their faith communities more sustainable. In the words of Sister Corinne Wright, manager of the Environmental Initiative for the Sisters of St. Francis of Philadelphia, which was designed though the efforts of numerous sisters serving on subcommittees that all helped research potential activities: "It was important that it was all done by committees because then there is more buy-in."

SUMMARY AND DOMAIN INTERACTIONS

How Congregations Affected Initiatives

WHEN A CONGREGATION BECAME INVESTED in a sustainability initiative, its members provided support in the form of human resources (participants and knowledge) and material resources (funds and supplies) that had significant effects on development and implementation of activities. Chapters 7 and 8 described factors that affected levels of congregational support. This section summarizes the findings from the two chapters, describing the effects that congregational support had on the sustainability initiatives and interactions between congregations and the other three domains.

CONGREGATIONS AS ARBITERS OF INITIATIVE CAPACITY

Congregations provided higher levels of support for initiatives in cases where they perceived a link between earth care and community identity and were involved in decisions to adopt earth care as a community ministry. Faith leaders defined past activities such as farming, prairie restoration, and social justice ministries as precursors to sustainability initiatives in order to persuade congregations that earth care fit with their community heritage and identity. Cases in which the members were actively involved in the decision processes through which the community adopted earth care as part of its mission had the strongest congregational support. Having played a role in deciding that care for the earth was an appropriate activity for their community, members felt a sense of ownership for the initiatives and were more likely to participate in activities and provide resources in support of projects.

Congregational investment affected how many individuals joined a green team and what types of actions they undertook. It also determined how many areas of the organization became venues for earth care activities and, in some cases, it influenced how consistently faith leaders promoted earth care. See Table 16 for an overview of factors that influenced levels of congregational support and how those factors interacted with other domains.

TABLE 16 CONGREGATIONAL SUPPORT FACTORS AND
THEIR INTERACTIONS WITH OTHER DOMAINS

FACTORS AFFECTING SUPPORT	EFFECTS ON THE INITIATIVE	INTERACTIONS WITH OTHER DOMAINS
Earth care linked with community identity	Earth care became embedded in community mission	*Faith Leaders:* religious messages
Involvement in decision to adopt earth care as a ministry/mission	Membership buy-in and increased resources: Participants Knowledge Material resources	*Champions:* affirmation and efficacy; critical mass on green team *Faith Leaders:* incentive to promote earth care *Organization:* integrate earth care into multiple activity areas and embed it in the organization

HOW CONGREGATIONAL SUPPORT AFFECTED RESOURCES

Congregational support determined initiative capacity by affecting the resources that were available for developing and implementing the initiative. High levels of congregational support correlated with increased contributions of human, knowledge, and material resources, which are often referred to as "time, talent, and treasure" in faith communities. Some members joined green teams and participated in earth-care activities while others contributed by providing financial and material support.

HUMAN RESOURCES. Congregational support affected available human resources in two ways: it influenced the experiences of champions and the number of participants. In cases where the entire congregation participated in the decision to authorize formation of a "green team" to pursue earth care as a community ministry, those teams were able to take action knowing that they had support from their congregations. On a practical level, this authorization meant that green teams and champions could react to opportunities for actions that were within the purview of their mission without going through time-consuming approval processes. Interviewees at the Madison Christian Community described their congregation as having a "permission-giving" culture that allowed individuals to take action of their own volition once sustainability became an established area of activity. Thus, for example, lay members planted native plants in an entryway garden bed at the Madison Christian Community without seeking staff approval. Similarly, because the covenant for the Earth Care House Church listed public advocacy work as an action through which to fulfill their mission, house church members joined efforts to prevent hydraulic fracturing in the Harrisonburg area and testified in a city council meeting that their opposition was rooted in both science-based health concerns and religious beliefs without worrying about whether their congregation would feel that Trinity Presbyterian Church was being misrepresented.

Congregational investment also influenced the number of people participating in initiatives, which affected champions' sense of efficacy. One way that green teams measured the success of their efforts was by the number of congregation members who participated in environmental activities they organized. At Trinity Presbyterian Church of East Brunswick, the Trinity Earth Shepherds were delighted when between seventy and eighty people attended a lunch-and-learn session on environmental stewardship; the high level of congregational participation served as an indicator that the congregation valued their efforts. Conversely, interviewees in a few cases were frustrated by low levels of participation in events they organized, which seemed to indicate a lack of congregational support for their efforts. Increased support could also mean more people serving on the green team, which mitigated the risk of burnout for individual sustainability champions.

In addition to its effects on champions, congregational participation affected initiative efficacy by determining the number and extent of activities that could be undertaken. At Holy Wisdom Monastery, volunteers came to workdays to prune and harvest orchards, tend gardens, and restore prairies, thereby increasing the scope of the earth-care initiative far beyond what could have been accomplished by the three sisters and their small staff. Support from congregation members who were active in various areas of a faith community intersected with the Organization domain and made it easier to integrate earth care into worship services, religious education programs, and facilities maintenance. Faith leaders in communities with high levels of congregational support for initiatives were motivated to preach more frequently about earth care as a religious issue, thereby reinforcing the links between sustainability and community identity. Religious education instructors, organizational staff, and volunteers who helped with facilities or ministries could also participate in initiatives by incorporating earth care into practices in their areas of the faith community. These supplementary activities expanded the capacity of an initiative and helped embed it in the religious organization.

KNOWLEDGE RESOURCES. One of the resources that congregational support provided was knowledge. When the Madison Christian Community calls for volunteers to help burn their restored prairie in the spring, the members who turn out already have experience with prairie restoration work because they have been involved with similar activities in other places around Madison. In this city where Aldo Leopold began restoration experiments at the university arboretum in the 1930s, patches of prairie are ubiquitous: they can be found in public parks and on private lands. MCC was also able to hire members of its own community who had professional training in environmental theology and in religious education with an emphasis on science and religion in order to develop formal environmental stewardship curricula for both children and adults. In other cases, members contributed their knowledge to apply for grants, install solar panels, create gardens, and develop forest management plans. These knowledge resources made it possible to translate ideas into coherent programs, thereby fostering a community's ability to move from theology to action.

MATERIAL RESOURCES. Access to material resources was another effect of congregational support for initiatives. At Villa Maria, one class (a group of sisters who had gone through their novitiate together) pooled funds to purchase cows for the Villa Farm and another class bought a tractor. Red Hill Farm, the community-supported agriculture project at Our Lady of Angels, also benefited from a tractor purchased with convent funds rather than farm income. At First Parish Church of Newbury, the community renovated the church basement so it could serve as the venue for an environmentally themed preschool. The project was time-consuming and cost more than expected because it had to meet strict state codes, but the congregation persevered because they saw it as an important way to fulfill their mission as Stewards of Earth and Spirit. At the Jewish Reconstructionist Congregation, a professional consultant estimated that the community would be able to raise $3–4 million to replace their building, but the members donated far more in order to reach a LEED platinum rating. According to Julie Dorfman, "The people who volunteered for fundraising were amazing. They raised $6 million! The green vision was part of what helped raise that much money—people really stretched to support it."[1] At the "green synagogue" and in the other case-study communities, financial backing was a significant indicator of congregational support for sustainability initiatives.

DOMAIN INTERACTIONS

The role of the Congregation domain in the development of the sustainability initiatives was intertwined with other domains. As described in Chapters 7 and 8, levels of congregational support were affected by faith leader messages about earth care as an aspect of community identity and by congregational engagement in decision processes that adhered to a community's organizational procedures. Moreover, the effects of congregational support played out through domain interactions. Congregations provided resources that affected the earth-care options champions could carry out, and their levels of participation determined whether green teams reached the critical mass

FIGURE 4 Interactions between Congregations and the Other Domains

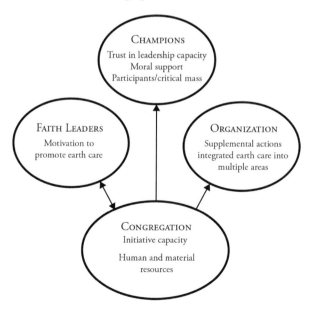

that helped prevent burnout. Congregational interest in earth care also influenced whether faith leaders felt motivated to promote sustainability initiatives; where environmental concern was "bubbling up" in a community, leadership teams and clergy were more likely to authorize initiatives and preach sermons on earth care as a faith issue. Finally, religious organizations supplied venues through which members of the congregation who were not on the green team could take action and contribute to the process of integrating earth care into their faith community. Figure 4 illustrates the interactions between congregations and the other three domains.

EARTH CARE EMBEDDED IN COMMUNITY MISSION

In case studies with strong congregational support for initiatives, sustainability became embedded in the community mission, thereby fulfilling the process of integration with community identity that began when individual champions and faith leaders framed community history and ministries as precursors to earth care. Although the data collected for this research project does not include surveys of whole congregations that would provide precise measures of how many members embraced earth care as a faith community mission, the ways environmental initiatives were integrated into mission statements and interviewees' comments about financial considerations that affected initiatives serve as indirect indicators of congregational attitudes.

EARTH CARE INTEGRATED INTO MISSION STATEMENTS. Mission statements provide one indicator of a congregation's perception that earth care has become part of its community identity. During the process of developing sustainability initiatives, the case-study communities created formal earth-care mission statements that were incorporated into their faith community missions in three different ways: as part of the overarching community mission, a subpart of a pre-existing ministry's mission, or a green team mission.

Five communities integrated earth care into their community mission statements, thereby defining it as a key component of community identity. Thus, for example, the Madison Christian Community mission is: "To live faithfully and lovingly with God, neighbors, and creation."[2] Seven communities integrated earth care into pre-existing ministries: five defined it as an area of social justice work, one defined it as a form of service to society, and one defined it as part of its tradition of small group ministry. In all twelve of these cases, formal statements incorporating earth care into the overarching community mission or pre-existing ministries were prominent on websites and in promotional materials through which the congregations publicly presented their communities.

In contrast, there was a final set of three cases that developed mission statements for their green teams but did not fully integrate earth care into a specific ministry or the community mission. Websites for these communities listed specific environmental activities on their social justice ministry pages but did not include formal mission statements or explanations of how earth care fit into the community's ministry work or religious mission. These were also the cases in which champions and faith leaders described lack of congregational support as a challenge for their initiatives. Consequently, adoption of mission statements defining earth care as an activity that fits into community missions or ministries seems to be an indicator of congregational support for initiatives.

SUPPORT TRANSCENDED FINANCIAL INTERESTS. Another indicator of how strongly congregations embraced the idea of a connection between sustainability and mission was evident in some interviewees' insistence that values, rather than economic considerations, determined whether their communities undertook environmental actions. For example, developers periodically offered to buy the one-acre prairie next to the Madison Christian Community. In 2010, the community turned down an offer for $300,000 because caring for the land had become part of their mission. According to church member Jill McLeod, they made the decision to keep the land because "God gave all of us this land, and he gave it to us for a reason. Not all religious lessons come out of a Bible; some of them come out of a garden."[3] John Moreira, land manager at Villa Maria, made a similar comment about the values that governed land use among the Sisters of the Humility of Mary:

> The sisters look at sustainability as being just as important as making money [from their farm and forest lands]. It's not because they don't care about finances. They've built hospitals and schools; they know how to earn money and make economic calculations. But sustainability is a priority for them, so they make decisions based on what is best for the health of the land and ecosystems, not just how to get the highest profit.[4]

A few interviewees contradicted these statements and stressed that economic considerations *were* a significant factor in community decisions about sustainability projects. However, even those who insisted that costs could be a barrier to environmental efforts said that values motivated their communities to upgrade facilities and appliances, pay for services such as composting, and purchase more sustainable products as long as those options only imposed moderate budgetary increases.

Thus, Tom Matthews, whose job as maintenance person for the Madison Christian Community required him to consider the cost of materials as he implemented earth-care projects, insisted, "With us, it's more of an ethical than an economic issue."[5] In this statement, he echoed his pastor, who felt that renewable energy was a valid investment for faith communities even if a congregation did not recover its financial costs because their calculations were based on religious teachings and concerns about the costs to the environment from using fossil fuels.[6] Consequently, for a religious organization, renewable energy had moral value as a public witness to the wider local community, demonstrating that the members were living in accord with their faith's principles. Because such an infrastructure investment could only be made with extensive support from the congregation, the sixty-four solar panels covering the roof at the Madison Christian Community attest to the congregation's investment in their mission to "live faithfully and lovingly with God, neighbors, and creation."[7]

By making decisions to authorize sustainability projects or adopt community-wide earth-care ethics, and by providing the resources to implement actions through the venue of their religious organizations, congregations contributed to the process of integrating earth care into the mission of their faith communities. The factors that influenced levels of support show the importance of the religious organization as a domain that affected development of the case-study initiatives. The organization determined what kinds of decision processes communities followed when they considered whether to adopt an earth-care ethic and what kinds of venues were available for implementing earth-care actions in a faith community. Therefore, the next section looks more closely at the contributions that religious organizations made to the development of these initiatives.

Part V

ORGANIZATIONS

Venues for Initiative Implementation

INTRODUCTION

During a weekend retreat in the mountains, members of Trinity Presbyterian Church discovered they shared concerns about the environment and began discussing the possibility of forming a group to explore how earth care connected with their religion. Their church's "house church" system provided a venue through which this group was able to put their plan into effect. House churches are lay-led ministry groups that are formed to address a specific area of ministry activity, such as providing clothing for low-income people. Each house church is supposed to consciously include four "marks": first, defining the mission of the house church; second, worship in the house church and with the whole congregation; third, nurture or study to deepen members' understanding of the issue in relation to religious life; and fourth, fellowship within the house church. Members of a house church create a ministry mission statement and develop a formal covenant that describes the activities through which they will fulfill their mission in accord with the four marks. At the time of this study, the covenant of the Earth Care House Church defined its mission as: "To promote Church and community awareness and involvement in restoring creation."[1]

The mission mark was fulfilled through specific activities such as: staying informed on environmental issues and sharing information by writing letters to the editor and to political representatives; attending public meetings to speak up for preserving the environment; encouraging youth to go on nature outings; promoting resource conservation practices like recycling and water conservation; installing a bicycle rack at the church; and assisting another house church with food for the local free clinic. The worship mark was fulfilled by including worship in house church meetings and leading an Earth Day Sunday service for the entire church. The covenant also included a study plan through which to address the nurture mark by cultivating "deeper theological understanding of the creation and our role in restoring its wholeness."[2] In accord with these plans, Earth Care House Church members studied eco-theological texts and environmental writings. The fourth mark, fellowship, was achieved through a meeting format that fostered attention to members' lives by celebrating birthdays and listening to each other's concerns. According to Judy LePera, "At the beginning of our house church meetings, we share joys and concerns. Often someone says, 'I feel discouraged because this terrible thing is happening or has happened to our environment.'"[3]

This house church system facilitated development of Trinity's earth care ministry by providing a procedure and format for organizing and managing an environmental affinity group. The structure of the four marks created a framework for formulating goals and corresponding actions, which facilitated implementation of ministry activities. Ideally, each house church had four marks leaders to lead its worship, nurture/study, mission, and fellowship activities. Meanwhile, formal presentation of the covenant and the opportunity to lead a Sunday service provided procedures for interactions between the house church and the congregation that fostered congregational support for earth care as a faith issue. Thus, the organizational context of Trinity Presbyterian Church, with its house church system, shaped development of the sustainability initiative in three ways. First, it determined the process for establishing earth care as an area of ministry work for the church. Second, it contributed operational procedures for establishing and managing an earth care affinity group and for regulating interactions between that group and the larger community. Third, its organizational structures provided opportunities to implement activities through venues such as worship services, community practices, and partnerships with other house churches. Thus, as the Trinity case demonstrates, faith community organizations made significant contributions that affected the emergence and development of initiatives.

CHARACTERISTICS OF RELIGIOUS ORGANIZATIONS

A faith community is an organization with the primary purpose of gathering people "to engage in the cultural activity of expressing and transmitting religious meanings."[4] Faith communities in the United States are voluntary associations that people join for a variety of reasons; in addition to providing a place for religious practice, individuals may seek the company and support of like-minded people or a place where their children can learn moral values. US faith communities tend to follow patterns adapted from the Protestant Christian model of religion.[5] They devote most of their resources to producing religious meaning through collective rituals that include scriptural readings, sermons, and music, and through religious education.[6] To produce these rituals and educational programs, they employ clergy, musicians, and educators, as well as staff to handle administrative duties and maintain facilities. The congregation members are the audience for the rituals and provide the funds that sustain the organization, so high-quality worship and educational programs that satisfy members are vital. Some faith communities also provide social services such as food assistance, legal aid, or low-cost daycare to people outside the congregation. A smaller number of faith communities engage in political activity. Monastic communities have the same primary purpose of expressing religious meaning but differ in that the members have taken up a life of full-time religious devotion that places them outside the mainstream social structures of family and secular labor.

Religious organizations have structures and procedures that help fulfill their goal of expressing religious meanings. The core elements of a religious organization's structure fall into two categories: 1) administration and facilities management to run the organization and maintain the physical infrastructure, and 2) religious program management to provide worship and educational programs for the members. Organizational structures for managing administrative and religious programs include governance systems to oversee the whole community as well as smaller units, such as committees, that manage specific long-term programs and short-term projects. Within these structures, people follow organizational operating procedures in order to perform administrative and programming functions.

The governance system of a faith community was one type of organizational structure that significantly affected development of sustainability initiatives. Religious organizations have polities, or forms of governance, that determine who has authority and what processes will be used to make decisions about activities and allocation of resources. There are three general types of governance, which differ according to where the focus of control is located.[7] "Congregational" polities place authority in the congregation itself. Ideally, although there may be a board to handle day-to-day management, major decisions are made by the entire congregation. A second governance structure, called "presbyterian" polity, is named for the central role of elected "elders" (*presbyters* in Greek). In communities with this polity, authority is held by a board comprised of the pastor and a group of lay representatives who are usually elected by the congregation. The elected board members may act according to their own consciences to govern the local religious organization. The characteristic that distinguishes this polity from the congregational type is the presence of a regional presbytery composed of all ordained clergy and ruling elders for congregations within a geographic area. The elected board has authority over its congregation, but local authority may be subject to review by the regional presbytery. "Episcopal" polity is the third form of governance. Its name comes from the Greek word for bishop (*episcopus*) and describes a hierarchical governance system in which authority flows from the top down. A central governing body sets policies that are implemented by regional representatives (bishops) who make decisions that affect local congregations.

Governance systems may affect decisions about patterns of worship, hiring of pastors, and control over material resources. In episcopal systems, material assets may belong to the regional or national organization rather than the local congregation, and pastors may be assigned by the regional bishop. Communities with congregational or presbyterian polities are more likely to own their buildings and hire pastors from a pool of candidates. However, as sociologist Nancy T. Ammerman notes, these neatly labeled categories can be misleading because communities with ostensibly local autonomy may rely heavily on denominational advice and support while congregations in hierarchical systems may be more strongly influenced by the local pastor than pronouncements from a bishop or higher official.[8]

In the case studies, the governance relationship between the local faith community and its denominational organization had only marginal effects on sustainability initiatives. Of greater importance were the governance structures and operating procedures within the communities, which affected the processes for adopting and implementing earth care ministries. The study sample included all three polity types, and aspects of more than one governance system were sometimes combined within a single community. St. Thomas Aquinas Catholic Parish, part of the Catholic Church, had an episcopal polity in which the pastor had authority over decisions. The three Jewish communities and most of the mainline Protestant communities followed a presbyterian polity that placed decision authority with elected boards and pastors. Saint John's Abbey had a form of presbyterian polity in which a leader handled daily administrative duties with assistance from a Senior Council, however it differed from the non-monastic systems because the abbot was a member of the community who had been elected to serve as long as physically possible. Furthermore, the monks periodically shifted to a congregational model and engaged the entire community for major decisions. Similarly, the prioress of Holy Wisdom Monastery handled day-to-day management but consulted with the other sisters and members of the extended community on larger matters. The Vineyard Church of Ann Arbor also had a variation on presbyterian polity. There, a pastor and board governed, however, the senior pastor had considerable authority because he controlled nominations for service on the board. Five cases, the First Universalist Church of Rockland, the First Parish Church of Newbury, and the three communities of Catholic women religious, blended presbyterian and congregational governance. Unitarian Universalist churches rely on boards for administrative leadership, however, many decisions are made by the congregations during annual meetings. The congregation at First Parish Church of Newbury had become so small that a large portion of its members served on the church council and the whole congregation was involved in many decisions. The convents followed a form of congregational-presbyterian polity in which an elected leadership team managed the communities in accordance with directional priorities established by the entire congregation.

In addition to governance systems, operating procedures and organizational structures within the case-study organizations affected development of sustainability initiatives. In order to coordinate management of administration and programming, faith communities develop procedures that define standardized practices for running an organization and its various committees. Some of these procedures are formally defined in bylaws that describe the roles and responsibilities of boards, leadership teams, staff, and congregation members. Others are informal traditions passed down through personal experience as new leaders adopt management practices learned from their predecessors or from experiences in their professional lives. Operational procedures that affected initiatives included processes for forming and managing affinity groups as well as protocols that determined how those groups would interact with the wider community and its governing system.

Organizational structure was another significant factor for initiatives. These structures, designed to support the administrative and worship functions of a faith community, became venues through which to enact various earth care activities. Administrative management included office work, purchasing, and maintenance of facilities and grounds. Religious programming could comprise worship services, music, religious education, and ministries for people in the congregation and the external community. Larger communities had more structural venues and had dedicated staff who could (if motivated) help integrate sustainability into organizational systems. For example, at Saint John's Abbey and St. Thomas Aquinas Parish, there were numerous office workers, priests, and educators to handle administrative management and religious programs, as well as custodians and groundskeepers to look after the buildings and grounds. Smaller communities, on the other hand, relied on volunteers to supplement a core staff that usually comprised a pastor, a religious education director, an administrative assistant, a maintenance person, and a music director. In many cases, some of these were part-time positions. The smallest case-study community, First Parish Church of Newbury, had a part-time pastor and a dedicated corps of volunteers who handled administration and maintenance of their historic church.

Organizational contexts provided opportunities and imposed constraints that affected all fifteen cases. Chapter 9 examines operational procedures that affected adoption of earth care ministry, formation of green teams, and community engagement in initiative implementation. Chapter 10 then explores how organizational structures defined the venues through which sustainability initiatives were implemented.

9 OPERATIONAL PROCEDURES

Countless devoted JRC members have worked tirelessly to prepare our new [green] synagogue building for this long-awaited day. Just as the ancient Israelites constructing the tabernacle in the wilderness, we have learned that it is not the building, but *the process* of building, that creates sacred community. (Emphasis in original)
—RABBI BRANT ROSEN, Jewish Reconstructionist Congregation

RELIGIOUS ORGANIZATIONS HAVE STANDARDIZED PROCEDURES for managing the administrative and programming functions necessary to the daily operations of a nonprofit organization designed to express and transmit religious meaning. Some of these procedures are formal operating protocols, recorded in policies and bylaws that ensure consistency in community decisions and staff duties, while others are informal behavioral norms, simply "the way things are done." These operating procedures affected development of initiatives in three ways. First, the procedures for making decisions about missions and ministry work influenced levels of congregational involvement in adopting and enacting earth care. Second, operational protocols affected the format and management of environmental affinity groups (green teams/ committees, environmental task forces, etc.). Third, normative protocols regulated interactions between green teams and the larger faith community. Thus, protocols for organizational operations were applied in ways that affected the internal workings of green teams and their engagement with the congregations, which, in turn, influenced congregational involvement and initiative capacity (see Table 17).

TABLE 17 ORGANIZATIONAL PROCEDURES
THAT AFFECTED INITIATIVES

PROTOCOL AREAS	NORMATIVE OPERATING PROCEDURES
1. Decision processes	Mission discernment
	Project approval
2. Green team management	Group format
	Management and planning
	Group study
	Religious rituals and fellowship
	Decision making
3. Community interactions	Communication with the congregation

1 DECISION PROCESSES

As described in the previous chapter, most of the case-study communities followed participatory decision processes that involved the congregation in the decision to adopt earth care as an area of activity. For five communities, these decisions emerged during periods of mission discernment, in which members worked together in well-defined processes designed to achieve consensus. Mission discernment processes do not, however, automatically require participatory processes, as evidenced by a sixth case in which a committee and board made decisions about mission on behalf of the congregation. A second path to initiative development began with specific projects rather than adoption of community-wide missions. In contrast to mission decisions, decision processes that focused on approval of single projects showed greater variation in levels of community participation, as illustrated in five cases. The diverse processes for project approval reflect differences in project scale and governance structures, which may help explain why four communities did not follow participatory processes in developing their sustainability initiatives.

Mission Discernment Processes

For Villa Maria, Nazareth, and Our Lady of Angels, Chapter meetings provided processes for engaging community members in evaluation of earth care as a potential area of activity. In the years since the Second Vatican Council, these women's religious orders have gradually shifted from a hierarchical governance structure that vested authority in a mother superior to participatory systems in which the members share responsibility for determining priorities and leading their communities. All sisters who are able gather at the motherhouse to participate in the multi-day Chapter meetings. These meetings include communal prayer and ritual in addition to discussion of how to update missions and allocate resources to best effect. Specific topics to consider, such as how earth care relates to a community mission, are proposed ahead of the Chapter. During the meeting, small groups engage in study and reflection on these topics then bring their conclusions back to the whole community for another round of discussions. If there is wide interest but some members do not agree on the best course of action, a task force may be created to further explore potential modes of activity for future consideration by the leadership team or in the next Chapter meeting. If there is consensus on the need to address an issue, the whole community may participate in the process of writing a directional statement describing this new priority before the close of the Chapter meeting. Due to the participatory decision processes in these convents, the congregations were actively involved in deciding to adopt earth care as a community mission and the leadership teams elected during the Chapter process had the task of implementing their communities' sustainability goals. Participatory processes were also central to mission discernment at Holy Wisdom Monastery and First Parish Church of Newbury, where, as described in Chapter 8, the congregations needed to be included in decisions about the futures of their communities.

In contrast to these five cases, one case followed a less participatory, representational process for mission discernment. At Trinity Presbyterian Church of East Brunswick, a volunteer committee examined three potential mission areas recommended by their denomination: hunger, peace-making, and environment. After study, they unanimously voted to recommend environmental stewardship as a new mission focus and made a presentation of their findings to the Session, the governing board comprised of the pastor, clerk, director of youth ministries, and twelve elected elders.[9] The Session approved the new mission, which was presented to the congregation. Throughout this discernment process, the mission committee was understood to be working on behalf of the wider community. The committee that recommended an environmental stewardship mission was authorized by the congregation, and the majority of the people on the Session board that adopted the new mission were elected by the congregation to serve as their representatives.

Five cases embarked on sustainability initiatives after following standardized processes for deciding whether or not the congregation would approve a specific project. These decision processes differed from the mission discernment processes in that a task force brought information to the board for approval prior to engaging the congregation. Despite less involvement of the congregation in the early stages of developing the idea for earth care, some of these processes were highly participatory at their later stages. Whether there were greater or lesser levels of participation seems to have been determined partly by the scale of the project and partly by community operating norms.

Although not part of a mission discernment process, the decision to create an educational arboretum at Saint John's Abbey led to adoption of earth care as a core ministry for the abbey. That decision would not have been possible without a participatory process that engaged the entire congregation. As described in Chapter 8, the abbot authorized formation of a task force to study the potential benefits of an arboretum. The task force presented their findings to the abbot and his Senior Council for approval. The Council then decided to present the idea to the Chapter, the whole community of monks. This process for approving the arboretum followed the standard decision process for the abbey, where the monks emphasize consensus in decisions about resources that they all hold in common. The abbot could set the process in motion, but only after the entire community approved the idea could abbey lands be converted into an arboretum.

A similar decision process unfolded at the Jewish Reconstructionist Congregation. There an environmental task force introduced the idea of using green building techniques for the new synagogue. They made a presentation to the board, which then presented the idea to the congregation. Decisions about construction of buildings are among the most participatory processes in faith communities; they require extensive community engagement to ensure that people are enthusiastic about the project and will provide the necessary financial support. The process includes community discussion of needs and preferences as well as several years of fundraising. The option of building green was integrated into these discussions and fundraising appeals so that the community had plenty of time to learn about alternative construction techniques. Neither the board nor the building committee made the decision to pursue LEED certification, the congregation voted to do so as part of the building decision process.

The scale of the projects combined with cultural traditions of congregational participation to ensure use of participatory decision processes at Saint John's Abbey and the Jewish Reconstructionist Congregation; only the congregations could make decisions that would fundamentally affect their resources and their futures. Nevertheless, cases where the sustainability projects being discussed were much smaller also employed participatory processes. The congregation at the First Universalist Church of Rockland was asked to vote on whether the church should enroll in the Green Sanctuary Program. This vote took place during the Annual Meeting, a gathering in which a congregation elects board members, approves the budget, reviews committee reports, and elects new committees. Holding the vote during the Annual Meeting ensured a high rate of congregational participation and allowed for immediate approval of a Green Sanctuary Committee to carry out the congregation's affirmative decision.

The decision process at Trinity Presbyterian Church in Harrisonburg also engaged the congregation during an annual community meeting. As previously noted, the process for "calling" a house church required presentation of a formal covenant describing its mission and proposed activities. This presentation took place in the fall, during a meeting in which the congregation would decide whether proposed house churches were appropriate ministries for fulfilling the church's mission. Through this process, the congregation annually engaged with and affirmed the Earth Care House Church mission to care for creation.

At the Madison Christian Community, some of the decisions about sustainability projects involved the whole congregation and others only involved the board. The difference had to do with the scale of the proposed projects. In this ecumenical community with two congregations, when an individual comes up with an idea for a project, he/she checks to see if others share interest in it and, if so, they form a task force to research costs, benefits, and drawbacks and take a proposal to the board. Unless the project costs more than $10,000, which requires a vote from the entire congregation, the board evaluates whether the idea fits with the community's mission and would be an appropriate use of resources. According to Tom Matthews, this format for interactions between task forces and board allows members to actively participate in church governance while also placing some reality checks on enthusiastic small groups. He commented, "It's good to have this review because sometimes the task force is made up of advocates who really want something but don't represent the congregation as a whole. The board thinks about the costs and opportunity costs, which means considering what we will not be able to spend money on if we spend it on this instead."[10] Matthews indicated that members of the Madison Christian Community perceived the elected board as a body that represented the congregation, with the result that congregational support was implied when the board made decisions.

Although the projects at First Universalist Church, Trinity Presbyterian Church, and the Madison Christian Community were smaller than those at Saint John's Abbey and the Jewish Reconstructionist Congregation, they still used participatory decision processes. Despite the variety of projects, these were all decisions about ministry emphases and, as Matthews notes, they involved tradeoffs in allocation of resources. Even if a project did not require large financial resources, it would draw on a community's limited reserves of staff and volunteer time and energy. Therefore, it was important for congregation members to be involved in choosing which projects they wanted to support.

Non-Participatory Decision Processes

In contrast to the eleven cases with participatory processes, there were four with standard operating procedures that did not require congregational participation in the decision to adopt an earth-care ministry. At St. Thomas Aquinas Catholic Parish, the senior pastor authorized formation of the Green Committee in response to a request from lay members. This top-down decision process is in keeping with the hierarchical structure of the Catholic Church. At the Vineyard Church of Ann Arbor, decision processes were handled by the pastors and a board. The pastors had authority over ministry decisions, and the board focused on fiscal management. In this case, the senior pastor encouraged an individual to found the Green Vineyard small group and, later, both pastors gave permission for another individual to create a community garden. Because both of these projects were designated as ministries, there was no need for board approval or for consultation with the congregation. The Vineyard board did participate in a decision to adopt a creation care policy that would require consideration of sustainability in choices about management of the building because this policy could affect finances. The congregation, however, played no part in the policy decision and it is probable that few people in the faith community were aware of it since policies are not visible to people who are not involved in their application.

Two final cases followed operating procedures that did not require congregational participation in earth-care decisions. Both of the Reform Jewish communities enrolled in the GreenFaith certification program after it was approved by their boards and rabbis. In these cases, the congregations were informed and were asked to support the programs after the decisions had been made. Decision processes in Reform temples vary depending on the issue; in general, the congregation empowers the board with decision-making authority and trusts it to make business decisions for the community. Perhaps these two communities did not perceive a need for congregational participation in the decision to seek green certification because the boards had already identified members who would lead the programs and there were no large financial considerations attached to the decisions.

POLITIES AND DECISION PROCESSES

Although governance structures determined some of the variations in decision processes, they are not sufficient to explain all of the differences among the case studies. It is, of course, possible to ascribe the lack of congregational participation at St. Thomas Aquinas to the episcopal structure of the Catholic Church, which gives authority to the priest. On the other end of the spectrum, the highly participatory processes in the women's monastic communities can be attributed to a form of congregational-presbyterian polity, in which the congregation makes decisions and elects a leadership team to implement them. Polity does not, however, explain the spectrum of participation among the nine non-monastic cases with presbyterian governance systems. For these communities, variations in levels of participation ranged from nearly as high as the women monastics to nearly as low as the Catholic parish, which suggests that other factors may also have influenced congregational involvement in decisions to engage in earth care.

The decision process at First Parish Church of Newbury was highly participatory. In this case, specific conditions contributed to congregational engagement: in addition to denominational emphasis on consensus decisions, the community had become so small that most members were regularly involved in the tasks necessary to sustain it, and a process for deciding whether the community would continue to exist naturally drew widespread interest. Community culture also combined with project scale to increase the likelihood of participation at the Jewish Reconstructionist Congregation and

Saint John's Abbey, where the projects under consideration would affect the resources and welfare of the entire communities. In these three cases, as for the women monastics, decisions to adopt earth care ministries were tied to decisions about the futures of the faith communities.

First Universalist Church of Rockland and Trinity Presbyterian Church of Harrisonburg had denominational cultural traditions that facilitated participatory decisions about ministry. The Unitarian Universalist Association's Green Sanctuary Program mandates a congregational vote before a church can enroll in the program because democratic processes are among the core principles of the denomination and because communities are more likely to succeed in attaining certification if there is buy-in from the congregation. Similarly, the Presbyterian house church system provided procedures for congregational approval of ministries so the whole community was engaged in decisions about how the church would implement its mission of service to the world. As with the Green Sanctuary vote, this process ensures that ministries are effective because congregation members are more likely to join and support house churches they have approved.

The middle of the spectrum includes a set of cases where boards played a more direct role than congregations. At the Madison Christian Community and Trinity Presbyterian Church of East Brunswick, task forces or committees reported to boards, which made decisions about approving sustainability projects. Despite the similarity of polity, these two communities followed dissimilar paths in development of their initiatives. In Madison, the sustainability initiative began with approval of solar panels, which led to efforts to conserve energy, then moved on to creation of extensive community gardening projects. As the number of activities increased, the community came to see earth care as an important part of its mission. Trinity, on the other hand, began with an earth care mission, adopted through mission discernment and approved by the board, then developed projects through which to fulfill it.

The work of the mission discernment committee at Trinity added an element of member participation that differed from the processes at Anshe Emeth Memorial Temple and Temple Shalom. In these Reform Jewish temples, the boards and rabbis decided to pursue green certification without consulting their congregations. Members were, however, expected to contribute to the certification process by participating in earth-care activities. That element of participation was less evident at the Vineyard Church of Ann Arbor, where the pastor authorized development of green ministries that interested specific individuals in the community without consulting the board or the congregation.

Comparing all fifteen cases suggests that the different levels of congregational participation derived from a combination of operating norms and scale. For some communities, such as the convents and First Parish Church of Newbury, participatory decision processes were standard operating procedures. Traditions of congregational input on ministries during annual meetings also provided opportunities for participatory decisions at First Universalist Church of Rockland and Trinity Presbyterian Church of Harrisonburg. For others, like St. Thomas Aquinas Catholic Parish and the Vineyard Church of Ann Arbor, standard operating procedures meant that most decisions were handled by the pastors. The majority of the communities had presbyterian polities that fell in between these poles. In these cases, the larger the scale of the project, the more likely the community would follow participatory decision processes instead of relying solely on the elected board. This issue of scale explains why participatory processes were prevalent in cases where communities made decisions about adopting a community-wide earth-care ethic or engaging in projects that would require significant investment of resources.

2 GREEN TEAM MANAGEMENT

Once a community decided to engage in earth-care activities, it needed a group to lead its efforts. These groups, whether called green teams, green committees, environmental task forces, earth teams, or some other term, took on formats for small groups or committees that were familiar to their communities. They also adopted standard organizational procedures for committee operations, which included meeting management protocols, practices of group study, religious ritual and fellowship cultivation, and inclusive decision making. Although some of these practices would be found in other types of organizations, the elements of religious practice woven into the operational procedures for these green teams are particular to religious organizations.

Green Team Group Format

Green teams took on formats that were familiar to their communities. Some of these formats facilitated development of earth care ministries by making it easy to establish a green team within the structure of a religious organization. The house church system facilitated creation of an Earth Care group at Trinity Presbyterian Church of Harrisonburg, and the tradition of small group ministry made it easy to establish a Green Vineyard group for people with shared environmental concerns. Other communities had long traditions of using task forces to study and implement specific projects, which provided models for creation of environmental task forces that often evolved into green teams. Thus, for example, an Environmental Task Force that began with an emphasis on scriptural study and incorporating earth care into liturgy at the Jewish Reconstructionist Congregation took the lead in promoting green practices for the new synagogue building. Similarly, a task force created to study the potential for installing a wind turbine at the Madison Christian Community evolved into a core group of members who implemented resource conservation practices and engaged in land stewardship. As the number of projects and involved people increased at MCC, it became necessary to have annual coordinating meetings that brought together the committees doing prairie restoration, food pantry gardening, community gardening, and children's garden programs so that there would be less chance of "stepping on each other's toes."[11]

It was relatively easy for individuals with shared environmental interests to adopt small group formats for exploring religious teachings about the environment or pursuing a specific project, however, finding an appropriate format for a green team with a mission to implement sustainability initiatives throughout a community could be more complicated. At St. Thomas Aquinas Parish, the Green Committee was created as a subcommittee of the Facilities Committee, with a membership comprised of volunteers and the director of facilities, and a mission to green the whole parish. Due to its place within the organizational structure, the operating norms for the Green Committee focused on recommendations to the Facilities Committee. In several of the monastic communities, green teams were shaped by the necessity of ensuring that their earth-care work fit organizational norms for generating income. At Villa Maria and Nazareth, the green teams became ministry committees that spent as much time developing eco-spirituality programs for retreat center ministries as working to make organizational operations more sustainable.

Familiar committee formats could also constrain green teams that tried to span multiple areas of a religious organization. In the three cases that enrolled in the GreenFaith Program, the green teams were required to include the heads of all other committees in their religious organizations. Over time, however, the mandated inter-committee format gave way to a more traditional pattern in which individuals with environmental concerns were the active green team members and did most of the work.

Management and Planning

Green teams used management and planning protocols adopted from previously established traditions within their communities. For example, the chairperson from the Human Concerns Committee was invited to serve as the chair of the Green Committee at St. Thomas Aquinas Parish during the inaugural year of the community's sustainability initiative. He instituted normative practices that included use of meeting agendas and minutes to organize information, designating a lead person to coordinate specific projects, and beginning meetings with a prayer. Adherence to similar foundational management practices was common across the cases and reflected the leadership knowledge of the individuals who championed these sustainability initiatives.

Group Study

In addition to standard meeting management practices, organizational procedures for green teams in many cases included group study. Sometimes these studies were aimed at specific projects, such as the potential installation of a wind turbine, but most green teams also incorporated some long-term study of eco-theology or environmental writings into their annual activities. For Trinity's Earth Care House Church, study was mandated under the nurture mark in order to build an understanding of the connections between religion and the house church's ministry focus. The materials the Earth Care House Church studied indicate how the group's interests evolved over two decades of activity. They started with theological texts such as the Presbyterian Church (USA) publications *Restoring Creation for Ecology and Justice*[12] and *Hope for a Global Future: Toward Just and Sustainable Human Development*[13] as well as more general works, like *Theology for Earth Community*[14] and *Earth Community, Earth Ethics*.[15] As the group members became increasingly interested in "doing something," they shifted their focus to texts that described ways to take action such as: *Animal, Vegetable, Miracle: A Year of Food Life*;[16] *Serve God, Save the Planet: A Christian Call to Action*;[17] and *Natural Saints: How People of Faith are Working to Save God's Earth*.[18]

Other green teams also engaged in study to explore connections between faith and earth care and to gain an understanding of environmental issues that would help them figure out how to take action. Thus, Green Vineyard engaged in Bible study to examine scriptural bases for creation care, and members of the First Universalist Church of Rockland formed a Green Chalice Circle in which to read and discuss environmental writings. At St. Thomas Aquinas Parish, Katia Reeves organized the Green Committee meetings around the St. Francis Pledge, which included instructions to "learn about and educate others on the causes and moral dimensions of climate change" and to "assess how each of us—as individuals or within our families, workplaces, or other organizations—is contributing to climate change."[19] For those who promote the St. Francis Pledge, learning and assessing are understood to be necessary precursors to action and advocacy. Similarly, men and women in monastic communities studied eco-theological teachings in study groups exploring whether to adopt earth care as a community ethic and on task forces working to develop sustainability initiatives.

Religious Rituals and Fellowship

Religious rituals and fellowship were regular components of group protocols that distinguish faith-based organizational procedures from those of secular groups. Most green teams began their meetings with prayer. At Trinity Presbyterian Church of East Brunswick, Debbie O'Halloran drew on practices used in Bible study classes for her leadership of the study group that examined whether to recommend earth care as a mission focus. In addition to investigating how environmental issues contributed to poverty, food insecurity, immigration, and violence, committee members were encouraged to engage in prayer and reflection about how these issues intersected with their religious lives. In its early days, prayers at the opening of the St. Thomas Aquinas Green Committee meetings varied from month to month, as different members took turns bringing in favorite prayers to share. Gradually, however, they adopted one standard prayer as part of their regular routine. As an alternative to prayer, the Green Sanctuary Committee at First Universalist Church of Rockland lit a chalice, the oil-filled vessel that is traditionally lit at the beginning of Unitarian Universalist worship services. Meetings also included fellowship practices such as personal "check-ins" in which members were invited to share joys and concerns that were affecting their lives. The Earth Care House Church celebrated birthdays and important events in members' lives as a way to fulfill the fellowship mark and build relationships within the group.

Across the cases, there was an emphasis on inclusive decision-making as part of green team operational practices. When interviewees were asked how they selected activities, they explained that all of the team members contributed ideas and the group supported each other in developing projects that addressed individual members' interests. Judy LePera, of Trinity Presbyterian Church in Harrisonburg, described the process by which one of the longest running groups selected its activities each year:

> We begin the year with a conversation about "What brought you to the Earth Care House Church?" The issues are all over the map: one person is concerned about water quality, another is interested in kids and nature, and for someone else it's about mountaintop removal mining. What gets chosen depends on who joins [for that year]. Different people take the lead in developing projects that go in different directions instead of having one narrow focus. Somehow it works, maybe because we all feel like we're part of a family.[20]

According to LePera, the Earth Care group sometimes worries that they will not be able to manage all the issues that get proposed, but it is important to them, as a group, to address the concerns of each member so they do not turn down anyone's request. Even in cases where activity selection was partially defined by green certification requirements, green teams made decisions based on the interests of their entire group. Mike Chodroff described the process for selecting sustainability activities at Anshe Emeth Memorial Temple: "We do it as a team. We talk about what we want to do. During the first year, we had all the requirements from GreenFaith. We had these amazing brainstorming sessions about how to fulfill the requirements. The ideas came from our interests and ideas from the congregation."[21] Across the cases, there was recognition of the importance of engaging people with diverse interests and talents in order to implement initiatives.

3 COMMUNITY INTERACTIONS

In addition to organizational procedures that provided guidelines for managing green teams, initiative development was facilitated by faith community protocols for interactions between affinity groups and the wider faith community. These interactions took place through presentations to the community and through communication media, primarily newsletters.

Presentations to the Community

Trinity's house church system offered a particularly effective model for fostering communication between small groups and the congregation. Every fall, the "calling" of house churches during a Sunday service gave the congregation an opportunity to formally affirm its support for each house church's ministry. The following summer, house church members presented reports summarizing their activities from the past year. These reports allowed for celebration of accomplishments while also increasing congregational awareness of house church activities. Moreover, because the congregation was asked to evaluate whether the house church was fulfilling an important ministry and should be recalled for another year, the annual summaries created a context in which the whole congregation actively endorsed earth care as a community mission.

Other faith communities had similar organizational processes for interacting with ministry groups. In many cases, committees proposed creation of green teams or submitted reports summarizing a team's accomplishments during a community's annual meeting. The First Universalist Church of Rockland sought community authorization to seek Green Sanctuary certification during such a meeting, which also raised awareness in the community and helped boost participation when the Green Sanctuary Committee subsequently organized a brainstorming meeting to ask the congregation to participate in decisions about the types of activities they should undertake. Likewise, the Anshe Emeth Memorial Temple Green Team used an annual meeting to inform the congregation that they were enrolling in the GreenFaith program and invited the wider community to share ideas for activities. Presentations during community meetings provided opportunities for people who did not have time to serve on the Green Team to make suggestions, thus leading to Chodroff's comment (above) that the ideas for their activities came from both the Green Team and the congregation. For cases in which organizational procedures did not allow green teams to make presentations to the whole community, there were alternative practices like that of St. Thomas Aquinas Parish, in which the Green Committee submitted written reports, summarizing the year's accomplishments, to the community leadership.

Newsletters provided green teams with a simple procedure for communicating with their faith communities. In most of the cases, green teams composed regular monthly articles to share information about their sustainability initiatives. These articles described their earth-care mission and its theological foundations, let people know about upcoming events they could attend, and provided tips for resource conservation behaviors that could be undertaken at home.

CONSTRAINTS:
MISALIGNMENT OF PROCEDURES AND INITIATIVES

Organizational procedures could create limitations where there was a misalignment between traditional practices and an emerging initiative, a situation that occurred in one case. At the Vineyard Church of Ann Arbor, Green Vineyard adopted a small group ministry format. In this faith community, small groups served as venues for Bible study in which people with shared interests, such as single mothers or gourmet cooks, gathered together to discuss scripture and engage in shared activities like cooking a meal. Unlike other small groups, Green Vineyard had a dual mission: to study the Bible in order to understand the scriptural basis for earth care and to undertake activities that would make the church more environmentally sustainable. The first part of this mission fit the traditional practice of small group ministry; however, the second part was out of sync with organizational norms because it included the expectation that people outside of the Green Vineyard group would participate in community-wide environmental activities. Green Vineyard members were distressed when church members did not join in projects such as outings to remove invasive species from nature preserves. However, one interviewee thought the problem had less to do with lack of interest than with a misperception caused by the church's small group norms. Gretchen Marshall-TothFejel suggested that "people didn't think they were supposed to take part in Green Vineyard activities because they didn't belong to the group,"[22] and normally only members of a small group would be expected to participate in its projects.

The experience at Vineyard suggests that a misalignment between a faith community's organizational norms and the mission of its green team could hinder implementation of an initiative. The small group model worked well to support individuals who wished to combine environmental interests with spiritual life but it posed limitations for the Green Vineyard mission of integrating creation care into the social norms of the wider Vineyard Church community. At the time of this study, Pastor Ken Wilson was trying to revive Green Vineyard, which had faded away due to member attrition, and was consciously looking for a new model that would integrate earth care into the entire faith community.

> The small group model worked well. They met at Phil and Cassie Brabbs' house and they really supported each other in their interests. That's what the small group is supposed to do, be a supportive community.
>
> The goal now is different. We want to have an overarching framework. That's why we liked the St. Francis Sustainability Model [a framework for greening a congregation developed by Michigan Interfaith Power and Light][23]; it has a whole framework. The key to ministry is naming and claiming various projects, naming all the things we do, like the organic garden and recycling, as part of Green Vineyard. Then people get a sense that it is integrated into the church and into life. It's not about having a separate group of environmentalists as a subgroup.[24]

Reverend Wilson recognized the need to replace the constraining format of the small group with a framework that better fit the goal of integrating creation care into the social norms of the whole Vineyard Church community. Like the Trinity Earth Shepherds who enrolled in the GreenFaith program and the Earth Care group at First Universalist Church of Rockland who enrolled in the Green Sanctuary Program, that meant turning to resources outside the faith community that could provide useful programmatic structures.

EFFECTS:
ORGANIZATIONAL PROCEDURES FACILITATED INITIATIVES

Supportive organizational procedures made it easier to integrate sustainability into faith communities and to create effective, durable initiatives. Processes for making decisions about adopting earth care ministry, establishing and managing green teams, and facilitating interactions between green teams and congregations were particularly significant (see Table 18).

The case-study experiences indicate that specific operating procedures facilitated the emergence and implementation of sustainability initiatives. First, participatory decision processes enabled congregational involvement in decisions about adopting earth-care ethics and ministry projects, a factor

TABLE 18 ORGANIZATIONAL PROCEDURES
THAT FACILITATED INITIATIVES

ORGANIZATIONAL PROCEDURES	EFFECTS ON INITIATIVES
Participatory decision processes	Involved congregation in adoption of earth care
Pre-existing formats for affinity groups	Enabled establishment of a green team
Procedures for group operations: Management and planning Rituals and fellowship practices Group study Inclusive decision processes	*Increased green team efficacy:* Facilitated implementation of activities Sustained team members
Procedures for interaction with congregation	Fostered congregational support

that was vital to fostering community support and gaining resources for implementation (see Chapter 8). Second, protocols for affinity groups with a specific task, such as committees, task forces, or small ministry groups, provided formats for creating green teams that would be recognized as legitimate groups for engaging in faith-based work. Third, these group formats contributed practical elements such as management processes that enabled champions to plan and implement projects effectively. They also provided inspirational practices of faith and fellowship that individuals cited as vital for dealing with despair and burnout; these practices helped people persevere in their work. In particular, religious practices such as prayer, which distinguish operational procedures of a faith-based group from those of a secular organization, reinforced the conviction that earth care was a religious activity and contributed to the sense of commitment that sustained individuals on green teams (see Chapter 3). Finally, some communities had organizational processes that created opportunities for regular interactions between green teams and congregations, thereby fostering greater community awareness of earth-care activities. These interactions contributed to the development of a sustainability social norm by reminding congregations of their decision to affirm earth care as a faith issue and by amplifying members' perceptions that sustainability is part of a community's practices.

Together, these supportive organizational procedures made significant contributions to initiatives. They facilitated creation, management, and maintenance of green teams that fit into the religious organization, thereby making it easier for champions to integrate earth-care activities into their faith communities. Moreover, they provided opportunities for cultivating the congregational support that was vital for effective, durable programs. Debbie O'Halloran stressed the importance of processes that fostered "across-the-board support" from the congregation in order to successfully implement the earth care mission at Trinity Presbyterian Church in East Brunswick.[25] The Trinity Earth Shepherds achieved this support through a participatory decision process. They asked all of the commission chairs who led ministry committees at the church to participate in the decision to join the GreenFaith program as a means of achieving the earth-care mission that the community had adopted. This process ensured that there was buy-in from all of the groups that carry out the administrative and religious programming for the faith community. As a result, commission chairs took responsibility for integrating environmental activities into their work. Thus, for example, the Deacons Commission decided to switch from disposable dishes to washable ones for coffee hour, and the Finance Commission, which handled building maintenance, upgraded the lighting to reduce energy consumption. The Trinity story not only illustrates the importance of participatory processes for gaining the support necessary to successfully integrate earth care into a faith community, it also reveals the critical role of organizational structures, which provided the venues through which to take action, a topic that will be explored further in the next chapter.

10 STRUCTURES AS VENUES FOR IMPLEMENTING INITIATIVES

[A] great aspect of what has happened here is that the temple administration has changed the purchasing practices. They'll only buy supplies
that are compostable or biodegradable. As lights need to be replaced,
they're being replaced with more efficient bulbs. And the cleaning supplies are green now.
—MICHAEL CHODROFF, Anshe Emeth Memorial Temple

A RELIGIOUS ORGANIZATION HAS STRUCTURES for maintaining itself and
for fulfilling its mission to cultivate members' religious lives. Maintaining
an organization requires administrative systems for governance, staff management, accounting, communications, and membership records as well as
maintenance of buildings and grounds. Fulfillment of religious missions
requires staff, volunteers, and management of programs. The case-study communities implemented their sustainability initiatives through the structures
of their religious organizations, and those structures affected development
and implementation of the initiatives.

VENUES FOR IMPLEMENTING INITIATIVES

The structures of the religious organizations included worship services,
religious education programs, ministries, administration, and facilities management (building and grounds). The first three venues are program areas
specific to faith communities; they serve the purpose of fulfilling the organization's religious mission. Administration and facilities, on the other hand, are
components of most organizations and are not unique to faith communities.

The following pages describe these two general areas and how they affected the initiatives.

I   *Religious Program Venues*

The programs through which religious organizations met the spiritual needs of their faith communities offered venues for integrating earth care into community culture. Messages about earth care as a religious practice were incorporated into worship services and religious education programs. Once members decided to develop a sustainability initiative, the community's ministries, the activities through which it expressed its religious values, also became venues for implementing earth-care actions (see Table 19).

TABLE 19 RELIGIOUS PROGRAM VENUES
FOR IMPLEMENTING INITIATIVES

	ACTIVITY VENUE	TYPES OF ACTIVITIES
1	Worship services	Earth-care themed services Sermons Rituals (e.g. bless gardens)
2	Religious Education Programs (for children and adults)	Sunday school activities, Faith-based environmental education Study groups: scripture, theology, ecology Informational events (films, presentations)
3	Ministries	Environmental education: preschools, summer camps Gardening and food donations Social Justice Retreat Centers: programs and infrastructure

1   *Worship Services*

Worship, especially through community rituals, is a core activity for religious organizations and served as a key venue for integrating earth care into the culture of a faith community. Part III of this book described a variety of mechanisms faith leaders used to share messages about the religious obligation to care for the earth. Worship services provided the context for message mechanisms that included sermons, spring and fall prayers for fruitful gardens, and blessing rituals for events such as installation of solar panels. In nine of the ten non-monastic communities, clergy incorporated earth-care messages into regular worship services by addressing the topic in sermons. Some religious traditions allow lay members to lead services occasionally, and, for Christian or Unitarian Universalist case-study communities with this option, green teams often took the lead in organizing an Earth Day Sunday service.

The liturgical calendar, with its yearly cycle of traditional holy days, also provided opportunities for integrating earth care into worship services. At the Jewish Reconstructionist Congregation, the Environmental Task Force organized a Tu BiShvat celebration, with some assistance from the rabbi.[1] Tu BiShvat, which falls on a day in late January or early February,[2] is the date that marks the "birthday" for trees.[3] Tracking tree age is important because biblical rules specify how old a tree must be before it is permissible to harvest fruit: "When you come to the land and you plant any tree, you shall treat its fruit as forbidden; for three years it will be forbidden and not eaten. In the fourth year, all of its fruit shall be sanctified to praise the L-RD[4]. In the fifth year, you may eat its fruit" (Lev. 19:23–25). This minor holiday is often celebrated with a ritual meal (*seder*) that includes seven "fruits" that the Torah describes as being abundant in Israel: wheat, barley, grapes (vines), figs, pomegranates, olives, and dates (or honey) (Deut. 8:8). In the early twentieth century, Israelis began a tradition of planting trees on this holiday, and, later, Jewish environmentalists adopted it as a time for raising environmental awareness. Because of this environmental tradition, the holiday served as an opportunity to integrate earth care into worship at the Jewish Reconstructionist Congregation. The Environmental Task Force began organizing Tu BiShvat seders that brought people together to eat while learning about the Jewish relationship to the environment through activities for kids and educational presentations for adults.

2 Religious Education Programs

Most of the faith communities had religious education programs for children and adults, and these programs offered opportunities for introducing information about sustainability to members. Communities incorporated environmental stewardship into curricula designed to teach children about the ethical codes of their religious traditions. They also organized educational events to share information with adults.

EARTH CARE EDUCATION FOR CHILDREN AND YOUTH. Religious education programs for children and youth were prominent venues for addressing earth-care missions in eight of the ten non–monastic cases. Teachers incorporated environmental ethics into curricula, often using materials that were available from denominational websites. At Anshe Emeth Memorial Temple, Mike Chodroff, the environmental educator leading the community's GreenFaith certification process, began teaching an elective course on Jews and Ecology for eighth- through eleventh-grade youth. He also worked with other members of the temple to incorporate earth care into the annual Mitzvah Day service project so that the donations children and parents packed and distributed to needy people in their New Jersey area were placed in reusable shopping bags. At Temple Shalom, Margo Wolfson's religious education classes for third through fifth graders regularly discussed green teachings in the weekly Torah readings, which included numerous references to caring for lands and animals that were important for the agricultural lives of the ancient Israelites. Rabbi Malinger also developed an environmentally themed course for teens during Temple Shalom's participation in the GreenFaith program. At the First Universalist Church of Rockland, children learned about caring for the earth in their Sunday school classes, during which they helped paint a banner proclaiming, "We believe in caring for our planet earth," to be hung over the entryway to the building.[5]

In addition to study of scriptures and wisdom teachings, youth engaged in environmentally themed activities as diverse as gardening, nature hikes, canoe trips to the Boundary Waters of Minnesota, field trips to local farms, service projects to clean up beaches, celebrating the birthday of Charles Darwin, and weatherizing a church building. The latter occurred at Trinity Presbyterian Church in Harrisonburg, where members of the Earth Care House Church led a Sunday school project focused on energy conservation. They showed middle-school students how to use various types of weatherization materials, such as caulk and weather stripping, and explained which materials were best suited to particular situations. They then turned the students loose on the older section of the church, an area of offices and meetings spaces, and let them decide how to use the available materials to make the building more energy efficient. After the students finished weatherizing the building, they were asked what they would do with their new skills. Several said they planned to repeat the activity at home. St. Thomas Aquinas Parish did not have a formal earth-care component to its Sunday school classes, but it developed environmental education programming for children at its annual picnics. The Green Committee organized activities such as a recycling game, in which kids received prizes if they sorted materials into correct categories of "recyclable or waste," and blind taste-testing of bottled versus tap water, to educate people about the advantages of tap water.

Despite general agreement that it was important to incorporate earth care into the moral education of children, one interviewee expressed concern that communities might perceive youth education as an adequate response to climate change, thereby absolving adults of the need to make significant changes in their personal behavior. She considered this "pediatric approach to sustainability" to be one of the greatest barriers to fostering real changes in the social norms of a faith community.

EARTH CARE EDUCATION FOR ADULTS. Adult education traditions also provided a venue for earth care action. Many of the faith communities organized regular educational programs for adults, often with a mix of formats, such as textual studies, film series, and guest presentations. Textual studies might involve weekly or monthly meetings to explore a specific section of scripture or the writings of select theologians. Anshe Emeth Memorial Temple had a practice of Kollel or "Jewish Learning with Scholars, Rabbis, and Community Leaders" in the form of an annual adult education course that "brings together great teachers and topics that help challenge and push curious adult minds towards further growth and knowledge."[6] During the period in which the community was working toward GreenFaith certification, Mike Chodroff organized an environmental course for the Kollel.

Film series, which are popular for adult education, might include overtly religious films or secular productions on topics of interest. Several green teams showed the documentary *Renewal* (2007), which presents eight stories of religious environmentalism focused on combating climate change, campaigning against mountaintop removal mining, promoting food security, recycling, reducing waste, advocating for environmental justice, and striving to preserve land, water, and trees. In 2011–12, some communities watched *Sun Come Up*, a documentary that highlights the moral implications of climate change by showing refugees from the Carteret Islands trying to find a place where their people can relocate as sea levels rise.[7] Green teams also organized film series using a variety of secular films about climate change, renewable energy, and organic farming.

3 Ministries

Religious organizations sponsor ministries through which members enact the moral teachings of their traditions. Some ministries, such as Bible study and retreats, focus on cultivation of personal spiritual insights. Others strive to address social needs by providing food, health care, and education to members and other people in the local community. Within the case-study communities, ministries that focused on education, food donations, social justice, and retreat centers became venues through which to implement sustainability initiatives.

ENVIRONMENTAL EDUCATION MINISTRY. Several faith communities developed environmental education programs for children that were separate from their Sunday school programs and were open to the general public. Some of these programs were religious and others were secular, but all were developed as forms of earth-care ministry with the goal of educating young people about earth care through a combination of outdoor experiences and educational curricula. In these cases, the buildings and grounds of the religious organizations served as resources for integrating environmental education into the ministry work of the faith communities.

At Trinity Presbyterian Church in East Brunswick, the community provided classroom space for the Little Earth Shepherds Preschool Learning Center as a means of fulfilling its environmental mission statement: *"We, as a family of faith, believe that it is the responsibility of all to Care for God's Creation through environmental education, conservation, and community outreach."*[8] The preschool program was designed to combine high-quality early education with an introduction to earth care in a Christian learning environment. According to the church website, an important aspect of that curriculum would involve time outdoors on the church grounds: "We will offer early childhood exposure to the concept of caring for creation and the world we live in. Children will have an opportunity to experience the beauty of the earth during outside activities in our on-site Vegetable Garden, as well as our Butterfly Garden—which has been designated as a Natural Wildlife Habitat by the National Wildlife Federation."[9]

Like Trinity, First Parish Church of Newbury sponsored a preschool that was created in response to the community's mission to be Stewards of Earth and Spirit, however Our Secret Garden Indoor/Outdoor Nursery and Preschool was a secular program. It used the renovated basement of the church, where large fish tanks divided the room into separate activity areas, as well as an outdoor play space in back of the church. As the program name indicates, the preschool combined indoor and outdoor activities to fulfill its educational philosophy, as described on the church website:

Our Secret Garden Indoor/Outdoor Nursery and Preschool (OSG) is a nature-based center aimed at nurturing children of all abilities to care for themselves, each other, and the earth in a quality educational program that kindles children's natural sense of wonder and intellectual curiosity. Experiencing nature hands-on and then taking that experience into the classroom sparks learning at the highest level of each individual child's potential. OSG is committed to environmental stewardship, believing that every child has incalculable worth and can make a positive difference in the community and in the world.[10]

Renovating the basement and acquiring the necessary permits to begin the preschool were expensive and time-intensive tasks, however the congregation members persevered because the project was perceived as an important contribution they could make to their local community.

Other cases also used their physical resources to provide space for environmental education programs that would expose children to nature. As described in previous chapters, Kids in the Garden was a summer program that brought children from a low-income neighborhood to the grounds of the Madison Christian Community, where they learned about growing fruits and vegetables and preparing healthy snacks. When the Sisters of the Humility of Mary began developing the Villa Maria Education and Spirituality Center, a couple of sisters and the farm manager created a Farm-Based Environmental Education ministry for children. One of their programs was a summer camp called GROW (Gardening, Responsibility, Once Weekly[11]) that brought elementary school children from nearby urban areas out to the Villa Farm to "learn the value of the land through gardening, nature crafts, swimming, plant and animal care, hayrides, and much more."[12] At Trinity Presbyterian Church in Harrisonburg, a member of the Earth Care House Church acquired a grant that supported a summer program to take urban youth on outdoor field trips during the summer.

GARDENING AND FOOD DONATIONS. Many religious organizations in the US contribute funds or supplies to food pantries and sponsor groups that take turns staffing soup kitchens, so there is a well-established precedent for food-related ministry work. Several faith communities were inspired to develop gardening ministries that added fresh produce to their pre-existing poverty alleviation ministries. Five of the case studies included creation of gardens for food pantry donations, and a sixth started a project growing herbs for a nearby soup kitchen. At Villa Maria, where the sisters had provided aid to people in need since the nineteenth century, the land manager was instructed to continue growing potatoes for the poor even after the convent's commercial farm operation was discontinued in the 1980s. With this heritage, it was natural that, when Sister Barbara O'Donnell and the land manager developed a new venture in organic gardening, a large portion of the produce would be donated to a local food pantry.

Partnerships with external food pantries facilitated distribution of garden produce for some faith communities. For example, the Green Team at Temple Shalom formed a partnership with a Methodist church that had a food pantry. Members from the two congregations helped in each other's gardens, and the produce from Temple Shalom's garden was donated to the Methodist church for distribution. Madison Christian Community also sent produce from its Food Pantry Garden to a nearby pantry for distribution. At the Vineyard Church of Ann Arbor, the Community Garden Ministry was begun in response to a presentation about a Faith and Food Program being organized through a county food pantry. Organizers of this program reached out to local faith communities, asking them to start community gardens and donate half of the resulting fresh, organic produce to the pantry. Participating houses of worship would receive assistance from experienced gardeners who could help them plan and set up their gardens, and the food pantry would arrange to pick up the donated produce and handle distribution to needy people in the community. Such partnerships with food pantries made it easier for faith communities to grow fresh produce that would benefit people in the community beyond their congregation membership.

SOCIAL JUSTICE. As discussed in the sections on Faith Leaders and Congregations, many case-study faith communities defined earth care as an extension of their social justice ministry work. Thus, organic food donations and garden programs for low-income children, like the GROW camp at Villa Maria and the Kids in the Garden program at Madison Christian Community, were ways to build a more just society. Pre-existing social justice ministries also provided opportunities for implementing an earth-care ethic. The Sisters of St. Francis of Philadelphia had a well-established ministry in Corporate Social Responsibility as part of their order's mission to "direct our corporate resources to the promotion of justice, peace, and reconciliation."[13] They purchased stock in corporations and attended stockholder meetings, where they encouraged the companies to become more socially responsible by adopting policies to ensure that workers throughout their supply chains were treated well. After the community adopted an earth-care ethic, the sister who led the Corporate Social Responsibility ministry added environmental justice to her stockholder advocacy efforts. During stockholder meetings, she submitted proposals to require that corporations provide information about the social and environmental impacts of their supply chains, with particular attention to examination of how the corporations might be contributing to climate change.

RETREAT CENTERS: PROGRAM CONTENT AND INFRASTRUCTURE. Retreat center ministries provided a venue for enacting an earth-care ethic through both programming and infrastructure. At Villa Maria and Nazareth, sisters developed eco-spirituality programs in which people came to the convents for retreats that included reflection on environmental spiritual teachings and time spent outdoors on the grounds. Offering retreats in which people gather for spiritual development was already a well-established form of ministry work that fit with community social norms: all five monastic communities had traditional practices in which members regularly went on retreats as part of their monastic lifestyle. By the late twentieth century, the monastic communities had begun ministries in which they sponsored retreats for non-members, and eco-spirituality programs were incorporated into those ministries. At Nazareth, the eco-spirituality ministry was combined with other retreat ministries to form the Transformations Spirituality Center, which offers organized retreats on a variety of topics throughout the year.

Connections with other areas of community ministry work facilitated development of eco-spirituality retreat ministries. At Villa Maria, Sister Barbara O'Donnell created and directed an eco-spirituality ministry called EverGreen that combined information about nature with spiritual practices and reflections. O'Donnell attributed some of EverGreen's popularity to its successful association with other program areas within the religious organization, explaining, "It was the fastest growing ministry on campus partly because of the integrative programs. For example, we had connections to the health programs and music therapy and food. Tons of people came for the seasonal rituals. We had lots of programs on food and also on alternative energy. Oh, and journaling."[14] Health care was a ministry area dating back to the nineteenth century. Many of the Sisters of the Humility of Mary (HM) living at Villa Maria had retired from careers in medical care or hospital administration, so connecting earth care to health care resonated with community members. The sisters also had a long tradition of work in education.

O'Donnell drew on her background in education when she and Frank Romeo, the land manager, created the Farm-Based Environmental Education ministry for children. As the environmental education and EverGreen ministries proved successful, the HM leadership team decided to merge them with the older Retreat Center and Education Center ministries. Together, the four programs became the Villa Maria Education and Spirituality Center (VMESC), with a centralized staff and coordinated vision: "VMESC is a sacred setting where God's grace is nurtured and abundant life unfolds. We seek to inspire lifelong learning and growth through relationships with God, others, self, and Earth."[15]

The infrastructure for retreat centers offered another opportunity for implementing an earth-care ethic. At Our Lady of Angels, the Sisters of St. Francis of Philadelphia constructed small hermitages on platforms jutting out over the side of a hill above an undeveloped woodland in order to "tread lightly on the earth" by not disturbing the soil. At Saint John's Abbey, a new guesthouse for retreat participants followed green building principles such as: including numerous windows for natural light; using wood harvested from the Abbey forests for ceilings, floors, wall panels, and furniture; and incorporating a rain garden with native plants into the landscaping where it serves as a settling pond for stormwater runoff. At Holy Wisdom Monastery, solar panels were installed on the roof of the renovated guesthouse and retreat center. All of these monastic communities added outdoor seating, often in native plant gardens, and created nature trails so retreat participants could spend contemplative time outdoors. Thus, the buildings and grounds that housed retreat ministries became venues for practicing earth care. As an additional benefit, these attractive environmental features were highlighted in promotional literature advertising the quality of the retreat facilities.

II *Organizational Management Venues*

Administration and facilities management provided venues through which to make a faith community's operational practices and physical systems more sustainable. Communities "greened" their religious organizations by integrating sustainability into their administrative practices for offices, custodial work, food service, and event planning. In the area of facilities management, they made improvements to building infrastructure, appliances, lighting, and landscaping. They also conserved resources by changing practices for purchasing supplies, using energy, and managing waste as well as adopting new methods for tending the grounds. See Table 20 for a categorization of administrative and facilities operations through which faith communities implemented their earth-care ethics.

TABLE 20 THE GREENING OF ADMINISTRATION
AND FACILITIES

ACTIVITY VENUE	TYPES OF ACTIVITIES
1 Administration	Purchasing policies and office management: recycled content supplies, non-toxic cleaning products, recycling, conservation behavior Kitchens/food: supplies and waste management Event planning (e.g. weddings, b'nai mitzvah, retreats)
2 Facilities (building and grounds)	Green infrastructure: building upgrades, renewable energy generation Technology upgrades: appliances, lighting Conservation behavior: energy, recycling, composting Land management: stewardship practices

1 *Administration*

Administration comprises all of the day-to-day activities necessary to make a religious organization function. These activities include office work, budgets, organizing programs and events, and managing staff. Thus, administration systems provided complex organizational structures where earth care could be integrated into faith communities through changes to policy and behavior. The case-study communities enacted earth care through administrative structures such as purchasing policies, office management, food sources and food service materials in kitchens, waste management, and event planning.

PURCHASING POLICIES AND OFFICE MANAGEMENT. At Anshe Emeth Memorial Temple, staff developed new policies to incorporate sustainability into decisions about supply purchases and building maintenance. In the quote at the beginning of the chapter, Mike Chodroff described the importance of administrative practices for greening the temple: "Another great aspect of what has happened here is that the temple administration has changed the purchasing practices. They'll only buy supplies that are compostable or biodegradable. As lights need to be replaced, they're being replaced with more efficient bulbs. And the cleaning supplies are green now."[16] Similar practices were adopted in all fifteen cases. Office and custodial staff began purchasing paper supplies with higher recycled content, as long as it did not exceed their budgets. They also reduced waste production through increased recycling, printing on both sides of paper, and switching to electronic communications. Communities that were already posting PDF versions of newsletters on their websites in order to improve communications made the online text the default version and reduced the number of copies they were printing. Thus, a practice that had begun for one reason (to make information more accessible) took on new meaning as the community sought ways to conserve resources and reduce waste generation. Anshe Emeth also revised its practice of mailing annual reports; instead, the temple replaced the mailing with an email message containing a link to an online version of the report and a message letting members know that they could request a hard copy if they wanted one. This system reduced printing and mailing costs while also preventing paper from being wasted on reports for people who were not actually interested in reading them.

KITCHENS AND WASTE MANAGEMENT. Kitchens were another venue for improving sustainability through changes in purchasing policies and resource management. Communities purchased fair-trade coffee and tea, encouraged use of local foods, and replaced Styrofoam coffee cups and paper plates with reusable dishes. The move away from disposable dishes was usually accompanied by installation of a new dishwasher, but the community at Trinity Presbyterian Church in East Brunswick organized teams of volunteers to hand wash the dishes.

Some communities with kitchen facilities further reduced waste production by developing composting programs. Often these were simple programs, such as arranging for members to take the used coffee grounds home for their gardens or placing kitchen scraps in compost bins for the community gardens at a house of worship. However, one of the monastic communities, Our Lady of Angels, had a more elaborate program. When the convent learned about a composting plant in Wilmington, Delaware, that would accept post-consumable waste, including food, they decided to create a comprehensive composting system. They designated a place in each office and living area for depositing paper and junk mail, which would be picked up by the housekeeping staff and taken to a bin for dry compostables. A separate bin was used for "wet" compostables like kitchen scraps and dining hall waste; it was centrally located so that sisters who did the cooking could bring scraps and waste to it. The maintenance staff loaded the bins on a truck and transported them to the composting facility. Sister Ruth O'Conner described the measurable difference in waste production that resulted from these practices: "There are about 60 sisters living here, and we feed lunch to 100 staff people every day. We also have the retreat center. So, there used to be *lots* of trash. Now the trash only goes out once a month while compost goes out about every fifteen days." The program succeeded for two reasons. First, it was designed to fit the daily activities of the organization: staff who generated waste or managed waste were provided with training so they knew which materials could be composted and which had to go in the trash. Second, the members were willing to make the effort to support the program because they thought it was important to reduce waste going to landfills, even though it cost more to send materials to the composting facility than to the dump. Thus, they supported the program through their personal efforts and their finances because they considered it "costly, but worth it."[17]

EVENT PLANNING. Along with changes in the daily operations of the organization, some case-study communities encouraged members to consider ways to incorporate earth care into their planning for special events. People who rented facilities for occasions like weddings and b'nai mitzvah[18] (coming of age rituals) were asked to follow guidelines that would uphold the earth-care values of the community. For example, the Jewish Reconstructionist Congregation developed a handout on "Greening Your Simcha" (celebration) to provide guidance on practices that would help members ensure that events were aligned with their community's sustainability ethic. The guide begins with the statement:

> Importantly, we view these guidelines as an opportunity to educate and inspire staff, congregants and guests as to the Jewish values that are at the heart of our JRC community, and to empower all to make conscious decisions in the life of the congregation. In doing so, may we be inspired to bring these values out into our work and home environments as well and truly live as stewards of the earth.[19]

The guide offers suggestions for conservation practices such as sending electronic invitations, selecting reusable decorations, and providing locally sourced food. The synagogue has a kitchen with dishwashers, and the guide informs people that it can provide table service for 100 people, including cloth napkins, if event organizers are willing to be responsible for washing and stacking the dishes. Interviewees also mentioned that JRC had a set of identical tablecloths they are able to use for synagogue events because a group of women in the congregation take turns laundering them at home. The Green Team at Anshe Emeth Memorial Temple also encouraged members to "green" their celebrations, which inspired one family to purchase yarmulkes (skullcaps) made from recycled materials for the guests who attended their daughter's bat mitzvah.

2 Facilities Management

Facilities provided a venue for implementing practices such as energy conservation and pollution prevention by making changes to management of the community's building and grounds. Energy efficiency in buildings is determined by three elements: the building envelope, building systems (appliances), and occupant behavior. To conserve energy, communities "greened" their building infrastructure, upgraded systems technology, and educated their members about ways they could help conserve energy in their houses of worship. Changes in land management policies could also turn community grounds into a venue for resource conservation and sustainable environmental practices.

GREEN INFRASTRUCTURE. Some communities replaced outdated facilities with new green buildings, while others incorporated green construction practices into building renovations or expansions. Three of the monastic communities and two of the non-monastic communities had installed solar panels at the time of this study, and two others were planning solar feasibility studies. Necessary repairs could present opportunities for making buildings more energy efficient, such as when the Vineyard Church added insulation while replacing a worn-out roof. Smaller projects included weatherization of buildings and installation of interior storm windows to prevent heat loss from windows.

TECHNOLOGY UPGRADES. Within the buildings, staff began replacing light bulbs with energy efficient CFL and LED bulbs. Such replacements were not always easy since older light fixtures often needed to be upgraded in order to accommodate new types of bulbs. Lighting, however, is one of the largest energy expenditures in houses of worship, and improvements in this area could make a significant difference in energy consumption.[20] Facilities staff and green teams also looked for Energy Star certified appliances when opportunities for upgrades arose during normal replacement cycles for boilers, water heaters, and air conditioning units. At St. Thomas Aquinas Parish, the women who presided over the church kitchens were aware that one kitchen had a stove with a pilot light that burned continuously and heated the kitchen even when the stove was turned off. The Green Committee researched possible replacement stoves with electric ignition systems that would fit the church's needs and meet budgetary guidelines provided by the facilities manager. They brought their recommendation to the facilities manager, who purchased the stove and later created a report documenting the decrease in the church's gas bill during the following year.

CONSERVATION BEHAVIOR. Weatherized buildings and new appliances significantly lowered utility bills, but behavior change was also a key component in community efforts to conserve resources. Conservation behavior was the least expensive way to save energy but that did not necessarily mean it was easy. Across the cases, communities encouraged staff and members to adopt new practices when using the community's facilities. Office personnel saved energy by using fewer lights, turning off computers at night, and printing fewer pages. Green teams also encouraged congregation members to keep doors closed to prevent loss of heat or air conditioning. "Doors-closed" campaigns were actually a challenge to implement, because there was a tendency to leave doors open before worship services to welcome people as they arrived, especially in milder climates. Consequently, door closing required changes to a long-standing social norm that was shared by a large portion of the faith community's members.

Because practices like leaving doors open and leaving heat on at night were so habitual, it took considerable time and effort to engrain new behaviors into community practices. Green teams wrote newsletter articles and created hand-outs to explain what people could do to conserve energy. They also developed signs that could be posted at appropriate locations to remind people to turn off lights and keep doors closed. At the Madison Christian Community, a sign directly over the dishwasher in the kitchen reminded members not to run the machine until after the lights in the sanctuary were turned off so they would not exceed their utility's threshold for base rate energy use and get charged a higher rate per kilowatt. Establishing new habits required patience, but the efforts paid off. St. Thomas Aquinas Parish reduced its energy use by twelve percent from 2009 to 2010 through a combination of upgrading to more efficient light bulbs, instituting practices such as turning off lights and office equipment when they were not in use, keeping exterior doors shut during cold weather, and posting information about thermostat procedures to remind people to decrease use of heat and air conditioning when buildings were empty.

LAND MANAGEMENT. Land management provided further opportunities for conservation practices. In addition to large-scale projects, such as designating 2,800 acres of land at Saint John's Abbey as an educational arboretum, case-study communities adopted a variety of practices through which to integrate stewardship into smaller scale land management. At St. Thomas Aquinas Parish, the Facilities Committee adopted a policy in which two trees would be planted to replace any one tree that had to be removed from parish grounds. Communities also replaced lawn areas with rain gardens or beds of native plants in order to prevent stormwater runoff, reduce greenhouse gas emissions from mowers, and provide habitat for pollinators. Such changes often required research and staff training. At Our Lady of Angels convent, Sister Corinne Wright, manager of the Environmental Initiative, focused on land management as an activity area where she could effectively implement the sisters' mission to care for creation. She explained, "Where I could have the most influence was here on the grounds of the motherhouse. For example, I could say that we are not going to use pesticides, and because the people who work on the grounds are your employees, they have to do what you say. But I also did it in an educational way, explaining that we wanted to reduce pesticide use to protect beneficial insects and birds."[21] Wright used information from the Pennsylvania State University College of Agricultural Sciences to develop an integrated pest management plan for the convent lands and shared that information with the grounds-keeping staff. According to Wright, once the groundskeepers had an understanding of "what was good and why," they could seek out additional information about ways to fulfill the sisters' earth-care ethic. Although the staff had not come to the convent with prior knowledge of stewardship practices, they became knowledgeable about native plants and alternative pest management in order to fulfill the faith community's goal of caring for the land in a way that was beneficial to the environment.

CONSTRAINTS IMPOSED BY ORGANIZATIONAL STRUCTURE

Just as organizational structures could offer opportunities for implementing earth care actions, so too could they impose constraints on sustainability initiatives. One constraint arose from the structures themselves when the venues available limited the types of actions that could be undertaken. A second constraint had to do with resource limits, both lack of funds and dearth of local services, that affected whether it was possible to make changes to a community's infrastructure and practices. Finally, the third issue that constrained implementation of actions came from inconsistent human behavior, which reduced the efficacy of conservation practices.

ACTION VENUE LIMITATIONS. In some cases, organizational structures constrained initiatives because the action venues available were not well suited to specific types of earth care. At St. Thomas Aquinas Parish, the Green Committee was designated as a subcommittee of the Facilities Committee. This location within the organization was beneficial for the committee's goal of conserving energy: they were able to research efficient appliances and submit recommendations for technology upgrades to the facilities manager, who followed through on recommendations whenever they were financially feasible. However, working through the Facilities Committee did not offer opportunities for environmental justice work even though social justice was one of the core missions of the Green Committee.

Environmental justice was among the most complicated areas of activity for faith communities to integrate into organizational systems. Although a few communities had pre-existing social justice ministries in Corporate Social Responsibility or food donation programs that were suitable venues for addressing environmental justice, others found it difficult to figure out how to take action. Debbie O'Halloran gave a detailed description of the challenges the Trinity Earth Shepherds faced when they tried to carry out environmental justice activities while participating in the GreenFaith program:

> We're very conscious of the environmental justice piece because it's a requirement for GreenFaith. We have an alcove in the church foyer dedicated to our greening efforts and we change the articles there regularly to keep people informed. We also do educational programs three times a year and these tend to focus on topics that are connected to environmental justice like fracking and its effects on low-income communities. We're good at keeping people informed, but I can't say we've kept up the action. GreenFaith organizes annual tours of the Ironbound area [a low-income area of New Jersey that is heavily polluted due to its long industrial history]. I was appalled. I had no idea there was an area like that so nearby. But one local woman who came on the tour bus and talked to us told us that we can't just come in as mid-

dle-class outsiders and try to solve their problems. She said that the people there would resent it. So, it's not easy to know what to do about environmental justice. It's not that you don't want to, it's that you don't know how to.[22]

Education was a type of action that could be easily incorporated into the organizational structure at O'Halloran's church, but there was no venue for political advocacy or campaigning to clean up centuries of pollution in a neighborhood that no church members lived in.

Distance from the daily lives of suburban, middle-class members combined with venue limitations made environmental justice actions a challenge. Some communities found solutions through partnerships with external organizations. The Madison Christian Community was able to engage in environmental justice work, helping low-income children gain access to green space and learn about raising and preparing healthy foods, through a partnership with a community center in a nearby neighborhood. The Lussier Neighborhood Center helped organize the summer program that brought children to the church to participate in the Kids in the Garden program. Similarly, the WindowDressers team at the First Universalist Church of Rockland collaborated with area Catholic churches to find low-income households that would benefit from receiving storm window inserts. As a trusted institution, the Catholic churches could contact low-income members who might need windows, which allowed the program to reach people beyond the social circles of First Universalist's largely middle-class membership. These partnerships helped compensate for limitations in the faith community's action venues, which did not include mechanisms for building long-term relationships with non-members.

LACK OF RESOURCES. Some initiatives faced constraints due to a lack of resources for funding or carrying out conservation practices. Interviewees consistently cited finances as a barrier to installing green infrastructure such as solar panels and new windows. A few communities had access to state or local resources such as the Wisconsin Focus on Energy grant that paid for the solar panels at the Madison Christian Community. Similarly, Saint John's Abbey benefited from Minnesota's renewable energy standard, which required utilities to increase the percentage of energy generated from renewable sources. As a result, Xcel Energy contacted the abbey to see if the monks would be interested in providing land for a solar field and, in 2009, they installed 1,820 panels that produce approximately 575,000 kilowatt-hours annually. The solar project was feasible because it was financed with $2 million in grant money from Xcel Energy's Renewable Development Fund and from Westwood Renewables; no money came from the abbey itself. In California, St. Thomas Aquinas Parish was able to afford technology and landscape improvements because of a municipal City Lights program that paid for installation of efficient LED light bulbs and offered rebates to offset the costs of upgrading to energy-efficient boilers and replanting grounds with water-conserving xeriscaping. By contrast, faith communities in states without such resources faced significant financial barriers to fulfilling their goals of generating clean energy onsite or upgrading buildings and grounds to conserve resources.

In some areas, lack of resources extended beyond finances to lack of local infrastructure, which created barriers for adopting other types of conservation behaviors. The Sisters of St. Francis at Our Lady of Angels in Aston, Pennsylvania, were very pleased when they heard about a new supply company that carried 100 percent recycled copy paper. Unfortunately, it was located in York, eighty-five miles from the convent, and the distance meant that shipping costs would make the paper too expensive. Thinking creatively, they worked out a financially viable solution by sending a convent truck to meet a delivery truck at a halfway point where they could pick up paper supplies three times a year. As the supply company grew, shipping costs declined, thereby making it possible to have supplies of copy paper, recycled-content toilet paper, and eco-friendly detergent delivered straight to the convent. Sister Ruth Bernadette O'Connor, the convent administrator at the time of this research, explained that the sisters were willing to invest time and effort in this complex delivery system because they were not only purchasing products that fit their values, they also felt it was important to provide support to "companies that are trying to be eco-friendly."[23]

In spite of such support, companies could go out of business. The composting facility to which Our Lady of Angels sent their paper and food waste closed down after nearby residents complained about odors and the city government declined to renew the company's permit. This experience prompted Sister Corinne Wright, former manager of the convent's Environmental Initiative, to comment that resource issues were a particular challenge for implementing their earth-care ethic: "It's not an easy task to keep up with all this stuff. Like the loss of the composting; once the arrangements fall apart, it's lots of work to find other options—if any exist at all. It seems like people are always making things difficult, so it's hard to keep our initiatives going."[24]

INCONSISTENT BEHAVIOR. Structures provided venues through which to take action, but the efficacy of the actions undertaken often depended on the behavior of congregation members. Weatherized doors only prevent heat loss if they are kept closed. Conservation practices for reducing use of paper, electricity, and water only work if people adopt the recommended behaviors. Because changes to member behavior were crucial for many of the sustainability projects undertaken, inconsistent behavior emerged as one of the challenges interviewees mentioned frequently. It took time and effort to replace habits with new behavior, and adherence to sustainable practices often fluctuated over time because people were unaware of the earth-care ethic and associated practices. For example, in order to conserve energy at St. Thomas Aquinas Parish, the Green Committee developed thermostat procedure guidelines to be distributed to all facilities users and implemented a closed-door procedure (with signage) to reduce heat loss during winter. Both of these projects required cooperation from building users, and the committee found that the messages had to be repeated regularly to foster consistent behavior change among the numerous people who used the facilities.

At Our Lady of Angels, one area of the Environmental Initiative focused on reducing lawn area and expanding wildlife habitat, which included increased use of native plants in garden areas. The Initiative manager worked with grounds staff, sharing information about native plants and developing an integrated pest management policy. However, consistency in practices was occasionally affected by changes in staff. Once the goals of the Environmental Initiatives had been achieved, Sister Corinne Wright stepped down from the position of Initiative manager. A few years later, she noticed that the mix of plants on the grounds was shifting back toward non-native plants:

> But now I see backsliding. For example, we recently raised the issue of the landscapers reducing the number of native plants on the grounds. They said, "Non-natives don't draw insects." They had replaced the native vines on a pergola with wisteria.
>
> "Natives draw insects!" Isn't that the point? They don't understand the big picture; they are just trying to make their work easier. The problem is that people change jobs, so the guy there now is not someone I worked with earlier and he does not know why we were doing things a certain way.[25]

The challenge of maintaining consistent conservation behavior highlights one of the benefits of physical infrastructure improvements—installing solar panels and efficient appliances is a one-time change that produces automatic reductions in energy use, whereas fostering new social norms can be a slow process with backsliding.

EFFECTS:
STRUCTURES FACILITATED INITIATIVE IMPLEMENTATION

As the examples above indicate, green team efforts to implement sustainability initiatives were facilitated by organizational systems in two ways. First, religious organizations provided suitable pre-existing structures through which to take action. Second, those structures offered the potential for collaboration between sustainability champions and other members of the congregation as well as people outside the faith community, which expanded the capacity for integrating earth care into the various activity areas of the community and embedding it in the community culture.

A faith community's organizational structure provided a variety of action venues through which to implement initiatives. The religious organization's regular worship services offered an arena for sermons and affirmations that integrated earth care into a community's religious values and practices, while religious education programs could present curricula to guide children and adults toward an understanding of the connections between earth care and their faith traditions. Communities found channels for enacting earth care in their social justice and spiritual development ministries where they added community gardens and organic food production to food donation programs, used building space for environmentally themed schools, designed environmental education curricula for summer camps, added environmental justice to Corporate Social Responsibility ministry, and developed eco-spirituality programs for retreat centers. Sustainability was also incorporated into daily operations for administering the religious organization. Staff adopted policies for purchasing greener supplies and revised the ways they carried out tasks in offices, custodial work, and grounds keeping. In addition to policy and behavior changes, earth care was integrated into maintenance of the organization's physical elements—its buildings, technologies, and grounds—so that the faith community's physical space became an important venue through which to enact its sustainability ethic. In effect, the buildings and grounds were transformed into media for ministry: solar panels and community gardens served as visible manifestations of a faith community's values. Thus, working within a faith community's organizational structures made it relatively easy to take action because there was no need for new staff, new programs, or extensive revision to operational procedures. The importance of supportive structures is underscored by cases where green teams encountered difficulties implementing social justice or environmental justice actions because the action venues available in their organizational structures were not well suited to these efforts.

These examples of conservation practices also reveal that community collaboration was a crucial factor in initiative implementation. Many of the actions undertaken were implemented by staff or community members who were not on the green team, yet were motivated to act in support of the community's sustainability ethic. Clergy, religious education directors, and teachers took the lead on integrating earth care into worship services and youth education programs. Congregational members who were involved in other ministries added sustainability to their work, thereby increasing the number of activities that could be undertaken and expanding the capacity of initiatives. As manager of the Environmental Initiative for the Sisters of St. Francis of Philadelphia, Wright described how helpful it was that community members in other ministry areas took action: "The investment group we belong to took up the fracking issue independently of us; that was a nice overlap. It gave me a chance to say, 'Should I take this up or leave it to Sister Nora?' It helps that people from other parts of the organization are also doing things to protect the environment."[26] The sisters involved in Corporate Social Responsibility perceived environmental justice as an aspect of their ministry and incorporated it into their work of their own volition, thereby expanding the areas through which earth care was integrated into community practices.

Cooperation from staff and members was equally important for implementation of conservation practices in administration and facilities management. Administrators, office workers, custodians, maintenance crews, and groundskeepers helped transform sustainability ethics into practical daily behaviors. Wright's story about new grounds-keeping staff who replaced native plants with "less insect-attracting" non-native plants further demonstrates the importance of collaboration to the continued success of initiatives. It was not enough to have individual community members take action; the new practices had to be integrated into policies and management procedures so they would become procedural norms for future staff and volunteers doing those same tasks. In non-monastic communities, members were as important as staff since these communities relied on volunteers to wash the dishes that replaced disposables, to sort compost and recyclables from trash, to donate their time to grow produce in community gardens, to adapt to new practices such as use of electronic newsletters, and to consider environmental impacts when planning for special occasions.

In addition to collaboration within the faith community, collaboration with external partners provided resources that facilitated initiative implementation. Administrators developed relationships with companies that could supply "green" products for offices and custodians. Facilities managers drew on city and state programs to offset costs for infrastructure improvements such as energy efficient appliances, lighting, and weatherization. Land managers turned to local agricultural programs and state foresters for information on best practices in sustainable resource management. Gardeners connected with food pantries that could help with distribution, environmental educators worked with community centers to coordinate outreach to low-income children, and the woodworkers crafting storm windows to make low-income housing more energy efficient benefited from partnerships with other religious organizations that could extend their capacity for outreach to the wider community. Thus, partnerships with external organizations helped faith communities find venues that enhanced their capacity to implement activities that would not have been possible solely through the structures of their own religious organizations.

SUMMARY AND DOMAIN INTERACTIONS

How Organizations Affected Initiatives

AS THE CONTEXT WITHIN which these faith-based sustainability initiatives were undertaken, religious organizations contributed procedures and structures that shaped initiative development and implementation. Sustainability became embedded in the social norms of a faith community when operational procedures facilitated community engagement with initiatives and earth-care actions were integrated into multiple areas of the organizational structure. Chapters 9 and 10 described organizational procedures and structures that contributed to the development of the case-study initiatives. This section summarizes the findings from the two chapters and describes how the factors that organizations contributed to initiatives interacted with other domains. Because champions, faith leaders, and congregations all participated in initiatives within the context of their religious organizations, Organization contributions and Domain Interactions are combined into one discussion instead of being treated separately, as in previous domain summaries.

ORGANIZATIONAL VENUES FOR IMPLEMENTATION AND DOMAIN INTERACTIONS

Religious organizations made significant contributions to initiatives by providing operational procedures for establishing and managing green teams and organizational structures that served as venues through which to implement earth-care actions. These organizational factors affected development of sustainability initiatives in ways that intersected with the other domains of activity. When organizational procedures and structures aligned well with individuals' plans, sustainability champions were able to operate effectively. Operational procedures offered opportunities for faith leaders to promote initiatives and influenced levels of involvement from congregations. Organizational structures provided venues for all three actor groups—champions, faith leaders, and congregations—to participate in initiatives. See Table 21 for an overview of enabling factors contributed by organizations and their interactions with other domains.

TABLE 21 ORGANIZATION CONTRIBUTIONS AND
THEIR INTERACTIONS WITH OTHER DOMAINS

CONTRIBUTIONS	EFFECTS ON INITIATIVES	INTERSECTION WITH OTHER DOMAINS
Operational procedures: Group protocols Communication Decision processes	Facilitated creation and implementation of initiative. Facilitated congregational involvement.	*Champions:* organize/ manage green teams, interact with congregation *Faith Leaders:* influence decisions *Congregation:* involvement, affirmation
Organizational Structure: Worship Religious Education Ministries Administration Facilities management	Venues suitable for implementing earth care. Collaboration integrated earth care into multiple areas of the faith community.	*Champions:* efficacy of actions *Faith Leaders:* opportunities for messages and organization management *Congregation:* contribute supplemental actions

Champions were able to act on their desire to address sustainability through the milieu of their faith communities by following operational procedures and integrating earth care into organizational structures, which contributed to the efficacy of their efforts. They created green teams by adopting affinity group formats and following practices that were customary in their communities. Application of established management and planning techniques that were not only familiar to members, but were also tried and true systems for organizing people and achieving goals, enhanced their ability to implement activities. Use of agendas and minutes kept data organized while project planning techniques facilitated development of initiatives. These techniques intersected with the Champions domain where they contributed to the leadership capabilities of sustainability champions and increased the sense of efficacy for all the members of the green team.

Champions were also affected by organizational protocols for groups, which integrated religious rituals, fellowship practices, group study, and inclusive decision processes into green team management. Green teams benefited from these normative practices in several ways. Religious rituals and group study of theology fostered commitment by reinforcing champions' conviction that faith and earth care were connected, which motivated them to take action and helped them persevere over time. Champions' commitment and perseverance were also enhanced by group study of theology and research into potential earth-care activities, which provided inspiration for their own initiatives. Selecting projects through inclusive decision processes enabled individuals to incorporate personal interests into the earth care initiatives, thereby adding to their motivation to participate. Finally, shared activities such as group study and fellowship practices fostered supportive relationships among members of green teams, a factor that previous research[1] has shown to be important for developing and maintaining successful collaborative projects.

Organizational procedures that provided opportunities for interactions within a faith community also affected development of initiatives. Processes for informing congregations about affinity group missions and reporting annual accomplishments fostered communication between green teams and the wider community memberships. At St. Thomas Aquinas Parish, where the Green Committee was particularly disciplined about posting meeting minutes and submitting annual reports, these practices increased member awareness of earth-care activities. Katia Reeves, leader of the St. Thomas Aquinas Green Committee at the time of this study, noted that: "We do a lot, and for the past couple of years I have heard comments that our committee is the most active in the parish."[2]

Just as supportive organizational norms facilitated initiatives, a misalignment between expectations about group behavior and a green team's actions could hinder initiatives. For example, adoption of a small group format associated with Bible study seemed to limit congregational participation in green team activities in one case. Thus, in some instances a poor fit between organizational norms for group behavior and the earth-care activities undertaken may have undermined efforts to integrate sustainability into the community's social norms and contributed to a perception that earth care was the purview of a small group rather than a community initiative requiring everyone's participation.

In addition to procedures for establishing and managing initiatives, organizational structures supplied the action venues for putting sustainability ethics into practice. These action venues made it possible for champions, faith leaders, and congregations to participate in earth care. Champions developed projects for implementation through the programmatic and administrative venues of their faith communities. They collaborated with clergy to integrate earth care into worship services, developed educational programs such as presentations and film series, and created new projects to supplement extant ministries like growing fresh produce for food pantries. Worship services provided faith leaders with a venue in which to share messages legitimating earth care as a faith issue through sermons and public affirmations while governance systems offered them a platform for promoting community-wide support for initiatives. Administrative systems and ministries also served as venues for members of the congregation to support initiatives by adding green practices to their work in offices, grounds keeping, and ministries. Actions by congregation members who were not on the green team, yet shared the

FIGURE 5 Interactions between Organizations and the Other Domains

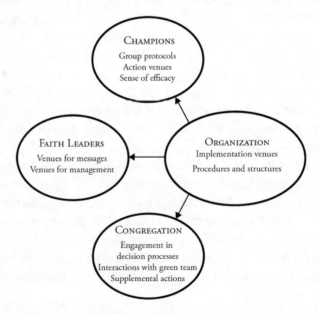

conviction that earth care was a community ethic, were vital for integrating sustainability into the religious organizations in the case studies. Figure 5 illustrates the interactions between the organization and the other three domains of activity.

EARTH CARE INTEGRATED INTO
THE RELIGIOUS ORGANIZATION

Religious organizations contributed processes for adopting earth care as a community mission, formats and procedures for effective green team operations, and structures through which to take action. When organizational norms aligned well with sustainability initiatives, green teams were able to operate effectively and enlist support from their communities. Efforts to implement initiatives were enhanced when green teams were able to collaborate with staff and other members of their communities to integrate earth-care activities into appropriate action venues provided by the structures of their religious organizations.

Earth care became embedded in the social norms of a faith community when it was integrated into action areas throughout the organization. One example of this embeddedness is illustrated by a story from the Madison Christian Community, where the death of a tree was woven into multiple, interconnected activities expressing the community's earth-care values. The community members were distressed to learn that the 175-year-old bur oak by their building was dying. The tree had a large cavity in its trunk and three independent arborists all agreed that it needed to be removed before it became a hazard to people walking under it to enter the church. In response to this sad news, members formed the Bur Oak Task Force and organized a series of practices through which to incorporate the final year of the tree's life into the community's faith life. A four-week adult education series focused on relationships between trees and a sense of place, and studied biblical references to trees. A community member who was a professional storyteller told biblical tree stories and coached other members in the art of recalling and telling personal tree stories. The tree also featured in the children's religious education program and in community-wide worship services:

> Children combed the grass under the tree like squirrels and filled grocery bags with acorns. One evening seventh- and eighth-grade confirmation students spread a large tarp on the education unit floor, separated good acorns

from bad acorns, cracked the shells open, and picked out small chunks of pulp. A mother and daughter found a Native American recipe for acorn bread, which, placed on the altar, became the bread of life at Sunday worship, nourishing our spiritual hunger. The taste of acorn reminded us of all the ways a single tree nourishes human and nonhuman life: sheltering birds, squirrels, and bugs, and by inviting people to repose under the shade of its outstretched limbs.[3]

In addition to education and worship activities, the congregation used the image of "tree as nourisher" as a theme for the financial stewardship campaign that year. The stewardship committee and the pastor explained that just as a tree transforms sun and rain into energy that sustains other creatures as well as itself, "so our gifts to our congregation not only sustain the life of this worshiping community, but are spread abroad to our neighbors, our community and the creation."[4]

Cross-organization projects like the tree activities were a hallmark of the earth-care mission at the Madison Christian Community, where Pastor Wild regularly brought experiences from time spent in the church gardens into sermons and education classes, but other cases had similar examples in which sustainability was integrated into multiple areas of the organization. Chapter 5 described the story of the children at the Jewish Reconstructionist Congregation, who brainstormed eighteen "pillars of their faith" that were written on cards and placed in each of the eighteen caissons supporting their green synagogue. Monastic communities like Villa Maria developed interconnected activities such as the Land Retreats in which the land manager took groups of sisters out to walk the boundaries of their property and learn about the ecosystems under their care, including the sustainably managed farmland and forests that had become venues for fulfilling their ministries to nurture people physically and spiritually. These examples of interconnected activities, implemented though multiple venues within the religious organizations, indicate that earth care had become embedded in these faith communities.

CONCLUSION

Pathways to Sustainability

THIS RESEARCH PROJECT SET OUT TO better understand the experiences of people of faith who promote and practice environmentally sustainable behavior by examining the motivations and processes through which fifteen faith communities in the United States developed sustainability initiatives. Although there may not be evidence to support the hypothesis that religious leaders' calls for action have inspired a widespread faith-based environmental movement that will transform the nation's climate action agenda, the stories described in this book demonstrate that some faith communities are going to great lengths to practice earth care. Knowing more about the empirical experiences of faith-based environmental activities that do arise can elucidate circumstances that affect religious environmental action. This project examined the experiences of congregation-level faith communities that developed exemplary sustainability initiatives, which included multiple activities sustained over at least four years. After conducting field research and comparing fifteen case studies, it seems clear that key contributions from champions, supportive leadership, and appropriate organizational systems were just as important as theology for the emergence and continuity of these initiatives.

This is not to say that religion was unimportant. Faith communities are religious organizations that exist for the purpose of supporting members' religious lives and, therefore, sustainability could only become part of the congregational social norm if it fit into the religious mission of a community. Earth care became integrated into the ministries of all fifteen case-study communities, but the process of adopting an environmental ethic did not unfold in the same way across the cases, and variations in the ways earth care was incorporated into community missions influenced the strength and durability of sustainability social norms. Despite variations in their paths to sustainability, a shared narrative threaded through the assorted cases. In each community, a few passionate individuals took the lead in proposing or organizing earth-care initiatives for their faith communities. The development and maintenance of those initiatives was affected by the characteristics of the champions who led the efforts and by their interactions with the faith leaders, congregations, and organizations that comprised the faith-community context in which they took action. Using these four domains of activity—Champions,

TABLE 22 KEY CONTRIBUTIONS AND ENABLING FACTORS IN THE FOUR DOMAINS OF ACTIVITY

	CHAMPIONS	FAITH LEADERS
MAJOR CONTRIBUTION	*Leadership*	*Legitimacy*
HOW CONTRIBUTION IS EVIDENCED	*Champions with ability to organize initiatives*	*Messages calling faith community to care for the earth because of:* Theology Community ministries and identity Special role of religion
KEY ENABLING FACTORS	*Commitment:* Motivations Environmental concerns Religion Personal windows of opportunity *Leadership Capability:* Sustainability knowledge Leadership skills Institutional knowledge Project management Embedded in community Trust Relationships	*Religious Authority:* Mechanisms for connecting earth care with values and practices Sermons Newsletters/blogs Affirmations *Organizational Manager:* Mechanisms for integrating earth care into practices Authorize initiatives or activities Advise Green Teams Advocate for support from other community groups
EFFECTS	*Ideas turned into action*	*Earth care integrated into social norms*

Faith Leaders, Congregation, and Organization—as an analytic framework made it possible to compare the cases and identify factors that enabled communities to develop effective earth-care initiatives as well as to understand why some initiatives were less durable.

CONTRIBUTIONS AND INTERSECTIONS OF THE FOUR DOMAINS

Each domain made specific contributions to the initiatives: champions led the efforts that turned idea into action; faith leaders legitimated earth care as a faith issue requiring action from the whole community; congregations

(Table 22 cont'd)	CONGREGATION	ORGANIZATION
MAJOR CONTRIBUTION	*Capacity*	*Implementation Venues*
HOW CONTRIBUTION IS EVIDENCED	*Resources made available* Human labor and knowledge resources Material resources Earth care activities by community members beyond Green Team	*Opportunities for actions that aligned with organizational systems*
KEY ENABLING FACTORS	*Earth care fit community identity:* Connections with previous activities Service ministries Environmental projects Land use *Ownership of initiatives:* Participatory decisions Shared learning Concerns addressed	*Operational procedures:* Decision processes Green Team format and management Communication with the congregation *Organizational structures as venues for action:* Worship services Religious education Ministries Administration Facilities management
EFFECTS	*Earth care integrated into community mission*	*Effective implementation of earth care actions*

supplied resources that determined the capacity for action; and organizations served as the venues for implementation. The extent and efficacy of these contributions was affected by enabling factors within the domains as well as interactions among the domains (see Table 22).

Champions

Individuals provided the leadership and effort that made sustainability initiatives feasible; they turned ideas into action. Without these champions, nothing would have happened. Comparing the cases indicated that champions who succeeded in developing initiatives shared two major characteristics: a sense of commitment to the task of taking action to care for the earth and a set of leadership capabilities suited to organizing an earth-care initiative within the venue of a faith community. Specific factors affected both of these characteristics. Commitment emerged from a mixture of environmental and religious motivations that inspired individuals to take action, and from whether their lives provided personal windows of opportunity that allowed them to devote time and energy to earth care. However, commitment alone did not ensure that champions could organize initiatives; their success also depended on leadership capabilities. These capabilities included factors such as sustainability knowledge and project management skills that provided the ability to plan and implement projects and coordinate volunteers. In addition, leadership capability was enhanced if the champions were longtime community members with institutional knowledge about organizational procedures and networks of personal relationships that facilitated their ability to integrate earth care into multiple areas of the religious organization. Champions who were embedded in the community benefited from relationships and trust that made it easier to gain approval for initiatives and to gather support from faith leaders and congregations.

Intersections with other domains affected the enabling factors that contributed to champions' commitment and leadership capabilities. Champions who were longtime community members were familiar with operational procedures and organizational structures in the Organization domain. The project management skills they employed were often drawn from these operational procedures and, therefore, were familiar to other community members. Similarly, champions' networks of relationships expanded the reach of sustainability initiatives into various areas of the organizational structure such as religious education programs and administration, increasing the number of activities beyond those the members of a green team could accomplish alone. Leadership capabilities and trust also intersected with the Congregation domain, where members who perceived the sustainability champions as effective leaders were more likely to join green teams, thereby increasing the likelihood the team would have the critical mass necessary for durability. Finally, there was a two-way relationship between champions and faith leaders. Faith leaders strengthened champions' commitment to sustainability by articulating religious messages describing earth care as an issue that required action from people of faith and reassuring them that acting on their faith was important even if the actions seemed inadequate. These messages contributed to champions' motivations to act through the venue of their faith communities and helped them persevere by reinforcing the sense of intrinsic satisfaction that arose from performing actions that expressed religious values. At the same time, the presence of individuals with environmental concerns motivated faith leaders to address earth care as a faith issue and assist their sustainability champions in taking action within the faith-community venue.

Faith Leaders

Faith leaders made an essential contribution to initiatives by legitimating sustainability as a religious issue. Since faith communities are, first and foremost, religious organizations that exist for the purpose of fostering members' religious lives, it was crucial to explain why caring for the earth was an expression of religious life. Faith leaders were able to legitimate earth care through their dual roles as religious authorities and organizational managers. As religious authorities, they explained how earth care fit into a community's religious values and practices. They made their case by invoking religious teachings that prescribed moral obligations to care for people and nature. In addition to these fundamental religious precepts, they connected earth care with extant ministry practices of personal devotion, social justice, and community service through which their faith communities enacted their religious values. Finally, they suggested that people of faith had a special role to play in making society more environmentally sustainable by speaking out about morality, environmental justice, and hopeful visions for the future.

Faith leaders further promoted community engagement with sustainability through their role as organizational managers. They authorized inclusion of environmental issues in mission discernment processes, encouraged individuals to create green teams, and approved proposals to undertake sustainability initiatives. They used their knowledge of religious organizations to advise champions and green teams about how to act on their desires to incorporate earth care into religious life by recommending appropriate options such as environmentally themed religious celebrations that fit into liturgical calendars or working through denominational organizations to address issues that could not be solved at the local level. As managers of their religious organizations, faith leaders were also able to advocate for support of initiatives from boards of trustees and other committees, thereby reinforcing the message that sustainability was an issue requiring action from the whole community, not just a core group of environmentalists.

Thus, faith leaders affected initiatives through interactions with the other three domains. Organizational structures provided opportunities for exercising religious and managerial authority. For example, worship services offered a venue for sharing authoritative religious messages about earth care as a faith issue in sermons and through affirming mechanisms such as announcements, celebrations of green accomplishments, and environmentally themed rituals. Faith leaders also enacted managerial roles as they headed administrative hierarchies or influenced boards of trustees in accord with the governance system of their denominations. The organization's operational procedures provided the means for managers to authorize consideration of earth care during mission discernment processes and presented opportunities for lay faith leaders to share earth-care messages with community members through study groups, educational presentations, and eco-theology retreats. Through these mechanisms, faith leaders interacted with the Congregation domain and encouraged the congregational membership to perceive earth care as a component of their religious values and practices, thereby integrating it into community social norms.

Faith leaders also influenced champions. Religious messages and affirmations strengthened champions' sense of commitment by contributing to their motivations to act. These messages also reinforced champions' sense of satisfaction from engaging in work that expressed their religious values. Moreover, faith leaders' advice on how to take action through the venue of religious organizations helped green teams develop and implement activities, which increased the efficacy of their efforts and helped sustain them over time. Even when some activities fell short, faith leaders bolstered individuals' commitment with a message that the actions themselves were valuable as expressions of faith, in spite of uncertain outcomes, because, "God calls you to be faithful, not successful."[1]

Congregations

Congregations contributed resources, both human and material, that determined the scale of earth-care activities undertaken within a community. For example, communities with extensive support had larger green teams, which meant more people to share knowledge and workloads, thereby expanding capacity while ameliorating burnout. Members also provided resources like funds and tractors to help implement initiatives, as well as endorsing administrative decisions such as giving up income from farm leases in order to replace agricultural fields with restored ecosystems. In addition, congregational support increased capacity because people beyond the green team supplemented sustainability initiatives by incorporating earth care into other areas of the religious organization such as office management, purchasing, grounds keeping, and religious education programs.

Two factors had a significant effect on the levels of support initiatives received from congregations: First, whether earth care became connected with community identity, and second, whether congregation members participated in the processes for adopting an earth-care ministry and incorporating sustainability into the community mission. The first of these factors affecting congregational support was closely intertwined with the Faith Leader domain; the second intersected with the Organization domain. Faith leaders across the cases, both clergy and lay champions, made presentations linking earth care to previous practices in ministries focused on justice and community service. In a smaller subset of cases with land holdings, they also framed previous environmental activities and past land uses as precursors to sustainable land stewardship, thereby encouraging the congregation members to perceive earth care as a continuation of historical traditions that defined the community. In cases where members engaged in outdoor activities like prairie restoration, gardening, tree planting, and beekeeping, there was extensive acceptance of earth care as an aspect of community identity. However, even in more urban areas where the "precursors to sustainability" invoked by faith leaders were social justice and community service ministries like food pantries and health care programs, many of the cases developed widespread congregational agreement that these ministries were connected to sustainability because environmental issues contributed to poverty, food insecurity, and ill health.

These precursor activities were entwined with community identity; they were ministry activities through which communities expressed their religious values. Cases that connected sustainability to prior ministries and, through them, to their community identity, had high levels of congregational support for their initiatives. The factor that influenced how widely the congregation accepted these connections came from the Organization domain, where a community's operational procedures determined the decision processes through which a community decided to adopt earth care as an area of activity. Communities that followed participatory decision processes, which allowed members to engage in shared learning about the connections between religious values and earth care and to address concerns about costs and activity selection, had higher levels of congregational support for initiatives.[2] Having participated in the decision to adopt earth care as an expression of their community mission, members of these congregations were more likely to contribute time and resources to support implementation of sustainability initiatives.

Organizations

The Organization provided opportunities for initiative implementation through its operational procedures and organizational structures. As noted above, operational procedures affected the processes for proposing and approving earth care as an area of activity for the community. They also provided formats for creating green teams and operational practices that were used to run meetings, plan and implement activities, and communicate with the congregation. These procedures intersected with other domains since knowledge of operational procedures enhanced the leadership capabilities of champions, while the organization's decision processes affected levels of support from congregations.

Organizational structures contributed venues through which to implement earth-care actions. Some of these structures connected earth care with the religious practices of the community. For example, worship services and religious education programs offered opportunities for faith leaders to share messages about earth care as a religious issue. Ministries served as channels for action. For example, environmental justice was incorporated into socially responsible investment practices, community gardens and organic farming were incorporated into poverty alleviation and food donation programs, and energy efficiency was incorporated into *tikkun olam*, healing the world.

Structures for the administration and maintenance of the religious organizations also served as implementation venues. Sustainability was integrated into community governance policies, where it affected supply purchases, office practices, building renovations, and facilities management. In cases with high levels of congregational support, these organizational structures made it possible for people beyond the green team to contribute to earth care by incorporating it into their work as administrators, custodians, groundskeepers, religious education teachers, clergy, and volunteers on ministry committees. These practices increased the number of activities undertaken without requiring additional effort from the green team, which added to the individual champions' sense of efficacy and satisfaction while helping to prevent burnout. By making it possible to integrate earth care into a wide range of community activities, these supportive organizational structures facilitated the process of embedding earth care in community social norms.

INTERPLAY OF THE FOUR DOMAINS

As the summary above makes clear, a dynamic interplay of enabling factors within the four domains facilitated development of initiatives (see Figure 6). Champions acted on their commitment and applied their leadership capabilities through the venues provided by religious organizations. If their actions aligned well with organizational procedures and structures, there was greater efficacy in the implementation of the earth care initiative. Faith leaders legitimated sustainability as a religious issue, which strengthened champions' commitment while also encouraging the congregation to see earth care as an activity that fit into community identity and deserved support from the whole congregation. Congregational support was influenced by previous activities and ministries linked to community identity and by members' involvement in development of initiatives. Congregational involvement was facilitated by organizational procedures for participatory decision processes. Appropriate organizational structures also made it easier for members of the congregation who were not on the green team to contribute to initiatives by incorporating sustainability into multiple areas of activity within the religious organization. Thus, earth care became embedded in the faith communities through the interplay of enabling factors across the four domains, which together produced durable sustainability initiatives. Among the fifteen case studies, those

FIGURE 6 Contributions and Interplay of the Four Domains

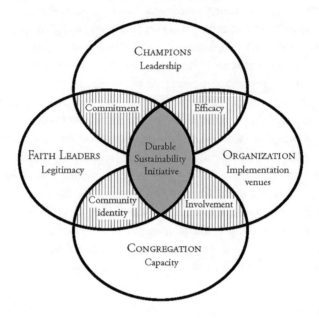

communities with enabling factors in all four domains developed strong sustainability social norms, while those lacking enabling factors in one or more domains had weaker social norms and less durable initiatives.

HOW EARTH CARE AFFECTED FAITH
COMMUNITIES AND RELIGIOUS LIFE

Although enabling factors such as decision processes and leadership capabilities were not inherently religious, religion did play an important role in motivating and sustaining these initiatives. Since they were implemented through religious organizations, it was crucial that sustainability be defined in relation to religious values and practices before it could be integrated into the faith community. These religious values combined with environmental concerns to motivate individuals to become sustainability champions. One of the characteristics shared by most of the champions who led these initiatives was their long-term membership and embeddedness in their faith communities. Religion was an important element in their daily lives and, consequently, may have been a stronger motivation for them than it would have been for "holiday" believers who only attend worship services on special occasions.

Clergy who became interested in sustainability had to examine religious premises for promoting environmental action before they could integrate earth care into their pastoral work. Once they were convinced of the theological bases for earth care, they could share those teachings with their congregations, thereby reinforcing the commitment of champions and encouraging the congregation to perceive earth care as an activity incumbent on people of faith. In faith communities with strong sustainability social norms, interviewees stressed that the congregation perceived earth-care activities as public expressions of their community's religious mission. Congregations were proud that their solar panels and community gardens showed that they "walked the talk" of their religious values. Moreover, people felt that their initiatives were important for the task of addressing environmental crises *because* they were faith-based. Interviewees interpreted unsustainable resource use and consumerism as symptoms of a cultural worldview that needed to be changed, and they argued that religion had a contribution to make by changing hearts and minds. In the words of Lucie Bauer, "This is where our spirit-filled lives come in. Without that, we can't make the changes that are needed. We need a sea change in consciousness, and that is a spiritual task."[3]

In addition to motivating action, religion played a vital role in sustaining initiatives. Interviewees stressed that religious messages calling them to "be faithful, not successful," made it possible for them to attempt new and difficult tasks, and helped them persevere when some of their efforts fell short. Moreover, the sense of satisfaction they derived from "living their values" strengthened their commitment and kept them going year after year. When asked whether practicing earth care through a faith community differed from practicing it through traditional environmental organizations such as the Sierra Club, interviewees said that religion helped them maintain a sense of hopefulness. Lynn Cameron summarized this perspective when she explained that, "You can't be frantically fighting all the time. We want to be hopeful." and taking time to thank God and realize that "you are related to all of creation" was what helped her be hopeful.[4]

Not only did religion affect development of sustainability initiatives, the stories of these faith communities indicate that participating in earth-care programs also affected religion. In particular, it affected faith leaders' theological perspectives, community membership, and interactions between the faith community and the wider community. For some faith leaders, exploring sustainability as a faith issue brought new theological perspectives. Reverend Jeff Wild noted that engaging in earth care had made him a better Trinitarian because he had become more aware of God as Creator of the earth and of the Holy Spirit present in nature in addition to the more traditional Lutheran focus on Jesus as savior. Several ministers and lay leaders became more observant of their physical environment and began to see spiritual teachings in natural processes because of congregational projects like prairie restoration and produce gardens. Others discovered new ways to love their neighbors as they learned about environmental injustices and recognized that environmental issues intersected with foundational moral precepts of their faith traditions. For these faith leaders, new theological emphases emerged in response to their faith communities' efforts to live more sustainably.

Earth care also influenced faith communities by affecting membership and relationships between the faith community and the wider community. At a time when congregations are shrinking in every US denomination, all ten of the non-monastic communities studied for this project had stable or growing memberships. Some interviewees theorized that their green activities might be one explanatory factor. At the Madison Christian Community, there have been instances in which people stopped to check out the church because they saw the solar panels and gardens while driving by. These visitors indicated that they wanted to be part of a church that engaged in such activities. Other interviewees were more circumspect about whether sustainability initiatives caused membership growth. At Trinity Presbyterian Church in East Brunswick, Debbie O'Halloran suggested their stable membership was not necessarily due to earth stewardship, but that their earth stewardship indicated to prospective members that they were a church that "walked their talk" and that this emphasis on faith in action was what drew people. An interviewee at the Reconstructionist Jewish Congregation expressed a similar view, explaining that she did not think people joined their congregation because they were "the green synagogue," but that media attention to their building drew people to visit "and they discover it is a beautiful building and they would like to worship here."[5] In all three of these cases, interviewees stressed that being green was not, in itself, the reason people joined their congregations. Earth care might draw people's attention because it connected to issues that people cared about, but faith communities also had to provide meaningful worship services and strong religious education programs for children in order for potential members to join.

The final way earth care affected religion was through new relationships with people and groups beyond the faith community. Earth care activities provided opportunities for increased interactions with people outside the congregation such as staff and program participants from neighborhood centers; retreat participants; school groups learning about sustainable forestry and farming; community supported agriculture members; volunteers from schools and civic groups who contributed to land stewardship work; and other faith communities that collaborated on food distribution, window inserts, and solar installations. For monastic communities, these interactions are serving as a basis for new kinds of relationships with individuals and community groups that may lead to opportunities for new organizational structures that will be able to continue these earth-care ministries even as the number of vowed members living in the communities decreases. For non-monastic communities, these interactions increased the sense of efficacy among members, who were pleased that their work was benefiting the wider community. In addition, these relationships increase the visibility of the faith communities, which may bring in new members and improve the likelihood of maintaining a stable membership.

DIRECTIONS FOR FUTURE RESEARCH

The research findings presented in this book can be used to develop a suite of best practices that would pay attention to factors in each domain to facilitate development of durable sustainability initiatives. These best practices could then be applied by faith communities seeking to develop their own earth care initiatives. As more communities apply the ideas, their experiences will provide data for insights into whether certain factors carry greater or lesser weight at different stages of initiative development or whether there are additional factors that were not identified in the original case sample.

There is also need for research to explore how congregation-level initiatives affect the lives of the people in the pews. The hope, as Laurel Kearns points out, is that "Religious groups can embed prescribed action in a story of living one's faith, following one's traditions, and being a moral exemplar. Once religious institutions, local congregations, mosques, and temples try something new such as installing solar power, or CFL bulbs, etc. and incorporate the action into the story of their missions and lived practice, it becomes easier for members to follow suit."[6] This expectation that institutional practices can influence the behavior of individual members has inspired the emergence of religious environmental movement organizations designed to encourage people of faith to engage in environmental behavior. Ellingson notes that congregation-level faith communities are a target audience for many of these organizations,[7] however, there has not yet been much research to determine whether these greening programs do indeed motivate changes in members' personal behavior or what kinds of actions members are most likely to undertake in their home and work lives.[8]

The sample biases in this project also open avenues for future research. The fifteen cases were predominantly white, middle-class congregations, most of which were located in northern Midwest and Northeast regions. The case selection criteria contributed to this uniformity. At the time of this study, the website resources used to identify potential sites did not include many examples of low-income faith communities or communities of color that fit the criteria of initiatives with multiple activities sustained over four or more years. Including cases with fewer activities or shorter time spans would widen the sample. For example, the African American pastors of Pilgrim Baptist Church in Detroit have worked with Michigan Interfaith Power and Light to make energy efficiency improvements to their church building and encourage other clergy in the region to join them in advocating for political action to address climate change because it will disproportionately affect low-income communities. Moreover, in 2010, African American church leaders began a Green the Church initiative that has grown to include member congregations in many states. Comparing cases with fewer activities, such as Pilgrim Baptist Church, and exploring the experiences of newer initiatives, such as communities that have joined Green the Church, would help determine whether there are additional factors that affect development of faith-based sustainability efforts in low-income areas or in communities of color. Conducting comparative studies to explore the experiences of sustainability initiatives among faith communities of color may help tease apart the influences of social groups, political identity, and religion in motivating earth care since there is some evidence that Black Protestants and Latinx Catholics have much higher levels of support for environmental policies and climate action than white church members, despite similar theological beliefs.[9]

A second limitation of the sample that should be addressed is the lack of regional diversity. Sociologists have frequently noted that, "Things are different in the South," and this observation may be particularly applicable to the role of religion in motivating behavior. Therefore, future research could examine cases of earth care in faith communities located in southern states, as well as other areas of the country not covered in this study, to determine whether regional differences affect the factors that enable development of initiatives.

It is also important to recognize that the fifteen case studies were affected by external variables such as tax codes, local resources for recycling and purchasing green supplies, and availability of knowledge resources through government agencies and universities. Research using cross-state comparison of single earth-care activities, such as sustainable forestry or solar panel installation, could assess the effects of specific external factors and provide information about how to improve policies and programs for promoting similar practices in more faith communities.

Along with comparing the book's fifteen cases with cases from other regions and demographics, there is opportunity for future research based on the analytical framework. The four domains could be used to analyze processes for integrating sustainability into social norms in other faith-based and secular organizations where individual champions interact with leaders, members, and organizational structures. It would also be interesting to explore whether the four domain contributions—leadership, legitimacy, capacity, and implementation venues—could be used to examine faith-based sustainability initiatives that take place outside of congregations. For example, Hinduism in India is not organized into congregations in the same way as American religions, yet there are Hindu earth-care initiatives.[10] An analysis that focuses on the four contributions associated with the domains could generate research questions that would reveal factors facilitating development of Hindu sustainability initiatives in accord with India's social structures. What characteristics make individual champions effective? What frames are used to legitimate action, and who are the appropriate messengers? What human and material resources determine capacity? What implementation venues are available, and how do they affect the efficacy of initiative development? Thus, even where the faith-community domains are not applicable, elements of the framework may provide a basis for research that can bring a better understanding of collective sustainability action.

SEEDS OF HOPE

This study identified four domain contributions and a matrix of enabling factors that facilitated development of earth-care initiatives in the fifteen cases, however, these results should not be interpreted as evidence that an initiative lacking in one or more of these factors would be a waste of effort. As the preceding chapters noted, there was tremendous variation across the case-study communities, and several of them earned green certification or achieved significant reductions in energy use despite low levels of support from clergy or congregations. Even if sustainability did not become deeply rooted in the social norms of their faith communities, the conservation accomplishments of the green teams in such cases are impressive. These variations also illustrate why this study did not rank the outcomes of the initiatives or suggest that some cases were more or less successful than others. There is no simple metric for defining "success" across the cases since, for example, a ranking that compared the strength of earth-care social norms would differ markedly from a ranking that measured reduction of energy use.

In all of the cases in this study, faith communities turned beliefs into action and implemented successful sustainability initiatives. The diverse pathways the initiatives followed and the variations in their activities indicate that there is no single "right way" to do this work. Communities were successful in developing and maintaining initiatives when they employed processes that were familiar and took action in ways that addressed individual champions' interests, fit into the structures of their religious organizations, and were suited to the conditions in their local communities.

The sustainability initiative at the First Universalist Church of Rockland illustrates the dynamic outcomes that are possible when people adapt their earth-care ethic to the local environment. The Green Sanctuary Committee developed projects focused on local food that helped a young couple start the first community-supported agriculture venture in Maine and helped local fishermen develop the first Community Supported Fishery (CSF) in the United States. They achieved these successes by involving the congregation in planning and selecting projects that aligned with faith-community interests in food and the local fishing economy. Lucie Bauer described how delighted the church members were that their efforts benefited their mid-coast regional community as well as the church: "We are part of rebuilding the historical resilience of our communities. It feels very, very important. It's a long way from where we started out, back in 2006. It's been amazing and wonderful and we're very grateful to have been a catalyst for both CSAs and CSFs because that little modest pilot CSF was the first CSF in Maine."[11] The "leap of faith" that the church and the fishermen took when they decided to try selling fish to CSF shareholders had effects that rippled down the coast and across the Atlantic Ocean as their story inspired development of a second Community Supported Fishery in Gloucester, Massachusetts, and eventually led to similar ventures in the United Kingdom after the British Broadcasting Corporation made a film about these two American CSFs.[12]

The ripples that spread outward from this church in Maine demonstrate the importance of sharing stories to compile a repertoire of faith-based actions. As

Revered Mark Glovin said in a sermon celebrating First Universalist Church's certification as a Green Sanctuary: "This is the gift of our community. The beauty of our work as a green sanctuary is that we'll form what Andrew Harvey calls a network of grace, brought together by passion, skill and serendipity to pool energies, triumphs, griefs, hopes and resources of all kinds. We can share our stories [to] encourage, sustain, and inspire each other in the course of what we believe is sacred action."[13] Hopefully, hearing about the diverse paths and actions undertaken by these fifteen communities will inspire others to think creatively about how to adapt these ideas into initiatives that are appropriate to their own communities. More Americans belong to religious organizations than any other type of voluntary association.[14] These religious organizations have, in the past, facilitated social change by challenging the status quo, articulating visions for a better society, and providing resources to help people adapt to changing social conditions. As more faith communities integrate sustainability into their social norms, they will help build capacity for making the institutional changes that are imperative in a world confronting a changing climate. In her analysis of how people in Maine respond to climate change, Bauer commented, "I guess on climate change, people go in and out of denial but we just have to have hope." She described how one of the people in her congregation was terribly depressed about climate change until he found the right project to work on, building storm window inserts to reduce energy use in churches and homes. Once he had a meaningful way to take action and a community to help support those actions, he became more hopeful. Consequently, Bauer had come to the conclusion that, "In doing is the seed of hope."[15]

For people of faith who express a desire to take action and experience frustration that they are not certain how to do so, the stories in this study may provide inspiration for finding a pathway toward sustainability. The matrix of four domains and analysis of enabling factors presented here are offered as a framework to help sustainability champions take action and integrate earth care into their faith communities so that they too can sow seeds of hope.

APPENDIX

BECAUSE THIS RESEARCH FOCUSED ON PROCESS, on *how* people translated intention into action, as much as on the motivations that inspired their desire to undertake sustainability initiatives, interviews were essential sources of data. Historical documents and sermons from faith communities, as well as media reports describing activities undertaken by congregations, tend to focus on 'why' questions. They try to explain why people of faith engage (or should engage) in earth care. These documentary materials were very helpful for understanding message framing related to theology and faith community identity and what kinds of events or experiences inspired pastors to speak about earth care. However, interviews were the primary source of information about the processes through which faith communities enacted earth-care practices.

The data collection and interview process conformed to grounded theory methodology in which theory emerges as data is systematically gathered and analyzed.[1] In this method, initial data is analyzed to discern patterns and these are then continuously compared with new data, which may lead to new insights that require revised analysis of earlier data. For this project, the earliest layer of data came from reading previous scholarship on religious environmentalism and environmental sociology, which was used to develop interview questions prior to fieldwork. For example, researchers examining natural resource management programs have identified social networks and decision processes as significant factors that influence collective action and program implementation,[2] therefore, these topics were included in the interview protocol to see whether they played a role in the processes for implementing earth-care programs within faith communities. The formal interviews were conducted using a semi-structured interview format that adhered to a prepared series of questions and topics but also allowed the conversation to follow topic trajectories that emerged from the respondents' own experiences. If new topics that came up seemed significant, they could generate additional questions that might then be included in subsequent interviews. Data from the interviews and documents collected at the study sites was organized into case studies ranging from thirty to fifty pages of text. These case studies were analyzed and coded into units and compared to identify similarities and differences.

The project and preliminary interview questions were submitted to the Institutional Review Board for the University of Michigan. Because the research focused on public ministry work, it received an IRB waiver. I piloted the interview questions during a trip to Trinity Presbyterian Church in Harrisonburg, Virginia, in 2012. There, I met with the minister and members of the Earth Care House Church, who shared the story of the work they had been doing since 1996. As I analyzed the field notes and wrote up a case study based on the data from this visit, it became evident that there were particular organizational features in this faith community that facilitated development of an Earth Care group. Therefore, I added questions about organizational structures and procedures for subsequent interviews at other study sites.

The interview questions were grouped into five topic areas. In the list below, the italicized questions form the general structure for the interviews, with subsidiary questions to be used as appropriate in order to probe for further information related to each topic.

1 ORIGINS
  – *How did these initiatives get started?*
  – *Who started the earth care projects here? Why?*
    - Did you have previous experience with this activity or something similar?
    - Why undertake this project in the context of a congregation?
    - Were there previous groups or activities related to this initiative in the congregation? In the community?
  – *Who joined in? (Information on age, gender, personality, education, family.)*
  – *Why did they get involved?*
  – *Do some people participate more/longer than others? If so, why?*

2 PROCESS/GENESIS (TOP-DOWN OR BOTTOM-UP?)
  – *How does this group/project fit into the congregation?*
    - How does it connect with the congregational structure?
    - Is there an established process for organizing groups/activities?
    - Is there interaction with the pulpit and/or other internal programs?
    - Are there interactions with denominational programs or resources?

3 PROCESS/FUNCTIONING
  – *How do you manage your projects/initiatives?*
    - Is there a core group (green team)? How is the group organized?
    - Were there previous structures/models/supports in place?
    - What types of activities were undertaken and why?
  – *How does the green team decide what to do?*
    - How are decisions made?
    - What happens at a meeting?
  – *Where do ideas for activities come from?*
    - What are the objectives of the activities?

4 FACTORS AFFECTING THE ACTIVITY
  – *What helps you in this effort?*
    - External resources/partners/knowledge
    - Internal resources/support/encouragement
  – *What challenges have come up and how have they been addressed?*
  – *What advice would you give others?*

5 OUTCOMES
  – *What do you see as significant accomplishments from this activity?*
    - How has it affected individuals/the green team/the congregation?
  – *How does engaging in this activity in the context of religion differ from a secular context?*
    - Has the sustainability initiative affected your perspective on religion?
    - Has the faith-context affected your perspective on the sustainability initiative?

The case study sample was mostly drawn from faith communities that were profiled on websites for three faith-based environmental organizations and an academic program that studies religious environmentalism: The National Religious Partnership for the Environment (NRPE), GreenFaith, Interfaith Power and Light (IPL), and the Yale Forum on Religion and Ecology (FORE). While reading the profiles of communities featured in accounts of stewardship

(NRPE), achievement of GreenFaith Congregation certification, winners of IPL Cool Congregations Awards, and engaged projects (FORE), I made lists of those that met the case study criteria for multiple earth-care projects. I then perused the websites of these communities to see how the projects had faired since the profiles were written. I found that many promising programs had faded away within two or three years, which suggested that program longevity was an important metric for gauging the success of efforts to embed earth care in faith community social norms. Consequently, I added duration to the case selection criteria, seeking cases where sustainability initiatives had been maintained for at least four years, in order to study factors that contributed to durability.

The case studies selected show a sample bias for white, middle-class communities, which reflects the communities profiled on these websites. This pattern probably has several causes. First, it may indicate that certain kinds of congregations have greater access to media coverage, thereby showing up in news stories that caught the attention of researchers from Yale and NRPE, who then profiled those communities. Second, it reflects the types of faith communities most likely to be early participants in the programs organized by GreenFaith and Interfaith Power and Light, both of which have been led by white, mainline clergy. If the sample selection process were to be repeated in 2020, there would be more communities of color, especially among African American churches that have joined the IPL-affiliated Green the Church movement since it launched in 2010.

Additional factors affected sample selection. I wanted to compare the experiences of communities that participated in green certification programs with those that developed their own sustainability initiatives. Many of the early participants in the GreenFaith certification program, which began in 2010, were near the organization's New Jersey headquarters and, consequently, the sample included three communities from New Jersey that met the four-year criterion. This clustering of communities is also indicative of an additional factor that affected the sample: research funding. I was fortunate to receive research support to study faith-based sustainable forestry in the Great Lakes region from the USDA McIntire-Stennis Program. This funding allowed me to include the five monastic communities in the study sample; all of them engaged in forest stewardship. In order to maximize time and financial resources, I chose urban and suburban case sites that could be reached within a day's drive of these monastic communities, thereby allowing for much of the fieldwork to be conducted during three road trips. The most geographically distant case was St. Thomas Aquinas Parish in Palo Alto, California, which was selected because the bishop had created a Catholic Green Initiative for the entire diocese that would allow me to compare a top-down initiative with the bottom-up action in other cases. Researchers who study natural resource management have identified top-down and bottom-up leadership as factors that significantly affect initiative outcomes,[3] so I wanted to see how this difference affected earth care in faith communities.

After doing preliminary data gathering from websites and media reports for each faith community, I made initial contact with the religious organizations through email. After explaining my research project, I asked for referrals to people who could share information about their sustainability initiatives. I was usually put in touch with one or two green team leaders. I asked them who else I should speak to and arranged to meet as many people as possible during multi-day site visits. In this way, I was able to interview green team members, pastors, administrative staff, facilities managers, CSA farm managers and workers, a member of a Maine fishing family, land managers, and retreat program leaders. Some of the interviewees had retired from active earth-care participation but were happy to share their historical knowledge. I met with interviewees individually or in small groups, depending on local circumstances. Most interviews were conducted indoors, where we could sit and I could take notes. At some sites, conversations also took place during tours of grounds and gardens and over meals. In a few cases, when a person with valuable knowledge was not available during my visit, I conducted interviews by phone.

I took notes during the interviews rather than using a recorder. I then typed up my notes the same day or the following day so that I could identify any quotes or topics that needed clarification. This method forced me to begin analyzing data immediately, instead of accumulating recordings for future transcription, which made it easier to discern similarities and differences among cases or recognize gaps in knowledge so I could ask follow-up questions while on site. I also conducted some follow-up interviews by phone if earlier data needed clarification or expansion based on new insights from later case study research.

I traveled to all of the sites, staying in guest houses at three of the monastic communities and in hotels for the other sites. Visiting in person allowed me to make observations about the scope and scale of projects, to see the size of gardens, forests, prairies, and solar arrays, to observe whether initiative displays were visible and well maintained, and to sit next to random congregation members during worship services and ask them what they thought about the green projects. In a few places, gardens were overrun with weeds and the people next to me in the pews looked blank when I mentioned their community's earth-care initiatives. But I also saw lots of families enjoying gardens after worship services, heard from people who were planning to get more involved in green activities the moment they retired, and met many young volunteers who were spending parts of their summers working to care for gardens, prairies, and forests at monastic communities.

The book uses the real names of the faith communities and the interviewees, most of whom have also spoken about these projects in newspaper interviews and congregational materials such as newsletter articles and blogs. However, there were times when respondents asked that specific sections of our conversations not be made public, and these wishes have been honored. Furthermore, names have not been included when describing experiences that seemed sensitive. In this way, I have tried to give a full accounting that addresses challenges as well as strengths in development of these fifteen sustainability initiatives, while being respectful of the generosity and trust shown by the people who shared their stories with me.

NOTES

PREFACE

1 Sarah McFarland Taylor, *Green Sisters: A Spiritual Ecology* (Cambridge: Harvard University Press, 2007).
2 Roger Gottlieb, *A Greener Faith: Religious Environmentalism and Our Planet's Future* (New York: Oxford University Press, 2006).
3 Jeremy Benstein, *The Way into Jewish Environmentalism* (Vermont: Jewish Lights Publishing, 2006).
4 Julia M. Wondolleck and Steven L. Yaffee, *Making Collaboration Work: Lessons from Innovation in Natural Resource Management* (Island Press, 2000).

INTRODUCTION

1 Pope Francis, *Laudato Si': On Care for Our Common Home* (Our Sunday Visitor Publishing Division, 2015), #15.
2 Pope Francis, *Laudato Si'*, #217.
3 David DeCosse, Edwin Maurer, and John Farnsworth, "Pope Francis' 'Common Home' encyclical is a game changer," Special to the *San Jose Mercury News*, June 18, 2015, accessed March 2016, http://www.mercurynews.com/opinion/ci_28341858/david-decosse-edwin-maurer-and-john-farnsworth-pope.
4 Stan Hirst, "Laudato Si—Hopefully a Game Changer," *Suzuki Elders*, July 26, 2015, accessed March 2016, http://www.suzukielders.org/laudato-si-hopefully-a-game-changer.

5 Sarah B. Mills, Barry G. Rabe, and Christopher Borick. *Acceptance of Global Warming Rising for Americans of All Religious Beliefs*, The Center for Local, State, and Urban Policy at the Gerald R. Ford School of Public Policy, University of Michigan, 2015, http://closup.umich.edu/files/ieep-nsee-2015-fa ll-religion.pdf.

6 Lynn White Jr., "The Historical Roots of Our Ecologic Crisis," *Science* 155 (March 10, 1967): 1203–7.

7 White, "Historical Roots," 1207.

8 Roderick Nash points out that Walter Lowdermilk created an Eleventh Commandment on environmental stewardship in 1939 and Joseph Sittler wrote about earth theology in the 1950s. Roderick Nash, "The Greening of Religion" in *The Rights of Nature* (Madison: University of Wisconsin Press, 1989). As early as 1934, Max Weber argued that religion played a role in the emergence of modern American capitalism in *The Protestant Ethic and the Spirit of Capitalism*, (1920) translated by Talcott Parsons (London: Unwin Hyman, 1930) and White had contemporaries such as Clarence Glacken and Roderick Nash who explored the intersection of religion and nature in Western culture. Clarence J. Glacken, *Traces on the Rhodian Shore: Nature and Culture in Western Thought from Ancient Times to the End of the Eighteenth Century* (Berkeley: University of California Press, 1967) and Roderick Nash, *Wilderness and the American Mind* (1967; New Haven, CT: Yale University Press, 2001).

9 Bron Taylor, "The Greening of Religion Hypothesis (Part One): From Lynn White, Jr and Claims That Religions Can Promote Environmentally Destructive Attitudes and Behavior to Assertions They Are Becoming Environmentally Friendly," *Journal for the Study of Religion, Nature and Culture* 10.3 (2016): 287.

10 John N. Black, *The Dominion of Man: The Search for Ecological Responsibility* (Edinburgh: Edinburgh University Press, 1970); Donald Worster, *Nature's Economy: A History of Ecological Ideas* (Sierra Club Books, 1977).

11 Examples of texts that present Asian and Native American traditions as inherently environmental include: David T. Suzuki, "The Role of Nature in Zen Buddhism," *Eranos–Jahrbuch*, Vol. 22 (1953): 293; Hwa Yol Jung, "The Ecological Crisis: A Philosophic Perspective, East and West." *Bucknell Review* 20 (1972): 25–44; and Theodore Roszak, *The Making of a Counter Culture* (Berkeley: University of California Press, 1969), in which the author contrasts white exploiters of nature with Native Americans who believe that the land is sacred and deserves respect. Tuan critiqued the assumption that Asian religions were pro-nature, pointing out that China became polluted despite the dominance of supposedly nature-friendly Taoist and Buddhist traditions. Yi-Fu Tuan, "Discrepancies between Environmental Attitude and Behavior: Examples from Europe and China," *The Canadian Geographer*, Vol. 12 (1968): 176–191. Reprinted in David and Eileen Spring, editors, *Ecology and Religion in History* (Harper Torchbook, 1974: 91–113).

12 "History," Creation Justice Ministries, accessed March 2016, http://www.cre ationjustice.org/history.

13 Carl Sagan et al., "Preserving and Cherishing the Earth: An Appeal for Joint Commitment in Science and Religion," National Religious Partnership for the Environment, (Global Forum, Moscow) January 1990.

14 National Religious Partnership for the Environment (NRPE), accessed March 2016, http://www.nrpe.org/history.html.

15 Alliance of Religions and Conservation, accessed March 2016, http://www. arcworld.org/about_ARC.asp.

16 "History," Interfaith Power and Light, accessed March 2016, http://www.inter faithpowerandlight.org/about/mission-history.

17 Evangelical Environmental Network, http://www.whatwouldjesusdrive. info/intro.php.

18 Taylor, "Greening of Religion Hypothesis (Part One)": 289.

19 In 1984, Hand and Van Liere surveyed people in Washington State and deter- mined that denominational differences influenced exposure to the dominance of nature doctrine. They argued that members of conservative churches, who encountered this doctrine most frequently, were least likely to express environmental concern. Carl M. Hand and Kent D. Van Liere, "Religion, Mastery-Over-Nature, and Environmental Concern," *Social Forces* 37 (1984): 555–70. In 1989, Eckberg and Blocker surveyed a random sample of residents in Tulsa, Oklahoma, and concluded there were links between conservative Christianity and decreased environmental concern after finding lower levels of concern among people who believed in biblical literalism. D. L. Eckberg and T. J. Blocker, "Varieties of Religious Involvement and Environmental Concerns: Testing the Lynn White Thesis," *Journal for the Scientific Study of Religion* 28 (1989): 509–17.

20 In 1995, Guth et al. tried to determine whether eschatological worldview affected environmental concern. They found that evangelicals were least concerned about the environment, followed by Protestants, Catholics, and seculars, however, there was variation within the groups so that more "engaged" members (those who attended church most frequently) were less likely to express concern even if they belonged to less eschatological tradi- tions. This finding led them to conclude that conservatism (associated with greater frequency of participation) was a better predictor of low environ- mental concern than denomination or doctrine. J. L. Guth, J. C. Green, L. A. Kellstedt, and C. E. Smidt, "Faith and the Environment: Religious Beliefs and Attitudes on Environmental Policy," *American Journal of Political Science* 39 (1995): 364–82. Shaiko pointed out that politics rather than religion might explain the findings in previous efforts to test the Lynn White thesis, a con- clusion that was further supported by Boyd, who found that denominational differences disappeared when studies included demographic and polit- ical variables, both of which could explain differing levels of concern. R. G.

Shaiko, "Religion, Politics, and Environmental Concern: A Powerful Mix of Passions," *Social Science Quarterly*, 68, no. 1–2 (1987): 244–62; Heather H. Boyd, "Christianity and the Environment in the American Public," *Journal for the Scientific Study of Religion* 38 (1999): 36–44. Eckberg and Blocker came to a similar conclusion after analyzing data from the 1993 General Social Survey, arguing that it was not possible to determine whether dominion statements in Genesis 1 or cultural conservatism caused fundamentalists to have lower levels of environmental concern than people with more liberal religious identities. Douglas Lee Eckberg and T. Jean Blocker, "Christianity, Environmentalism, and the Theoretical Problem of Fundamentalism," *Journal for the Scientific Study of Religion* 35, no. 4 (1996): 343–55.

21 Laurel Kearns, "Saving the Creation: Christian Environmentalism in the United States," *Sociology of Religion* 57 (1996): 55–69.

22 For example, Mary Evelyn Tucker, *Worldly Wonder: Religions Enter Their Ecological Phase* (Master Hsuan Hua Memorial Lecture), (Chicago: Open Court Publishing Company, 2003); Roger Gottlieb, *A Greener Faith: Religious Environmentalism and Our Planet's Future* (New York: Oxford University Press, 2006).

23 Roger Gottlieb, "Religious Environmentalism: What It Is, Where It's Heading, and Why We Should Be Going in the Same Direction," *Journal for the Study of Religion, Nature, and Culture* 1, no. 1 (2007): 81–91; Laurel Kearns, "Saving the Creation: 55–69.

24 The most prominent critique of the "greening of religion" hypothesis comes from Bron Taylor et al., who made a thorough examination of literature on religion and ecology and argue that despite the emergence of pro-environmental religiosity, there is little evidence for a widespread religious environmental movement in the United States. Bron Taylor, Gretel Van Wieren, and Bernard Zaleha, "The Greening of Religion Hypothesis (Part Two)," *Journal for the Study of Religion, Nature and Culture* 10, no. 3 (2016): 306–378.

25 Michael DeLashmutt, "Church and Climate Change: An Examination of the Attitudes and Practices of Cornish Anglican Churches Regarding the Environment," *Journal for the Study of Religion, Nature and Culture* 5, no. 1 (2011): 61–81.

26 Carr et al. conducted interviews with pastors and lay members of evangelical churches in Dallas, Texas, to examine relationships between religious beliefs and views on climate change. The interviewees were skeptical of non-evangelical scientists and generally unaware of organizations like the Evangelical Climate Initiative or evangelical leaders who are advocating for climate change action. Some were uninterested in climate issues, which they saw as a distraction from their primary focus on building a relationship with God. Others indicated that they would be interested in hearing about climate change from their own pastors but did not trust scientists. Wilkinson found

similar patterns in her book-length study of the Evangelical Climate Initiative. Focus group interviews with evangelicals revealed that few lay people had heard of the Evangelical Climate Initiative. The interviewees were skeptical about climate change, and their attitudes seemed to have more to do with a distrust of science than theological teachings of dominion or eschatology. Wylie Carr, Michael Patterson, Laurie Yung, and Daniel Spencer, "Evangelical Religious Beliefs and Perceptions of Climate Change," *Journal for the Study of Religion, Nature and Culture* 6, no. 3 (2012): 276–99; Katherine Wilkinson, *Between God and Green: How Evangelicals Are Cultivating a Middle Ground on Climate Change* (New York: Oxford University Press, 2012).

27 John M. Clements, Aaron M. McCright, and Chenyang Xiao. "An Examination of the 'Greening of Christianity' Thesis Among Americans 1993–2010," *Journal for the Scientific Study of Religion* 53, no. 2 (2014): 373–91.

28 In the editor's introduction to a 2011 issue of the *Journal for the Study of Religion, Nature and Culture,* Bron Taylor points out that much of the research hypothesizing the existence of a greening trend is "based not on randomized datasets but on cases where religious individuals and small groups are demonstrably environmentally concerned and active" (255). Consequently, the data does little to explicate what proportion of a religious group has environmentally positive attitudes and behavior, nor does it compare religious and secular groups or track changes over time. He is concerned that the studies assume religion is the variable responsible for environmental practices and beliefs, thereby overlooking other potential variables such as the possibility that "environmental concern by religious actors" may just as easily be explained as "a *reflection* of the culture in which the religious actors are situated, not the *result* of the religion's ethical ideals" (255; emphasis in original). Bron Taylor, "Toward a Robust Scientific Investigation of the 'Religion' Variable in the Quest for Sustainability," *Journal for the Study of Religion, Nature and Culture* 5, no. 3 (2011): 261.

29 Ellingson, Stephen, *To Care for God's Creation,* (Chicago: University of Chicago Press, 2016), 12.

30 Environmental Ministries, Earth Care Congregations. The website keeps count of certified congregations. Accessed November 2018, https://www.pres byterianmission.org/ministries/environment/earth-care-congregations/#

31 UUA Green Sanctuary Program, accessed November 2018, https://www.uua. org/environment/sanctuary/introduction/history-acknowledgements.

32 Mark Chaves, *Congregations in America* (Cambridge: Harvard University Press, 2004), 1.

33 Pew Research Center, "The Future of the World Religions: Population Growth Projections, 2010–2050," Religion and Public Life (April 2, 2015).

34 Amanda Baugh, *God and the Green Divide: Religious Environmentalism in Black and White* (Oakland: University of California Press, 2016), 12.

35 Ellingson, *To Care for God's Creation.*

36 Sarah McFarland Taylor, *Green Sisters: A Spiritual Ecology.* (Cambridge, MA: Harvard University Press, 2007).

37 Amanda Baugh, *God and the Green Divide: Religious Environmentalism in Black and White* (Oakland: University of California Press, 2016), 3.

38 Robert K. Yin, *Case Study Research: Design and Methods*, 2nd ed. (Thousand Oaks, Sage Publications, 1994).

39 Definition from IUCN/UNEP/WWF, *Caring for the Earth: A Strategy for Sustainable Living.* (Gland, Switzerland, 1991).

40 Chaves, *Congregations in America*, 1–2.

41 When this background research was conducted in 2012, there were numerous case studies on the webpages for the National Religious Partnership for the Environment and Creation Justice Ministries. Both of these organizations subsequently developed new webpages that have fewer posted cases.

42 Further details about the case selection process are presented in the Appendix.

43 See the Appendix for more information on the interview questions.

CHAPTER ONE

1 Informational brochure, Trinity Presbyterian Church, 2013.

2 Informational brochure, Trinity Presbyterian Church, 2013.

3 Lynn Cameron, interview by author, August 21, 2012.

4 Cameron, interview.

5 Cameron, interview.

6 Cameron, interview.

7 Madison Christian Community website, http://www.madisonchristian-community.org.

8 Jeff Wild, interview by author, May 9, 2013.

9 Brant Rosen, quoted in Pauline Dubkin Yearwood, "Chicago's Green Synagogue," *The Chicago Jewish News: Special Issue* (no date): 4.

10 LEED stands for Leadership in Energy and Environmental Design.

11 Our Secret Garden Indoor/Outdoor Nursery and Preschool webpage, accessed December 9, 2015, http://www.oursecretgarden.org/aboutus.html.

12 Ken Wilson, "The Evangelical Awakening to Environmental Concern," unpublished essay presented at the "Let's Tend the Garden" Conference, Boise, ID, Sept. 20, 2007.

13 Trinity Earth Shepherds webpage, https://www.trinity-pc.org/environmental-stewardship.

14 Trinity Presbyterian Church, East Brunswick, NJ, "How our church is structured," accessed December 2015, http://www.trinity-pc.org/who-we-are/how-our-church-is-structured.

15 Deborah O'Halloran, interview by author, July 26, 2013.

16 Rob Carter, email message to author, July 15, 2013.

17 Trinity Presbyterian Church, East Brunswick, NJ, "How our church is structured," accessed December 2015, http://www.trinity-pc.org/who-we-are/how-our-church-is-structured.

18 Trinity Presbyterian Church, "How our church is structured," accessed December 2015. http://www.trinity-pc.org/who-we-are/how-our-church-is-structured.

19 Michael Chodroff, interview by author, July 24, 2013.

20 Margo Wolfson, interview by author, July 27, 2013.

21 Technically, the Catholic Church uses the term *nun* specifically for vowed religious women who are cloistered from the outside world, but in vernacular English it has come to be used for all vowed women in Roman Catholic religious orders. This book uses the latter, common understanding, but more frequently uses the term *sisters*, a general term for vowed religious women.

22 The Second Vatican Council, or Vatican II, gathered together Catholic Church leaders to evaluate relations between the Roman Catholic Church and the modern world. It produced recommendations for institutional changes to make the Church more compatible with current social contexts.

23 Southwest Michigan Land Conservancy, "Bow in the Clouds Preserve," http://swmlc.org/project/bow-in-the-clouds-preserve.

24 Virginia Jones, interview by author, Jan. 25, 2013.

25 Congregation of St. Joseph, "Our Mission," accessed November 2018, https://www.csjoseph.org/our-mission.

26 Virginia Jones, "Sisters of St. Joseph" in *Religious Congregations on the Land: The Practical Links Between Community, Sustainable Land Use, and Spiritual Charism* (National Catholic Rural Life Conference, August 1996), 17.

27 Jones, "Sisters of St. Joseph," 17.

28 Southwest Michigan Land Conservancy, "Bow in the Clouds Preserve."

29 Mary Kroll, "In the Beginning," *Sagatagan Seasons* 10, no. 2 (Spring 2007): 1.

30 Kyle Rauch, "Here Comes the Sun," *Sagatagan Seasons* 20, no. 3 (Summer 2017): 3–4.

31 At five-year intervals, herbicides may be used in hay field preparation to suppress weeds. Yearly weed management relies on crop rotation and tilling; consequently, field crops are not fully organic but are generally chemical-free for three out of each five years.

32 Barbara O'Donnell, interview by author, July 1, 2013.

33 Frank Romeo, interview by author, June 29, 2013.

34 O'Donnell, interview.

35 Holy Wisdom Monastery webpage, http://benedictinewomen.org.

36 Mary David Walgenbach, interview with author, May 11, 2013.

37 Walgenbach, interview.

38 Sisters of St. Francis of Philadelphia, "Peace and Justice," accessed May 2015, http://www.osfphila.org/justice_peace/csr2.

39 Environmental Initiative brochure, Sisters of St. Francis. (No date).

40 Sisters of St. Francis of Philadelphia, Environmental Initiative webpage, accessed May 2015, https://osfphila.org/justice-and-peace/eco.

CHAPTER TWO

1 Going Green Helps Church Bloom," United Church of Christ Massachusetts Conference Newsletter, Dec. 7, 2011, http://www.macucc.org/newsdetail/112206.

2 The estimated number of congregations in the US is based on records collected by the National Council of Churches, Office of Research, Evaluation and Planning, *Yearbook of American and Canadian Churches*, (Nashville: Abingdon Press, 1998).

3 There are no formal statistics for the number of congregations that have undertaken sustainability efforts throughout the United States, however the National Religious Partnership for the Environment, Yale Forum on Religion and Ecology, Interfaith Power and Light, and GreenFaith Program all collect case studies. These case databases represent a tiny percentage of American congregations.

PART II

Barbara O'Donnell, interview by author, July 1, 2013.

CHAPTER THREE

1 Although the term "calling" may be used to describe a strong desire to do any type of work, it is particularly common as a way to describe the motive for doing religious work. Cf. Merriam Webster Dictionary.

2 Texts studied included: General Assembly Report, *Restoring Creation for Ecology and Justice* (Presbyterian Church (USA), 1990); General Assembly Report, *Hope for a Global Future: Toward Just and Sustainable Human Development* (1996); Matthew Fox, *Original Blessing* (New York: Penguin Putnam Inc., 1983); and Dieter T. Hessel, *Theology for Earth Community: A Field Guide* (New York: Orbis Books, 1996).

3 Lynn Cameron, interview by author, August 21, 2012.

4 Cameron, interview.

5 Margo Wolfson, interview by author, July 27, 2013.

6 Wolfson, interview.

7 Coalition on the Environment and Jewish Life, "Mission Statement," accessed July 2015, http://www.coejl.org.

8 Gerard McGuire, interview by author, March 4, 2013.

9 Barbara O'Donnell, interview by author, July 1, 2013.

10 Quoted in Debra Illingworth Greene, "Church Starts Egg-cellent Ministry." *The Lutheran* (November 2010), accessed June 15, 2013, http://www.theluth eran.org/article/article.cfm?article_id=9480.

11 Kimberly Eighmy, telephone interview by author, June 17, 2013.

12 Sonja Keesey-Berg, interview by author, May 9, 2013.

13 McGuire, interview.

14 Katia Reeves, email letter to the author, May 6, 2013.

15 O'Donnell, interview.

16 Ken Wilson, "The Evangelical Awakening to Environmental Concern," unpublished essay presented at the "Let's Tend the Garden" Conference (Vineyard Church, Boise, Idaho, Sept. 20, 2007).

17 Wilson's framing of his calling to care for creation as a form of spiritual transformation accords with evangelical social norms. Evangelicals emphasize the possibility of dramatic changes in an individual's perspective on an issue, with the understanding that such changes lead to new actions for individuals and faith communities.

18 Wilson, "The Evangelical Awakening to Environmental Concern."

19 Debbie O'Halloran, interview by author, July 26, 2013.

20 O'Halloran, interview.

21 O'Halloran, interview.

22 Bread for the World is a Christian citizens' movement in the United States that advocates for policy changes to reduce hunger and poverty. (http://www.bread.org/what-we-do/).

23 O'Halloran, interview.

24 Gretchen Marshall-TothFejel, interview by author, Jan. 4, 2013.

25 Cameron, interview.

26 Champions' responses to the challenge posed by insufficient knowledge are described in more detail in Chapter 4.

CHAPTER FOUR

1 Chuck Tully, interview by author, March 4, 2013.

2 Ann Thayer-Cohen, interview by author, July 29, 2013.

3 Margo Wolfson, interview by author, July 27, 2013.

4 Jeff Wild, interview by author, May 9, 2013.

5 Kimberly Eighmy, telephone interview by author, June 17, 2013.

6 Julia M. Wondolleck and Steven L. Yaffee, *Making Collaboration Work* (Washington DC: Island Press, 2000), 163–5.

7 Asher Siebert, interview by author, July 24, 2013.

8 The Human Concerns Committee at St. Thomas Aquinas Church focuses on alleviating hunger, homelessness, and disease, and addressing deficiencies in housing and health care.

9 Brian Keeley, *Human Capital: How What You Know Shapes Your Life* (Paris: OECD Publishing, 2007). https://www.oecd.org/insights/humancapitalhow-whatyouknowshapesyourlife.htm.

10 Gretchen Marshall-TothFejel, interview by author, Jan. 4, 2013.

11 Marshall-TothFejel, interview.

12 Marshall-TothFejel, interview.

13 Marshall-TothFejel, interview.

14 See, for example Icek Ajzen, "The Theory of Planned Behavior," *Organizational Behavior and Human Decision Processes* 50 (1991): 179–211, and Paul C. Stern, "Understanding Individuals' Environmentally Significant Behavior," *Environmental Law Reporter: News and Analysis*, 35 (2005): 10785–10790.

15 Debbie O'Halloran, interview by author, July 26, 2013.

16 Wolfson, interview.

17 Wolfson, interview.

18 Frank Mundo, telephone interview by author, August 5, 2013.

19 Cameron, interview.

20 Virginia Jones, interview by author, Jan. 25, 2013.

21 Jones, interview.

22 Cameron, interview.

23 Mundo, interview.

24 Mundo, interview.

25 According to Elizabeth Sim, Tom Kroll had years of experience working in forestry when he was hired as land manager and arboretum director after Fr. Paul Schwietz died. He had previously worked for the Minnesota Department of Natural Resources, where he served as supervisor of the State Forest Nursery and Private Forest Management Program. He had extensive experience assisting private landowners with land management plans, plant inventories, and regeneration effort. Moreover, when interviewed, Kroll explained that he was a lifelong resident of the area, born into an old German farming family. This heritage helped him build a local community network focused on preservation of the Avon Hills ecosystems, with the abbey as a key resource for teaching about land stewardship. Elizabeth Sim, "Saint John's Hires New Land Manager and Arboretum Director," *Sagatagan Seasons* 4.2 (Summer 2001), 1, 3; Tom Kroll, interview by author, May 13, 2013.

26 See for example, Raymond De Young, "Expanding and Evaluating Motives for Environmentally Responsible Behavior," *Journal of Social Issues* 56, no. 3 (2000): 509–26, and Stephen Kaplan, "Being Needed, Adaptive Muddling, and Human-Environment Relationship," in R. I. Selby, K. H. Anthony, J. Choi, and B. Orland, eds., *Coming of Age.* (Oklahoma City, OK: EDRA 21,1990): 19–25.

27 Mundo, interview.

28 Tom Matthews, interview by author, May 9, 2013.

29 Lynn Cameron, telephone interview by author, April 8, 2013.

30 Greg Armstrong, interview by author, July 25, 2014.

31 Jeff Wild and Peter Bakken, *Church on Earth: Grounding Your Ministry in a Sense of Place* (Minneapolis: Augsberg Fortress, 2009), 60.

32 Wild, interview.

1 The leadership capabilities that contributed to champions' success in organizing these cases are similar to the characteristics Ellingson observed among
   founders of other types of religious environmental movement organizations. Stephen Ellingson, *To Care for God's Creation: The Emergence of the
   Religious Environmental Movement* (Chicago: University of Chicago Press,
   2016): 29–30.

PART III

1 LEED is an abbreviation for Leadership in Energy and Environmental
   Design, a formal program for "green" building construction that ranks buildings based on incorporation of design features and construction practices that
   reduce resource consumption.
2 The processes for legitimating sustainability observed in these cases help
   explain how these communities overcame one of the biggest challenges for
   religious environmentalism. In Ellingson's study of religious environmental
   movement organizations, he notes that demonstrating environmentalism is
   critical to religious life is essential for motivating earth care in the context of
   religious organizations where associations with liberal politics and religious
   emphases on conversion and interior life create barriers for religious environmentalism. Stephen Ellingson, *To Care for Creation: The Emergence of
   the Religious Environmental Movement* (Chicago: The University of Chicago
   Press, 2016): 18.
3 Some religions have oral traditions rather than written scriptures, however
   the traditions studied in this research all use written texts.
4 Some Christians also authorize clergy who attain their status through non-
   academic systems. For example, Ken Bailey notes that in the nineteenth
   century some evangelical denominations only required that potential ministers have a spiritual calling. Kenneth K. Bailey, *Southern White Protestantism
   in the Twentieth Century* (New York: Harper & Row, Publishers, 1964): 7.
   By the twentieth century, most evangelicals adopted seminary training for
   clergy, however some nondenominational evangelical churches are still
   suspicious of educational institutions and prefer to emphasize a call from
   God and preaching skills as criteria for church leadership. Randall Balmer,
   "Evangelicals: Current Trends and Movements," *Encyclopedia of Religion in
   America* (Washington DC: CQ Press, 2010): 792.
5 Lynn Cameron, interview by author, August 21, 2012.
6 Ann Thayer-Cohen, interview by author, July 29, 2013.
7 Virginia Jones, interview by author, Jan. 25, 2013.
8 This observation accords well with research by Andrew Szasz, which indicates
   that pastors in denominations with strong environmental messages (Catholic
   and United Methodist Churches) were more likely to deliver environmental

sermons and encourage efforts to green facilities if they thought congregants already agreed with the message. In "less hospitable communities," ministers avoided a subject they perceived as potentially divisive. Andrew Szasz, "Novel Framings Create New, Unexpected Allies for Climate Activism," in *Reframing Climate Change: Constructing Ecological Geopolitics,* edited by Shannon O'Lear and Simon Dalby (London: Routledge, 2016), 164.

9 Michael Chodroff, interview by author, July 24, 2013.

CHAPTER FIVE

1 These first three motifs align with the theological ethics of Christian steward-ship, creation spirituality, and eco-justice that Laurel Kearns identified in her study of Christian environmental activism in the 1980s: "Saving the Creation: Christian Environmentalism in the United States," *Sociology of Religion* 57 (1996): 55–70. However, the term "nature spirituality" is used here rather than Kearns' "creation spirituality" in order to include non-theists such as Unitarian Universalists.

2 Because faith leaders shifted among message frames, it is not easy to identify a community as solely anthropocentric or ecocentric in its worldview. Most could be described as predominantly anthropocentric because they perceived humans as having a special role in creation, but some champions might be more ecocentric. The prevalence of stewardship and social justice ethics as message frames promoting sustainability complicates Bron Taylor's argu-ment that Christianity is too anthropocentric to serve as an effective green religion. Bron Taylor, *Dark Green Religion* (Berkeley: University of California Press, 2009).

3 Organizations such as the Coalition on Environment and Jewish Life, the National Council of Churches' Creation Justice Ministries, the Catholic Climate Covenant, and the Evangelical Environmental Network have devel-oped resources to provide scriptural support for faith-based environmental action. The biblical creation story features prominently in these materials.

4 Rebecca Epstein, "Rosh Hashanah, Second Day Sermon," (Sept. 10, 2010/5771).

5 As discussed in the Introduction, the classic example of this argument was presented by Lynn White. Lynn White Jr., "The Historical Roots of Our Ecologic Crisis," *Science* Vol. 155 (1967): 12–37.

6 In the Hebrew Bible, the first man is called *"ha adam"* or "the man," which is usually translated as the name Adam in English versions of the text. The word for man is closely related to the word *adamah*, "ground, earth, soil, land." Brown-Driver-Briggs Hebrew and English Lexicon, Unabridged, Electronic Database. Biblesoft, Inc.

7 Epstein, "Rosh Hashanah, Second Day Sermon."

8 Laurence Malinger, "Temple Shalom and Greenfaith," Sermon for Rosh Hashanah 5771 (Sept. 9, 2010).

9 Brant Rosen, "Is the Bible Destroying Creation?" Yedid Nefesh Blog (Sept. 2, 2011).

10 Malinger, "Temple Shalom and Greenfaith."

11 Malinger, "Temple Shalom and Greenfaith," emphasis in original text.

12 Ken Wilson, "A Biblical Basis for Creation Care," in Boorse et al. *Loving the Least of These: Addressing a Changing Climate*, National Association of Evangelicals (2011), 9.

13 Mark Glovin, "The Technology of Community: A Reflection on Our Green Sanctuary Certification," Sermon delivered Jan. 31, 2010.

14 Jeff Wild, interview by author, May 9, 2013

15 Wilson, "A Biblical Basis for Creation Care," 9.

16 Margaret, Pirkl, OSF, "The Cosmic Christ" (undated essay).

17 Pirkl, "Cosmic Christ."

18 Pirkl, "Cosmic Christ."

19 Pirkl, "Cosmic Christ."

20 Mary David Walgenbach, interview with author, May 11, 2013.

21 Walgenbach, interview.

22 Quoted in webpage article about Bow in the Clouds Preserve, Southwest Michigan Land Conservancy, accessed June 3, 2015, https://swmlc.org/project/bow-in-the-clouds-preserve.

23 Ann Reed Held, interview by author, August 21, 2012.

24 Quoted in Jeff Wild and Peter Bakken, *Church on Earth: Grounding Your Ministry in a Sense of Place* (Minneapolis: Augsberg Fortress, 2009), 60.

25 Wild, interview.

26 Villa Maria Education and Spirituality Center homepage, accessed November 28, 2020, https://www.vmesc.org/Web/home.

27 Barbara O'Donnell, interview by author, July 1, 2013.

28 Paul Boutwell, interview by author, May 8, 2013.

29 Boutwell, interview.

30 Wilson, "A Biblical Basis for Creation Care," 11.

31 O'Donnell, interview.

32 Sisters of St. Francis of Philadelphia, "Corporate Social Responsibility," accessed November 26, 2020, https://osfphila.org/corporate-social-responsibility.

33 Epstein, "Rosh Hashanah, Second Day Sermon."

34 Quoted in Pauline Dubkin Yearwood, "Chicago's Green Synagogue." *The Chicago Jewish News: Special Issue* (no date): 11.

35 Mark Glovin, "The Technology of Community: A Reflection on Our Green Sanctuary Certification," Sermon delivered Jan. 31, 2010.

36 Brant Rosen, Rosh Hashanah Sermon (Oct. 2008/5769).

37 Wilson, "The Evangelical Awakening to Environmental Concern," 3.

38 Quoted by anonymous author, "Ecology in Action," *Catholic Rural Life Magazine* (Summer 2014): 14

39 "Ecology in Action," 14.

40 Malinger, "Temple Shalom and Greenfaith."

41 Glovin, "The Technology of Community.

42 Glovin, "The Technology of Community.

43 The phrase "healing the world," *tikkun olam*, refers to the Jewish vision of creating an ideal society that adheres to religious ethics. Christians have a similar vision of transforming earth into "the Kingdom of God." Dr. Martin Luther King Jr. popularized a vision of "the beloved community" as a society in which poverty and racism are eliminated and all people share earth's resources. King's vision has been adopted by many US religious groups, including Unitarian Universalists.

44 Malinger, "Temple Shalom and Greenfaith."

45 Glovin, "The Technology of Community.

46 Wild and Bakken, *Church on Earth*, 42.

47 T. Lowe, K. Brown, S. Dessai, M. de Franca Doria, K. Haynes, and K. Vincent, "Does Tomorrow Ever Come? Disaster Narrative and Public Perceptions of Climate Change," *Public Understanding of* Science, 15 (2006): 435–457.

48 I. Lorenzoni, S. A. Nicholson-Cole, and L. Whitmarsh, "Barriers Perceived to Engaging with Climate Change among the UK Public and Their Policy Implications," *Global Environmental Change* 17 (2007): 445–459.

49 Saffron O'Neill and Sophie Nicholson-Cole, "Fear Won't Do It: Promoting Positive Engagement with Climate Change Through Visual and Iconic Representations," *Science Communication* 30, no. 3 (2009): 355–79.

50 Wilson, "The Evangelical Awakening to Environmental Concern."

51 Stephen Ellingson, *To Care for Creation: The Emergence of the Religious Environmental Movement* (Chicago: The University of Chicago Press, 2016), 94.

52 In his description of religious environmental movement organizations (REMOs), Ellingson says that nearly all proponents of Jewish environmentalism use the concept of *tikkun olam* as the central ethical principle of their organizations. Ellingson, *To Care for Creation*, 93.

53 Sisters of the Humility of Mary, "Mission Statement," accessed November 2018, https://www.humilityofmary.org/who-we-are/our-spirituality/mission-statement.

54 Ellingson identified this process of "expanding the mission" as a key element for integrating environmentalism into religious organizations. *To Care for Creation*, 49–51.

55 Ellingson describes frames used to bridge denominational teachings and environmentalism in REMOS that match up well with the general theological foundations found in these case studies, however, the REMOs are larger

organizations and do not seem to use the kinds of community identity frames that appear in messages from congregation-level faith leaders.

CHAPTER SIX

1 Ann Cohen, interview by author, July 29, 2013.
2 Lynn Cameron, interview by author, August 21, 2012.
3 Cohen, interview.
4 Ticia Brown, interview by author, May 10, 2013.
5 Brant Rosen, *JRC Construction Diary #26* (Nov. 16, 2007).
6 Brant Rosen, "What Makes a Green Shul Green?" *JRC Construction Diary* (Feb. 6, 2008).
7 Brant Rosen, *JRC Construction Diary #2* (posted Nov. 26, 2006).
8 Asher Siebert, interview by author, July 24, 2013.
9 Cohen, interview.
10 Cameron, interview.
11 Minnesota DNR, "Two Mile Trail and Dike," *Restored Wetlands* (March–April 1990).
12 Tom Matthews, interview by author, May 9, 2013.
13 Icek Ajzen, *Attitudes, Personality and Behaviour*, (Milton Keynes: Open University Press 1988); Icek Ajzen, "The Theory of Planned Behavior," *Organizational Behavior and Human Decision Processes* 50 (1991): 179–211.
14 Robert B. Cialdini, Raymond R. Reno, and Carl A. Kallgren, "A Focus Theory of Normative Conduct: Recycling the Concept of Norms to Reduce Littering in Public Places," *Journal of Personality and Social Psychology* 58, no. 6 (1990): 1015–1026.
15 Ajzen, "Theory of Planned Behavior."
16 Jeff Wild, interview by author, May 9, 2013.
17 Wild, interview.
18 Jeff Wild and Peter Bakken, *Church on Earth: Grounding Your Ministry in a Sense of Place* (Minneapolis: Augsburg Fortress, 2009): 21.
19 The curriculum is available as a downloadable PDF: https://www.madison-christiancommunity.org/PDF/11-27-13%20CornerCreation.pdf.

SUMMARY AND DOMAIN INTERACTIONS:
HOW FAITH LEADERS AFFECTED INITIATIVES

1 Lynn Cameron, interview by author, August 21, 2012.
2 Malcolm Cameron, interview by author, August 21, 2012.
3 Judy LePera, interview by author, August 21, 2012.
4 Brant Rosen, "Tu B'shevat in the Diaspora: Celebrating the Unseen," *Yedid Nefesh* (blog). January 25, 2013.
5 Brant Rosen, "Is the Bible Destroying Creation?" *Yedid Nefesh* (blog). Sept. 2, 2011.

PART IV

1 Jeff Wild, interview by author, May 9, 2013.
2 Sonja Keesey-Berg, interview by author, May 9, 2013.
3 Michael R. Greenberg, "Concern about Environmental Pollution: How Much Difference Do Race and Ethnicity Make? A New Jersey Case Study," *Environmental Health Perspectives* 113, no. 4 (2005): 369–374.
4 Anthony Leiserowitz and Karen Akerlof, *Race, Ethnicity and Public Responses to Climate Change*, Yale University and George Mason University (New Haven, CT: Yale Project on Climate Change, 2010).
5 This research project did not gather data on community members' political leanings, a factor that is known to influence attitudes toward the environment, however the diversity of denominations in the sample suggests it is unlikely that uniformity of political identity accounted for the faith communities' shared affinity for earth care. According to a 2014 Pew research report, 48 percent of white mainline Protestants identify or lean Republican, and 40 percent identify or lean Democratic. White, non-Hispanic Catholics mirror these numbers with 50 percent Republican and 41 percent Democratic. In contrast, 65 percent of Jewish voters and 82 percent of Black Protestants identify or lean Democratic. Pew Research Center. "A Deep Dive into Party Affiliation." April 7, 2015.
6 Michael Chodroff, interview by author, July 24, 2013.
7 These statistics come from the Center for Applied Research in the Apostolate, Georgetown University, as cited in Michael Lipka, "U.S. Nuns Face Shrinking Numbers and Tensions with the Vatican," Pew Research Center (August 8, 2014), accessed February 2015, https://www.pewresearch.org/fact-tank/2014/08/08/u-s-nuns-face-shrinking-numbers-and-tensions-with-the-vatican.
8 Barbara O'Donnell, interview by author, July 1, 2013.

CHAPTER SEVEN

1 Jeff Wild, interview by author, May 9, 2013.
2 The Madison Christian Community is an ecumenical community composed of the Advent Lutheran congregation (Evangelical Lutheran Church in America) and the Community of Hope congregation (United Church of Christ). It grew out of an ecumenical (unifying) movement in the 1970s that focused on bringing people from diverse Christian traditions together.
3 David Keesey-Berg, "This Gifted Land," unpublished essay (2003).
4 Madison Christian Community website, http://www.madisonchristian-community.org.
5 David Keesey-Berg, interview by author, May 9, 2017.
6 Sonja Keesey-Berg, "Garden History," unpublished essay (no date).
7 Mary Kroll, "In the Beginning," *Sagatagan Seasons* 10, no. 2 (Spring 2007): 1.
8 Quoted in Kroll, "In the Beginning," 1.

9 Saint John's Abbey, "Sustainability," http://www.saintjohnsabbey.org/our-work/sustainability.

10 Conifers are not native to the region; the pasture was originally maple-basswood forest.

11 Jennifer Delahunty Britz, "EverGreen!" *Saint John's Magazine* 41, no. 2 (Winter 2003): 6.

12 Quoted in Alex Evenson, "Saint John's History: Brother George Primus," *Sagatagan Seasons* 2.3 (Autumn 1999): 5.

13 Evenson, "Saint John's History," 5.

14 Saint John's Abbey, "Garden," accessed May 27, 2013, http://www.saintjohns abbey.org/working/garden.html.

15 Saint John's Abbey, "Mission Statement," http://www.saintjohnsabbey.org/info/mission-statement.

16 Barbara O'Donnell, interview by author, July 1, 2013.

17 A charism is the founding purpose of a religious order.

18 O'Donnell, interview.

19 John Moreira, interview by author, June 30, 2013.

20 Villa Maria Land Ethic, unpublished document (2009).

21 Villa Maria Land Ethic.

22 Neal Smith, "Care for the Earth: A Longstanding Monastery Tradition," *Benedictine Bridge* (April 15, 2010).

23 Smith, "Care for the Earth."

24 Walgenbach, interview.

25 According to Sarah McFarland Taylor, this movement to conserve convent lands is widespread among US monastic communities, and sisters from various communities educate each other about land trusts and conservation easements. *Green Sisters*, 93f.

26 Corinne Wright, interview by author, January 2015.

27 Taylor, *Green Sisters*, 10–11.

28 Taylor, *Green Sisters*, 61ff.

29 O'Halloran, interview.

CHAPTER EIGHT

1 Earth Care House Church Covenant, unpublished document, Trinity Presbyterian Church, Harrisonburg, Virginia, 2011.

2 The size is larger than ideal for a house church. A large group means fewer opportunities for members to take turns at leadership and, because of an inclusive format, meetings are long. There are periodic discussions about whether to create two separate groups.

3 Tom Matthews, interview by author, May 9, 2013.

4 U.S. Energy Information Administration, "How Much Energy is Consumed in U.S. Buildings?" accessed November 2020, https://www.eia.gov/tools/faqs/faq.php?id=86&t=1

5 Julie Dorfman, interview by author, April 9, 2013.

6 Pauline Dubkin Yearwood, "Chicago's Green Synagogue," *The Chicago Jewish News: Special Issue* (no date), 4.

7 Yearwood, "Chicago's Green Synagogue," 4.

8 Tom Kroll, interview by author, May 13, 2013.

9 Saint John's Arboretum Task Force, "A Green Banner: Values of an Arboretum at Saint John's," unpublished document (1997).

10 Arboretum Task Force, "A Green Banner."

11 John Kulas, OSB, "The Abbey and Its Land," *Sagatagan Seasons* 10, no. 2 (Spring 2007): 4.

12 United Church of Christ, Massachusetts Conference, "Going Green Helps Church Bloom," online newsletter. Dec. 7, 2011.

13 Quoted in Elizabeth Rose, "A Matter of Faith," *The Newburyport Current* (Newburyport, MA: GateHouse News Service, posted September 11, 2008).

14 God speaks to Elijah in a "still small voice" in 1 Kings 19:12 (KJV). Newer versions of the Bible translate the phrase as a "gentle whisper" (ESV). The passage is understood to mean that God's voice can be heard in quiet reflection, not just in dramatic manifestations like great winds. http://www.gotquestions.org/still-small-voice.html.

15 First Parish Church of Newbury, "Congregationalism," accessed September 28, 2015, http://firstparishofnewbury.org/about-us/congregationalism.

16 Quoted in Rose, "A Matter of Faith."

17 Mary David Walgenbach, interview with author, May 11, 2013.

18 Walgenbach, interview.

19 Use of the term *Chapter* differs slightly among the monastic cases. At Saint John's Abbey, the Chapter is the entire community of members, whereas in the women's convents, a Chapter is a community discernment process. The two uses overlap because both refer to gatherings of members who make decisions about the welfare of the community. It should be noted that this democratic process is not universal, and some religious orders rely on committees of representatives instead of a vote by the whole membership.

20 "A Living Document," *HM Voice* 30, no. 1 (Summer 2013): 5.

21 Readings came from authors such as Teilhard de Chardin (SJ), Thomas Berry (CP), and Sandra Schneiders (IHM).

22 Direction Statement for the Sisters of the Humility of Mary, 1989, unpublished document.

23 Virginia Jones, "Sisters of St. Joseph," in *Religious Congregations on the Land* (National Catholic Rural Life Conference, 1996).

24 Debbie O'Halloran, interview by author, July 26, 2013.

25 Lucie Bauer, interview by author, August 4, 2013.

26 Brant Rosen, quoted in Pauline Dubkin Yearwood, "Chicago's Green Synagogue," *The Chicago Jewish News: Special Issue* (no date), 11.

27 Yearwood, "Chicago's Green Synagogue," 11–12.

28 Sisters of St. Francis of Philadelphia, "Environmental Initiatives" brochure (Aston, PA: Our Lady of Angels Convent, 2000).

29 Corinne Wright, interview by author, January 2015.

30 Sisters of St. Francis of Philadelphia, "Environmental Initiatives" brochure.

31 Chodroff, interview.

32 Temple Shalom website, accessed November 2020, http://templeshalomnj.org.

33 Wright, interview.

34 Wright, interview.

35 Wright, interview.

36 Quoted in Yearwood, "Chicago's Green Synagogue," 12.

37 Quoted in Yearwood, "Chicago's Green Synagogue," 12.

38 *Kashrut* is a term for the dietary laws prescribed in the Torah. They delineate foods that may and may not be eaten as well as rules for preparing foods.

39 Quoted in Yearwood, "Chicago's Green Synagogue," 12.

40 Lewis Grobe, interview by author, May 12, 2013.

41 Grobe, interview.

SUMMARY AND DOMAIN INTERACTIONS: HOW CONGREGATIONS AFFECTED INITIATIVES

1 Julie Dorfman, interview by author, April 9, 2013.

2 Madison Christian Community, "Purpose Statement" (Madison, WI, 2011), accessed November 2018, https://www.madisonchristiancommunity.org/about_mcc.aspx.

3 Quoted in Doug Erickson, "Madison Church Emphasizes Call to Land Stewardship," *Wisconsin State Journal* (July 9, 2010).

4 John Moreira, interview by author, June 30, 2013.

5 Tom Matthews, interview by author, May 9, 2013.

6 Wild and Bakken, *Church on Earth*, 40.

7 Madison Christian Community, "Purpose Statement."

PART V

1 Trinity Presbyterian Church, "Earth Care House Church Covenant," unpublished document (Harrisonburg, VA, 2011).

2 "Earth Care House Church Covenant."

3 Judy LePera, interview by author, August 21, 2012.

4 Mark Chaves, *Congregations in America* (Cambridge, MA: Harvard University Press, 2004), 8.

5 Nancy Tatom Ammerman, *Pillars of Faith: American Congregations and Their Partners* (Berkeley: University of California Press, 2005), 3.

6 Chaves, *Congregations in America*, 9.

7 This description of polities is drawn from H. Paul Chalfant, Robert E. Beckley,

and C. Eddie Palmer, *Religion in Contemporary Society*, 3rd ed., (Itasca, IL: F.E. Peacock Publishers, Inc., 1994), 117–120.

8 Nancy T. Ammerman, *Congregation and Community* (New Brunswick: Rutgers University Press, 1997), 52.

9 Trinity Presbyterian Church, https://www.trinity-pc.org.

10 Tom Matthews, interview by author, May 9, 2013.

11 Jeff Wild, interview by author, May 9, 2013.

12 Presbyterian Church (USA), *Restoring Creation for Ecology and Justice* (General Assembly Report, 1990).

13 Presbyterian Church (USA), *Hope for a Global Future: Toward Just and Sustainable Human Development* (General Assembly Report, 1996).

14 Dieter T. Hessel, *Theology for Earth Community* (New York: Orbis Books, 1996).

15 Larry L. Rasmussen, *Earth Community, Earth Ethics* (New York: Orbis Books, 1996).

16 Barbara Kingsolver, Steven L. Hopp, and Camille Kingsolver, *Animal, Vegetable, Miracle: A Year of Food Life* (New York: HarperCollins, 2007).

17 Matthew Sleeth, *Serve God, Save the Planet: A Christian Call to Action* (White River Junction, VT: Chelsea Green Publishing, 2006).

18 Mallory McDuff, *Natural Saints: How People of Faith are Working to Save God's Earth* (New York: Oxford University Press, 2010).

19 Catholic Climate Covenant, "St. Francis Pledge," accessed May 2012, catholic-climatecovenant.org.

20 LePera, interview.

21 Michael Chodroff, interview by author, July 24, 2013.

22 Gretchen Marshall-TothFejel, interview by author, Jan. 4, 2013.

23 St. Francis Catholic Parish in Ann Arbor organized a green team and implemented green activities such as conserving resources and incorporating earth care into religious education classes. Staff from Michigan Interfaith Power and Light adapted ideas from the sustainability initiative at St. Francis into a Sustainability Framework that could be shared with other houses of worship.

24 Ken Wilson, interview by author, October 17, 2013.

25 Debbie O'Halloran, interview by author, July 26, 2013.

CHAPTER TEN

1 In the Jewish tradition, laity often help organize holiday celebrations, which are less formal than Sabbath services. Sabbath observance is performed in fulfillment of a biblical commandment: "Remember the Sabbath day to sanctify it" (Exod. 20:8), whereas many holidays are post-biblical.

2 Because Judaism uses a lunar-solar calendar with shorter months than the Gregorian calendar, dates for holidays shift from year to year. Tu BiShvat is the fifteenth day of the month of Shevat.

3 Judaism 101, "Jewish Holidays," http://www.jewfaq.org/holiday8.htm.

4 Many Jews follow a custom that prohibits writing the name of the deity. Instead, they use substitutes and abbreviated versions of divine names that omit vowels.

5 Lucie Bauer, interview by author, August 4, 2013.

6 Anshe Emeth Memorial Temple, "Kollel," https://www.aemt.net/learning/adult-education/kollel.

7 The Catholic Coalition on Climate Change (now renamed Catholic Climate Covenant) helped with distribution and promotion of *Sun Come Up*. The Carteret Islanders are predominantly Catholic, and the Bougainville Catholic Diocese has been active in resettlement efforts. Sharon Abercrombie, "Film Screening to Raise Awareness of Plight of Islanders," *EarthBeat* (August 20, 2012), accessed November 2020. https://www.ncronline.org/blogs/earthbeat/eco-catholic/film-screening-raise-awareness-plight-islanders.

8 Trinity Presbyterian Church, Harrisonburg, "About Us," accessed December 9, 2015, http://www.trinity-pc.org/les/about/.

9 Trinity Presbyterian Church, "About Us."

10 Trinity Presbyterian Church, East Brunswick, "Our Secret Garden Preschool," accessed December 9, 2015, http://www.oursecretgarden.org/aboutus.html.

11 This program was later renamed Growing in Reverence for Ourselves and the World. Villa Maria Education and Spirituality Center, "GROW Camp" Program, Event Calendar 2019, accessed November 2020. https://www.vmesc.org/Web/home/programs-retreats?id=628.

12 Villa Maria Education and Spirituality Center, "GROW Camp," unpublished brochure (Villa Maria, PA: no date).

13 Sisters of St. Francis of Philadelphia, "Corporate Social Responsibility," accessed November 18, 2015, https://osfphila.org/corporate-social-responsibility/.

14 Barbara O'Donnell, interview by author, July 1, 2013.

15 Villa Maria Education and Spirituality Center, "Vision Statement," https://www.vmesc.org/Web/home.

16 Michael Chodroff, interview by author, July 24, 2013.

17 Ruth Bernadette O'Conner, interview by author, June 25, 2013.

18 The bar/bat mitzvah (Son/Daughter of the Commandment) is a ritual to celebrate that a Jewish child has reached the age at which he/she becomes personally responsible for practicing Jewish rituals, traditions, and ethics. For boys, this ritual occurs at age 13; for girls it occurs at 13 in Reform communities and 12 in Orthodox and Conservative communities.

19 Jewish Reconstructionist Congregation, "Greening Your Simcha: JRC's Environmentally Preferred Simcha Plan," (Downloadable PDF: No date). https://images.shulcloud.com/1321/uploads/uploaded_documents/green_simcha_guide.pdf

20 According to the Department of Energy, in 2012 lighting accounted for 10 percent of the energy used in commercial buildings, down from 25

percent in 2008 because new lightbulbs are much more efficient. Heating and cooling together made up 34 percent of energy use, an amount that did not change significantly from 2008. Natural gas provides some of the heat; lighting uses electricity. US Energy Information Administration, *2012 Commercial Buildings Energy Consumption Survey.* https://www.eia.gov/consumption/commercial/.

21 Wright, interview.
22 Debbie O'Halloran, interview by author, July 26, 2013.
23 Bernadette O'Conner, interview by author, June 25, 2013.
24 Wright, interview.
25 Wright, interview.
26 Wright, interview.

SUMMARY AND DOMAIN INTERACTIONS: HOW ORGANIZATIONS AFFECTED INITIATIVES

1 Julia M. Wondolleck and Steven L. Yaffee, *Making Collaboration Work: Lessons from Innovation in Natural Resource Management* (Washington DC: Island Press, 2000).
2 Katia Reeves, email communication, April 6, 2013.
3 Wild and Bakken, *Church on Earth*, 55.
4 Wild and Bakken, *Church on Earth*, 56.

CONCLUSION

1 Reverend Ann Held, quoted by Lynn Cameron, interview by author, August 21, 2012.
2 Szasz noted that Catholic clergy tended to avoid the topic of climate change because they worried about offending or even losing conservative parish members and that pastors were more likely to support greening efforts when they saw it as something their congregants wanted. Andrew Szasz, "Novel Framings Create New, Unexpected Allies for Climate Activism," in *Reframing Climate Change: Constructing Ecological Geopolitics,* edited by Shannon O'Lear and Simon Dalby (London: Routledge, 2016). Participatory decision processes that allowed members to work through disagreements and make a consensus or majority decision about adopting an earth-care ethic would make it easier for clergy to know how many people in a congregation were interested in sustainability. If the topic drew wide support, there would be more incentive for clergy to support it.
3 Lucie Bauer, interview by author, August 4, 2013.
4 Cameron, interview.
5 Dorfman, interview.

6 Laurel Kearns, "The Role of Religions in Activism," in *The Oxford Handbook of Climate Change and Society*, edited by John S. Dryzek, Richard B. Norgaard, and David Schlossberg (Oxford University Press, 2011), 415.

7 Ellingson points out that a REMO needs to connect with its audience in order to successfully mobilize people. *To Care for God's Creation*, 19.

8 Amanda Baugh does offer some information about changes in individual behavior among congregation members in Chicago, although it is not clear whether the healthy food practices she describes might have occurred even without the Faith in Place programs. Many of her interviewees indicated that they already used healthy cooking techniques and were not particularly fond of traditional "soul foods." *God and the Green Divide*, 94.

9 This difference in perspectives was highlighted by Laurel Kearns based on the work of R. P. Jones, D. Cox, and J. Navarro-Rivera, *Believers, Sympathizers, and Skeptics: Why Americans Are Conflicted about Climate Change, Environmental Policy and Science; Findings from the PRRI/AAR Religion, Values, and Climate Change Survey* (Washington, DC: Public Religion Research Initiative, 2014) in Veronica Kyle and Laurel Kearns, "The Bitter and the Sweet: Weaving a Tapestry of Migration Stories," in *Grassroots to Global: Broader Impacts of Civic Ecology*, edited by Marianne E. Krasny (Ithaca, NY: Cornell University Press, 2018), 58.

10 One long-running environmental project in India has focused on restoration of the forests in Vrindavan, an area closely associated with Krishna worship. See, for example, Ranchor Prime, "Saving Krishna's Forests," *DownToEarth* June 7, 2015, accessed November 2020, https://www.downtoearth.org.in/coverage/saving-krishnas-forests-21430. Georgina Drew's research examines efforts to prevent pollution of a sacred river and Pankaj Jain describes Hindu communities that protect trees and wildlife. Georgina Drew, *River Dialogues: Hindu Faith and the Political Ecology of Dams on the Sacred Ganga* (Tucson: The University of Arizona Press, 2017); Pankaj Jain, *Dharma and Ecology of Hindu Communities: Sustenance and Sustainability* (New York: Routledge, 2016).

11 Lucie Bauer video interview by Eric C. Smith, "A Leap of Faith: Community Supported Fisheries," Maine Council of Churches (2010), accessed August 2013, https://vimeo.com/10041016.

12 Landis provides a good overview of the history of CSFs that describes the success of the CSF in Gloucester Mass. Information about the BBC documentary came from an interview with Kim Libby who was a key organizer for the first CSF, which emerged out of the partnership between the First Universalist Church of Rockland and fishermen from Port Clyde, Maine. Benjamin Young Landis, "Community Supported Ingenuity," *Coastwatch* (Winter 2010), accessed August 12, 2013, https://ncseagrant.ncsu.edu/coastwatch/previous-issues/2010-2/winter-2010/community-supported-ingenuity/; Kim Libby, interview by author, August 3, 2013.

13 Mark Glovin, "The Technology of Community: A Reflection on Our Green Sanctuary Certification," Sermon delivered at First Universalist Church (Rockland, Maine: Jan. 31, 2010).

14 Robert D. Putnam, *Bowling Alone: The Collapse and Revival of American Community* (New York: Simon and Schuster, 2000), 66.

15 Bauer, interview.

APPENDIX

1 Anselm Strauss and Juliet Corbin, "Grounded Theory Methodology," in *Handbook of Qualitative Research,* ed. N. K. Denzin & Y. S. Lincoln (Thousand Oaks, CA: Sage Publications, 1994), 273.

2 Part II of Wondolleck and Yaffee, *Making Collaboration Work*, analyzes the importance of decision processes and social interactions for successful collaborative resource management in a diverse collection of management projects.

3 Wondolleck and Yaffee, *Making Collaboration Work.*

Abbate, Michael. *Gardening Eden: How Creation Care Will Change Your Faith, Your Life, and Our World.* Colorado Springs, CO: WaterBrook Press, 2009.

Abercrombie, Sharon. "Film Screening to Raise Awareness of Plight of Islanders." *EarthBeat.* August 20, 2012. Accessed November 25, 2020. https://www.ncronline.org/blogs/earthbeat/eco-catholic/film-screening-raise-awareness-plight-islanders.

Agyeman, Julian and Briony Angus. "The Role of Civic Environmentalism in the Pursuit of Sustainable Communities." *Journal of Environmental Planning and Management* 46, no. 3 (2003): 345-63.

Ajzen, Icek. *Attitudes, Personality and Behaviour.* Milton Keynes: Open University Press, 1988.

——. "The Theory of Planned Behavior." *Organizational Behavior and Human Decision Processes* 50 (1991): 179-211.

Ajzen, I. and M. Fishbein. "A Theory of Reasoned Action." In *Understanding Attitudes and Predicting Social Behavior.* Englewood Cliffs, NJ: Prentice Hall, 1980.

Albanese, Catherine L. *Nature Religion in America: From the Algonkian Indians to the New Age.* Chicago: University of Chicago Press, 1990.

Alliance of Religion and Conservation. "About ARC." http://www.arcworld.org/about_ARC.asp.

Ammerman, Nancy Tatom. *Congregation and Community.* New Brunswick, NJ: Routledge University Press, 1997.

——. *Pillars of Faith: American Congregations and Their Partners.* Berkeley: University of California Press, 2005.

Anshe Emeth Memorial Temple. "Kollel." https://www.aemt.net/learning/adult-education/kollel.

Armitage, Christopher J., and Mark Conner. "Efficacy of the Theory of Planned Behaviour: A Meta-Analytic Review." *British Journal of Social Psychology* 40, no. 4 (2001): 471–499.

Baer, Richard A. "Land Use: A Theological Concern." *Christian Century* 83 (1966).

Bailey, Kenneth K. *Southern White Protestantism in the Twentieth Century*. New York: Harper & Row, Publishers, 1964.

Balmer, Randall. "Evangelicals: Current Trends and Movements." In *Encyclopedia of Religion in America*. 4 vols. Washington DC: CQ Press, 2010.

Ban Ki-moon. "Papal Encyclical Calls for Climate Action." 2015. Accessed March 2016. https://www.linkedin.com/pulse/papal-encyclical-call-climate-action -ban-ki-moon.

Bauer, Lucie. Video interview by Eric C. Smith. "A Leap of Faith: Community Supported Fisheries." Maine Council of Church, 2010. Accessed August 2013. https://vimeo.com/10041016.

Baugh, Amanda. *God and the Green Divide: Religious Environmentalism in Black and White*. Oakland: University of California Press, 2017.

Benedictine Women of Madison. "Holy Wisdom Monastery." Accessed March 2016. http://benedictinewomen.org.

Benstein, Jeremy. *The Way into Judaism and the Environment*. Woodstock, VT: Jewish Lights Publishing, 2006.

Berry, Thomas. *The Dream of the Earth*. San Francisco: Sierra Club Books, 1988.

———. *The Great Work: Our Way into the Future*. New York: Random House, 1999.

Black, John. *The Dominion of Man: The Search for Ecological Responsibility*. Edinburgh: Edinburgh University Press, 1970.

Boyd, Heather H. "Christianity and the Environment in the American Public." *Journal for the Scientific Study of Religion* 38 (1999): 36–44.

Britz, Jennifer Delahunty. "EverGreen!" *Saint John's Magazine* 41, no. 2 (Winter 2003): 6–15.

Brown, Edward R. *Our Father's World: Mobilizing the Church to Care for Creation*. Downers Grove, IL: IVP Books, 2006.

Brune, Michael. "Sierra Club Statement on Pope Francis' Encyclical." 2015. Accessed March 2016. http://content.sierraclub.org/press-releases/2015/06/ sierra-club-statement-pope-francis-s-encyclical.

Caring for the Earth: A Strategy for Sustainable Living. IUCN—The World Conservation Union, UNEP—United Nations Environment Programme, and WWF—World Wide Fund for Nature. Gland, Switzerland, 1991.

Carr, Wylie, Michael Patterson, Laurie Yung, and Daniel Spencer. "Evangelical Religious Beliefs and Perceptions of Climate Change." *Journal for the Study of Religion, Nature and Culture* 6, no. 3 (2012): 276–99.

Catholic Climate Covenant. Accessed March 2016. https://catholicclimate- covenant.org/.

Center for Applied Research in the Apostolate, Georgetown University. Accessed February 2015. http://cara.georgetown.edu/caraservices/requested-churchstats.html.

Chalfant, H. Paul, Robert E. Beckley, and C. Eddie Palmer. *Religion in Contemporary Society*, 3rd ed. Itasca, IL: F. E. Peacock Publishers, 1994.

Chaves, Mark. *Congregations in America*. Cambridge, MA: Harvard University Press, 2004.

Cialdini, Robert B., Raymond R. Reno, and Carl A. Kallgren. "A Focus Theory of Normative Conduct: Recycling the Concept of Norms to Reduce Littering in Public Places." *Journal of Personality and Social Psychology* 58, no. 6 (1990): 1015–1026.

Clements, John M., Aaron M. McCright, and Chenyang Xiao. "An Examination of the 'Greening of Christianity' Thesis Among Americans 1993–2010." *Journal for the Scientific Study of Religion* 53, no. 2 (2014): 373–91.

Coalition on the Environment and Jewish Life. "Mission Statement." Accessed March 2015. http://www.coejl.org/.

Cohen-Kiener, Andrea. *Claiming Earth as Common Ground: The Ecological Crisis through the Lens of Faith*. Woodstock, VT: Skylight Paths Publishing, 2009.

Creation Justice Ministries, National Council of Churches. "History." Accessed March 2016. http://www.creationjustice.org/history.

DeCosse, David, Edwin Maurer and John Farnsworth. "Pope Francis' 'Common Home' Encyclical Is a Game Changer." Special to the *San Jose Mercury News*. June 18, 2015. Accessed March 2016. http://www.mercurynews.com/opinion/ci_28341858/david-decosse-edwin-maurer-and-john-farnsworth-pope.

DeLashmutt, Michael. "Church and Climate Change: An Examination of the Attitudes and Practices of Cornish Anglican Churches Regarding the Environment." *Journal for the Study of Religion, Nature and Culture* 5, no. 1 (2011): 61–81.

De Young, Raymond. "Expanding and Evaluating Motives for Environmentally Responsible Behavior." *Journal of Social Issues* 56, no. 3 (2000): 509–26.

Drew, Georgina. *River Dialogues: Hindu Faith and the Political Ecology of Dams on the Sacred Ganga*. Tucson: The University of Arizona Press, 2017.

Eckberg, Douglas L. and T. Jean Blocker. "Varieties of Religious Involvement and Environmental Concerns: Testing the Lynn White Thesis." *Journal for the Scientific Study of Religion* 28, no. 4 (1989): 509–17.

———. "Christianity, Environmentalism, and the Theoretical Problem of Fundamentalism," *Journal for the Scientific Study of Religion*, 35, no. 4 (1996): 343–55.

"Ecology in Action." (No Author.) *Catholic Rural Life Magazine*. Summer 2014. https://catholicrurallife.org/wp-content/uploads/Ecology-in-Action.pdf.

Ellingson, Stephen. *To Care for Creation: The Emergence of the Religious Environmental Movement.* Chicago: University of Chicago Press, 2016.

Epstein, Rebecca. "Rosh Hashanah, Second Day." Sermon delivered at Anshe Emeth Memorial Temple, New Brunswick, New Jersey. Sept. 10, 2010/5771.

Erickson, Doug. "Madison Church Emphasizes Call to Land Stewardship." *Wisconsin State Journal* (July 9, 2010). https://madison.com/wsj/news/local/environment/madison-church-emphasizes-call-to-land-stewardship/article_.31a5f49a-8ae2-11df-b262-001cc4c002e0.html.

Evangelical Environmental Network. "What Would Jesus Drive?" Accessed June 2014. http://www.whatwouldjesusdrive.info/intro.php.

Evenson, Alex. "Saint John's History: Brother George Primus." *Sagatagan Seasons* 2, no. 3 (Autumn 1999): 5.

First Parish Church of Newbury. "Congregationalism." Accessed September 28, 2015. http://firstparishofnewbury.org/about-us/congregationalism/.

———. "Our Secret Garden Indoor/Outdoor Nursery and Preschool." Accessed December 9, 2015. http://www.oursecretgarden.org/aboutus.html.

Fowler, Robert Booth. *The Greening of Protestant Thought.* Chapel Hill: University of North Carolina Press, 1995.

Fox, Matthew. *The Coming of the Cosmic Christ: The Healing of Mother Earth and the Birth of a Global Renaissance.* San Francisco: Harper & Row, 1988.

Francis. *Laudato Si'.* Vatican City: Vatican Press, 2015. Retrieved March 2016.

Glacken, Clarence. *Traces on the Rhodian Shore: Nature and Culture in Western Thought from Ancient Times to the End of the Eighteenth Century.* Berkeley: University of California Press, 1967.

Glovin, Mark. "The Technology of Community: A Reflection on Our Green Sanctuary Certification." Sermon delivered at First Universalist Church, Rockland, Maine. Jan. 31, 2010.

Gottlieb, Roger. *A Greener Faith: Religious Environmentalism and Our Planet's Future.* New York: Oxford University Press, 2006.

———. "Religious Environmentalism: What It Is, Where It's Heading, and Why We Should Be Going in the Same Direction." *Journal for the Study of Religion, Nature, and Culture* 1, no. 1 (2007): 81–91.

Greeley, Andrew. "Religion and Attitudes toward the Environment." *Journal for the Scientific Study of Religion* 32, no. 1 (1993): 19–28.

Greenberg, Michael R. "Concern about Environmental Pollution: How Much Difference Do Race and Ethnicity Make? A New Jersey Case Study." *Environmental Health Perspectives*, 113, no.4 (2005): 369–374. http://doi.org/10.1289/ehp.7611.

Greene, Debra Illingworth. "Church Starts Egg-cellent Ministry." *The Lutheran.* Nov. 2010. Accessed June 15, 2013. http://www.thelutheran.org/article/article.cfm?article_id=9480.

GreenFaith. "GreenFaith Certification Program." Accessed March 2014. http://greenfaith.org.

The Guardian. "The Guardian View on Laudato Si': Pope Francis Calls for a Cultural Revolution." Editorial. *The Guardian*. June 18, 2015. Accessed March 2016. http://www.theguardian.com/commentisfree/2015/jun/18/guardian-view-on-laudato-si-pope-francis-cultural-revolution.

Guth, James L., John C. Green, Lyman A. Kellstedt, and Corwin E. Smidt. "Faith and the Environment: Religious Beliefs and Attitudes on Environmental Policy." *American Journal of Political Science* 39, no. 2 (1995): 364–82.

Hand, Carl M. and Kent D. Van Liere. "Religion, Mastery-Over-Nature, and Environmental Concern." *Social Forces* 37, no. 1 (1984): 555–70.

Harper, Fletcher. "Beyond Belief: Effective Religious Leadership on Energy and Climate Change." In *Sacred Acts: How Churches Are Working to Protect Earth's Climate*, edited by Mallory McDuff. Gabriola Island, BC: New Society, 2012.

Harrison, Peter. *The Bible, Protestantism, and the Rise of Natural Science.* Cambridge: Cambridge University Press, 1998.

Hessel, Dieter T. *Theology for Earth Community.* New York: Orbis Books, 1996.

Hines, Jody M., Harold R. Hungerford, and Audrey N. Tomera. "Analysis and Synthesis of Research on Responsible Environmental Behavior: A Meta-Analysis." *Journal of Environmental Education* 18, no. 2 (1987): 1–8.

Hirst, Stan. "Laudato Si—Hopefully a Game Changer." *Suzuki Elders.* July 26, 2015. Accessed March 2016. http://www.suzukielders.org/laudato-si-hopefully-a-game-changer/.

Interfaith Power and Light webpage. http://www.interfaithpowerandlight.org/.

———. "Mission and History." http://www.interfaithpowerandlight.org/about/mission-history/.

Jain, Pankaj. *Dharma and Ecology of Hindu Communities: Sustenance and Sustainability.* New York: Routledge, 2016.

Jewish Reconstructionist Congregation. "Greening Your Simcha: JRC's Environmentally Preferred Simcha Plan." Evanston, IL, No date.

Jewish Virtual Library. "Kashrut." Accessed February 5, 2016. https://www.jewishvirtuallibrary.org/jsource/Judaism/kashrut.html.

Jones, Virginia. "Sisters of St. Joseph." In *Religious Congregations on the Land: The Practical Links Between Community, Sustainable Land Use, and Spiritual Charism.* National Catholic Rural Life Conference, August 1996.

Judaism 101. "Tu B'Shevat." Accessed February 5, 2016. http://www.jewfaq.org/holiday8.htm.

Jung, Hwa Yol. "Ecology, Zen, and Western Religious Thought." *Christian Century* 89 (1972): 1153–6.

———. "The Ecological Crisis: A Philosophic Perspective, East and West." *Bucknell Review* 20 (1972): 25–44.

Kanagy, Conrad L. and Fern K. Willits. "A 'Greening' of Religion? Some Evidence from a Pennsylvania Sample." *Social Science Quarterly* 73, No. 3 (1993): 674–83.

Kaplan, Stephen. "Being Needed, Adaptive Muddling, and Human-Environment Relationships." In *Coming of Age*, edited by Robert I. Selby, Kathryn H. Anthony, Jaepil Choi, and Brian Orland. Oklahoma City, OK: EDRA 21 (1990): 19–25.

———. "Human Nature and Environmentally Responsible Behavior." *Journal of Social Issues*, 56, no. 3 (2000): 491–508.

Kearns, Laurel. "Noah's Ark Goes to Washington: A Profile of Evangelical Environmentalism." *Social Compass*, Vol. 44, No. 3 (1997): 349–66.

———. "Saving the Creation: Christian Environmentalism in the United States." *Sociology of Religion* 57 (1996): 55–69.

———. "The Role of Religions in Activism." In the *Oxford Handbook of Climate Change and Society*, edited by John S. Dryzek, Richard B. Norgaard, and David Schlossberg. Oxford University Press, 2011: 414–28.

Keeley, Brian. *Human Capital: How What You Know Shapes Your Life*. Paris: OECD Publishing, 2007. https://www.oecd.org/insights/humancapitalhow-whatyouknowshapesyourlife.htm.

Keesey-Berg, David. "This Gifted Land." Unpublished essay. Madison Christian Community, Madison, WI, 2003.

Keesey-Berg, Sonja. "Garden History." Unpublished essay. Madison Christian Community, Madison, WI, No date.

Kempton, Willett, M. James S. Boster, and Jennifer A. Hartley. *Environmental Values in American Culture*. Cambridge: MIT Press, 1995.

Kingsolver, Barbara, Steven L. Hopp, and Camille Kingsolver. *Animal, Vegetable, Miracle: A Year of Food Life*. New York: HarperCollins, 2007.

Kinsley, David. *Ecology and Religion: Ecological Spirituality in Cross-Cultural Perspective*. Englewood Cliffs, NJ: Prentice-Hall, 1996.

Kroll, Mary. "In the Beginning." *Sagatagan Seasons* 10, no. 2 (Spring 2007): 1, 6.

Kulas, John, OSB. "The Abbey and Its Land." *Sagatagan Seasons* 10, no. 2 (Spring 2007): 4.

Kyle, Veronica and Laurel Kearns. "The Bitter and the Sweet: Weaving a Tapestry of Migration Stories." In *Grassroots to Global: Broader Impacts of Civic Ecology*, edited by Marianne E. Krasny. Ithaca, NY: Cornell University Press, 2018.

Landis, Benjamin Young. "Community Supported Ingenuity." *Coastwatch* (Winter 2010). Accessed August 12, 2013. https://ncseagrant. ncsu.edu/coastwatch/previous-issues/2010-2/winter-2010/community-supported-ingenuity/.

Laser, Rachel. "Reform Movement Welcomes Vatican's Environmental Encyclical." Religious Action Center of Reform Judaism. June 18, 2015. Accessed March 2016. http://www.rac.org/reform-movement-welcomes -vaticans-environmental-encyclical.

Leiserowitz, Anthony and Karen Akerlof. *Race, Ethnicity and Public Responses to Climate Change*. Yale University and George Mason University. New

Haven, CT: Yale Project on Climate Change, 2010. Accessed March 23, 2016. http://environment.yale.edu/uploads/RaceEthnicity2010.pdf.

Lipka, Michael. "U.S. Nuns Face Shrinking Numbers and Tensions with the Vatican." Pew Research Center. August 8, 2014. Accessed February 12, 2015. https://www.pewresearch.org/fact-tank/2014/08/08/u-s-nuns-face-shrinking-numbers-and-tensions-with-the-vatican/

"A Living Document." *HM Voice* 30, no. 1 (Summer 2013): 5.

Lorenzoni, Irene, Sophie A. Nicholson-Cole, and Lorraine Whitmarsh. "Barriers Perceived to Engaging with Climate Change among the UK Public and Their Policy Implications." *Global Environmental Change*, 17, no. 3–4 (2007): 445–459.

Lowe, Thomas, Katrina Brown, Suraje Dessai, Miguel de Franca Doria, Kat Haynes, and Katharine Vincent. "Does Tomorrow Ever Come? Disaster Narrative and Public Perceptions of Climate Change." *Public Understanding of Science* 15, no. 4 (2006): 435–457.

Madison Christian Community website. Accessed June 11, 2014. http://www.madisonchristiancommunity.org/.

Madison Christian Community. "Purpose Statement." Madison WI, 2011. June 11, 2014. https://www.madisonchristiancommunity.org/about_mcc.aspx.

Malinger, Laurence. "In the Middle." Sermon delivered at Temple Shalom, Aberdeen, New Jersey. 2010.

———. "The Rabbi Writes." Sermon delivered at Temple Shalom, Aberdeen, New Jersey. Sept. 4, 2010.

———. "Temple Shalom and Greenfaith." Sermon for Rosh Hashanah delivered at Temple Shalom, Aberdeen, New Jersey. Sept. 9, 2010/5771.

McDuff, Mallory. *Natural Saints: How People of Faith Are Working to Save God's Earth.* Oxford: Oxford University Press, 2010.

McFadden, Steven. "The History of Community Supported Agriculture." Rodale Institute, 2004. Accessed March 20, 2016. http://www.newfarm.org/features/0104/csa-history/part1.shtml.

McFague, Sallie. *Life Abundant: Rethinking Theology and Economy for a Planet in Peril.* Minneapolis: Fortress Press, 2001.

McHarg, Ian. L. *Design with Nature.* Garden City, NY: Natural History Press, 1969.

McKenzie-Mohr, Doug and William Smith. *Fostering Sustainable Behavior: An Introduction to Community-Based Social Marketing.* Gabriola Island, BC: New Society, 1999.

McNutt, Marcia. "The Pope Tackles Sustainability." *Science* 345, no. 6203 (2015):1429. Accessed March 5, 2016. https://science.sciencemag.org/content/345/6203/1429.abstract.

Mills, Sarah B., Barry G. Rabe, and Christopher Borick. *Acceptance of Global Warming Rising for Americans of All Religious Beliefs.* The Center for Local, State, and Urban Policy at the Gerald R. Ford School of Public Policy. Ann Arbor: University of Michigan, 2015. Accessed March 2016. http://closup.umich.edu/files/ieep-nsee-2015-fall-religion.pdf.

Minnesota DNR. "Two Mile Trail and Dike." *Restored Wetlands* (March–April 1990).

Moody, Michael. "Caring for Creation: Environmental Advocacy by Mainline Protestant Organizations." In *The Quiet Hand of God: Faith-based Activism and the Public Role of Mainline Protestantism,* edited by Robert Wuthnow and John H. Evans. Berkeley: University of California Press, 2002.

Morris, Aldon. *The Origins of the Civil Rights Movement: Black Communities Organizing for Change.* New York: Free Press, 1984.

Morris, Aldon D. and Carol McClurg Mueller, eds. *Frontiers in Social Movement Theory.* New Haven: Yale University Press, 1992.

Nash, Roderick F. "The Greening of Religion." In *The Rights of Nature: A History of Environmental Ethics.* Madison: The University of Wisconsin Press, 1989.

———. *Wilderness and the American Mind,* 4th ed. New Haven: Yale University Press, 2001.

Nasr, Seyyed Hossein. *Man and Nature: The Spiritual Crisis of Modern Man.* Kuala Lumpur: Foundation for Traditional Studies, 1968, and New York: Harper Collins, 1991.

National Council of Churches. *Yearbook of American and Canadian Churches.* Nashville: Abingdon Press, 1998.

National Religious Partnership for the Environment. "History." Accessed March 2016. http://www.nrpe.org/history.html.

Nigbur, D., E. Lyons, and D. Uzzell. "Attitudes, Norms, Identity and Environmental Behaviour: Using an Expanded Theory of Planned Behaviour to Predict Participation in a Kerbside Recycling Programme." *British Journal of Social Psychology* 49, no. 2 (2010): 259–284.

O'Neill, Saffron and Sophie Nicholson-Cole. "Fear Won't Do It: Promoting Positive Engagement with Climate Change Through Visual and Iconic Representations." *Science Communication* 30, no. 3 (2009): 355–79.

Palmer, Martin with Victoria Finlay. *Faith in Conservation: New Approaches to Religions and the Environment.* Washington DC: The World Bank, 2003.

Passmore, John. *Man's Responsibility for Nature: Ecological Problems and Western Traditions.* New York: Scribner, 1974.

Pew Research Center. "A Deep Dive into Party Affiliation." April 7, 2015. https://www.people-press.org/2015/04/07/a-deep-dive-into-party-affiliation/

———. "The Future of the World Religions: Population Growth Projections, 2010–2050." Religion and Public Life. April 2, 2015. https://www.pewforum.org/2015/04/02/religious-projections-2010-2050/

Pirkl, Margaret, OSF. "The Cosmic Christ." September 19, 2006. Document downloaded from https://osfphila.org/justice-and-peace/eco/.

Presbyterian Church (USA). *Restoring Creation for Ecology and Justice.* Louisville KY: Office of the General Assembly, 1990.

———. *Hope for a Global Future: Toward Just and Sustainable Human Development.* Lousiville KY: Office of the General Assembly, 1996.

Prime, Ranchor. "Saving Krishna's Forests." *DownToEarth* June 7, 2015.
Accessed November 26, 2020. https://www.downtoearth.org.in/coverage/
saving-krishnas-forests-21430.

Proctor, James D. and Evan Berry. "Social Science on Religion and Nature." *The
Encyclopedia of Religion and Nature*. London and New York: Continuum,
2005: 1571–1577.

Putnam, Robert D. *Bowling Alone: The Collapse and Revival of American
Community*. New York: Simon and Schuster, 2000.

Rauch, Kyle. "Here Comes the Sun." *Sagatagan Seasons* 20, no. 3 (Summer 2017):
3–4.

Rasmussen, Larry L. *Earth Community, Earth Ethics*. New York: Orbis
Books, 1996.

Robinson, Tri and Jason Chatraw. *Saving God's Green Earth: Rediscovering the
Church's Responsibility to Environmental Stewardship*. Norcross, GA:
Ampelon Publishing, 2006.

Rose, Elizabeth. "A Matter of Faith." *The Newburyport Current*,
Newburyport, MA.

(GateHouse News Service). Sept. 11, 2008.

Rosen, Brant. "What Makes a Green Shul Green?" *JRC Construction Diary*. Feb.
6, 2008. Accessed February 2014. https://rabbibrant.com/2008/02/06/
what-makes-a-green-shul-green/.

———. "That I May Dwell Among Them." *JRC Construction Diary*. Feb. 8,
2008. Accessed February 2014. (https://rabbibrant.com/2008/02/08/
that-i-may-dwell-among-them/.

———. Rosh Hashanah Sermon. Delivered at Jewish Reconstructionist
Congregation, Evanston, Illinois. Oct. 2008/5769.

———. "As Long as There are Slaughterhouses, There Will Be Battlefields."
Yedid Nefesh. August 26, 2011. Accessed February 2014. https://ynefesh
.com/2011/08/26/as-long-as-there-are-slaughterhouses-there-will-be
-battlefields/.

———. "Is the Bible Destroying Creation." *Yedid Nefesh*. Sept. 2, 2011.
Accessed February 2014. https://ynefesh.com/2011/09/02/is-the-bible
-destroying-creation/.

———. "Tu B'shevat in the Diaspora: Celebrating the Unseen." *Yedid Nefesh*.
January 25, 2013. Accessed February 2014. https://ynefesh.com/2013/01/25/
tu-bshvat-in-the-diaspora-celebrating-the-unseen/.

Roszak, Theodore. *The Making of a Counter Culture: Reflections on the
Technocratic Society and Its Youthful Opposition*. Berkeley: University of
California, 1969.

Sabin, Scott C. *Tending to Eden: Environmental Stewardship for God's People*.
Valley Forge, PA: Judson Press, 2010.

Sagan, Carl et al. "Preserving and Cherishing the Earth: An Appeal for Joint
Commitment in Science and Religion." National Religious Partnership for

the Environment, (Global Forum, Moscow). *January 1990*. http://earth renewal.org/Open_letter_to_the_religious_.htm.

Saint John's Abbey. "Garden." Accessed May 27, 2013. http://www.saintjohnsabbey. org/working/garden.html.

Saint John's Arboretum Task Force. "A Green Banner: Values of an Arboretum at Saint John's." Unpublished document. Collegeville, MN: Saint John's Abbey, 1997.

Santmire, Paul H. *Brother Earth: Nature, God and Ecology in Time of Crisis*. New York: Thomas Nelson, 1970.

Shaiko, R. G. "Religion, Politics, and Environmental Concern: A Powerful Mix of Passions." *Social Science Quarterly*, 68, no. 1–2 (1987): 244–62.

Sherkat, Darren E. and Christopher G. Ellison. "Structuring the Religion-Environment Connection: Identifying Religious Influences on Environmental Concern and Activism." *Journal for the Scientific Study of Religion* 46, no. 1 (2007): 71–85.

Shirley, Betsy. "Sister Act." *Sojourners*. April 2011. Downloaded from https://bene dictinewomen.org/wp-content/uploads/2015/03/Sister-Act-Sojourners.pdf.

Sim, Elizabeth. "Saint John's Hires New Land Manager and Arboretum Director." *Sagatagan Seasons* 4.2 (Summer 2001).

Sisters of St. Francis of Philadelphia. "Corporate Social Responsibility." Accessed November 18, 2015. https://osfphila.org/corporate-social-responsibility/.

———. "Environmental Initiatives." Brochure published by the Environmental Initiatives Core Group, Aston PA: Our Lady of Angels, 2000.

———. "Environmental Initiative Statement of Commitment." Accessed May 29, 2015. https://osfphila.org/justice-and-peace/eco/.

Sittler, Joseph. "A Theology for Earth." *Christian Scholar* 37 (1954): 177–79.

———. "The Care of the Earth." In *The Care of the Earth and Other University Sermons*. Philadelphia: Fortress Press 1964 (reprinted 2004): 49–62.

———. "Ecological Commitment as Religious Responsibility." *Zygon* 5 (1970): 5–17.

Skolimowski, Henryk. *Eco-Theology: Toward a Religion of Our Times*. Madras, India: Vasanta Press, 1985.

Sleeth, Matthew. *Serve God, Save the Planet: A Christian Call to Action*. White River Junction, VT: Chelsea Green Publishing, 2006.

Smidt, Corwin E. *Religion as Social Capital: Producing the Common Good*. Waco, TX: Baylor University Press, 2003.

Smith, Lynne, OSB. "Benedictine Sisters Share Leadership at Holy Wisdom Monastery." *Benedictine Bridge*. March 15, 2010. https://benedictinewomen. org/blog/benedictine-sisters-share-leadership-at-holy-wisdom-monastery/.

Smith, Neal. "Care for the Earth: A Longstanding Monastery Tradition." *Benedictine Bridge*, April 15, 2010. https://benedictinewomen.org/blog/ care-for-the-earth-a-longstanding-monastery-tradition/.

Snow, David. A., Calvin Morrill, and Leon Anderson. "Elaborating Analytic Ethnography: Linking Fieldwork and Theory. *Ethnography* 4, no. 2 (2003): 181–200.

Southwest Michigan Land Conservancy. "Bow in the Clouds Preserve." Preserve Features, Southwest Michigan Land Conservancy, Kalamazoo, MI (2007). Accessed June 3, 2015. http://www.swmlc.org/content/bow-clouds.

St. Thomas Aquinas Parish. "Green Committee Annual Report 2012–13." Accessed December 31, 2015. http://paloaltocatholic.net/documents/2015/5/ Green%20Committe%20Annual%20Report%202012-2013.pdf.

———. "Green Committee Mission Statement." Accessed December 31, 2015. https://paloaltocatholic.net/green-committee.

Stern, Paul C. "Understanding Individuals' Environmentally Significant Behavior." *Environmental Law Reporter: News and Analysis* 35 (2005): 10785–10790.

Stoll, Mark. Protestantism, Capitalism, and Nature in America. Albuquerque: University of New Mexico Press, 1997.

Strauss, Anselm and Juliet Corbin, "Grounded Theory Methodology." In *Handbook of Qualitative Research*, edited by N. K. Denzin & Y. S. Lincoln. Thousand Oaks, CA: Sage Publications, 1994.

Suzuki, David T. "The Role of Nature in Zen Buddhism." *Eranos-Jahrbuch* 22 (1953): 291–321.

Szasz, Andrew. "Novel Framings Create New, Unexpected Allies for Climate Activism." In *Reframing Climate Change: Constructing Ecological Geopolitics,* edited by Shannon O'Lear and Simon Dalby, 150–70. London: Routledge, 2016.

Tarakeshwar, Nalini, Aaron B. Swank, Kenneth Pargament, and Annette Mahoney. "The Sanctification of Nature and Theological Conservatism: A Study of Opposing Religious Correlates of Environmentalism." *Review of Religious Research.* 42, no. 4 (2001): 387–404.

Taylor, Bron. *Dark Green Religion: Nature Spirituality and the Planetary Future.* Berkeley: University of California Press, 2010.

———. "Toward a Robust Scientific Investigation of the 'Religion' Variable in the Quest for Sustainability," *Journal for the Study of Religion, Nature and Culture* 5, no. 3 (2011): 261–279.

———. "The Greening of Religion Hypothesis (Part One): From Lynn White, Jr. and Claims that Religions Can Promote Environmentally Destructive Attitudes and Behavior to Assertions They Are Becoming Environmentally Friendly." *Journal for the Study of Religion, Nature and Culture* 10, no. 3 (2016).

Taylor, Bron, Gretel Van Wieren, and Bernard Zaleha, "The Greening of Religion Hypothesis (Part Two)," *Journal for the Study of Religion, Nature and Culture*, 10, no. 3 (2016): 306–378.

Taylor, Sarah McFarland. *Green Sisters: A Spiritual Ecology*. Cambridge: Harvard University Press, 2000.

Trinity Presbyterian Church, East Brunswick, New Jersey. "Little Earth Shepherds Preschool Learning Center." Accessed December 9, 2015. http://www.trinity-pc.org/les/about/.

———. "Who We Are." Accessed December 9, 2015. http://www.trinity-pc.org/who-we-are/how-our-church-is-structured/.

Trinity Presbyterian Church, Harrisonburg, Virginia. "Earth Care House Church Covenant." Unpublished document, 2011.

Tuan, Yi-Fu. "Discrepancies between Environmental Attitude and Behavior: Examples from Europe and China." *The Canadian Geographer* 12 (1968): 176–191. Reprinted in *Ecology and Religion in History*, edited by David Spring and Eileen Spring, 91–113. New York: Harper Torchbook, 1974.

Tucker, Mary Evelyn. *Worldly Wonder: Religions Enter Their Ecological Phase* (Master Hsuan Hua Memorial Lecture, Pacific School of Religion, Berkeley, CA, March 2002). Chicago, Illinois: Open Court Publishing, 2003.

Tveit, Rev. Dr. Olav Fykse. "Statement on the Encyclical Laudato Si'." General Secretary of the World Council of Churches. June 18, 2015. Accessed March 2016. https://www.oikoumene.org/en/resources/documents/generalsecretary/statements/statement-by-the-wcc-general-secretary-rev-dr-olav-fykse-tveit-on-the-encyclical-letter-laudato-si2019-of-the-holy-father-francis-on-care-for-our-common-homencis.

United Church of Christ Massachusetts Conference. "Going Green Helps Church Bloom." Online newsletter. Dec. 7, 2011. Accessed July 3, 2013. http://www.macucc.org/newsdetail/112206.

United Nations General Assembly. "Report of the World Commission on Environment and Development: Our Common Future; Transmitted to the General Assembly as an Annex to document A/42/427—Development and International Co-operation: Environment; Our Common Future, Chapter 2: Towards Sustainable Development." March 20, 1987. https://sustainabledevelopment.un.org/milestones/wced.

United States Conference of Catholic Bishops. "Universal Prayer." Accessed December 31, 2015. http://www.usccb.org/prayer-and-worship/the-mass/order-of-mass/liturgy-of-the-word/universal-prayer.cfm.

United States Energy Information Administration. "How Much Energy Is Consumed in U.S. Buildings?" Accessed November 26, 2020. https://www.eia.gov/tools/faqs/faq.php?id=86&t=1.

United States Energy Information Administration, *2012 Commercial Buildings Energy Consumption*. Accessed November 26, 2020. *Survey*. https://www.eia.gov/consumption/commercial/.

Veldman, Robin Globus, Andrew Szasz, and Randolph Haluza-DeLay. "Introduction: Climate Change and Religion—A Review of Existing

Research." *Journal for the Study of Religion, Nature and Culture* 6, no. 3 (1012): 255–75.

Villa Maria Education and Spirituality Center Website. Accessed December 10, 2015. https://www.vmesc.org/Web/home.

Walgenbach, Mary David, OSB. "Leadership in a Benedictine Community." *Benedictine Bridge*, March 15, 2010.

White, Lynn, Jr. "The Historical Roots of Our Ecologic Crisis." *Science* 155 (1967): 12–37. Reprinted in Roger S. Gottlieb, (Editor). *This Sacred Earth*. New York: Routledge, 1996.

Wild, Jeff and Peter Bakken. *Church on Earth: Grounding Your Ministry in a Sense of Place*. Minneapolis: Augsberg Fortress, 2009.

Wilkinson, Katherine. *Between God & Green: How Evangelicals Are Cultivating a Middle Ground on Climate Change*. New York: Oxford University Press, 2012.

Wilson, Ken. "A Biblical Basis for Creation Care." In *Loving the Least of These: Addressing a Changing Climate,* edited by Dorothy Boorse, 9–14. National Association of Evangelicals, 2011. http://nae.net/wp-content/uploads/2015/06/Loving-the-Least-of-These.pdf.

———. "The Evangelical Awakening to Environmental Concern." Unpublished essay presented at the Let's Tend the Garden Conference. Vineyard Church, Boise, Idaho (Sept. 20, 2007).

Wondolleck, Julia M. and Steven L. Yaffee. *Making Collaboration Work: Lessons from Innovation in Natural Resource Management*. Washington DC: Island Press, 2000.

Worster, Donald. *Nature's Economy: A History of Ecological Ideas*. Cambridge: Cambridge University Press, 1977.

Yale Forum on Religion and Ecology webpage. Accessed April 2012. http://fore.research.yale.edu.

Yardley, Jim, and Laurie Goodstein. "Pope Francis, in Sweeping Encyclical, Calls for Swift Action on Climate Change." *The New York Times*. June 18, 2015. Accessed March 2016. https://www.nytimes.com/2015/06/19/world/europe/pope-francis-in-sweeping-encyclical-calls-for-swift-action-on-climate-change.html.

Yearwood, Pauline Dubkin. "Chicago's Green Synagogue." *The Chicago Jewish News: Special Issue,* no date.

Yin, Robert K. *Case Study Research: Design and Methods*, 2nd ed. Thousand Oaks, CA: Sage Publications, 1994.

INDEX

Champions (*cont'd*)
 and despair, 98, 102, 104–106, 245
 environmental interests of, 75–80
 factors that sustained efforts, 106, 109–
  12, 245
 and faith communities as venues for
  earth care, 73, 85
 and knowledge deficits, 98, 99–102, 109
 leadership skills/capabilities, 89–93, 95,
  97, 114, 272–73, 280
 motivations for earth care, 73–74, 85
 personnel challenges, 106–108, 109
 religious interests and earth care,
  80–84, 286
 relationships within the community,
  93–97, 114
 support from faith leaders, 104, 108,
  109, 114
 and sustainability knowledge, 86, 89,
  102, 280
 trusted by faith leaders, 93, 94, 96
 and windows of opportunity, 74, 84–85,
  106, 108, 114, 280
Chittister, Joan, 104
Chodroff, Michael (Mike), 40, 41, 88, 90,
  94, 95, 107, 123, 207, 241, 247, 250,
  251, 257
Climate Reality Project, 32, 78, 89, 92
Cohen, Ann, 149, 150, 153
Community gardens. *See* Gardens
Community supported agriculture (CSA)
 and First Parish Church of Newbury,
  29, 79
 and First Universalist Church of Rockland, 36, 112, 203, 292
 Red Hill Farm at Our Lady of Angels,
  53, 54, 62, 185, 218
 type of land stewardship, 11, 190
Community Supported Fishery, 36, 292
Congregation of St. Joseph at Nazareth
  (CSJ)
 adoption of an earth-care ethic, 45, 177,
  179, 201, 202
 Bow in the Clouds Natural Area, 44,
  45–46, 58, 85, 124, 179, 186
 case summary, 43–46

 and champion's career, 58, 59, 75
 community mission (charism) and
  earth care, 44–45, 144, 179
 congregational support for earth care,
  growth of, 124–25, 179
 connections between healing of earth
  and humans, 45
 eco-spirituality programs, 59, 85, 124,
  179, 238
 farming history, 44, 184
 and first Earth Day, 44, 75, 179
 land stewardship, 44–45, 59, 179
 leadership team and earth care, 155
 mission discernment processes, 231–32
 organic farming, 179
 resource conservation, 46, 59
 Transformations Spirituality Center,
  255
Congregations
 and activities undertaken, 203–205, 217
 and adoption of earth-care ethic, 199–
  203, 206–207
 and authorization of projects, 194–99,
  217–18, 242
 case sample, characteristics of, 171–73
 champions, effects on, 25, 217
 community identity and land use, 179–
  87, 190
 community identity and religious tradition, 176
 community identity and ministries,
  187, 284, 285
 connecting sustainability with community identity, 190–91, 193, 208, 215,
  220–21, 283, 284
 contributions to initiatives, 69, 170, 175,
  193, 216, 222, 283–84
 influence on faith leaders, 217–18, 220
 and financial support for initiatives,
  215, 218–19, 221–22
 fluctuations in initiative support,
  208–209
 greening members' behavior, 210–11,
  212
 and human resources, 173, 215, 216–18
 involvement in initiatives, 193–94, 214

place attachment, 187–89
previous environmental activities, 176–79, 189–90, 215, 283
and size of green team, 219
support for initiatives, 170, 175, 190, 191, 212, 215, 246, 284
Corporate Social Responsibility. *See* Our Lady of Angels

Dorfman, Julie, 197, 219

Eighmy, Kimberley (Kim), 92, 93
Einerson, Jean, 92–93
Ellingson, Stephen, 7, 8, 142, 289, 311n1, 314n52, 314n54, 323n7
Environmental education
  and gardening, 29, 49, 59, 100
  programs for adults, 38, 41, 47, 179, 251
  programs for kids, 25, 42, 77–78, 93, 112, 137, 250, 253, 254, 264
  public preschool programs, 252–53
Environmental interests that influenced initiatives
  climate change, 78, 82–83, 105–106, 166
  descendants' welfare, 75, 80, 83
  gardening, 79–80, 92, 100
  greening organizations, 76–78
  outdoor activities for children, 25, 27, 30
  outdoor hobbies, 122, 165, 178, 181
  protecting nature 75–76, 77
  spiritual development of children, 79, 112
Environmental justice
  challenges of, 263–64, 268
  and congregation-level earth care, 6, 8
  educational programs on, 41, 213, 251, 264
  facilitated through partnerships, 264
  Faith Leader message theme, 166, 280, 281
  and GreenFaith program, 38, 263
  and Green Sanctuary Program, 35
  and National Council of Churches Ecojustice Ministry, 3
  and Presbyterian Church (USA), 24

Epstein, Rebecca (rabbi at Anshe Emeth Memorial Temple), 129, 137, 149, 150
Evangelical Christianity
  and climate change, 6, 30
  decision processes in, 157
  theology of, 84, 131, 142
Evangelical Environmental Network, 4

Faith leaders
  advice to champions, 155–56
  authorization of initiatives, 154–55
  benefits of initiatives for, 159–60
  blogs as message mechanisms, 150–52
  connecting sustainability with community identity, 137, 142, 143–44, 145, 159, 164
  connecting ministries and sustainability, 138, 143
  connecting theology and sustainability, 127
  and congregational support for initiatives, 164
  contributions to initiatives, 68, 120, 127, 147, 161–62, 164, 281–83
  definition of, 120–21
  denominational theology, 142–43
  encouraging community support, 156–57, 158
  legitimating sustainability, message themes, 128, 145 (*see also* Nature spirituality, Social justice, Stewardship ethic)
  mechanisms for promoting sustainability, 147–48, 158–59, 162–63
  message cadence, 164–67
  moral support of champions, 153, 163
  motivations for earth care, 121–25
  newsletters as message mechanism, 150–52
  as organizational managers, 120, 148, 154, 157, 159, 162
  and outdoor activities, 135, 165
  positive religious vision and initiative durability, 141–42
  public affirmations of initiatives, 152–53
  as religious authorities, 120, 127, 147, 161

Faith leaders (*cont'd*)
rituals and earth care, 153–54
sermons as message mechanism,
148–49
and special role of religion, 139–42,
144–45, 287
study groups as message mechanism,
149
and sustainability social norm, 145, 147,
149, 158–59, 161–63, 282
First Parish Church of Newbury (FPC)
case summary, 29–30
champions, role of, 79, 91, 102
adopting mission to be Stewards of
Earth and Spirit, 29, 61, 155
community garden, 29, 61, 62–63, 79
congregational support for initiative,
218
Congregationalist decision processes,
200
mission discernment process, 155, 200,
231, 235, 237
Our Secret Garden preschool, 30, 218,
252
outdoor worship services, 30, 154
partnerships with community groups,
29–30
and place attachment, 188
polity, 227, 237
revitalization through earth care, 159
First Universalist Church of Rockland
(UUR)
case summary, 35–37
and community supported agriculture,
36, 112, 292
and community supported fishery,
36–37, 188, 292
decision processes, role of congregation, 195, 203, 233, 234, 236, 237, 242
despair and fellowship, 104–105
earth care as social justice ministry,
138, 140, 143
environmental education for kids, 250
and environmental justice, 264
and Green Chalice Circle, 240

Green Sanctuary Committee rituals,
240
and Green Sanctuary Program, 35, 64,
101, 195, 236, 244, 293
genesis of the initiative, 63–64
and knowledge deficits, 99, 100–101
and place attachment, 188, 292
polity, 227
reduction of activity, 107
storm window project, 37, 105–106, 110,
264, 293
Unitarian Universalist Values (Seventh
Principle), 131, 141, 143
Four domains. *See also* Champions,
Congregations, Faith leaders, Operational procedures, Organizational
structures
as analytical framework, 13, 67, 70,
278–79, 290
contributions to initiatives, 58, 67
interplay of facilitated initiatives,
285–86
intersections among, 278–84
and sustainability social norms, 286,
291
Francis I (pope), 1, 2, 32

Gardens
butterfly garden, 39
children's garden programs, 27, 57, 93,
112, 169, 253, 254, 264
community gardens, 27, 29, 31, 39, 61,
62–63, 79, 92, 96–97, 153–54, 178,
254
food pantry gardens, 43, 57, 80, 170,
253–54
management of, 92
and partnerships with food pantries,
138, 254
as visible witness to earth-care mission, 39
and volunteers, 79–80, 92–93, 97, 169,
170, 217
Glovin, Mark, (pastor at First Universalist
Church), 138, 140, 143

Green building, 28, 51, 62, 197, 203–204,
256 (*see also* Holy Wisdom Monastery, Jewish Reconstructionist
Congregation)
GreenFaith Program
and case study selection, 11, 19, 295–96
certification requirements, 40, 42, 95, 238
and champions' burnout, 102–103
and champions' leadership, 77–78, 88,
90, 94, 101, 123
congregational involvement in, 203–
204, 207, 235
and environmental education, 250, 251
and environmental justice, 38, 263
faith leader role in, 149, 150, 152, 157
and initiative structure, 34–35, 38, 40,
42, 77
as knowledge resource, 34–35, 38, 39,
61, 77, 101–102, 202
and Union for Reform Judaism, 40, 42,
65, 124
See also Anshe Emeth Memorial Temple, Temple Shalom,
Trinity Presbyterian Church East
Brunswick
Green Sanctuary Program
certification requirements, 35
congregational support for, 195, 203,
233, 236, 242
and initiative structure, 34, 36 64
as knowledge resource, 101, 102
See also First Universalist Church of
Rockland
Grobe, Lewis (monk at Saint John's
Abbey), 182, 212

Haverington, Nancy (pastor at First Parish
Church), 29, 159, 200
Held, Ann Reed (pastor at Trinity Presbyterian Church in Harrisonburg), 24,
25, 75–76, 95, 104, 105, 121, 122, 134,
153, 156, 163, 165
Holy Wisdom Monastery (HWM)
adoption of an earth-care mission, 50,
143
Benedictine values and earth care, 143

case summary, 49–51
congregational involvement in activities 217
decision processes, 173, 200, 201, 231
earth care and community relationships, 51
earth care in worship services, 149
evolution of initiative, 62
initiative implementation challenges,
61
green infrastructure, 51, 256
land management, history of, 50, 184–
85, 186
land stewardship, 49–50, 185, 186
nature spirituality, 134
organizational leadership and earth
care, 154, 155
polity, 227
partnerships with local organizations,
50, 101
prairie restoration, 50, 101, 111
sacred space, 51, 136
staff role in earth care, 61–62

Interfaith Power and Light
and case study sample, 11, 295, 296
and greening of religion, 4, 306n3

Jewish Reconstructionist Congregation
(JRC)
bar/bat mitzvah, 210
case summary, 27–28
congregational involvement in initiative, 193, 196, 197–98, 204, 210–11,
212, 213, 232, 235
congregational support, 218–19, 235
decision processes, 28, 197, 203–205,
213, 232, 233, 234, 236
earth care integrated into spiritual
practices, 99, 100, 249
environmental education, 249
Environmental Task Force, 28, 94, 99,
119, 150, 155, 238
evolution of initiative, 63
green construction process, 60–61, 151,
197–98, 204, 213, 229

Organizations, religious. *See also* Operational procedures, Organizational structures
purpose of, 225
as venues for sustainability initiatives, 224, 247
Our Lady of Angels (OLA)
adoption of environmental mission, 51, 61
case summary, 51–54
challenges of implementing environmental mission, 61, 265, 266
composting, 53, 258–59, 265
congregational participation in initiative, 205, 208, 209, 218
Corporate Social Responsibility, 53, 137, 254, 263, 267, 268, 271
discernment processes and earth care, 155, 201, 230
environmental justice, 62, 255, 284
Environmental Initiative, 51, 205
Franciscan worldview and earth care, 51–52, 54, 144, 205
guiding principles for environmental mission, 52
integrated pest management, 53, 262
land managed for wildlife habitat, 52–53, 262, 266
land management, history of, 184, 185
Neuman University, collaboration with, 51
Red Hill Farm (CSA), 53, 62, 185, 218
resource conservation, 53, 265
retreat center, 256
staff role in initiative, 62, 209, 262, 266

Partnerships with external organizations, 27, 30, 254, 264–65, 269

Reeves, Katia, 73, 80, 81, 107, 240, 273
Resource conservation, 11, 31, 207
energy conservation, 31, 33, 34, 64, 250, 260
rain gardens, 256, 262
recycling programs, 34, 38, 40, 250
storm window inserts, 37, 106, 264

waste reduction, 82
See also solar panels
Robinson, Lenore, 43, 92
Romeo, Frank, 48–49, 79, 100, 184, 202, 256
Rosen, Brant (rabbi at Jewish Reconstructionist Congregation), 28, 100, 119–20, 130, 138, 139, 151, 155, 156, 166, 193, 197, 204, 210, 211, 229

Saint John's Abbey (SJA)
Benedictine traditions and sustainability, 47, 139–40, 143, 180, 198
case summary, 46–48
champion's career and initiative, 58–59, 75, 85
creation of Saint John's Arboretum, 46–47, 180–81
decision processes, 196, 198–99, 212, 227, 232, 233, 236
environmental education, 47
faith leader support of initiative, 121, 123, 149, 154, 155
green building, retreat guesthouse, 256
land management, historical, 47, 143, 179, 180–81
land stewardship and habitat restoration, 46, 59
monks' outdoor hobbies, 181–82
partnership with Saint John's University, 46, 47, 198
polity, 227
resource conservation, 47–48
solar farm, 48, 264–65
staff role in initiative, 108, 182, 228
stewardship as community ethic, 153, 180, 182, 232
Schwietz, Paul (monk at Saint John's Abbey), 46, 47, 59, 75, 84–85, 89, 108, 123, 180, 182, 198, 199, 213
Siebert, Asher, 94, 152
Sisters of St. Francis of Philadelphia. *See* Our Lady of Angels
Sisters of the Humility of Mary. *See* Villa Maria
Smith, Neal, 185